The Spirit of Magic

Rediscovering the Heart of Our Sacred Art

Virgil

List of Titles by Virgil

- *The Spirit of Magic,* (1st Edition), Falcon Books Publishing, 2017
- *The Elemental Equilibrium,* Falcon Books Publishing, 2017
- *The Covert Side to Initiation*, Falcon Books Publishing, 2018

Future titles:

- *The Tao of Universal Magic,* Falcon Books Publishing.

All titles are available at www.falconbookspublishing.com

The Spirit of Magic

Rediscovering the Heart of Our Sacred Art

Virgil

Falcon Books
Publishing
2019

Copyright © 2019 by Virgil
All rights reserved. This book or any portion thereof may not be reproduced or used in any manner whatsoever without the express written permission of the publisher except for the use of brief quotations in a book review or scholarly journal.
First Printing: 2018
Second Edition 2019

Cover Design by Tanya Robinson

FALCON BOOKS PUBLISHING LTD
71-75 Sheldon Street Covent Garden.
London, WCH 9JQ

www.falconbookspublishing.com
Copyright © 2019 Virgil
All rights reserved.

ISBN-13: 978-986-94925-7-7

FALCON BOOKS
PUBLISHING
2019

Ordering Information:
Hardback copies are only available on the Falcon Books Publishing website.:
www.falconbookspublishing.com.

(Ebooks and paperback books are also available on www.amazon.com)

Contents

Acknowledgments..vii
The Orison of the Aspiring Magician..................xi
Foreword..xiii
Preface...xvii
Introduction..xxvii
Chapter 1: The Practice of Asana......................1
Chapter 2: The Purified Elemental Equilibrium..13
Chapter 3: Introspection...................................37
Chapter 4: The Six-Pronged Attack.................45
Chapter 5: The Importance of Magical Training Systems...53
Chapter 6: Magical Training Systems – the Alternative to the Shotgun Approach...............57
Chapter 7: Thought-Observation.....................73
Chapter 8: Magical Training Tips and Advice..83
Chapter 9: The Magician's Life........................99
Chapter 10: Working Magic...........................127
Chapter 11: Talismans...................................151
Chapter 12: Lessons from the Tarot.............159
Chapter 13: Becoming a Guardian Angel.......173
Chapter 14: Wisdom.......................................185
Chapter 15: Caring for Your Garden.............195
Chapter 16: Heaven on Earth........................205
Chapter 17: The Golden Key..........................211
Chapter 18: Becoming Hermes Trismegistus.283

Epilogue..........293
Appendix A: Summary of IIH..........295
Appendix B: An Example Black Soul Mirror...299
Appendix C: A Council of Angels..........311
Appendix D: A Conversation with an Archdemon..........315
Appendix E: Useful Articles and Essays..........317
References..........325
Chapter 3: The Importance of Present Mindedness..........332

Acknowledgments

In the process of preparing this book, I was blessed to receive the assistance of many individuals who were very generous with their time and knowledge. I am grateful for the help they gave me, and would like to thank them and give them credit for their efforts.

First and foremost, I must thank William Mistele for corresponding with me over the course of several years, for his insights into the nature of magic, and for letting me quote relevant passages from his writings in this book.

I must thank Martin Faulks for helping me break into the business of being an esoteric author, for introducing me to Falcon Books Publishing, and for the support he has continued to give me.

I must thank Tanya Robinson for publishing this book. Without her help, this book would never have been anything more than a giant Microsoft Word document on my laptop.

I must thank Sam for the time she has spent helping me proofread and revise both the first and second edition of this book, and for writing the foreword to this book's first edition.

I must thank my friend Crystalf Maibach for reading the first edition of this book and giving me helpful feedback regarding what changes I should make when creating this second edition.

I must thank my friends Tom and Bailey B. for accepting me in all my weirdness, and for their support in my endeavors, whether related to magic, writing, or understanding aerosol science. Tom, your ability to make great scientific advances with incomplete chicken nuggets taught me that anything is possible. Bailey, chemistry is cool, but I think you'd make a great actress.

I must thank Krishna D. for her conversations about spirituality with me, for being open-minded and considerate about my unconventional views about the subject, and for sharing her thoughts about enlightenment, happiness, and meditation with me.

I'd also like to thank all of the authors, living and deceased, whose works I quote, and who took the time to share their knowledge with the world. Thanks you Franz Bardon, Rawn Clark, Eliphas Levi, Frater Acher, John O'Donohue, Daskalos, George MacDonald, Paracelsus, Frank MacEowen, Stephanie Leon Neal, Ursula Le Guin, José Luis Stevens, Melita Denning, Osborne Phillips, Nathaniel Branden, J.K. Rowling, Christopher McIntosh, Paulo Coelho, Goethe, and Patsy Rodenburg.

Finally, I'd like to thank all of my awesome readers, and especially those readers who correspond with me frequently via my online presence and give me feedback about my books and encouragement to continue writing. In particular, I'd like to thank Melanie Laskowski, Sapnali Chetia, Ewen Barling, Cass VanBaal, Eden VanBaal, Wayne O'Boogie, Eduardo Ballena, Eric Summers, Gabriel Moreira, Pakpoom Poolsong, Ioan Rocsoreanu, Lucas Augusto, Jacob Scully, Guido Cesano, Marc Pugliese, Eric Willis, Steve Vadney, R.H. Andrew, Mario Kulash, Nathan Quick, Johannes Kul, Colter Davis, Philip Raquinel, Fabio Salvi's Tricks, Charles Freeman, Nenad Vasin, Devin Kelly, Mahazou Mahaman, Paul Sutherland, Kerrie O'Sullivan, and Cheri Burns. Thanks a lot for your support guys. I appreciate it greatly; it allows me to continue doing what I do.

They do not tell you this – the universe is a very big place and we as a human race have barely begun to read the preface to the book of wisdom. No matter how ritualized, systematized, institutionalized, or laid out in a step-by-step guide, magic is always exploratory. You are crossing a boundary, leaving behind the familiar world, and entering the unknown.

– William Mistele

Magic is the divinity of man conquered by science in union with faith; the true Magi are Men-Gods, in virtue of their intimate union with the divine principle.

– Eliphas Levi

The Orison of the Aspiring Magician

The following orison appears in William Mistele's essay *The Shadow in Psychology and Magick*. This essay's eloquent and insightful discussion of the deeper aspects of magical training has made it a popular and frequently discussed piece of writing in the Bardon community. I'd like to share this orison here because many of the values, dreams, and principles at the heart of magic are reflected in its words.

May the work I perform in training to be a magician serve the highest light of Divine Providence. May divine justice, fair play, and harmony shine through and within all that I do. May the words I speak, the breath I breathe, the light in my eyes, and the love in my heart transform the world around me. May my path be anointed with Divine beauty.

May all who enter my life see divine peace reflected through me. May the truth of the universe, the mystery of creation, the light which sustains and shines within every created being use me as its servant. May my will be so perfected that in the end there is no distinction between the satisfaction of my desires and the work of Divine Providence on Earth.

When it comes to understanding the heart of magic, contemplating the statements in this orison is a good place to start. It will give you a sense of what it means to be a magician, and of the sort of work students of this art engage in upon completing their basic training.

Foreword

When Virgil approached me a year ago and asked me for a list of everything I wish I had known when I first began my training in the Bardon system of magic, I naturally wanted to know why he wanted this list. When he told me about his plans to write a book designed to aid beginning students of magic, I was delighted. As a longtime friend of his, I knew he was one of the few people truly qualified to write this book.

The current state of the esoteric world is a sorry sight, and the low standards most teachers and systems abide by constitute one major reason for this. In laya yoga, the process of raising the kundalini energy takes years of dedicated training and asceticism. These days, there exist numerous books insisting all you have to do to raise the kundalini energy is visualize red light rising up your spine. People who know no better do this visualization and then think they are advanced yogis. A similar thing has happened with magic. There are countless people who believe they are adepts, but only because they do not know what it means to be an adept.

Magical training is not for the lazy. It requires persistent daily practice over many years in order to reach the level of an initiate. While getting the hang of an exercise is a good starting point, too many people think they have mastered an exercise just because they have gotten the hang of it. For those students who intend to become adepts, this will never suffice. Over the course of many years, the student practices visualization, pore breathing, accumulation, condensation, transplantation of consciousness, depth-point meditation, and exteriorization over and over again. At some point along the way, each exercise will become second nature. At some further point, they will become first nature. The skills they develop will become burned into the student's DNA. They will become a veritable part of who she is. At this point, the student can call herself an initiate. She can, to use Virgil's extended metaphor, begin ascending up the rainbow in the same manner as Tangle and Mossy. Eventually, when she ascends high enough, she will reach the Sphere of the Sun and learn the lessons contained within it. At this point, she can rightfully refer to herself as an adept.

The Spirit of Magic by Virgil

This book reveals a crucial fact about serious magical training – standards exist and they are important. For every exercise, there are hard and fast rules that allow you to definitively know whether or not you are proficient enough to move on. No guesswork is involved. Magic is an art. Every magical exercise is designed to develop a specific skill useful to the magician. If those skills are not developed well, then the artwork of the magician will be of low quality. Instead of creating beauty, she will create ugliness. We see this in the many instances where magicians have attempted to work magic for good and created more suffering than they alleviated as a result of the unforeseen negative side effects of their workings. A higher level of wisdom would have allowed them to calculate a better approach, and an adherence to worthwhile standards of training would have allowed them to work with greater precision.

The history of occultism during the past century has been dominated by a handful of trends, orders, tenets, and idolized figures. This book presents a breath of fresh air for those searching for something new and different. For this same reason, this book will also upset many. There will be those who criticize this book because what Virgil writes contradicts this traditional belief or that standard dogma.

It takes courage to write a book like this. To claim that any magical system which neglects to teach introspection is a waste of time is very bold indeed, after all, most purportedly "magical" systems give no heed to introspection. Regardless, Virgil is correct in making this claim. The student who does not know himself is lost, and there is no other way to know oneself than through introspection.

Although this book is not specifically intended for Bardonists, Virgil's background in the Bardon system inevitably shows itself throughout this book. In particular, it is clear to me that this book was written for the same type of people Bardon wrote his books for. Bardon did not write his books for anchorites and hermits who spend all day hiding in their oratories. He wrote them for people who wanted to engage those around them, follow their dreams, transform the world in tangible ways, attain their goals, build connections, explore, and spread joy through their words, actions, careers, decisions, and undertakings.

Everyone has several talents that they can develop and expand with effort and practice. Everyone has the capacity to love and be loved.

Everyone has the ability to be active in society. Everyone has the potential to care for their family and loved ones, to pursue their hobbies, to travel the world, and to seize every second of every day. Magical

Foreword

training should not prevent you from doing any of these things by vampirizing your time. On the contrary, magical training aids you in doing all of these things more efficiently and effectively.

In light of this, it is apparent that an underlying theme of this book is time. The time of a student can be roughly divided into three categories. The first category is time spent actually doing magical exercises. The second category is time spent reading about magic. The third category is everything else – the time you are not doing formal magical exercises or reading about magic. This book teaches the student how to get the most out of any of these categories.

It is easy to put a lot of effort into practicing magical exercises and then get nothing out of it at all. To truly benefit from practicing magical exercises, a student must practice the right exercises at the right time in a serious manner. It does no good to practice arbitrary exercises collected from a mishmash of books and systems. For beginning students, the right exercises are the basic exercises, and Virgil highlights this by providing an in-depth commentary on several basic exercises including thought-observation, asana, and the creation of the soul mirrors. Without becoming proficient in these exercises, the student would only be wasting his time and endangering himself if he were to attempt more advanced exercises like accumulating the elements, depth-point meditation, exteriorization, and electromagnetic volting.

The same principles apply to the second category of time. Although reading is an essential part of the magical path, it is easy to spend a lot of time reading and still end up no better off than you were before. It is important to read the right books at the right time. What the "right" books are for you depends on what system you ultimately choose to follow to the end.

Wise use of one's time leads to something too few students of magic experience – progress. Through a combination of self-suggestion and cognitive dissonance, many people trick themselves into believing they are advancing steadily along the path. Such long-term self-deception continues indefinitely because they do not know what true progress is, and therefore, have no basis for comparison. In some instances, a student will realize they are no better off than before after years of occult study and practice and then lose faith in everything.

The Spirit of Magic by Virgil

This is a book for those whose will is to advance steadily and safely. The best way to ensure this is to pick a complete and balanced system and stay focused on it. This message is embedded into every chapter of this book. To reach a destination, one must pick a path and then stay on it. Even then, one is bound to come across obstacles. Since every person's path is unique, no book can cover every single obstacle a student could possibly face. Virgil does, however, discuss the more common ones and provides many generic tips for dealing with them in the eighth chapter. My own years of training have taught me that no one can tell you how to approach magical training. They can only give advice about the less personal aspects. Your own life will tell you how to approach magical training. You just need to learn to listen. I find this same lesson woven into this book's emphasis on developing inner silence and acquiring the adaptive power of water.

Human society is complex. There are many aspects of it that are pleasant and delightful. There are also many aspects of it that are dismal and bleak. The circumstances of my life have often forced me to confront the darker and more appalling aspects of society. These are the aspects that could really benefit from a blessing. If society is a garden, then these are the regions that could use some more fertilizer, water, or love.

This book was written for people who are intent on playing their part in ensuring that those troubled regions of the garden also flourish and prosper. It is a book written for those determined to provide blessings when they are needed, and to ensure the blessings they provide ring with power – the power of a veritable adept. If this divine mission resonates with your heart and will, then you will find much useful information herein.

Samantha P.
Vancouver, August 2016

Preface

We swallow greedily any lie that flatters us, but we sip only little by little at a truth we find bitter.

~Denis Diderot

    A well-known alchemical axiom states "Whoever has no knowledge of the correct beginning will never reach the desired ending." When it comes to magical training, the desired ending is to become an adept, yet few aspiring magicians ever succeed in reaching this desired ending. It's not that they don't have what it takes to reach this desired ending. The problem is that they don't know the correct beginning. People search their whole lives exploring various traditions, paradigms, and styles of magic without ever learning how to begin their training. They may try a few workings, and some of those workings may manifest results, which can be cool, but they never come close to acquiring "the freedom and discretionary power of a spirit who watches over and guides human evolution."

    If you think about it, the magical world is kind of a mess. There are thousands of books, YouTube videos, blogs, and websites about the subject of magic. There are numerous orders, lodges, and organizations. The internet is filled with forums and chatrooms for people who want to discuss magic. There are many knowledgeable people giving out good advice, and many ignorant people giving out bad advice. It is very difficult for the aspiring magician to sort through this mess and find the correct beginning.

    This book was written to help fix this problem. This book won't guide you all the way to the desired ending, but it will help you find the correct beginning. Once you find the correct beginning, you are so close yet so far from the rainbow. It is only a matter of walking the path step by step until you enter the house of wisdom and begin ascending to the country whence the shadows fall.

    This is not meant to be a book that is dense or difficult to read. I want this book to be easy to understand so that those who read it can assimilate the information it contains without unnecessary mental strain.

The Spirit of Magic by Virgil

To make the experience of reading this book easier and more enjoyable, I've provided a few clarifying comments in the sections below that will help you understand the following chapters.

Occultism vs. Magic (Linguistic Drift is a Thing)

In this book, I make a distinction between occultism and magic. Several people who read the first edition of this book had an issue with this distinction, claiming that my definition of occultism is incorrect, and that magic is not separate from occultism, but a part of occultism.

Those who assert that my definition of occultism is incorrect usually insist that occultism means "the study of hidden subjects." They base their definition on the word's etymology. The word "occultism" comes from the Latin word "occulere," which means "to hide." This is because the original meaning of occultism was indeed "the study of hidden subjects." That was back in the Middle Ages and in Victorian times. In those days, religious authorities and governmental bodies could persecute you for studying certain esoteric subjects or possessing books about those subjects. Therefore, the resources needed to study those subjects were hidden well, and the people who studied those subjects did so while hidden from the view of the public. It's not surprising those esoteric subjects came to be called "occultism."

However, the definitions of words change over time. For example, the word "nice" used to mean "silly" instead of "good," and the word "eerie" used to mean "feeling creeped out" instead of "creepy." We currently live in a world where people wear occult jewelry to show off the fact that they are occultists, and where any large bookstore is bound to have a section filled with occult books. Those things that fall under the category of occultism are no longer hidden, but displayed in full view of the public. More importantly, the way people use the word "occultism" is different from the way the word was used in the past. This is all that is needed to prove that the definition of the word, for all practical purposes, has changed. The study of esotericism-themed miscellanea, which is what is referred to as "occultism" these days, has little in common with magic, which is the art of using a balanced combination of inner and outer power wisely to fulfill the purposes of love. And if we examine communities of occultists and communities of magicians, it becomes even clearer that the two types of communities are formed from two very different types of people. In one type of community, you see people arguing about what color corresponds to what Hebrew letter, bragging about their grades, and speculating about the inner realms. In the other

Preface

type of community, you see people giving each other practical advice for improving mental discipline, discussing practical ways of acquiring self-knowledge, and passing on information about the inner realms they acquired through direct experience during the course of their practices.

Sorcery vs. Magic

I also make a distinction between sorcery and magic. During the course of this book, I explain that many of the esoteric authors of the past, including Paracelsus, Abraham, and Bardon, also distinguished between sorcery and magic for the same reasons I have, so this distinction is neither new nor revolutionary. Although this distinction is old, it is not necessarily universal. In other words, there are people out there who use the terms "sorcery" and "magic" interchangeably, resulting in magicians who call themselves sorcerers and sorcerers who call themselves magicians. Therefore, if you want to learn more about magic, you should not ignore someone just because he calls himself a sorcerer, and you should not listen to what someone says just because he calls himself a magician. If you want to determine if someone is a magician or a sorcerer, examine what they do, as opposed to what label they put on themselves. At the end of the day, one can add labels and change labels with little effort, but it is what you do that reflects your values and reveals what you really are.

A Note on Terms

I make use of different terms to differentiate between different types of people. An aspiring magician is someone who wants to become a magician but may not yet have chosen a magical training system to work through. A student is someone who has chosen a good (complete and balanced) system and is working through it. A Bardonist is a student of the Bardon system. A magician is anyone who has successfully finished working through any good magical training system. An initiate is someone who is proficient at mental wandering (this is Bardon's definition of the word). An adept is someone who possesses the level of maturity and magical skill needed to travel to the Sphere of the Sun via mental wandering (also Bardon's definition). A full adept is someone who possesses the level of maturity and magical skill needed to travel to the Sphere of Uranus via mental wandering.

The Spirit of Magic by Virgil

This Book's Point of View

Some people who have written reviews of the first edition of this book have remarked that it is written from a Bardonist point of view. I disagree. This book is written from MY point of view. Yes, I am a Bardonist. However, I am also an engineer, a former actor, a poet, an aspiring novelist, a lover, a karateka, an avid reader, someone trying to learn how to cook better, a volunteer tutor, a Natalie Portman fan, an Ariana Grande fan, and lots of other things. The point of view of this book is influenced by all of my life experiences, and not just the experiences that involve sitting in a chair practicing the exercises of IIH. No one is just a Bardonist, or just a Golden Dawn magician, or just a shaman, or just a vitki. Each person is many things, and his of view reflects all of the things he is.

Why I Reference the Bardon System so Much

Although I prefer to think of this book as being from my point of view as opposed to a Bardonist point of view, I do make regular references to the Bardon system in this book, which might be annoying for readers unfamiliar with the Bardon system. I do this for a simple reason. Over the past few years, I have seen many people who have never spent time working through the Bardon system making comments about this system. Usually, their comments are inaccurate and misleading, and reflect a complete lack of understanding of the system. I wouldn't have expected anything other than this to be the case; after all, they never spent time working through the system. To really understand the Bardon system enough to make accurate and intelligent comments about it, you need to have a decent understanding of the system, and a decent understanding of the system can only be acquired by working through it.

I have no doubt that this is true for other magical training systems as well. This is why I try not to comment on other magical training systems. Whenever I make general comments that apply to all magical training systems, I use examples from the Bardon system to illustrate my point. For this reason, to understand this book, you do need to familiarize yourself with how the Bardon system is set up. That way, whenever I write something like "Step 3" or "Sphere of the Moon," you will know what I am referring to. It would be best to read through IIH and PME before reading this book, but for those who want to hold off on doing that, I will present a brief overview of the Bardon system, and of the

Preface

initiatory and magical work contained in those two books later in this preface.

What is the Bardon System?

The Bardon system is a magical training system created by the Czech adept Franz Bardon, who lived in the early half of the twentieth century. Like any magical training system, it consists of various exercises that should be practiced daily in order to gradually develop the skills, abilities, and qualities of a genuine magician. The instructions for these exercises can be found in three books – *Initiation into Hermetics*, *The Practice of Magical Evocation*, and *The Key to the True Quabbalah*.[1]

One of the most unique things about the Bardon system is its origins. Bardon received the information and guidance he needed in order to create his system from various knowledgeable spirits. The spirits who primarily helped him were the ruling genii of the Earthzone and of the planetary spheres. While many of the other people who created magical training systems looked to the traditions and teachings of the past for information and guidance, Bardon chose to seek information and guidance from a significantly different source. While there are very important reasons for this choice, a discussion of those reasons is beyond the scope of this book.

Initiation into Hermetics (IIH)

The work of this book constitutes the basic training of a magician, and is divided into ten steps that must be worked through in sequence. Each step contains several mental, astral, and physical exercises. Unless stated otherwise, all of the exercises in a step must be mastered before the student can move on to the next step.

IIH, being a complete system of basic magical training, is also a system of initiation. In the modern esoteric world, "initiation" is a buzzword that is often thrown about but has no clear meaning. In the Bardon system, however, the word "initiation" does have a very specific meaning. In PME, Bardon writes the following.

> *There are only a few people in our physical world, who, with their spirit, are able to penetrate the borders of human existence and to proceed to other zones. People who are able*

The Spirit of Magic by Virgil

to do this consciously are called initiates from the point of view of Hermetics.

Thus, an initiate is someone who has mastered the technique of mental wandering, and initiation is the process of learning mental wandering. Since mental wandering is an important skill for all magicians to have, any complete magical training system will contain exercises to develop this skill. Therefore, all complete magical training systems are also systems of initiation, which is why I often use "magical training" and "initiation" interchangeably throughout this book. Remember that the word "initiation" may have a different meaning in the context of other systems and magical circles unrelated to the Bardon system.

The Practice of Magical Evocation (PME)

The magician must have completed the eighth step of IIH before he can begin the work contained in this book. The work of PME consists of learning from the ruling spirits, or "genii," of various realms on the inner planes. These realms are as follows.

  The Elemental Kingdoms
  The Zone Girdling the Earth (also called the Earthzone)
  The Sphere of the Moon
  The Sphere of Mercury
  The Sphere of Venus
  The Sphere of the Sun
  The Sphere of Mars
  The Sphere of Jupiter
  The Sphere of Saturn

The order of the realms listed above is the order the magician must follow when learning from their ruling spirits. For example, if a magician has not yet learned from the ruling spirits of the Sphere of Venus, then he is not yet ready to learn from the ruling spirits of the Sphere of the Sun. There are two ways the magician can learn from these spirits. He can use evocation to bring them to him, or he can use mental wandering to go to them. The instructions for both of these techniques are described in great detail by Bardon in PME.

Preface

Since the magician has already completed his basic training (or at least most of it) when he begins learning from these spirits, he can work magic to improve the world. Often, he will work together with the spirits he meets. The spirits, being powerful, can do things the magician can't. The magician, having a physical body, can do things it is difficult for the spirits to do. A magician and spirit working together make a fantastic team that can do a lot to bless society.

The Key to the True Quabbalah (KTQ)

This book teaches a powerful magical technique called Creative Speaking. It's not possible to fully understand Creative Speaking before one has completed Step 8 of IIH or reached the equivalent level in another magical training system because it is a form of advanced energy work, and the more nuanced aspects of energy work can't be explained in words, but must be understood through practical experience.

Esoteric theory teaches us that the universe is like a projection. If you have ever seen a projector projecting an image onto a wall, you will know that the image is sustained by a constant flow of light. If this flow of light were to stop, then the image on the wall would disappear. If you could manipulate the flow of light emanating from the projector, then you could also manipulate the image projected onto the wall.

A beam of light can be divided (via a prism) into different aspects, which we see as different colors. You can manipulate the flow of light sustaining the universe by manipulating the different aspects of this light. The magicians of various cultures have used the letters of their alphabet as names for these aspects. The Kabbalists used the Hebrew alphabet. The vitkar used the Elder Futhark. The Druids used Ogham. Bardon, adopting this system, used the German alphabet. All of these alphabets have different numbers of letters, but just as you can divide a pie into as many pieces as you want, you can divide the spectrum of light into as many colors as you want, so there is no contradiction.

The reason Bardon said this book is about Quabbalah is because Creative Speaking was indeed practiced by the Kabbalists.[2] However, there are many things besides Creative Speaking, such as gematria and angel work, that are also a part of the rich spiritual tradition that is Kabbalah but have nothing to do with Creative Speaking. Furthermore, there are many non-Jewish cultures that practiced Creative Speaking. For this reason, I think a better name for the book would have been *The Key to True Creative Speaking*. I don't mention KTQ too frequently in this book, so you don't really need to know anything about it. I only include a brief overview of the work of KTQ for the sake of completion, having already given overviews of Bardon's other two books.

The Astral Plane/Body vs. the Mental Plane/Body

> *The Sages will tell you*
> *That two fishes are in our sea*
> *Without any flesh or bones.*
>
> ~The Book of Lambspring

In the modern esoteric world, the astral plane and the mental plane are often collectively referred to as the "astral plane," and the astral body and the mental body are often collectively referred to as the "astral body." This has led to a lot of confusion, and a poor understanding of the inner worlds and the occult anatomy. While there is no single correct way to divide the range of vibrational density between the akashic/spiritual plane and the physical plane, models that divide this range into two levels (Kabbalah's Yetzirah and Briah, Bardon's astral and mental, Daskalos's psychic and noetic) are usually far more useful than those that treat this range as one level. This is because the higher and lower regions of this range really do have very different properties. For example, in the mental plane, the principle "like attracts like" holds all of the time, but in the astral plane, that principle holds only half of the time while the principle "opposites attract" holds the other half of the time. Furthermore, the limitations imposed by the dimensions of time and space are much less stringent on the mental plane than they are on the astral plane.

The astral and mental bodies, similarly, have very different properties and different uses. The astral body cannot travel beyond the Earthzone or else the astral matrix connecting it to the physical body will break, resulting in death. The mental body, on the other hand, can travel beyond the Earthzone. Furthermore, the processes that each of these two bodies undergoes after death are different. A lot of people have emailed me in the past asking questions about "astral projection." I am never able to answer those questions because I have no idea what they mean by "astral projection." Sometimes, people use the term "astral projection" to refer to the exteriorization of the mental body alone (what Bardonists call "mental wandering"). Other times, people use the term "astral projection" to refer to the exteriorization of the astral body as well as the mental body (what Bardonists call "astral wandering"). The answers to

Preface

their questions are often different depending on whether they are referring to the exteriorization of the astral body or the exteriorization of the mental body alone.

For the purposes of this book, you don't need a deep understanding of the difference between the astral plane and the mental plane, or of the difference between the astral body and the mental body, but you should understand that a difference exists. Thus, when I use the word "mental," you will know I am talking only about the mental level, and when I use the word "astral," you will know I am talking only about the astral level. When I am talking about both levels, I will use the term "astra-mental."

A Note Regarding Bardon System Jargon

I use a number of terms throughout this book that are a part of the jargon of the Bardon system. Some examples that come to mind are "exteriorization," "akashic trance," "depth-point meditation," "electromagnetic volt," "dynamide," and "fluid condenser." In most cases, it should be easy to figure out the meaning of a word from context alone. In the cases where it didn't seem to me that context was enough to figure out the meaning of a word, I've provided an explanation, either close by the word's first appearance or in an endnote. For those who want greater clarification regarding the meaning of an unfamiliar word, consulting IIH, typing the word in the search bar of AbardonCompanion.de, or requesting an explanation in an online Bardon forum are possible options for finding a more thorough and detailed definition.

Introduction

But as for the magician, he sees the purpose of the moral laws in ennobling the mind and the soul, for it is in an ennobled soul only that the universal powers can do their work, especially if the body, mind, and soul have been equally trained and developed.

~Franz Bardon

Magic is one of several disciplines that fall under the general category of esotericism. Esotericism is the study of the greater mysteries – the profound truths about God, nature, and man that the masses are not yet ready to behold and experience. Many of the greatest esoteric teachers, such as Jesus Christ, taught the greater mysteries to small groups of students who were mature enough to comprehend those mysteries. These same spiritual teachers gave the lesser mysteries to the masses. This wasn't because they selfishly wanted to keep the greater mysteries within an elite and exclusive group, but because it's pointless to present the greater mysteries to those who aren't ready to receive them. Jesus compared this to "casting pearls before swine." Any attempt to penetrate into the greater mysteries before one is ready to is a dangerous waste of time. There are numerous instances where individuals who lacked the maturity and balance needed to penetrate into the mysteries of magic tried to anyway by pursing magical training, only to acquire deranged minds and fragmented personalities.

The lesser mysteries are a preparation for the greater mysteries. Until a person has fully penetrated into the lesser mysteries and made their lessons his own, he cannot penetrate into the greater mysteries. Several esoteric masters founded religions as vehicles through which the lesser mysteries could be preserved for each new generation of seekers. In the modern forms of these religions, the lesser mysteries are often buried under piles of dogma that have been added over the years and have nothing to do with the founder's original teachings. However, the lesser mysteries are still there and if you peer through those piles of dogma, you will find them.

The lesser mysteries, in essence, concern the basic qualities of soul and spirit that need to be developed before it is possible to penetrate into

The Spirit of Magic by Virgil

the greater mysteries. Aspiring magicians who want to penetrate into the mysteries of magic rarely want to be told that they need to become compassionate, generous, humble, righteous, patient, and kind. If they wanted to be told that, they would go to a church, a synagogue, a mosque, or a temple, but not into a magical lodge. Aspiring magicians, however, do want to be told what Hebrew letter corresponds to the sign of Leo in the zodiac, and they do want to be told what ancient Egyptian deity corresponds to the 27th path of the Tree of Life. They memorize this information eagerly, thinking themselves far more enlightened than their religious neighbors who waste their time organizing food drives to feed the hungry and volunteering at local retirement homes to keep the elderly company. In truth, their religious neighbors have penetrated at least partially into the lesser mysteries, while these aspiring magicians have not done even that.

Anyone can memorize tables of correspondences and wave a wand around in the air while vibrating Hebrew names, but not everyone can penetrate into the mysteries of magic. The lesser mysteries deem it vital for the aspiring magician to possess certain qualities before he is truly capable of doing this. Of these qualities, the most important is the one that the master Jesus called "love." In 1 Corinthians, Paul summarizes one of Jesus's most important teachings as follows.

> *If I speak in the tongues of men or of angels, but do not have love, I am only a resounding gong or a clanging cymbal. If I have the gift of prophecy and can fathom all mysteries and all knowledge, and if I have a faith that can move mountains, but do not have love, I am nothing.*

Take a good look around the magical community. You will find many aspiring magicians spending hours of their time studying languages like Enochian that are supposedly spoken by angels. You will find many aspiring magicians spending hours of their time learning to divine using Tarot cards, horoscopes, or runes. You will find many aspiring magicians spending hours of their time trying to move candle flames with their minds. Yet, you will find few aspiring magicians striving to develop the quality of love and actively trying to treat others with love. It is no mystery why so few aspiring magicians succeed in becoming adepts.

There are many different types of love. There is the empathic love of the water element. There is the romantic love of the sephirah Netzach.

Introduction

There is the compassionate love of the sephirah Tiphereth. It is this latter type of love that Jesus, Krishna, Buddha, and so many other past masters of the greater mysteries spoke about. Compassionate love, or compassion for short, is the golden key that will open the doors to the greater mysteries. Once those doors are open, you still need to do all the walking required to penetrate into the realms behind them; but at least you have the opportunity to do that walking. This would not be the case if those doors remained closed.

Imagine if the most revered mathematicians in the world could not do basic arithmetic. This would be a ridiculous situation, yet we find an analogous situation in the magical community. Historically, many of the individuals revered as adepts were people who were just plain mean. Even to this day, there are quite a few individuals revered as adepts who are, again, just plain mean. Needless to say, an individual who has not even penetrated into the lesser mysteries cannot lead people into the greater mysteries. This is why so much of the magical world is just the blind leading the blind in circles.

Compassion isn't just about being nice to people. Don't get me wrong, being nice to people is the first level of acquiring compassion, and you do need to reach that first level if you want to develop the deep and profound compassion that characterizes the true adept. However, developing compassion doesn't end with learning to be nice to people. The compassion of a magician is a voice that wakes him up to the atrocities that go unnoticed in the world and compels him to embody divine levels of power and wisdom so that he can recreate the world into a better world filled with beauty, joy, and wonder. Many aspiring magicians spend decades reading countless books about chakras, sacred geometry, the Tree of Life, the Tarot, Egyptian deities, shamanism, yoga, evocation, qigong, sigils, astrology, and alchemical symbolism. They also practice the exercises they find in these books. However, despite all this reading and all this practicing of exercises, they decide at the end of their lives that they have wasted their time and that they haven't done anything productive. Instead of walking systematically and intelligently toward adepthood, they spent their years walking in circles.

Compassion is necessary because compassion prevents you from spending years walking in circles. Compassion demands that you develop genuine power and wisdom so that you can protect, serve, support, heal, and guide those you love. Compassion will cause you to continually examine yourself objectively and ruthlessly to assess just how successful you have been in developing that power and wisdom. If you have failed to gain in power and wisdom, then compassion will

The Spirit of Magic by Virgil

continue prodding you to explore until you find the path that will give you those two things. And when you do find that path, compassion will prod you to keep walking that path, even when the path becomes difficult and steep. It will remind you that there are people suffering, and it will remind you that the more you walk, the more power and wisdom you will have to help those people. The desire to be a hero is not strong enough to keep people walking this difficult path. The desire for praise and acknowledgement is not strong enough to keep people walking this difficult path. Only genuine love for others is strong enough to keep people walking this difficult path, and if you do not find this genuine love within yourself, you will not reach adepthood.

Chapter 1: The Practice of Asana

An asana is a posture. The practice of asana involves remaining in a posture for a set amount of time. To make steady progress in the practice of asana, you must practice every day. Choose an asana and remain in it for ten minutes each day. Do this until you can remain in it fairly comfortably and fairly still throughout the ten minute period. At this point, increase the amount of time you spend in the asana by one minute each day until you have reached thirty minutes. Continue to remain in the asana for thirty minutes each day until you can remain in it perfectly comfortably and perfectly still throughout the entire thirty minute period. When you have reached this level, you have become proficient enough at the practice of asana for the purposes of the beginning stages of magical training. However, you should continue to deepen your proficiency throughout the rest of your magical training. Eventually, you should reach the point where you can remain in the asana perfectly comfortably and perfectly still for an indefinite amount of time. When you can do this, you have mastered the asana.

There are many possible asanas the student of magic can choose when he begins the practice of asana. The curriculum of Hatha Yoga contains hundreds. Some of the more well-known asanas include padmasana (lotus posture), vrikshasana (tree posture), tadasana (mountain posture), and virabhandrasana (warrior posture). The practice of asana is a great way to improve one's health, and different asanas have different health benefits, which is the reason many people practice Hatha Yoga. As far as our purposes go, however, improved health is not the primary reason we practice remaining in an asana. Magic often requires us to enter deep states of meditation and use our minds in very precise and focused ways. This is impossible to do if our bodies are always distracting us. If we master an asana, then we know that while we are in that asana, our bodies are perfectly comfortable and perfectly still. Thus, there are no bodily discomforts (itches, cramps, restlessness, etc.) that can distract us as we enter deep states of meditation and use our minds to work powerful magic.

For these reasons, you should not choose a bizarre and difficult asana that will take you many years to master. Instead, you should choose a simple asana that you can master relatively quickly. The specific asana I use is known in many magical systems as the "throne posture," and I will refer to it by this name throughout this book. Bardon has students of his system using this posture in their asana practice when they reach Step 2. Crowley also has students of his system master a variation of this posture at the beginning of their training (he calls it the "god posture").[3]

The throne posture is very simple. Sit in a chair with your back straight, knees slightly apart, and palms facing downward on your thighs. Look ahead, point your toes forward, and make sure your lungs are unrestricted enough for you to breathe easily. According to Crowley, the adjective "braced" is a good way to describe the state your body should be in during your asana practice – firm, and neither too stiff nor so relaxed you are slouching.

How Not to Master an Asana

Many magicians attempt to master their asana by sitting in it for thirty minutes or an hour each day right from the start. It is much better to start with ten or even five minutes and gradually work your way up to half an hour by adding a minute each day. If you attempt to sit for an entire half hour at once the first time, the practice session will be very painful. You want to associate your asana with the idea of comfort, and practicing in this way will only cause you to associate your asana with discomfort and pain. I am not saying you will never experience discomfort or pain while mastering your asana, because you probably will. All I am saying is there is no need to feel more discomfort or pain than is necessary. This is the case for many other physical activities like jogging, tennis, basketball, or swimming. If you push yourself during your training because you want to excel, you're going to experience some discomfort and pain, but if you experience unnecessary discomfort and pain, you are probably training incorrectly. This can even result in injury if continued for a long time. A weak swimmer who wants to improve does not start by swimming the English Channel. A student of magic who wants to master an asana like the throne posture should not start by trying to sit in it for a half hour or an hour right off the bat. Like I said in the previous section, start with ten minutes and then gradually work your way up to half an hour or longer.

Chapter 1: The Practice of Asana

Some Benefits of the Practice of Asana

Those students who intend to advance beyond the beginning stages of magical training will find this basic exercise to be of the utmost importance. For one thing, the intermediate and advanced exercises take it for granted that the magician can at least sit still without fidgeting. Furthermore, the practice of asana will help the student develop many important traits, including the following.

1. Self-discipline
2. Patience
3. Persistence
4. Focus
5. Peace
6. Decisiveness

Self-discipline is absolutely vital in the study of magic. The student of magic needs to p⁴ractice his magical exercises every day. At the beginning of his training, his laziness will often tempt him to skip a day or two. When this happens, his self-discipline will be the primary weapon he has to overcome his laziness and force himself to practice. During the advanced stages of training, the student will have acquired a great deal of power. His self-discipline will often be one of the major safeguards that prevent him from using his power to destroy himself. If you are currently at the beginning of your training, you most likely will not fully understand what I mean by that. However, if you train correctly each day and develop magical power, wisdom, and understanding, then in a few years, you will see why the stories of those who reach for magical power before they have mastered themselves always end tragically. The practice of asana provides the student with an excellent way to begin the process of developing self-discipline. The lower animal self is always restless and those who are under its control ceaselessly move about and never stay still. Before we can express the nature of our higher selves, we must first gain control over our lower animal selves, and because it is restless, learning to sit perfectly still goes a long way toward achieving this control.

The practice of asana is a basic exercise, and as I will show later on, the basic exercises in magic are never flashy or dramatic. They are always simple – so simple that those who cannot see their value ignore and pass over them, thus ensuring they never make any real progress. This is a good thing, and is one of the ways the art of magic protects itself from those who are not suited to delve into its mysteries. It takes little effort to make a wand and carelessly walk around a circle while absentmindedly drawing pentagrams in the air and singing divine names you do not know the meaning of. Sitting perfectly still for half an hour, on the other hand, is a very difficult task for many. It's no wonder that so few people bother attempting such a feat.

Patience is another important trait that all students should possess. Lust for results often leads to no results at all, and the desire to make rapid progress in his training may compel a student to skip exercises or even entire steps as he attempts to advance toward adepthood.[5] If he is lucky, this impatient approach to his training will lead him nowhere at all. If he is unlucky, as is often the case, this impatient approach will lead him into great danger. Since it takes patience to sit perfectly still for a long time, asana is a great way to develop this trait.

Persistence is another important trait to have. The student trying to master an asana will find that steady progress only comes with daily practice. This is true of most exercises he will encounter later on his path, regardless of how basic or advanced they are. It's best for the student to realize this at the beginning of his training, and to establish the habit of daily practice right from the start.

With more complex exercises, the lower self can make many excuses to persuade you to skip practice. Perhaps you have run out of the necessary ingredients for a ritual, or you can't find the tools you need, or you don't have enough space, or you are afraid that your neighbors will hear you vibrating divine names. With something as simple as asana, there are few excuses the lower self can make for skipping practice, so it is a good exercise to work on as you make daily practice a part of your life.

The student's ability to focus is also developed to a great extent by the time he has mastered his asana. Whenever one's attention strays from the exercise, the tendency is to slouch and move around, even if the student is not aware he is doing this because he is not paying attention. To ensure that he has indeed remained perfectly still throughout the duration of the exercise, the student must be able to keep his attention on his body the whole time.

A magician's asana is his home, and all homes should be peaceful. When the student has mastered his asana, he will find that the stillness of his body leads to a stillness of the emotions and a stillness of the mind.

Chapter 1: The Practice of Asana

This stillness will provide him with peace. With further practice, he will be able to carry this peace with him throughout his daily life, even when he is not sitting in his asana.

Success in magic requires the student's full commitment to the path. He must be resolute and determined to succeed despite all obstacles. This is reflected in the practice of asana. During a student's first few practice sessions, his body may itch and cramp up. He may feel uncomfortable and wish to stop. If this is not enough to cause him to give up, his mind may also come up with many excuses to end the exercise. Regardless of what happens, he has already made the decision to remain in his asana for a predetermined amount of time and must do so until that time has passed.

The Purpose of the Practice of Asana

As useful and important as all of the qualities listed above are, developing those qualities is merely a nice bonus that comes with the practice of asana. They are not the primary reason we engage in this practice. In the context of magical training, the purpose of this practice is not to develop self-discipline, patience, persistence, improved focus, peace, and decisiveness, nor is it to promote health and physical fitness. The purpose is to ensure there is at least one posture the student is able to remain in comfortably for an extended period of time. Having mastered his asana, he should remain confident that he will not be disturbed or distracted by his body when performing the various exercises of the magical training system he has chosen – plastic imagination exercises, depth point meditation, pore breathing, VOM, exteriorization, etc. Some of these exercises are impossible to master if your body is distracting you while you are practicing them; however, your body cannot distract you if you are in an asana you've mastered because your body is perfectly comfortable and perfectly still. If this isn't the case, then you haven't truly mastered that asana.

Many magical exercises involve entering altered states of consciousness. Not too long ago, I was reminded of just how important it is to be physically comfortable when entering altered states of consciousness. No, I was not meditating or performing a ritual. I was lying in bed sick and trying to fall asleep; however, my migraine and my constant need to cough kept me from drifting off into the bliss of sleep. Similarly, itches and cramps in your body may impair your efforts to achieve altered states of consciousness such as VOM, the akashic trance, or the various planetary levels of consciousness.

Understanding the purpose of the practice of asana will help you choose a good asana to master. Some people feel compelled to master padmasana because this asana is traditionally used for spiritual practices. However, when you understand the purpose of the practice of asana (in the context of magical training), then you realize that the throne posture fulfills this purpose just as well as padmasana does. The throne posture is easier to master than padmasana because with the throne posture, you don't have to spend a period of time increasing the flexibility of your hips and legs. Therefore, the throne posture makes more sense as a first asana to master than padmasana does. The sooner you move on from the practice of asana to more advanced exercises, the sooner you will become an adept. There is no reason to spend an unnecessarily long time on the practice of asana by choosing an unnecessarily difficult asana to master.

I've seen people claim that it's better to choose an asana that is difficult to master because mastering a difficult asana strengthens your willpower more than mastering an easy asana does. While it's true that less willpower is required to master an easy asana than a difficult asana, this assertion reflects a lack of understanding of the purpose of the practice of asana for students of magic. We master an asana so we can practice later magical exercises in that asana without our bodies distracting us. If you want to spend time mastering difficult asanas to improve your willpower, that's great. However, first master a simple asana so you can move on from this stage of your training to the later stages in which you have to use your asana.[6]

Comments on the Throne Posture

The throne posture requires the magician to keep his back straight. In traditional yoga, the explanation for keeping the back straight while sitting in an asana had to do with "prana," the vital force animating the body. The idea was that if the back was straight, prana would be able to flow better through the channels around the spine, promoting good health. This is true, but there are less esoteric reasons why a student should keep his back straight while doing this exercise.

A Harvard professor named Amy Cuddy specializes in body posture and differentiates between "low power poses" and "high power poses." A low power pose, according to Cuddy, is any posture that makes

Chapter 1: The Practice of Asana

someone feel weaker and less confident simply by being in that posture. In her works, she gives several examples of low power poses. Nearly all of them involve slouching and crossing the arms over the chest to form a shield. These are things people do when they are trying to make themselves small or hide.

The high power poses are much more varied, but many of them involve a straight back and an open unrestricted chest. Cuddy recommends that everyone spend a few minutes in a high power pose before any stressful encounter like an interview because the pose itself is enough to make a person feel confident and powerful. The throne posture obviously leans much more toward being a high power pose. Think about its very name – "throne posture." Look at pictures of kings and gods seated upon their thrones. Do any of them seem unconfident? Do any of them look like they doubt their power and authority? Do any of them slouch?

An asana is more than just a physical body position. It is also a feeling and a state of mind. When the throne posture is assumed correctly, it should result in a feeling of confidence, power, and stability. This is much more important than one might think because a student's confidence in himself will greatly impact how well his magical training goes. Whether or not you are confident in your ability to successfully complete an exercise may make all the difference in whether or not you actually do so.[7]

This is also why frustration is very detrimental. If you continually become frustrated while practicing an exercise, you will quickly lose confidence in your ability to do it. The proper thing to do whenever you feel frustrated is to immediately relax. Remind yourself that you will inevitably master the exercise if you persist, and that magical advancement is not meant to be a race. Repeat to yourself "I am confident." In fact, if you have doubts about yourself before even starting the exercise, which may be the case if you have been repeatedly unsuccessful in the past, then repeat the affirmation to yourself several times before starting and imagine that you have already mastered the exercise. You will never successfully master any exercise if you practice it with a negative attitude. In fact, if your frustration ever gets too bad, stand up, go to the nearest sink, turn the water as cold as possible, and use the technique of magical washing to wash the frustration down the drain, as well as any sense of failure or doubt you have.

The Spirit of Magic by Virgil

A Mastered Asana is Like a Home

Earlier, I compared a magician's asana to his home, and this is indeed the way I have come to think of my asana over the years. Just as it is important for a person to feel comfortable in his home, it is important for a magician to feel comfortable in his asana. Not everyone wants the same sort of home. Some people prefer homes by the bright sunny beach. Others prefer homes in the dark quiet forest. Some people want large mansions with expensive furniture. Others prefer simple huts. Similarly, there is no asana that is perfectly suited for everyone. Some asanas (e.g. the throne posture) involve sitting in a chair. Others involve sitting (e.g. padmasana) or kneeling on the ground (e.g. seiza). Pick one that suits you and stick with it. Someone who changes homes all the time without ever settling in will find it very difficult to build up a family life. Likewise, someone who changes asanas all the time without ever mastering it will never build up a magical life.

A person should also be able to engage in whatever activities he wants in his home. I like to sing, but I am terrible at it so you will never find me singing karaoke in front of a large crowd. At home, I can sing whenever I want and as much as I want without feeling self-conscious. Likewise, a magician in his asana should be able to do whatever exercises he wants – breathing exercises, visualization exercises, concentration exercises, meditation, etc. Some people require a special room or even an entire building just for their magical exercises, but I have never found that necessary. Whenever I am sitting in my asana, the external outside world fades from my awareness anyway, so it does not matter where I am sitting.

Life is a rollercoaster, and several times, my life has taken a sharp turn for the worse. The first time this happened, I was in the middle of mastering my asana. The practice was painful, but the pain was physical and it distracted me from the emotional pain I was going through at the time which was much worse. In this way, I came to seek refuge in my asana.

This continued on through the next few years, even after I had mastered my asana and sitting in it was no longer painful. Whenever I went through dark times, my asana became more than a home. It became a veritable fortress. Whatever anxieties or worries were on my mind would immediately vanish upon assuming my asana. It eventually got to the point where I was hiding from life by sitting in my asana. Whenever I felt I couldn't handle life, I'd just sit in my asana and let the outside

Chapter 1: The Practice of Asana

world fade away. During this time, I wasn't practicing any magical or spiritual exercises like visualization, meditation, or japa. I was just sitting. I might as well have just slept my life away, as most people do when depressed, but I preferred siting in my asana even to sleeping! Of course, in retrospect, it is never a good idea to hide from life in any way. I bring this up only to show just how comfortable I am in my asana, and why I have come to think of my asana as a home.

Later on, when I experimented a little in ritual magic, I ended up thinking of my circle in the same way – as a home. As with any good home, I felt comfortable and "at home" in my circle. I personalized it so it appealed to me and called in energies that resonated well with me. I designed it using symbols and patterns that were aesthetically pleasing to me and brought in objects that were meaningful to me when I performed my rituals. My circle also became a fortress against the outside world. When I drew that line of golden fire in the air around me and closed it, I was sealing out anything related to work, school, or relationships so I could focus on the magical task I wished to accomplish.

The practice of constructing circles is one that is found in many traditions of magic, and one that is given great importance. New members of the Golden Dawn were given the Lesser Ritual of the Pentagram to practice the act of creating a ritual circle right at the beginning of their training. Some Wiccan systems also teach this practice at the beginning of their training because it can be a powerful tool for enhancing the effectiveness of a magical working. I am sure most practitioners of magic would agree with me that a magician's circle should feel like a home to him, but how can a magician feel at home in his circle if he does not even feel at home in his own body?

No one wants to remain in a home that is not safe. Likewise, no magician wants to remain in an asana that is injurious or unhealthy. Remaining slouched is terrible for the back.[8] At one point, sitting with the back straight was considered to be the position healthiest for the back. For this reason, schoolchildren were told to sit in this manner. It has since been discovered that this position puts a lot of pressure on the lower back, which has to support a lot of weight, but it is still much better than slouching. Just be sure to stretch your back before and after practicing. The best position for the back is laying down flat, but the problem with using this as an asana is that it is very easy to fall asleep in such a posture.

The Spirit of Magic by Virgil

The Practice of Asana and Concentration

The Bardonist who has read up to this point might be wondering why Bardon put the practice of asana in Step 2 instead of in Step 1 if it's so important. As I've stated earlier, someone who is absent-minded or daydreams while practicing asana is wasting his time because his body will begin to slouch and fidget without him noticing it. Therefore, Bardon wanted the student to have some rudimentary skill in concentration before practicing this exercise. In Liber ABA, Crowley also discusses this problem of drifting attention during the practice of asana. His suggestion was for the student to choose an awkward and cramped posture to master so that the uncomfortableness would constantly draw his mind to his body and prevent it from wandering around. I have already explained why I disagree with this solution.

If you have decided to work through the magical training system Bardon lays out in IIH, then do practice the exercises in order. There is a very clear logic behind the sequence Bardon chose. The Step 1 mental exercises are relatively simple and do not require the student to sit still for long periods of time, but for later exercises like depth point meditation and accumulating the elements, it is imperative that the student has mastered an asana and feels completely at home in it.

Exercises Resembling the Practice of Asana

Throughout your exploration of the magical world, you will likely come across many exercises and practices that resemble the practice of asana but aren't the practice of asana. It's important not to confuse these with the practice of asana, because if you do, this indicates you don't properly understand the practice of asana, and therefore are more likely to do it incorrectly.

For example, in Israel Regardie's book *The One Year Manual*, there is a body awareness exercise that also involves sitting in a chair. Many people confuse this exercise with the practice of asana, but it is a different exercise. In the practice of asana, your focus is on keeping your body perfectly still. In Regardie's body-awareness exercise, your focus is on being aware of the sensations felt by your body. These are two different things to focus on, and therefore, the two exercises develop two different skills. One exercise is designed to teach you how to keep your body still for a long period of time. The other exercise is designed to teach you how to be aware of bodily sensations.

Chapter 1: The Practice of Asana

Final Comment

In bringing this chapter to a close, I'll point out that when Crowley says getting into a mastered asana is like getting into a nice hot bath when tired, he is not exaggerating. When the student has mastered his asana, it will provide him with the stillness of earth, the clarity of air, the alertness of fire, and the serenity of water.

Chapter 2: The Purified Elemental Equilibrium

If an individual is easily susceptible to anger, depression, obsession, sorrow, confusion, fear, and so forth, then as he increases his exposure to primal energies, out of control emotions and mental states will also increase in strength. Consequently, knowing oneself and developing wisdom should precede the development of power and control over the elements.

~William Mistele

Life is THE test of your elemental equilibrium. When you achieve the equilibrium, you will know it beyond a doubt.

~Rawn Clark

The journey to adepthood is a difficult one filled with many challenges. This journey turns from difficult to impossible, however, if the student neglects to build a strong foundation. A very important part of building a strong foundation is the process of developing a purified elemental equilibrium

The Personality

Like all things in the created universe, your mental body is made of the four elements – fire, water, earth, and air. If you think about all the different people you know, you might notice that they all have different sets of mental traits. Some people possess positive mental traits such as optimism, open-mindedness, intelligence, being able to think rationally, being able to discriminate, and having a good memory. Other people possess negative mental traits such as pessimism, narrow-mindedness, paranoia, stupidity, gullibility, and having a poor memory. What mental traits you possess depends on how balanced and pure the elements constituting your mental body are.

The Spirit of Magic by Virgil

Your astral (emotional) body is also made of the four elements. If you think about all the different people you know, you might notice that they all have different sets of emotional traits. Some people possess positive emotional traits such as patience, compassion, and cheerfulness. Other people possess negative emotional traits like irritability, greed, and arrogance. What emotional traits you possess depends on how balanced and pure the elements constituting your astral body are.

Your mental traits and emotional traits are collectively referred to as personality traits, and the collection of your personality traits is your personality. In your magical studies, you're going to come across many adepts who will tell you (either via their writings or maybe even in person) that it is important to become balanced and pure, and to remain balanced and pure throughout your magical career. This means balancing and purifying your personality, and keeping your personality balanced and pure.

Balancing One's Personality

Consider a person whose personality is represented in Table 1.

Fire Traits	Self-discipline, charisma, assertiveness, vigilance, courage
Air Traits	Intelligence
Water Traits	Empathy, serenity
Earth Traits	Patience

Table 1: Unbalanced Personality

Clearly, this person's personality is not very balanced. He has many fire traits, but relatively few air, earth, and water traits. To become more balanced, he should develop some (positive) air, earth, and water traits. If he does this, his personality might look like the personality represented in Table 2.

Fire Traits	Self-discipline, charisma, assertiveness, vigilance, courage
Air Traits	Intelligence, open-mindedness, creativity, cheerfulness, optimism
Water Traits	Empathy, kindness, adaptability, serenity, vivaciousness

Chapter 2: The Purified Elemental Equilibrium

Earth Traits	Patience, down-to-earth, thorough, humble, dependable

Table 2: Balanced Personality

The personality in Table 2 is well-balanced.[9] In this personality, there are just as many fire traits as there are air, earth, and water traits.

Purifying One's Personality

Consider the personality represented in Table 3.

Fire Traits	Irascibility, jealousy, lustfulness, arrogance
Air Traits	Addiction to daydreaming, tendency to gossip, frivolity, shyness
Water Traits	Complacency, conformity, self-restricting, passive-aggressiveness
Earth Traits	Greed, laziness, dullness, apathy

Table 3: Impure Personality

This personality is technically balanced; however, nobody would say that a person with a personality like this one is highly spiritually evolved or mature enough to handle any magical power the universe might give him. The elements are equally strong in his personality, but they are impure, so the traits arising from the elements are the sorts of negative traits you would find on a black soul mirror rather than on a white soul mirror. The personality represented in Table 2 is pure, as well as balanced.

What is a Purified Elemental Equilibrium?

A purified elemental equilibrium is a state in which all of one's personality traits are positive, and the presence of each of the four elements is equally strong in the personality traits constituting one's personality. The personality in Table 2 is an example of a personality in a state of purified elemental equilibrium. There are an equal number of fire, water, earth, and air traits, so th personality is balanced. Furthermore, all of the personality traits are positive, so the personality is pure.

For the sake of concision, most magicians shorten the phrase "purified elemental equilibrium" to just "elemental equilibrium." From this point forward in the book, I also use the phrase "elemental "equilibrium" to refer to a purified elemental equilibrium.[10] However, it is important to remember that one's personality must be pure as well as balanced.

The Pentagram

There are two symbols often used in modern Western magic to illustrate the concept of an elemental equilibrium. One of these symbols is the pentagram.

The pentagram symbolizes a human being and has five points. The top point corresponds to akasha, and each of the lower four points corresponds to one of the four elements. This represents the fact that a person is made up of akasha, fire, water, earth, and air.

<u>The Balanced Pentagram</u>

A balanced pentagram is a pentagram in which all points are the same size. Let's say that a person has many fire traits but few air, water, or earth traits (e.g. Table 1). This person is not a balanced pentagram. Instead, he is a pentagram in which the fire point is very big, and the air, water, and earth points are very small.

A person with a personality like that represented in Table 2 is a balanced pentagram. He has an equal number of fire, water, earth, and air traits. Therefore, his fire, water, earth, and air points are all the same size.

<u>The Upright Pentagram</u>

An inverted pentagram is a pentagram that is upside down. In other words, the point corresponding to akasha is at the bottom, and the other four points are on top of it. There are certain traits that do not arise from the four elements, but from the presence of divine spirit within us. These traits are sometimes called "higher

Chapter 2: The Purified Elemental Equilibrium

faculties." Two examples of higher faculties are will and reason, which are the two most relevant to this sectiom.[11]

In an upright pentagram, the akasha point is above the four elemental points, meaning that the personality traits arising from the elements do not supersede one's will and reason.[12] It's not hard to see why this is a good thing. Irritability (the tendency to become angry) is a fire trait. Let's say you are at work and your coworker makes fun of your shoes. Your irritability might compel you to punch your coworker. Clearly, this is not a reasonable way of handling this situation. If you are an upright pentagram, then your will and reason supersede your irritability. Your irritability might create within you an impulse to punch your coworker, but your ability to reason allows you to come up with a more reasonable way of handling the situation, and with your will, you can overcome the impulse to punch your coworker and force yourself to handle the situation in the more reasonable way you came up with.

Greed presents us with another example of the importance of being an upright pentagram. Greed is an earth trait. Your greed might create impulses within you to take more than your fair share of an allotted resource. Clearly, it is not reasonable to take more than your fair share of the resource. However, with the power of your reason, you can determine what is a reasonable/fair amount of the resource to take, and with your will, you can fight the impulses by forcing yourself to take only a reasonable amount of the resource and no more.

If you are an inverted pentagram, then your elemental traits superseded your higher faculties. In this case, you can never will yourself to act reasonable. You always act however your elemental traits compel you to act. This is a bad situation to be in if your elemental traits are mostly negative (e.g. if you're like the person represented in Table 3). If your elemental traits are mostly positive, then it's not as bad of a situation to be it, but becoming spiritually evolved still requires you to place your elemental traits under the dominion of your higher faculties.

The "Blazing Star"

If the elements constituting a person's astra-mental body are impure, then he is represented by a dull pentagram. The purer the elements constituting a person's astra-mental body are, the brighter the pentagram representing him is. Very bright pentagrams are sometimes called "blazing stars."

The Spirit of Magic by Virgil

When discussing inverted vs. upright pentagrams, I stated that if you possess the trait of irritability, you can use your will to overcome the angry impulses coming from your irritability. In this way, you can force yourself to act calmly and patiently, even if your irritability is trying to compel you to act angrily. This is good, but if you never root out your irritability, then each time you get angry, a battle between your will and your anger will occur. This can be exhausting and stressful. Therefore, you should also purify the fire element in your astra-mental body so that instead of manifesting as negative fire traits like irritability, it manifests as positive fire traits like assertiveness. The more you purify an element, the brighter that element's point on the pentagram becomes until eventually it is blazingly bright.

The Ideal Pentagram

A person with an elemental equilibrium is represented by an ideal pentagram. This is a pentagram that is...

1) Balanced (equal number of fire, water, earth, and air traits)
2) Bright (traits are all positive)
3) Upright (traits are under the dominion of one's will and reason)

The Cross of Equilibrated Forces

The second symbol that is often used to illustrate an elemental equilibrium is the Cross of Equilibrated Forces.[13] This is a Greek (equal-armed) cross where each arm represents an element. Usually, the top arm represents air, the bottom arm represents earth, the right arm represents fire, and the left arm represents water. The center point where all four arms merge represents akasha. Right now, symbolically speaking, everyone stands somewhere on this cross. If you are a very "fiery" person, in other words if you possess a lot of fiery traits like assertiveness, self-discipline, charisma, and enthusiasm, then you stand on the fire arm of the cross. Likewise, if you are a very "airy" person, in other words if you possess a lot of airy traits like intelligence, creativity, and open-mindedness, then you stand on the air arm of the cross. If you are a fiery person, then you are imbalanced toward the fire element. To become balanced, you should develop more (positive) air, water, and

Chapter 2: The Purified Elemental Equilibrium

earth traits. Similarly, if you are an airy person, then you should develop more (positive) fire, water, and earth traits to become balanced. When you are balanced, there is no single element dominating your personality, so you don't stand on any arm of the cross. Instead, you stand at the center of the cross. One of the documents of the Hermetic Order of the Golden Dawn tells its initiates the following.

> *Establish thyself firmly in the Equilibrium of Forces, in the center of the Cross of the Elements; that Cross, from whose center, the Creative World issued in the birth of the Dawning of Time.*

To stand at the center of the cross is to have established an elemental equilibrium. The center point is the part of the cross that represents akasha. Akasha is, in a sense, the source of the created universe – the universe of space and time.[14] This is why the center of the cross is described in the document as the place where "the Creative Word issued in the birth of the Dawning of Time." Akasha is also the medium through which Divinity interacts with the created universe, and therefore the medium through which the created universe (which we are a part of) can interact with Divinity. Thus, the center of the Cross of Equilibrated Forces can be seen as a window to Divinity. When we stand at this center point, we can interact with Divinity, access Divinity, and even assume the power and authority of Divinity by temporarily merging with Divinity through this window. This is why Mouni Sadhu writes the following.

> *The mystical authority of Man is based on the fact, that he should stand in the center of the Hermetic Cross, then being present in all its elements, and so become the master of them, as is the case with the central point which belongs to all of the cross.*

This comment on the elemental equilibrium puts the concept in the context of those traditional practices that deal with spirits. In many grimoires there is this idea that one must have authority to conjure and command spirits, and that this authority comes from God. In the Goetia, there is a line in one of the conjurations that goes "Also I, being made after the image of God, endued with power from God and created according unto his will, do exorcise thee [...]" Well, are you really made in the image of God? Of course not! God is perfectly balanced, and this balance is seen in the four divine elemental qualities of omnipotence (fire), omniscience (air), omnipresence (water), and eternity (air). Until you have balanced and purified the elements that form you, you are at best a very poor image of God, and that is not enough for you to access the authority of God.

Why Establishing an Elemental Equilibrium is Done at the Beginning of One's Training

Eliphas Levi is the first esoteric author I am aware of to explicitly describe the concept of an elemental equilibrium. In D&R, he writes the following,

To overcome and subjugate the elementary spirits, we must never yield to their characteristic defects. Thus, a shallow and capricious mind will never rule the Sylphs; an irresolute, cold and fickle nature will never master the Undines; passion irritates the Salamanders; and avaricious greed makes its slaves the sport of Gnomes. But we must be prompt and active, like the Sylphs; pliant and attentive to images, like the Undines; energetic and strong like the Salamanders; laborious and patient, like the Gnomes: in a word, we must overcome them in their strength without ever being overcome by their weaknesses.

This is an eloquent and accurate description of an elemental equilibrium. According to Levi, only after achieving this state can the magician begin working with the powers of the elements. Those who ignore this natural order of progress put themselves at risk. Note that in Bardon's system, only after achieving this state (via Steps 1 and 2) can the magician begin accumulating, condensing, and projecting the elements (Steps 3 through 5), and later working with the elemental spirits when he develops clairvoyance and learns mental wandering (Steps 7 through 10). To do so earlier is dangerous. One must first master the elements in the microcosm before attempting to master them in the macrocosm. Although this is a very common mindlessly repeated concept, few people bother to learn what it means and put it into practice. People will pay enormous sums of money for rituals designed to control

Chapter 2: The Purified Elemental Equilibrium

the elements in the macrocosm, but will not spend even a few seconds thinking about what it means to master the elements in the microcosm first.

The Golden Dawn included a variation of the above passage by Levi in its Practicus document *On the General Guidance and Purification of the Soul*. For reference, the latter part of the passage is as follows.

> *Be thou therefore prompt and active as the Sylphs, but avoid frivolity and caprice; be energetic and strong like the Salamanders, but avoid irritability and ferocity; be flexible and attentive to images as the Undines, but avoid idleness and changeability; be laborious and patient like the Gnomes, but avoid grossness and avarice. So shalt thou gradually develop the powers of thy Soul, and fit thyself to come in contact with the Spirits of the Elements. For wert thou to summon the Gnomes but to pander to thine avarice, thou wouldst no longer command them, but they would command thee.*

Mathers also makes the following remarks about this passage in a footnote.

> *This paragraph must not be taken to mean that the Sylphs themselves are necessarily frivolous and capricious; that the Salamanders are irritable and ferocious; the Undines idle and changeable; the Gnomes gross and avaricious; but that contact with these races without due preparation and self-control might easily tend to increase and foster such defects in ourselves to an undesirable extent.*

In other words, Mathers himself also understood, at least on an intellectual level, the importance of establishing an elemental equilibrium. He realized that if one were to interact with elemental forces or elemental beings prematurely, this contact would "increase and foster" the impurities and imbalances (AKA "defects") within us. This same Practicus document also tells the student to "establish thyself firmly in the Equilibrium of Forces, in the center of the Cross of the Elements; that Cross, from whose center, the Creative World issued in the birth of the Dawning of Time." Thus, we see that the order did explicitly tell its students to establish an elemental equilibrium. However, despite this, the

The Spirit of Magic by Virgil

order gave no methods or instructions for actually establishing an elemental equilibrium. Therefore, despite being told to establish an elemental equilibrium, the members of this order had no idea how to even begin the process of doing that. As a result of this incompleteness in the system, many of them failed at this task. Unsurprisingly, if you examine the politics and dynamics of the order while it existed, much of it was driven by frivolity, caprice, irritability, ferocity, and grossness. The resulting effects of this are seen in the bickering, feuding, and general immaturity that characterizes its history. It was not until Bardon collected together the techniques of autosuggestion, conscious eating, conscious breathing, magical washing, and assumption, and presented them all in IIH that the magical world had a clearly defined set of tools and instructions for establishing the previously elusive state of an elemental equilibrium.

In spiritual alchemy, the godly and noble part of an individual is symbolized by gold, while the gross and impure part of an individual is symbolized by lead. It is often said that to make gold, one must first have gold. What is not often said, but equally true, is that to make lead, one must first have lead. Therefore, if you intend to create gold, use the six-pronged attack to transform the lead within you into gold. Only then are you in a position to create more gold. Otherwise, you will only end up with more lead.

If a person is irritable, lustful, and violent, then the practice of pore breathing the fire element will cause him to become more irritable, lustful and violent.

If a person is assertive, charismatic, and courageous, then the practice of pore breathing the fire element will cause him to become more assertive, charismatic, and courageous.

If a person is greedy, lazy, and dull, then the practice of pore breathing the earth element will cause him to become more greedy, lazy, and dull.

If a person is hardworking, patient, and calm, then the practice of pore breathing the earth element will cause him to become more hardworking, patient, and calm.

Your body is the athanor in which your soul and spirit are placed to be transformed. The elemental forces you bring within the athanor of your body via the Step 3 pore breathing exercises serve in part to transform the soul and spirit housed within this athanor. Whether you end up with more lead or more gold after this transformation process depends on what you began with.

Do you now see why establishing an elemental equilibrium is so important? If you attempt the practice of pore breathing the elements

Chapter 2: The Purified Elemental Equilibrium

before you are ready to do so, you will turn into a monster. If you are an angry or violent individual, then having such traits strengthened by pore breathing the fire element will turn you into a veritable danger to those around you. The wise will heed my warnings. The foolish will not.

Rooting out most but not all of a negative trait is often no better than rooting out none of it at all. If you root out most but not all of a negative trait, then when you move on to Step 3, the work of pore breathing the elements will strengthen the weakened negative trait. It will grow strong again, and all of your hard work will have been for nothing. A student of magic should be serious, and a serious student strives for excellence. Someone striving for excellence is not going to be satisfied with mostly conquering irascibility. He will only be satisfied when he has completely rooted out this negative trait from himself.

The ideas I put forth in the last few paragraphs are by no means new in the world of modern Western magic. Besides the previously quoted note by Mathers, there are quite a few books that explain to readers that constantly working with the fire element or some other fiery energy like Mars, Geburah, or Aries, may cause you to become irascible and develop violent tendencies. A warning is given for the magician to keep this in mind and be very careful. One book I am aware of even advises the magician to make use of magic very infrequently in order to minimize the dangers of becoming too unbalanced from contact with magical energies. The actual solution to this problem is to develop an elemental equilibrium. This should be common sense, really. Someone trying to work with intense magical energies without an elemental equilibrium is like a knight riding into battle without armor or a firefighter entering a burning building without his protective suit.

The bottom line is this. Working with the fire element, whether through pore breathing or ritual magic, will not cause you to become irritable. It will augment and strengthen the irritability already within you. However, if you root out the trait of irritability so that it no longer exists within you, then there will be no irritability within you for the fire element to augment. Therefore, working with the fire element, or a fiery energy like Mars, Geburah, or Aries, will not cause you to become more irritable.

Life as the Test of One's Elemental Equilibrium

The second epigraph of this chapter is a quote from one of Rawn's articles in which he states that life is the definitive test that will reveal whether or not you have an elemental equilibrium. This is something that all Bardonists must realize before they move on to Step 3 because otherwise, they can never be certain that they do have an elemental equilibrium and are therefore ready to move on to Step 3.

I want to now discuss what is mean by the statement that life is the ultimate test of whether or not you have an elemental equilibrium. There are two ways of thinking about this. When you have an elemental equilibrium, you have rooted out all of the impurities and imbalances in your astra-mental body, including impurities and imbalances like impatience, greed, and social anxiety. Life will put you in frustrating situations that may cause you to become impatient. Life will provide you with temptations that may cause you to act greedily. Life will put you in the presence of many other people, possibly causing you to feel anxious as a result. In this way, you will come to know whether or not there is impatience, greed, or social anxiety in your personality, or whether you have truly rooted out these impurities/imbalances. This is one thing that is meant when Bardonists say that life is the ultimate test of whether or not you have an elemental equilibrium. By objectively observing the ways you think/feel/act in various life experiences, you will be able to tell if there are still major impurities/imbalances (negative personality traits) you possess and need to root out, or if you have rooted out all the major ones and are left with only minor and trivial ones (no one is ever perfectly pure and balanced).

Another way of thinking about how life is the definitive test is that the better of an elemental equilibrium you have, the more successful you are in life. That's because the impurities/imbalances you root out of your personality are the traits that often cause people to fail in their endeavors, and the positive personality traits you develop that are indicative of a pure and balanced personality (e.g. assertiveness, organization, self-discipline, intelligence, etc.) are the traits that often help people accomplish their goals and achieve their dreams. As another example in Bardonist literature of this idea that life is the definitive test of your elemental equilibrium, Bill writes the following in his extended essay about the elemental equilibrium.

> *What kind of imbalance might throw a wrench into one's life work? One would be a Shakespearean character flaw. Envy and greed destroy Macbeth. Hamlet suffers from indecision. He is unable to take action because his feelings are troubled by uncertainty, ambiguity, and the responsibility suddenly imposed upon him. These two claimants to the throne obviously were not working on their magical equilibrium.*

Chapter 2: The Purified Elemental Equilibrium

There are rumors that Shakespeare was an initiate of some sort. While I'm not aware of any substantial evidence to support this claim, I have found that many of the life lessons in his writings can be extremely valuable for those walking the magical path. The Greek poet Homer, another supposed initiate, wrote epics that also contained heroes with tragic flaws, which in terms of the occult anatomy can be viewed as impurities/imbalances in the astra-mental body. The tragic flaw of Achilles, for example, was arrogance. Had these heroes rooted out their tragic flaws with the six-pronged attack (discussed in Chapter 4), they would have been fine. After you create your black soul mirror, you will have a whole list of tragic flaws that you can root out so you don't end up like Macbeth, Hamlet, or Achilles.

The Elemental Equilibrium and Practical Magic

Practical magic is often seen as the art of controlling the forces/energies of the astra-mental plane. Therefore, many people believe that the entirety of practical magic training consists of learning to control these forces. That is only half of it. Before you can control these forces, you must first break the control they have over you and free yourself from their influence. This is what establishing an elemental equilibrium is all about. The tendency to overlook this crucial first step is the reason many magical systems fail to produce genuine adepts. If you do not have an elemental equilibrium, the exercises that were designed to increase your control over the elements will do the opposite. They will increase the control the elements have over you. Instead of becoming liberated from their influence, you will become further enslaved. If you spend some time in the occult world, you're going to come across people who try to establish control over the fire element through powerful fire rituals, only to become irritable power-hungry egomaniacs. You're going to come across people who try to establish control over the water element through powerful water rituals, only to become frigid, socially inept, and depressed. When you observe these sorts of phenomena, you'll know their cause.

In the Bardon system, the word "initiation" refers to the process of learning to sense, influence, and move on the inner planes. The establishment of a basic elemental equilibrium is the first step in initiation. Think about the ocean. It is filled with waves and currents that will pull and push you every which way. Only a very strong person can successfully resist these waves and currents and swim wherever he will without straying off course. The inner planes are like an ocean. They too have their currents, waves, and cycles that will push and pull travelers off course if they are not strong enough to resist them. These currents, waves, and cycles of inner forces are personified by Nahash, the great writhing astral serpent. While physical strength is determined by the amount of muscle one has, inner strength is determined by the magician's elemental equilibrium. If the magician possesses a genuine elemental equilibrium, then he has no reason to be afraid of Nahash because his elemental equilibrium will serve as a strong foundation which will allow him to not only resist the movements of the astral serpent, but also to control it and wield and direct the forces constituting it.[15] This is why Eliphas Levi called the pentagram "the Man-Sun, the monarch of light, the supreme magus, the master and conqueror of the serpent."

Consider the following statement from *The Magical Ritual of the Sanctum Regnum*,

> *You will now need to learn the last secret of magical force and the final grade of human will power. It is Resistance to the Universal Attraction; this is the conquest of nature, it is the Royal Authority of Soul over Body—it is Continence. To have the power and opportunity to do what give pleasure, yet to abstain because one wills it; this shows the Royal power of Soul over body.*

The secret of magical force is the ability to resist the "Universal Attraction," that is to say, the influence of Nahash. Either you are able to resist Nahash, or you are not. Those who are able to resist Nahash are not under the astral serpent's control, and therefore, are in a position to begin learning how to control the serpent. The influences of Nahash upon us manifest as impulses to act in certain ways.[16] Therefore, the first step in acquiring magical power is to acquire mastery over ourselves, and especially our impulses. From this point onwards, we extend this mastery outward until we are Hermes Trismegistus – master of the three planes.[17]

The Elemental Equilibrium as a Source of Magical Protection

> *Magicians often use magic circles during their evocational practices. The four directions often symbolize the four elements. But establishing magical equilibrium within yourself is a way of internalizing the magic circle. It offers a great deal*

Chapter 2: The Purified Elemental Equilibrium

of protection by insuring that your aura is not vulnerable to being influenced or infiltrated by outside energies.

~William Mistele

In pop culture, the pentagram is often associated with magic, and not without good reason. Within magic, it is used for many purposes. The most well-known of these is its role as a symbol of protection and defense against attacking forces. In any case, it must be remembered that the magician who wishes to use the full power of this symbol must be an ideal pentagram himself. In other words, he must have an elemental equilibrium. The pentagram as a tool is an expression of the magician's elemental equilibrium, but if the magician does not possess an elemental equilibrium, then the pentagram, regardless of whether it is drawn in the air or etched in gold, is a meaningless expression of nothing at all. The thing is, the magician who possesses an elemental equilibrium has very little need to use the symbol of the pentagram for defensive purposes because the inner strength conferred by an elemental equilibrium will make him resilient to most magical attacks, and the reflection of Divinity seen in his perfect tetra-polar balance will ensure that no negative spirits would dare attack him. Notice that when a certain man was overcome by the negative influences of the astral plane, the master Jesus Christ redirected those influences toward a group of pigs. Being animals, they were less balanced and weaker of will than humans, and therefore more susceptible to such influences. A balanced person who has placed the lower/elemental aspects of his being under the authority of his will (is an upright pentagram), is not susceptible to such influences because these influences manipulate him through his passions (negative personality traits), but his passions are under the control of his will.[18]

According to Mouni Sadhu, if two magicians get into a duel, the one with the stronger elemental equilibrium will be the winner. Of course, in reality, if they were both genuine magicians, they wouldn't waste their time with something as stupid as magical duels. Ignoring that, there is a lot of truth in his statement.

These days, you see a lot written about magical defense or "psychic self-defense." There is a big market for books about these subjects because people are always worried about being magically attacked.

Consider the following two people,

1. A man who is very weak but knows a handful of karate moves

The Spirit of Magic by Virgil

2. A man who knows nothing about martial arts, but is a very strong bodybuilder with enormous muscles

If you make these two people fight each other, who is going to win? Obviously the second man will. If the difference in strength is great, the second man might not even feel the punches of the first man.

Many people dream of learning an easy martial arts technique that will instantly stop any mugger, kidnapper, or assailant. They want a technique that they don't have to practice, and that works every time. No such technique exists. However, having a lot of physical strength will always be helpful in a physical fight.[19] This fact is not lost on martial arts practitioners. Practitioners of kung fu stand in a horse stance regularly to strengthen the muscles in their legs. They do push-ups to strengthen the muscles in their arms. Even practitioners of martial arts like Aikido and Wing Chun which are designed to rely less on strength still do exercises to strengthen their muscles.

Similarly, a lot of people dream of learning an easy ritual or spell that will allow them to neutralize any magical attack and defend themselves from people trying to work black magic on them. No such ritual or spell exists. However, having a lot of inner strength will give you an enormous advantage in any magical fight. A magician who possesses great inner strength may not even feel or notice the silly hexes and curses sent his way by immature dabblers. Some people who are paranoid about magical attack spend hours reading books about defensive magic and devote a lot of effort to memorizing protective rituals and spells. In reality, the most effective way they could prepare themselves for a potential future attack is to develop inner strength. Inner strength comes from one's elemental equilibrium.[20]

In traditional Kabbalah, Joseph is associated with the concept of righteousness, and was seen as a shining example of a *tzadik*. Righteousness is a trait that arises from having an elemental equilibrium. If you have an elemental equilibrium, then you stand on the point at the center of the Cross of Equilibrated Forces. This is the position on the cross corresponding to akasha, the spiritual power that connects everything in the created universe with Divinity. It is through akasha that we commune with Divinity, and therefore, anyone who stands at the center of the Cross of Equilibrated Forces can listen to the voice of Divinity and access the divine guidance that comes with it. It is by following this divine guidance that one becomes righteous and leads a righteous lifestyle. One popular legend states that because Joseph was so righteous, he was invulnerable to curses like the evil eye. It is not hard to

Chapter 2: The Purified Elemental Equilibrium

see the message contained in this legend. Joseph's righteous lifestyle did not protect him from the evil eye. The elemental equilibrium that gave rise to his righteous lifestyle is what protected him from the evil eye.

The Elemental Equilibrium and Ritual Magic

In modern Western magic, there are certain names and symbols like Eheieh, AGLA, Metatron, and the spirit wheel that are associated with akasha. No matter how loudly you scream/vibrate/chant/sing these names, or how many times you do so, or how many times you draw these symbols, you will not be able to access akasha if you do not have an elemental equilibrium. This can be clearly seen if you examine the Cross of Equilibrated Forces. The point at the center of the cross is the position corresponding to akasha. A person with an elemental equilibrium stands at the center of the cross, since it is also the position of balance. Therefore, he has access to akasha. The more unbalanced he is, the farther away from the central point he is positioned, and therefore the farther away he is from being able to access akasha.

In ritual magic, the ritual circle is very similar to the Cross of Equilibrated Forces. Just as each arm of the cross corresponds to an element, each quadrant of the circle also corresponds to an element (the eastern quadrant corresponds to air, the southern quadrant corresponds to fire, etc.). Each quadrant is the same size, and therefore the circle is balanced. The center of the circle is the position of akasha. As you can see, the whole circle is a symbol that represents the magician's elemental equilibrium (four quadrants) and his connection with Divinity (central point). For a lot of people, that's all the circle is – a symbol representing something that is not real. It is empty of substance and truth. When a genuine magician stands in a magic circle, he is asserting that he possesses an elemental equilibrium and is connected with Divinity. When a typical modern pseudo-magician stands in a ritual circle, he is making the same assertion, but in his case, the assertion is not true because he neither has an elemental equilibrium nor is connected to Divinity. Therefore, he is lying. The circle he stands in is not a magic circle, but an occult circle.

When a magician who has been properly trained in the use of this kind of ritual magic activates such a ritual circle, the circle does not just represent his elemental equilibrium; it is an extension of his elemental equilibrium.[21] Although he is not always at the center of the circle in a physical sense, he is always at the center of the circle in a magical sense because his depth point is one with the center of the circle, and he has moved his consciousness into the position of his depth point (akashic

The Spirit of Magic by Virgil

trance). When used in this way, the ritual circle turns from a charming and intellectually pleasing symbol to a powerful reality that will support the magician during his ritual. Throughout the ritual, he stands at the center point, which is the point Archimedes was referring to when he said "Give me a point on which to stand and I will move the world." And the magician does move the world, or at least a part of it.

That said, I must emphasize the fact that this is only the case for the properly trained magician. Many people believe that rituals are the entirety of magic so they jump into ritual magic right from the start because, well, where else would you start? Thus, there are many books that try to teach complete beginners how to do ritual magic. Maybe the first chapter teaches them how to sew their own robe and make a wand, and then the second chapter teaches them how to draw pentagrams in the air, etc. In reality, the practice of rituals is advanced work and should be held off until the student has mastered the basics of magic. Given the amount of time, money, and resources that can go into rituals, the magician practicing ritual magic should seek to get the most out of any ritual, and this can only be done if he has mastered the basics and built a solid foundation for himself. If this is not the case, then the ritual goes from an act of magic to mere roleplaying and theater. This is one common example of what Bill calls "pretend magic."[22]

This principle can be seen in any field. Let's say there is a literate person who has no experience with math. He could pick up a calculus textbook and try to understand it. If he studies it very diligently for a lifetime, then he will probably succeed in understanding it in the end. However, he could have saved himself vast amounts of time and trouble if he first learned arithmetic and then algebra before trying to tackle calculus. It is the exact same case with ritual magic. First learn the basics of magic before jumping into more complex things like ritual magic. First build up a solid foundation before you try to climb high. A large portion of the process of building this foundation consists of establishing an elemental equilibrium within oneself.

The Process of Establishing an Elemental Equilibrium

Although IIH was designed to help the student establish an elemental equilibrium, which is the first major step in the work of initiation, Bardon did not invent the idea of an elemental equilibrium. This concept does appear in the writings of the alchemists, magicians, and adepts of old, but it is merely hinted at and alluded to with symbols so that only those who were already in the know would understand. For example, in the vision of Ezekiel, the prophet sees a shining being sitting

Chapter 2: The Purified Elemental Equilibrium

on a throne which hovers over four angels representing the elements. In more recent times, other writers like the previously mentioned Eliphas Levi, G.O. Mebes, and Rudolf Steiner also mention this concept, and it is clear that they understood its utmost importance. Where Bardon differs from these authors is that instead of only explaining the concept, he actually gives a systematic series of practical step by step instructions for attaining it.

The initial stages of the process of establishing and elemental equilibrium will be examined and scrutinized in detail in Chapters 3 and 4; however, I want to discuss one aspect relating to these initial stages here. This part of the process is found in the first two steps of IIH. As I have already shown, the student is expected to have already attained a strong elemental equilibrium before moving on to Step 3. The process for achieving this strong elemental equilibrium is relatively simple. In Step 1, you make the black and white soul mirrors by listing all of your positive and negative traits and then categorizing them. Each negative trait reflects an elemental impurity or imbalance. For example, irascibility is usually indicative of an impure fire element, while a lack of empathy is usually indicative of having too little of the water element. In Step 2, you use the six-pronged attack to eliminate your elemental impurities and imbalances, which again are listed in your black soul mirror. All of this is very simple and straightforward. There is nothing specifically occult about analyzing yourself and listing your traits. Autosuggestion is a widely accepted technique of self-change that is used by many people who have no interest in magical subjects. The same is true for the other prongs. Conscious breathing, conscious eating, and magical washing are all simple and unshowy techniques that are also found in a number of non-magical spiritual traditions. My point is, you don't need elaborate secret rituals to develop a basic elemental equilibrium, and if anyone ever claims you do, he is probably trying to sell you such a ritual, or membership into an order than supposedly possesses such a ritual. One of the things you will discover throughout your training is that oftentimes, the most magical and important techniques you will learn are those that are the simplest and most unassuming.

The Elemental Equilibrium and the Bardon System

Equilibrium is the basis of the Great Work.
~Esoteric Axiom

The Spirit of Magic by Virgil

In Step 1, you create your black and white soul mirrors. Any impurities and imbalances in the elements within you will manifest as your negative traits – your vices, flaws, defects, bad habits, and weaknesses. When you create your black soul mirror, you write down as many of these negative traits as you can think of. Once you know your negative traits, you can work to eliminate them, thus eliminating the elemental imbalances or impurities that gave rise to those negative traits.

In Step 2, you use the six-pronged attack (discussed in Chapter 4) to eliminate your negative traits, and therefore the elemental imbalances and impurities at the root of those traits as well. When you have done this, then you have established an elemental equilibrium within yourself.

In Step 3, you begin working with the elements by learning to accumulate them. This elemental work will strengthen your elemental equilibrium.

In Step 4, you learn to condense the elements after accumulating them, and in Step 5, you learn to project the elements and create elemental dynamides. This more intense work with the elements strengthens your elemental equilibrium even further.

In Step 5, you also learn how to enter an akashic trance by practicing depth-point meditation. The depth-point is analogous to the point at the center of the Cross of Equilibrated Forces. Therefore, the depth-point work of this step also strengths your elemental equilibrium by reinforcing your position at the center of the Cross of Equilibrated Forces.

In Step 6, you begin working with akasha. Since you already have an elemental equilibrium (you've had one since Step 2), you stand at the center of the Cross of Equilibrated Forces, which is the part of the cross corresponding to akasha. This allows you to access akasha. Your work with akasha in this step also reinforces your position at the center of the cross, and therefore also strengthens your elemental equilibrium.

In the work of Step 8, the student learns to pore breathe, accumulate, and wield the electric and magnetic fluids. These are MUCH more refined and potent than the elements, and it takes a MUCH more balanced individual to work with them safely. They are the Yin and Yang of the Taoists. They are the Love and Strife of Empedocles. They are the Luna and Sol of the alchemists. Every civilization and culture in history has had its own names and symbols for the universal expansive and contractive principles. In the Bardon system, they are more than just abstract concepts and ideas. They are real forces that can be manipulated and controlled by the magician. They are the black and white sphinxes in The Chariot that bear the rider to victory and the throne of the Most High. The end result, after completing this step, is an even more

Chapter 2: The Purified Elemental Equilibrium

balanced individual – an individual so balanced he is able to merge with Divinity in the last two steps of IIH, win the respect of spirits during evocations, and begin training in the true Quabbalah, also known as the art of Creative Speaking. When the student goes from being a magician to a true Quabbalist, he learns to use the original language of creation. For this reason, the pentagram is also called the "Sign of the Word."

In the last two steps, the student builds into his personality the four divine qualities of omnipotence (fire), omniscience (air), omnipresence (water), and eternity (earth). This work of divinizing his subtle bodies greatly enhances their purity, resulting in the student's elemental equilibrium becoming extraordinarily strong.

The entirety of IIH is designed to help the student develop an elemental equilibrium and continually strengthen and perfect it. This is reflected in the image of the first Tarot card at the beginning of the book, which Bardon says his book is designed to reveal. Four ribbons of color represent the four elements. Above these ribbons of color is a violet pillar representing akasha, which is the source of one's higher faculties. In more conventional images of the Magician card, the elements are represented by tools on an altar. Akasha is represented by the magician's hat, which is in the shape of an infinite sign and alludes to the infinite transcendent nature of akasha.

How Not to Establish an Elemental Equilibrium

Let's now turn to the topic of occultism in relation to the elemental equilibrium. If you went up to a modern-day occultist, explained to him what an elemental equilibrium was, and challenged him to design an exercise to help someone establish an elemental equilibrium, he would probably come up with something like this,

> *Visualize a circle in front of you divided into four sections that are colored yellow, red, green, and blue. Go to the center of the circle and feel yourself balanced. Then go to the yellow quadrant of the circle and feel yourself light and airy. Then go to the red quadrant and feel yourself hot and energetic. Then go to the green section and feel yourself grounded and solid. Then go to the blue quadrant and feel yourself cold and peaceful. Then go back to the center, imagine yourself turning into a ray of violet light, and focus on the sensation of being centered.*

The Spirit of Magic by Virgil

There are many books that contain similar exercises. In other words, exercises that use elemental correspondences (e.g. divine names, colors, regions of the body, symbols, mantras, etc.) to magically manipulate the elements constituting one's astra-mental body into a balanced and purified state. Admittedly, this approach to balancing the elements seems logical; however, it is ineffective. An examination of the systems that espouse techniques like these and the state of balance of their practitioners will make this obvious. While certain types of elemental work can strengthen your elemental equilibrium if you already have one, you cannot just magically force the elements constituting you into a balanced state through the use of elemental correspondences. This is due to conditions/limitations arising from the complexity of one's subtle bodies, as well as the connection between one's karma and one's state of balance. In other words, one's state of elemental balance and purity is not arbitrary, but caused by one's karma, so establishing an elemental equilibrium is also process of working through one's karma. This process of working through one's karma is done by eliminating one's negative traits and developing positive traits, after all, karma teaches us important lessons, and many of those lessons concern the benefits of eliminating one's negative traits and developing positive traits.

It is important for me to emphasize this point. If you have assimilated what I have said throughout this chapter, then you now understand the importance of establishing an elemental equilibrium and are probably eager to begin the process. Without a doubt, you will take an interest in anything that will help you do this. Throughout your magical studies, you will find that many magical teachers and adepts consider discrimination to be a very important quality to develop, and recommend that students develop this quality as early on in their training as possible. This is true for many reasons. One of them is that discrimination can prevent you from wasting large amounts of your time. There are certain practices and exercises that will help you develop an elemental equilibrium. There are also many practices and exercises that purportedly will help you develop an elemental equilibrium, but that really won't. Life is short. Do not waste your time practicing those exercises, or you may find that you have no time left that you can use to practice effective exercises. In Chapter 4, I elucidate an effective approach that will provide you with an elemental equilibrium good enough for you to move on to Step 3 (if you are using IIH) or the equivalent level in whatever magical training system you are using.

Chapter 2: The Purified Elemental Equilibrium

The Magician and The Universe

The cards of the Major Arcana are said to depict an individual's journey to complete spiritual maturity. The individual himself is represented by The Fool. The first major stage of his journey is represented by The Magician. The last major stage of his journey is represented by The Universe.

If we examine the imagery of The Magician, we see a magician standing over an altar with four tools representing the elements. The pentacle represents the earth element. The cup represents the water element. One of the long straight things represents the fire element. The other long straight thing represents the air element. Regarding the magician in this card and the state of personal development represented by the elemental tools on the altar in front of him, Bill writes the following.

> *Before him are symbols of each of the four elements. He can pick up one, evoke its powers, and enter its mysteries and ecstasies. He can do this freely with any of the four in any combination – earth, air, fire, and water. With earth – solidity, practicality, and quiet ecstasy. With air – freedom, harmony, and the delight in each moment unfolding. With fire – strength courage, resolve, and the brilliance of the light that illuminate the world. With water – an innocence and purity of love that has no end to its giving.*

The last card, The Universe, shows a figure in the midst of a circle surrounded by four animal symbols representing the elements. The beginning of one's magical journey is the establishment of an elemental equilibrium (The Magician), and its end is the absolute perfection and completion of that elemental equilibrium (The Universe).

Chapter 3: Introspection

Life is filled with constant, unrelenting change and the only way to keep apace with the internal changes is through constant, unrelenting introspection.

~Rawn Clark

You must practice introspection every night!

~Daskalos

The previous chapter should have made it clear why it is important to transform yourself into a balanced and pure individual. As a general rule, you aren't qualified to transform something if you don't understand it. This rule applies to you yourself as well. You aren't qualified to transform yourself if you don't know/understand yourself. In the next chapter, I will teach you some powerful techniques you can use to transform yourself. In this chapter, I will teach you how to acquire self-knowledge. The more self-knowledge you possess, the more qualified you are to transform yourself, and the more intelligently you can go about the process of transforming yourself.

Know Thyself

Throughout the ages, teachers of magic and esotericism have told their students to acquire an understanding of themselves. In ancient times, the phrase "Know Thyself" was inscribed over the threshold of the temple of Apollo at Delphi. It was hoped that all who came to the temple seeking spiritual guidance would see this imperative and acquire an important key to their personal development. In modern times, teachers of magic and esotericism continue to assert the importance of knowing oneself. For example the Astrum Argenteum, a magical order founded by Aleister Crowley, divides its training program into different levels called "grades." Each grade has a task that students must complete before moving on to the next grade. The first grade is called the Probationer grade. According to Crowley, the task of the Probationer is "to obtain a scientific knowledge of the nature and powers of my own being." From this task, it is clear that Crowley designed his order's magical training system in such a way that its students' first goal is to know themselves. Bardon, too, makes his students know themselves at the very beginning of their training by observing their minds (thought-observation) and analyzing their personalities (creating the soul mirrors).

What is Introspection?

Self-knowledge is gained via the systematic analysis and examination of oneself and one's life. In magic, this process of systematic analysis and examination is called "introspection." Introspection exercises are exercises that involve analyzing and examining yourself or your life. In the next section, I will describe an important introspection exercise you should do at the very beginning of your training. Regardless of what magical training system you are working through, you can benefit from this exercise. If you are working through the Bardon system, then this exercise is already a part of the magical training system you are working through. If you aren't working through the Bardon system, then this exercise will be a great supplemental exercise to practice in addition to the introspection exercises of whatever system you are working through.

Creating the Soul Mirrors

What are those Shakespearean character flaws you possess that inevitably bring you down?

~William Mistele

In the Bardon system, students begin learning how to introspect by creating two lists called "soul mirrors." There are two soul mirrors the student should create – the black soul mirror and the white soul mirror.

Chapter 3: Introspection

The instructions for creating the black soul mirror are as follows.

(#1) Make a list of as many of your negative personality traits as you can think of. This can include vices, character flaws, bad habits, deficiencies, and weaknesses.

(#2) Next to each negative trait, write the element that you feel best reflects the nature of the trait.[23]

(#3) Next to each negative trait, write a number between 1 and 3 that indicates how strong the trait is. If the trait is really strong, write a 3 next to it. If the trait is weak, write a 1 next to it. If the trait is neither weak nor really strong, write a 2 next to it.

The instructions for creating the white soul mirror are as follows.

(#1) Make a list of as many of your positive personality traits as you can think of. This can include virtues, strengths, skills, and talents.

(#2) Next to each positive trait, write the element that you feel best reflects the nature of the trait.

(#3) Next to each positive trait, write a number between 1 and 3 that indicates how strong the trait is. If the trait is really strong, write a 3 next to it. If the trait is weak, write a 1 next to it. If the trait is neither weak nor really strong, write a 2 next to it.

There is no official lower limit for how many items you should put in a soul mirror before you are finished making it; however, it is generally agreed that each mirror should have at least 100 items or it probably will not be complete enough to give an accurate reflection of your good or bad side.

Over the course of the past few decades, numerous aspiring magicians have taken the first step towards knowing themselves by creating their soul mirrors. In the process of creating their soul mirrors, they have discovered or come up with dozens of tips, suggestions, and tricks to make the process easier and more efficient. If you want more information, tips, or advice regarding the soul mirror creation process, I suggest reading the instructions Bardon gives for making the soul mirrors in his book *Initiation into Hermetics*. Once you have done this, I suggest reading the chapter of Rawn Clark's book *A Bardon Companion* about the soul mirror creation process. If you still want more tips and advice regarding the soul mirror creation process after reading Bardon's instructions and Rawn's comments on those instructions, my book *The Elemental Equilibrium: Notes on the Foundation of Magical Adepthood*

The Spirit of Magic by Virgil

contains a chapter filled with tips and advice to help aspiring magicians create their soul mirrors.

An example black soul mirror can be found in Appendix B. A white soul mirrors looks just like a black soul mirror, but the traits listed on the white soul mirror are positive instead of negative. Note that each of the traits is as specific as possible. One of the biggest mistakes aspiring magicians make when creating their soul mirrors is that the traits they write in their soul mirrors are too general and vague.

After Creating the Soul Mirrors

After creating your soul mirrors, don't just store them somewhere and forget about them. In order to really know yourself, you need to familiarize yourself with the contents of your soul mirrors. Merely making them is not enough to do this. Begin by reading and rereading your soul mirrors several times. After doing this, reflect on the contents of your soul mirrors and study them. Contemplate the connections between the various items on them. One good way to do this is to photocopy your soul mirrors and read through the photocopies while annotating them. Jot notes in the margins of the photocopies. Highlight or underline important words. Draw arrows to show connections between different items. Etc.

It may help to type up a copy of your soul mirrors so you can print out a copy to read, study, and annotate whenever you desire to. Typing up a copy of your soul mirrors also gives you the opportunity to create different versions of your soul mirrors by organizing the items in different ways. This makes it easier to see the connections between the various items listed in each mirror.

Do Not Neglect the White Soul Mirror

Most students of magic understand why they need to create the black soul mirror. You can't eliminate your negative traits if you don't know what your negative traits are. The important thing to remember is that it is equally important to create your white soul mirror. You should spend just as much effort creating and studying your white soul mirror as you do your black soul mirror. Knowing yourself requires that you know your positive traits as well as your negative traits, so if you don't know your positive traits, you will never fully know yourself.

Chapter 3: Introspection

Besides this, your positive traits are your tools, and the better you know your tools, the more effectively you can use them. For example, when I made my white soul mirror, I found that one of my greatest strengths was my ability to dissect complex issues into smaller issues that I could deal with one by one. Once I realized this was a strength I had, I used this strength at every opportunity and got a lot more out of it. As you can see, the white soul mirror does have its practical uses as well.

What "Know Thyself" Does Not Mean

Some people think that "Know Thyself" means something along the lines of "Come to a full realization of the divine and eternal nature of your true self." Perhaps at the later stages of one's training, that is what "Know Thyself" means. However, at the beginning stages of one's training, that is certainly not what the phrase means and it is counterproductive to think so. At the beginning stages of one's training, "Know Thyself" means the following.

- Know your positive and negative personality traits.
- Know which aspects of your personality help you succeed in life and which prevent you from succeeding in life.
- Know your strengths and weaknesses.
- Know what sorts of things influence you and how they influence you.
- Know how you react in various situations.
- Know what you do well and what you don't do well.
- Know how you behave around others and how well you relate to others.
- Know what sorts of things distract you.
- Know what you want in life.
- Know why you want those things.
- Know what things you value and consider important.
- Know what kind of person you aspire to be.

This is the kind of knowledge I am referring to when I use the phrase "self-knowledge." There is no better way to begin acquiring self-knowledge than to create one's soul mirrors.

The Spirit of Magic by Virgil

Why a First Date Didn't Go Well for Mirrors

Those who correspond with me regularly know I tell this story a lot, so bear with me if you've heard it before.

When I first began my magical training via IIH, I understood the importance of creating my soul mirrors right away. Some students underestimate the importance of creating their soul mirrors, and this comes back to bite them in the butt later when they are forced to learn the importance of this exercise the hard way. I wasn't one of those students. In order to rid myself of my negative traits, I first needed to learn what my negative traits were by creating my black soul mirror. This made sense to me and was obvious. In order to get the most out of my positive traits, I needed to learn what they were so I could consciously draw upon their support whenever I needed to. This also made sense to me and was obvious. As you can see, I had no trouble appreciating the importance of creating my soul mirrors and studying my soul mirrors carefully.

Sometime after I had made my soul mirrors and spent a long period of time studying them regularly, I went on a date with a woman I really liked. When two people go on a first date, the purpose of the date is to get to know each other better. For the date to go well, both people have to be able to talk about themselves in a smooth and engaging manner.

This date didn't go so well for me. I wasn't able to talk about myself in a smooth and engaging manner because I didn't know myself that well, and you can't talk in a smooth and engaging manner about a subject you don't know much about. Of course, I was an expert on my negative traits and positive traits because I had spent so much time making and studying my soul mirrors, but this didn't help me too much because spending the whole date telling her all about my negative traits would clearly have been a bad idea, and spending the whole date telling her all about my positive traits would have made me seem narcissistic and arrogant. There's more to knowing yourself than knowing your negative traits and your positive traits. Creating your soul mirrors is the first step to knowing yourself, but it's only the first step. If you stop after taking this first step, then you will only know what negative traits and what positive traits you possess, but you won't know any of the colorful and interesting aspects of yourself that aren't necessarily "negative" or "positive." To learn about those aspects of yourself, such as what inspires you, or what your dreams are, or what your values and priorities in life are, you have to do other introspection exercises besides creating

Chapter 3: Introspection

the soul mirrors. Those other introspection exercises will provide you with the self-knowledge you need to be able to talk about yourself in a smooth, engaging, and truthful manner when you're on a date. Of course, no one undergoes magical training just because they want their dates to go better, but magical training improves all areas of your life when it is approached correctly, and this does include the romance aspect of your life.

Regarding Complete Magical Training Systems

In Chapter 6, I will explain what magical training systems are, and why a magical training system has to be complete in order to be good. Given the vast importance of introspection, it should be clear that a magical training system that does not include introspection exercises is incomplete.

Chapter 4: The Six-Pronged Attack

Knowing is not enough; we must apply.

~Goethe

When we love, we always strive to become better than we are. When we strive to become better than we are, everything around us becomes better too.

~Paulo Coelho

In Chapter 2, I explained the importance of becoming a balanced and pure individual. In Chapter 3, I explained how to create your soul mirrors. Your black soul mirror is a list of your negative traits. These traits arise from the elemental impurities and imbalances within you. When you eliminate a negative trait, you eliminate the elemental impurity or imbalance at the root of the trait. In this chapter, I will teach you a set of six powerful self-transformation techniques, known as the "six-pronged attack." These six techniques will allow you to root out the negative traits listed in your black soul mirror one by one.

More detailed explanations of these techniques can be found in Franz Bardon's book *Initiation into Hermetics* and in my own book *The Elemental Equilibrium: Notes on the Foundation of Magical Adepthood*.

Prong 1: Conscious Eating

This technique can be used to develop a positive trait. The idea behind this technique can be found in the saying "You are what you eat." If you want to become patient, eat patience. If you want to become compassionate, eat compassion. If you want to become assertive, eat assertiveness. When the great magician Jesus Christ attended the wedding at Cana and the wine ran out, Jesus transformed water into wine. Using the same technique, you can transform food into any positive trait.

The Spirit of Magic by Virgil

The gist of the technique is that you look at the food and transmute it into a positive trait through focused intent. There isn't exactly one single correct way to do this. Bardon suggests holding the idea of the positive trait in your mind and then impressing this idea into the essence of the food. This will cause the essence of the food to "absorb" this idea, which will result in the food transforming into the positive trait. Other people will the food to transform into the positive trait. Some people reach into the food with their minds and adjust the "vibration" of the food so that it becomes the "vibration" of the positive trait. Your mind can change the world directly if it is focused and used correctly. With this technique, you use it to transform the food into a positive trait using whatever approach works best for you. The process of transforming food into a positive trait is called "impregnation" in the Bardon system because Bardon saw a parallel between the process of imbuing an idea into the essence of the food and the process of impregnation.

After transmuting the food into the positive trait, you eat the food while believing with full conviction that you are eating the positive trait. This reinforces the impregnation. In other words, it makes the transformation more thorough, which makes the technique more effective.

While this technique is designed to develop positive traits, it can also be used to get rid of negative traits. To do this, you use the technique to develop the negative trait's opposite positive trait. For example, if you are an impatient person, you can use conscious eating to develop patience. If you are a mean person, you can use conscious eating to develop compassion. If you are a greedy person, you can use conscious eating to develop generosity.

This technique should be used at every meal. Furthermore, I highly recommend using it when eating snacks between meals, even if the snack is something as small as a candy bar. Regardless of what you are eating or when you are eating it, impregnate your food with a positive trait to turn it into the positive trait before eating it.

Prong 2: Conscious Breathing

Normal breathing has two phases – inhalation and exhalation. With conscious breathing, each phase serves a different purpose. In the inhalation phase, you breathe in a positive trait and assimilate it into your personality. In the exhalation phase, you breathe out the opposite negative trait.

Chapter 4: The Six-Pronged Attack

For example, let's say you want to become more patient. You begin by transmuting the air in the room around you into patience by impregnating it with patience. Then you inhale while believing with full conviction that you are inhaling patience, bringing the patience within you so that it can be assimilated into your personality. After that, you exhale while believing with full conviction that you are exhaling out impatience, removing this trait from your personality. You continue to breathe in this manner until the conscious breathing session is done.

Start with seven breaths for your first session. You can use a string of beads to count breaths. This way, instead of worrying about how many breaths you've taken, you can focus all of your attention on breathing in the positive trait and breathing out the negative trait. Slowly increase the number of breaths you take per session until you can breathe in this way for ten minutes each session.

Prong 3: Magical Washing

This is a great technique that can be used to remove negative traits from your personality. Every time you wash your hands, turn the knob of the sink until the water is cold. Then, wash your hands while imagining, feeling, and believing that the water is pulling the negative trait out of you and carrying it down the drain. Whenever you shower, do the same thing.

Water has a magical attractive quality that is strongest when it is cold. In this technique, you take advantage of this quality by using your mind to direct it to absorb the negative trait, in this way removing it from you.

Some people use visualization to enhance the effectiveness of this technique. There are several ways to do this. One way is to imagine the water growing darker and murkier as it pulls the negative trait out of you and absorbs it.

There is a variation of this technique. Instead of washing a negative trait out of yourself, you imbue water with a positive trait and then bathe in the water while washing the positive trait into yourself. I wanted to bring this variation to your attention in case you like it, but since I've never actually used this variation myself, I can't really comment on it.

The Spirit of Magic by Virgil

Prong 4: Autosuggestion

This is a technique that can be used to develop a positive trait. First, design an affirmation containing the idea that you already possess that trait. For example, if you are impatient and want to develop patience in order to rid yourself of your impatience, an appropriate affirmation is "I am patient." The affirmation should be worded in the present tense, so "I will be patient" is an incorrectly worded affirmation because it is in the future tense. Furthermore, the affirmation should not contain negative words (not, don't, no, etc.), so "I am not impatient" is an incorrectly worded affirmation because it contains the negative word "not."

When you have come up with a correctly worded affirmation, repeat the affirmation at least forty times immediately before falling asleep and at least forty times immediately after waking up. These are the two periods in the day when the barrier between your subconscious mind and conscious mind is weakest. Therefore, when you repeat the affirmation during those two times, the affirmation sinks into your subconscious mind with greater ease.

In addition to repeating the affirmation before falling asleep and immediately upon waking up, repeat the affirmation regularly throughout the day whenever you get the chance to. Each time you repeat the affirmation, it sinks into your subconscious mind, takes root there, and begins to reprogram your subconscious mind in such a way that you develop the trait.

Prong 5: Assumption (Volition)

The name of this technique comes from a line in Shakespeare's play *Hamlet*. In this line, Hamlet says "Assume a virtue, if you have it not." In modern English, this can be reworded as follows – "If you don't possess a trait, act like you possess the trait." This will eventually cause you to develop the trait. For example, if you are impatient, you don't possess the trait of patience. However, if you force yourself to act like a patient person, you will eventually become a patient person. In this way, you can rid yourself of your impatience.

This prong is also called "volition," and you might still see people referring to this prong by that name. The reason for this other name is that this prong does require willpower. Forcing yourself to act patiently when you are an impatient person requires willpower. Forcing yourself to be outgoing when you are shy requires willpower. Forcing yourself to

Chapter 4: The Six-Pronged Attack

be generous when you are greedy requires willpower. It takes willpower to assume a trait, which is one of many reasons the student of magic should have strong willpower.

Prong 6: Non-magical methods

This just refers to all other non-magical methods and techniques you can use to rid yourself of your flaws. For example, if you have poor leadership skills, you can take a leadership class, hire someone to coach you to become a better leader, read a book about how to be a good leader, etc. If you are disorganized, you can start using a planner, buy expandable folders and plastic bins to store your papers and belongings, buy smartphone apps that will help you organize and stick to your schedules, etc.

Putting it All Together

In this section I present two examples of how all six prongs can be used together to root out a negative trait.

Let's start by looking at how the six prongs can be used to root out arrogance from your personality.

Conscious eating: At each meal, transmute your food into humbleness before eating it. While eating it, believe with full conviction that you are consuming humbleness.

Conscious breathing: Transmute the air around you into humbleness. Inhale while believing with full conviction that you are breathing in humbleness. Exhale while believing with full conviction that you are breathing out arrogance. Continue to breathe in this manner for a few minutes.

Magical washing: Whenever you shower or wash your hands, turn the water cold and will it to draw arrogance out of you, absorb it, and carry it down the drain.

Autosuggestion: Repeat the affirmation "I am humble" forty times before falling asleep at night and immediately upon waking up in the morning. In addition, repeat the affirmation regularly throughout the day.

Assumption: Live as if you were a humble person. In other words, use willpower to force yourself to act like a humble person. Be especially sure to do this in situations where you are tempted to boast or to look down on others.

The Spirit of Magic by Virgil

Non-Magical Methods: Sometimes arrogant behavior arises from insecurities. See if this is the case and, if so, identify and work through the insecurities that give rise to your arrogant behavior. Also, read about the benefits of humbleness and the negative effects of arrogance. Introspect regularly so you have an accurate image of yourself. Review your black soul mirror regularly to remind yourself that you aren't perfect.

Now let's look at how the six-pronged attack can be used to remove irascibility from your personality.

Conscious eating: At each meal, transmute your food into patience before eating it. While eating it, believe with full conviction that you are consuming patience.
Conscious breathing: Transmute the air around you into patience. Inhale while believing with full conviction that you are breathing in patience. Exhale while believing with full conviction that you are breathing out irascibility. Continue to breathe in this manner for a few minutes.
Magical washing: Whenever you shower or wash your hands, turn the water cold and will it to draw irascibility out of you, absorb it, and carry it down the drain.
Autosuggestion: Repeat the affirmation "I am patient" forty times before falling asleep at night and immediately upon waking up in the morning. In addition, repeat the affirmation regularly throughout the day.
Volition: Live as if you were a patient person. In other words, use willpower to force yourself to act like a patient person. Be especially sure to do this in situations that make you angry.
Non-Magical Methods: Read Swami Sivananda's book *Conquest of Anger*. Learn to think of everyone around you, including those who anger you, as divine sparks incarnate. Learn to view every situation in which you become angry as an opportunity to exercise patience and therefore develop it. Contemplate the negative consequences of anger. Contemplate the positive benefits of patience. Learn to see the big picture. Get enough sleep each night so you don't wake up cranky. Stop using drugs that mess with your mood and weaken your emotional stability.

Chapter 4: The Six-Pronged Attack

Final Note

You don't have to rid yourself of every negative trait in your black soul mirror in order to become a magician, but you do need to rid yourself of most of them. By "most," I mean all of your major negative traits and a significant portion of your minor negative traits. This needs to be done at the beginning of your training or else you will not be able to safely work with powerful energies and spirits in the intermediate and advanced stages of your training. The more powerful an energy or spirit is, the more balanced, pure, and mature you need to be in order to work with that energy or spirit safely. The techniques of the six-pronged attack are extremely effective. If you apply all six of them to any negative trait, you should be able to rid yourself of it relatively quickly. In this way, you can rid yourself of your negative traits one by one, causing you to gradually become a more balanced, pure, and mature person.

Chapter 5: The Importance of Magical Training Systems

As a student of magic, one of your goals is to become an adept – a master magician. To understand the process of becoming an adept, consider the following metaphor.

Let's say you are in a country called Magic Land. This country has many locations, including a city called Adepthood. In order to get from one location in Magic Land to another location in Magic Land, you have to walk. Therefore, if you want to get to Adepthood from wherever you are, you need to walk there. Walking represents doing something magic-related. If you are reading a book about magic, you are walking. If you are practicing a magical exercise, you are walking. If you are doing a magical working, you are walking.

Here's the thing – just because you are walking doesn't mean you are walking in the right direction. Many people make the erroneous assumption that this is the case, when it is not true at all. Magic Land is filled with many aspiring magicians who want to reach Adepthood. Some of them are walking in the right direction – the direction of the city. Others are walking in the wrong direction. Many people are just walking in circles.

Adepts have balanced personalities and excellent minds. They also have their lives together. The process of walking to Adepthood is in part a process of balancing your personality, developing your mind, and getting your life together. Those who intend to get to Adepthood and are walking in the right direction should be able to examine themselves objectively after a long period of walking and notice that their personalities are more balanced, their minds are better, and their lives are more organized. Such people are in a much better situation than the misguided or unguided individuals who are walking in the wrong direction or walking in circles.

The people who walk in the wrong direction end up very far from Adepthood. These are the people who unbalance their personalities, destroy their minds, and wreck their lives by approaching magical training incorrectly. If they want to reach Adepthood, the first thing they should do is stop walking. This means giving up magic, at least temporarily. Standing still is better than walking in the wrong direction

The Spirit of Magic by Virgil

because if you are standing still, at least you are not moving farther away from Adepthood.

The people who walk in circles don't end up as demented or deranged as the people walking in the wrong direction, but they still end up in a pitiable situation. The fact that they are wasting their time eventually becomes so obvious that they can no longer remain in denial about it. After decades of magical study and practice, they reflect back on their journey and cannot help but conclude that they never gained anything meaningful from it. They lose their faith in magic and regret that they did not give up their studies years earlier.

If you wish to become an adept, you must make sure you are walking towards Adepthood, and that you are not walking in the wrong direction or walking in circles. Most aspiring magicians are not walking in the right direction. They read whatever book about magic they want to read whenever they want to, they practice whatever magical exercise they want to practice whenever they want to, and they perform whatever magical ritual they want to perform whenever they want to. This is like walking north whenever you feel like walking north, walking south whenever you feel like walking south, walking east whenever you feel like walking east, and walking west whenever you feel like walking west. No one who does this will ever reach their destination. They will be wandering around forever.

To get to your destination, you need walk north whenever you should walk north, walk south whenever you should walk south, walk east whenever you should walk east, and walk west whenever you should walk west. You need some sort of guidance such as a map or a GPS device to tell you what direction to walk at any given point in time. When it comes to your magical training, it's not about doing whatever you want whenever you feel like it. It's about doing what you need to do when you need to do it. This is training systematically. Magic is an art, and mastery of any art requires systematic training. Those students of magic who are fortunate enough to have studied an art in the past, whether it was acting, ballet, or wushu, have an advantage because they have been through systematic training, and therefore understand and appreciate the importance of systematic training. To train systematically in the art of magic, you need to work through a magical training system. A magical training system will tell you what you should do, and when you should do it. It will tell you what exercises to practice, and when you

Chapter 5: The Importance of Magical Training Systems

should practice them. It will tell you what information you should learn, and when you should learn it. To go back to our Magic Land analogy, a magical training system will tell you what direction to walk and when you should walk in that direction. This is necessary, because if you walk in whatever direction you feel like walking in whenever you feel like it, you will never reach Adepthood. Again, you will always be wandering around aimlessly.

Good magical training systems guide students, while bad magical training systems misguide students. People who are misguided never reach their destination, so it is important to be able to discriminate between good and bad magical training systems. In the next chapter, I explain in detail what magical training systems are and how to tell whether a magical training system is good or bad.

Chapter 6: Magical Training Systems – the Alternative to the Shotgun Approach

Practicing IIH is not about making little changes that upgrade your life and make you a better person. You really do not need this caliber of magical training to do something positive and constructive with your life. IIH is altogether different. It gives you the ability to act as a divine being and to interact with all aspects of human evolution.

~William Mistele

Many aspiring magicians spend their time trying different exercises and practices from the Solomonic grimoires, yoga, Kabbalah, esoteric Taoism, ceremonial magic, alchemy, and other miscellaneous spiritual and magical traditions in hopes of hitting upon something that makes them clairvoyant, or teaches them to "astral project," or allows them to evoke spirits, or does anything else that brings them even the tiniest bit closer to adepthood, which is where they long to be. This approach to training is what I call the "shotgun approach." As you can see, it's very unsystematic. You're trying random stuff from random sources and just hoping that somehow something you do will take you a little bit closer to where you want to be.

If you're the kind of person who can easily see why this approach is inefficient, fear not. Besides the unsystematic shotgun approach, there *are* systematic approaches out there. These approaches can be found in magical training systems. The best way to ensure you are training systematically is to pick a magical training system and work through it.

What is a Magical Training System?

Magical training systems have three components.

1. Practices
2. Knowledge

The Spirit of Magic by Virgil

3. Structure

The practices component of a system consists of exercises designed to effect a transformation in the student such as the evolution of consciousness or the development of magical skills and abilities. Introspection exercises, concentration exercises, meditation exercises, energy manipulation exercises, clairvoyance exercises, and exteriorization exercises are examples of some of the types of exercises you might find constituting the practices component of the magical training systems you come across.

The knowledge component of a system consists of information taught to the system's students. This information can include theories about how magical faculties work, models illustrating how the inner planes interact with each other, tables of correspondences showing the inner connections between various objects and concepts, diagrams showing the anatomy of the one's subtle bodies, or teachings regarding the nature of different entities. Needless to say, this information should be accurate. How accurate the information constituting a system's knowledge component is often depends on where the founder of the system acquired the information. If the source of the information comes from many years of intelligent magical practice, or if it was received from knowledge spirits, then it is probably accurate. If the source of the information is speculation and conjecture on the founder's part, then it is probably not accurate.

A calculus course is not just a collection of lectures and homework assignments. It's a collection of lectures and homework assignments that must be worked through in a specific order. This order is the course's structure. Similarly, a building is not just a collection of bricks and steel. It is a collection of bricks and steel arranged in a specific manner. This manner of arrangement is the building's structure.

A magical training system is not just a collection of practices and knowledge. Magical training systems also have a structure. The structure is the order in which the student works through the process of mastering the system's practices and assimilating the system's knowledge. If you examine the Bardon system, you see a structure consisting of ten steps to be worked through in order. If you examine the Golden Dawn system, you see a structure consisting of various grades to be worked through in order. If you take away a building's structure, it is no longer a building, but a pile of bricks and steel. If you take away a magical training

Chapter 6: Magical Training Systems – the Alternative to the Shotgun Approach

system's structure, it is no longer a magical training system, but a collection of magical practices and magical knowledge. If you assimilate the knowledge contained in a system and practice the exercises in a system but you don't do this in the correct order, then you are not working through the system because you are not adhering to the system's structure. A system's structure is really what makes the system a system.

A Brief Overview of Existing Magical Training Systems

There are many magical training systems the aspiring magician can choose to work through in order to become an adept. In the West, the most well-known magical training systems were developed by magical orders and are meant to be used by the orders' members. Examples of such systems include the Golden Dawn system, the Argenteum Astrum system, and the Aurum Solis system. Each of these systems is named after the magical order that developed the system and teaches the system to its members. If you intend to work through such a system of magical training, it is usually considered best to actually join the order that developed and teaches the system, after all, the system was designed to be taught by that order rather than worked through alone.

However, if you don't want to join a magical order, there's no need to worry. There are many magical training systems that can be worked through alone. These magical training systems are usually found in books. For example, Bardon's magical training system can be found in his book *Initiation into Hermetics*.

There is a common misconception in the esoteric world that no magical training system is inherently better than another. The important thing for aspiring magicians to remember is that this common misconception is wrong. In fact, some magical training systems are significantly better than others. Let's examine why this might be the case.

Balanced Systems are Better than Unbalanced Systems

Think about a strength training regimen. When it comes to any antagonistic pair of muscles (such as the biceps and triceps), the regimen should require you to strengthen both muscles in the pair. If you don't do this, you can injure yourself. A strength training regimen that always has you strengthening one muscle in an antagonistic pair but not the other is not balanced.

The Spirit of Magic by Virgil

Now think about a high school curriculum. An ideal curriculum would have science classes, humanities classes, math classes, and art classes. Any student going through such a balanced curriculum would become a well-rounded individual. If a high school curriculum included only art classes, it would not be balanced. Students going through such a curriculum would not be well-rounded and therefore would not function as effectively in the world as a well-rounded individual would.

Magical training systems are like the strength training regimen because if a magical training system is not balanced, it is inevitable that those who try to work through the curriculum will injure themselves. Magical training systems are also like the high school curriculum because a magician who trained using an unbalanced system will not be able to function in the magical world as effectively as a magician who trained using a balanced system would. Some magical training systems are balanced. Other magical training systems are unbalanced. Therefore, some magical training systems are better than others.

Complete Systems are Better than Incomplete Systems

A complete magical training system is one that provides that student with all of the knowledge and practices needed to achieve proficiency in magic. An incomplete magical training system is one that is missing crucial practices or is unable to provide the student with crucial pieces of knowledge. If you insist on using an incomplete magical training system, you will have to draw from other outside sources to fill the gaps in the system. Identifying the gaps and figuring out how to fill them can be frustrating.

Some magical training systems are complete. Other magical training systems are incomplete. Therefore, some magical training systems are better than others.

Safe Systems are Better than Unsafe Systems

There are many reasons a magical training system can be unsafe. One reason a magical training system can be unsafe is that it is unbalanced. Another reason magical training systems can be unsafe is that they contain exercises that are unsafe. For example, I know of one magical training system that contains breathing exercises that can permanently injure the lungs of anyone who tries them. I know of another magical training system that includes energy exercises that can

Chapter 6: Magical Training Systems – the Alternative to the Shotgun Approach

seriously disrupt the harmony of one's astra-mental body. I know of another magical training system that includes exercises that, if practiced regularly, will result in the development of mental illnesses. The people who created these magical training systems were not qualified to do so. However, there are magical training systems created by people who knew what they were doing. These systems are safe, and clearly preferable to those systems that are not safe.

Efficient Systems are Better than Inefficient Systems

An efficient magical training system is one that does not force the student to spend an unnecessarily long amount of time on his training. An inefficient magical training system is one that forces the student to spend an unnecessarily long amount of time on his training. There are many possible reasons an inefficient system could be inefficient, but by far the most common one is that it contains exercises that are a waste of time. Efficient systems only contain productive exercises, and do not contain exercises that are a waste of time. Efficient systems also do not contain redundant exercises or unnecessarily complicated exercises. Those are all things that can cause a student to spend an unnecessarily long amount of time on his training.

Considerations When Picking a Magical Training System

To become an adept, or at least a well-trained and competent magician, you need to choose a magical training system and work through it. Needless to say, you should choose the magical training system that is best for you. When evaluating magical training systems to determine which one is best for you, consider the following three things.

1. Whether the system is good or bad
2. Whether the system is compatible with your life
3. Whether or not you like the system

If a system is bad, it's not going to be the best one for you. This should be obvious. A good system is complete, balanced, safe, and efficient.

Sometimes, a system is good but you cannot work through it because it is not compatible with your life. If you are constantly moving around or you have very little privacy, a system that incorporates a lot of ritual or ceremonial work is probably not compatible with your life. This ended up being my situation. I love to travel, so a system that incorporated a lot of ceremonial work and required me to have an oratory I could practice in daily would not have been compatible with my life.[24] The exercises of IIH can all be done while sitting in a chair – no oratory, altar, or forest grove required. I could do them in my home, in a hotel, in an airport while waiting for my plane, on a plane, at work, in a car, at my girlfriend's house, on a park bench, and even in a bathroom if I really needed to. Although I travelled a lot, no matter where I was, I could do the exercises of IIH, so it was one of the few systems compatible with my unpredictable life.[25]

Even if a system is compatible with your life, you might not like it for some reason. IIH was compatible with my life, and fortunately, I also liked the system. If this hadn't been the case, it wouldn't have been the right system for me. For me, each of the exercises of IIH is like an onion. The exercises may seem simple on the outside, but they have many layers, and the more you practice the exercise, the more of these layers you uncover and master. I find this fun and exciting. However, some people may be bored by IIH-esque exercises no matter what. Perhaps these people would prefer a Druidry-themed magical training system that involves a lot of work in nature, or a magical training system with exercises that involve movement, instead of sitting in the throne posture. There are some forms of shamanism that weave powerful magic through dance.

Picking a Magical Training System is a Serious Endeavor

Think about the process of picking a college to attend. This requires paying the college thousands of dollars in tuition fees, so you're not going to pick a random college and hope you like it. Instead, you're going to do a lot of research on each college you could attend and then make an informed decision regarding which college you'll pay your tuition fees to. This research could involve visiting the campus of each college, talking with current students, and sitting in on a few classes to get a sense of what it's like to be a student there.

Picking a magical training system to work through is a lot like picking a college. Time is money. You're going to be spending hundreds of hours over the course of several years working through the magical training system you ultimately choose. Therefore, it makes no sense to

Chapter 6: Magical Training Systems – the Alternative to the Shotgun Approach

pick a random system and hope you like it. I've gotten a few emails in the past from people who want my opinion on whether the Bardon system is the right system for them. That's a dangerous question to ask other people. If you tell me your values, dreams, and interests, I can certainly give you my prediction regarding whether or not you'll like the Bardon system, but you shouldn't pick a system just because someone else thinks you'll like it. Instead, you should investigate the system on your own. If the system you are investigating is the Bardon system, this requires at the very least reading through IIH and PME.[26] If the system you are investigating is an order-based system, this requires at the very least reaching out to current members of the order to discuss the system, and maybe even visiting the order's temple to meet the members in person and observe what they do.

An Important Purpose of Magical Training Systems

Magical training systems have many purposes. They help you develop basic magical skills and abilities. They help you become more mature. They increase your magical power. They help you acquire wisdom and understanding. They also prepare you to contact entities and teach you how to contact entities. This last purpose is, in my opinion, one of the most important purposes of magical training systems, and I'm not the only one who views magical training systems in this way. In the Bardon community, it's often said that your real magical training doesn't begin when you start working through IIH. Your real magical training begins when you start working through PME. Let me elaborate on what this means.

In *Memories of Franz Bardon*, Dr. M.K. writes that during the time he knew Bardon, Bardon would go to an unknown location every evening and perform evocations. The spirits Bardon evoked provided him with knowledge and guidance that he used to accomplish important tasks. Whatever knowledge Bardon received from the spirits he evoked is not knowledge that can be found in books or received from human teachers. The spirits he evoked are the same spirits described in PME, and when the descriptions of spirits like Ugali, Elason, and Akahimo are studied, it becomes clear that they are far more knowledgeable about the magical arts than any human could ever dream of becoming. When you work through the magical training system Bardon lays out in IIH, or through any other good magical training system, you become ready to

The Spirit of Magic by Virgil

learn from these spirits. You can do this by bringing these spirits to our realm via evocation, or by travelling to their realm via mental wandering.

In other words, IIH does teach you a bit of magic, but more importantly, it prepares you to contact those who will teach you more magic. You never stop learning, and when you walk the path of a magician, you do a lot of learning. Most of this learning isn't done while working through a magical training system. It's done after you've finished working through a magical training system and begin exploring the various spiritual resources available on the inner planes. In his book *Twenty-Five Earthzone Spirits*, Bill shares a small portion of the magical knowledge and wisdom he received while studying with 25 of the ruling genii of the Earthzone. When you finish working through a good magical training system, you gain the ability to perceive, move, and effect change beyond the physical. The inner planes are opened up to you. Within the inner planes are many regions and many types of entities. Some of those entities, such as the ruling genii of the planetary spheres, deities, and elemental sovereigns possess vast amounts of knowledge, including knowledge no human has ever possessed before.

Some people can't decide between two magical training systems they like, so they wonder if they can work through both. It is not really an intelligent decision to do so. The sooner you work through one magical training system, the sooner you have access to the vast spiritual resources on the inner planes, which means the sooner you can really begin learning. There is an old saying – "The hunter who chases two rabbits catches neither one." To work through a magical training system, you must stay focused. You can't be focused on working through two magical training systems at the same time because being focused, by definition, means that your attention is centered on one thing, and not split between two things. Basically, what I'm saying is this. There might be many good magical training systems that appeal to you, but you shouldn't feel sad that you can't work through all of them and learn all that they can teach you. Once you work through one good magical training system, the inner plane entities you learn to contact can teach you far more than you could learn working through another magical training system. Regardless of how much you can learn about charging talismans from a particular magical training system, you won't learn as much as you could learn from Saris. Regardless of how much you can learn about modifying karma from a particular magical training system, you won't learn as much as you could learn from Milon. Regardless of how much you can learn about how the elements work on the magical

Chapter 6: Magical Training Systems – the Alternative to the Shotgun Approach

plane from a particular magical training system, you won't learn as much as you could learn from Erimihala.[27] How quickly you are able to contact these spirits productively depends on how quickly you complete your training. The more efficiently you train, the sooner you will be able to contact these spirits, and trying to work through two systems simultaneously is not an efficient way to train.

Magical Training Systems vs. Magical Traditions

A magical training system is not the same as a magical tradition, and it is important not to confuse the two. In his book *Swimming with the Whale*, Daniel Joseph does a good job explaining the difference between spiritual systems and spiritual traditions. Part of his explanation, when applied/adapted to magic, is as follows. A magical training system is just a tool that you use to aid you in your magical advancement. You use this tool, but you don't really become attached to it. A tradition, on the other hand, is something you can become attached to. This isn't immediately a bad thing, but it can cause you to self-restrict yourself and prevent you from innovating or exploring in ways that fall outside the bounds of the tradition. Magical traditions can build up around magical systems, but it is possible to work with a magical system without becoming a part of the tradition associated with it. There are potential benefits that can come with becoming part of a tradition, for example, interacting with other people who are part of the tradition can provide you with companionship. This isn't really the place for me to get into an in-depth explanation of what a magical tradition is. I simply want to make it clear that they do exist, and that they aren't the same as magical training systems.

The Training of a Magician vs. the Training of a Sorcerer

There are books (e.g. IIH) designed to teach aspiring magicians how to be magicians, and there are books designed to teach aspiring sorcerers how to be sorcerers. A comparison of these two types of books will show that they are very different in their contents and in their structures.

The astral plane is formed from a substance many call the "astral light." Changes effected in the astral plane result in corresponding changes on the physical plane, as asserted in the Hermetic axiom "As above, so below." Sorcery training books are often a collection of tricks to nudge the astral light in ways that produce the effect you want in the

The Spirit of Magic by Virgil

physical world, whether the effect is getting a new car, getting a date, obtaining money, or whatever.

Books containing magical training systems, on the other hand, do not contain a collection of tricks for nudging the astral light. Bill writes the following in his essay about negative spirits.[28]

> *The way to escape evil is to say 'I am committed to a higher purpose. I identify with it with my whole being. If you proceed against me, you proceed against the powers behind me.' In other words, once you encounter evil – a highly potent negativity – it is no longer life as usual. You have to make an enormous commitment if you want to regain balance and harmony. This commitment must transcend your own life. It must be to the highest light you can imagine and your commitment must be sufficient that your life then becomes a vehicle for this light's expression. In other words, you need to find a source of power greater than the one which has control of you. If you are on a spiritual path, then you need a source of spirit of greater power and might.*

The entire essay is a very important one for aspiring magicians to read since the information in it can save you from a lot of unnecessary grief (I know this from experience). I want to discuss this passage in particular because it brings up the idea of a "higher purpose." Many sorcerers (not all, there are always exceptions) apply their art for the purpose of getting a girlfriend, or acquiring money quickly, or hexing their enemies, or getting a promotion, or seducing someone they like. Being able to nudge the astral light is enough to fulfill many of these purposes, so that is all sorcerers need to be able to do. However, the path of the magician is very different from the path of the sorcerer. The magician often comes across dangers the sorcerer never dreams of. To survive, the magician often has to commit to a higher purpose for the reasons explained by Bill in the passage above.

The thing is, fulfilling these higher purposes requires more than the ability to nudge the astral light with a collection of neat tricks. The magician needs advanced magical skills and abilities. Advanced magical skills and abilities are developed by practicing advanced magical exercises. However, the advanced exercises of magic can only be

Chapter 6: Magical Training Systems – the Alternative to the Shotgun Approach

practiced after one has mastered the intermediate exercises of magic, and the intermediate exercises of magic can only be practiced after one has mastered the beginning exercises of magic.[29] Therefore, if you examine a book like IIH, what you see is beginning exercises followed by intermediate exercises that build off of those beginning exercises, which are in turn followed by advanced exercises that build off of those intermediate exercises. This is the structure of magical training systems, which I discussed earlier. When it comes to the training of a sorcerer, the tricks a sorcerer uses to nudge the astral light can be learned in any order, so the training of a sorcerer does not need to be as structured as the training of a magician. If you rearrange the chapters of a sorcery training book, the book will remain essentially the same. For example, it does not matter if the chapter with the love spells comes before or after the chapter with the hexes, and it does not matter if the chapter with the weather spells comes before or after the chapter with the money spells. However, if you rearrange the steps of IIH so that Step 8 comes before Step 1, or Step 7 comes before Step 3, what you have is an incoherent mess because you have destroyed the system's structure.

The System Produces Magicians, not the Practices/Exercises

Many occult authors have cherry-picked exercises from IIH and included them in their own books, promising readers that if they practice these exercises, they will become magicians. This is not only erroneous, but also irresponsible because many of the exercises of IIH are dangerous if the practitioner has not completed the prerequisite exercises. For example, the Step 3 elemental pore breathing exercises are dangerous for those who have not completed the Step 2 elemental equilibrium work. This isn't an empty claim that I am pulling out of thin air, but an assertion Bardon makes in several warning throughout IIH. For example, at the beginning of Step 3, he gives the following warning.

> *Before starting on the training for this step, the astral equipoise of the elements in the soul has to be established by introspection and self-control unless you wish to do mischief to yourself. If it is absolutely sure that none of the elements is prevailing, you ought to keep working on the refinement of the character, in the course of the development, but you might as well go on to work with the elements in the astral body.*

The Spirit of Magic by Virgil

The people who cherry-pick exercises from IIH to practice because they think they can become magicians this way must remember that it is the system that produces magicians, and not the exercises alone.[30] Part of a system is its structure. When you cherry-pick exercises from a system, you remove those exercises from the system's structure. Without a structure, there is no system, and without a system, there is no way of training systematically. That's the key idea to grasp. Magical training isn't a process of mastering exercises and acquiring knowledge. It's a process of mastering exercises and acquiring knowledge systematically. If you understand this, then you will understand why it's not enough to practice random magical exercises from random books. You must pick a magical training system and work through it.

A Conversation Regarding Clairvoyance

The most common way people give up their power is by thinking they don't have any.

~Alice Walker

Some time ago, I had an interesting conversation with a person I will call Ben. The conversation, paraphrased for concision, went like this.

Virgil: Anyone can become clairvoyant if he finds the right approach to becoming clairvoyant.

Ben: Hogwash! Some people are born with the knack for clairvoyance. Only those people can become clairvoyant. If you weren't born with the knack for clairvoyance, you won't become clairvoyant, no matter how hard you try!

Virgil: You seem to be firmly convinced that this is the case. May I ask why?

Ben: Because I have spent over a decade trying to become clairvoyant. I have tried every exercise in every book.

Virgil: Ok, but have you tried every approach to becoming clairvoyant?

Ben: Yes. I told you already. I tried every exercise I came across.

Chapter 6: Magical Training Systems – the Alternative to the Shotgun Approach

Virgil: I heard that. However, you did not say you tried every approach. It seems like your approach to becoming clairvoyant is to find the right exercise. Perhaps you should instead try to find the right system.
Ben: ...

Ben was like a missionary. In the occult organization he was a member of, he went around preaching his belief that some people can't become clairvoyant no matter how hard they try or for how long. It's not because he was an asshole. In fact, the situation was the complete opposite. Ben was actually a thoughtful person and just wanted to prevent people from wasting many years of their lives trying to become clairvoyant if they seemingly couldn't. He didn't want people to go through the long frustrating period he went through before giving up and concluding that he would never become clairvoyant. Without a doubt, there are hundreds of people out there who are just like Ben in that they tried for a long time to become clairvoyant before giving up and concluding they just didn't have the "knack" for it.

Here's the interesting and ironic thing. Opening your astral senses is extraordinarily easy. In fact, of all the things you will do during your magical training, opening your astral senses will probably be the easiest. Why? Because it takes no effort whatsoever. Yes, you read that correctly. Opening your astral senses takes no effort because when you have reached a certain level of magical advancement, your astral senses will open on their own.[31]

Now, you might be saying, "Wait a minute Virgil. If your astral sense of sight (clairvoyance) will open on its own, why is there an exercise in Step 8 of IIH that is designed to open that astral sense?" Ok, you might've caught me there. But let's look at Bardon's comments regarding the Step 8 clairvoyance exercise. Two of those comments are as follows.

> *A very particular topic we shall deal with in this step concerns the development of the astral senses [...]. The magician's astral senses have been trained and developed in any case in the course of all the preceding exercises; nevertheless there is need of an extraordinary drill in cases of poor abilities for one or the other faculty, because every human being has different talents.*

The Spirit of Magic by Virgil

The magician ought not to forget that all the [exercises] mentioned here are nothing but poor expedients. By no means, however, are they the real factor that produces the desired result of genuine clairvoyance.

As the above passages from IIH show, Bardon states that in the vast majority of cases, the student who has reached this level of magical advancement won't have to become clairvoyant because the student's clairvoyance will have already opened on its own. However, many people have a weak area, or several weak areas. For example, my weak area while working through IIH was the Step 3 vital force condensation exercises. Some people's weak area will pertain to their astral senses. If this is your weak area, then there is a small chance that your astral sense of sight won't have fully opened when you reach Step 8. If this is the case, then Bardon's exercise is designed to give your astral sense of sight just the little nudge it needs in order to fully open. As you can see, even the people who have no knack for clairvoyance whatsoever will just need to give their astral sense of sight a little nudge when they reach Step 8 in order to open this astral sense fully.

It's clear that Ben's approach to becoming clairvoyant was wrong. Like many aspiring magicians, he was asking himself the wrong questions. The question he was asking himself was "What exercise do I need to practice in order to become clairvoyant?" The question he should have been asking himself is "How can I reach the level of magical advancement where my astral senses will open on their own?" The shotgun approach is not going to get you there.

Don't deprive yourself of the power to become clairvoyant by believing you don't have the power to become clairvoyant. And don't listen to the people who try to deprive you of this power by getting you to believe that.[32] You do have the power to become clairvoyant, to exteriorize your subtle bodies, to transplant your consciousness, to unite with Divinity, and to master any other skill that any competent magicians would have. You just need to find the right approach. If your approach so far has been to search for the right exercise, perhaps you should vary your approach by searching for the right system instead.

Chapter 6: Magical Training Systems – the Alternative to the Shotgun Approach

Beware of Scams

Proponents of some systems claim that their systems can turn people into adepts overnight. These are scams. Don't buy into them. Of course, depending on how you define "adept," it could be possible to become an "adept" overnight, but if you use a set of meaningful standards (e.g. Bardon's standards) to evaluate whether the proponents of those systems are genuine adepts, then you will find that they never meet the standards required for that level of advancement.

Magical training is in part a process of becoming more mature. The process of becoming more mature cannot be rushed. It can only be facilitated. This is why magical training takes time. Adepthood is a level of magical advancement that is very much worth achieving, but anything worth achieving requires effort to attain. Those who are looking for an instant and effortless way to adepthood will never find it.

Concluding Remarks

I learned fairly early on in my magical studies that maturity is vital in this art. True magical power is only given to the mature, because only the mature can be trusted to use it maturely. This is why when I studied the history of Western magic, I was so surprised to see it characterized by drama; after all, drama is always started and propagated by immature behaviors. What was worse, despite how often the phrase "Know Thyself" appears in so many books on Western magic, many of the immature individuals engaging in these immature behaviors seemed to have no idea how immature they were. Did magicians actually care about becoming mature and acquiring self-knowledge, or was all this talk about knowing oneself and evolving spiritually a bunch of smoke and mirrors?

Knowing what I know now, it no longer surprises me that so much of the history of Western magic is characterized by drama. When magical training is approached correctly, the student becomes more balanced. When magical training is approached incorrectly, the student becomes more unbalanced because the imbalances existing within him become strengthened and exacerbated. Numerous students approach magical training incorrectly because the systems they are using are incomplete, unbalanced, or improperly structured. This has been the case for decades and perhaps much longer.

Many common magical training systems were created by people who were unqualified to create magical training systems. They lacked

The Spirit of Magic by Virgil

the genuine initiatic knowledge needed to ensure that their systems were complete, balanced, and properly structured. When students rely on these systems for guidance, they approach magical training incorrectly, which strengthens and exacerbates the imbalances within them that cause them to behave immaturely. Common imbalances include egotism, arrogance, and pettiness - three qualities that are often at the root of drama. This explains the prevalence of drama in the history of modern Western magic.

If you are reading this book, my guess is that you don't want to become like the unfortunate occultists of the past who spent their lives quarrelling with other self-proclaimed adepts, starting feuds with rival orders, and engaging in the politics of their own orders. Instead, you want to live a life that is actually productive, and realize that while pretend magic has little to offer you, real magic can help you achieve your goals. The road to genuine adepthood is long, and since there is only so much time in a human lifetime, the amount of time wasted should be minimized. Find a path that helps you eliminate your imbalances, as opposed to a path that strengthens them. Proper magical training is such a path, but improper magical training is not. In the end, much of it boils down to the integrity of the magical training system you use.

Chapter 7: Thought-Observation

You master the mind by both understanding and being free of every mental vibration which can occur within it.

~William Mistele

In my opinion, the most important thing that differentiates Bardon's system from most all of the other modern systems of magic is that it begins at the beginning.

~Rawn Clark

Mental training is a big component of magical training, and the end goal of this component of magical training is complete mastery over one's mind. The beginning of the long journey to this end goal is learning to observe the contents of one's mind. In the Bardon community, this exercise is called "thought-observation," and it is the first mental exercise in Step 1.

Back when I was active on several Bardon-themed Facebook groups, I would often receive messages asking for advice or help on various exercises in IIH. A lot of the messages looked like this,

Dear Virgil,

I recently began working through IIH, but I am encountering a problem with the first mental exercise. Bardon writes in IIH that you're supposed to sit down and observe your thoughts for five minutes. Every time I sit down and try to observe my thoughts though, I find that I don't have any thoughts. How can I observe my thoughts if I don't have any thoughts? Should I just move on to the next exercise? I would appreciate your advice.

Regards,
Horace

The Spirit of Magic by Virgil

I've lost track of the number of people who have messaged me with this exact same problem. Students sit down to observe their thoughts, find that they have no thoughts because their mind is seemingly empty, and then wonder what to do. Some try to create thoughts to observe. Others try to move on to the next exercise.

First, let's review what exactly this exercise entails based on the instructions in IIH. These instructions, as found in the Radspieler translation of IIH, are as follows.

Take a seat in a comfortable chair or lie down on a settee. Relax the whole body, close your eyes and observe the train of your thoughts for five minutes, trying to retain it. At first, you will find that there are rushing up to you thoughts concerning everyday affairs, professional worries, and the like. Take the behavior of a silent observer toward these trains of thoughts, freely and independently. According to the mentality and the mental situation you happen to be in at the moment, this exercise will be more or less easy for you. The main point is not to forget yourself, not to lose the train of thoughts, but to pursue it attentively. Beware of falling asleep while doing this exercise.

Alright. So basically, you sit down in a chair and you observe your thoughts for five minutes. Gradually, you increase the length of the exercise until you can easily observe your thoughts for ten minutes without losing focus. That's the whole exercise, or so it seems...

First, let me say that this exercise is EXTREMELY important. It's the foundation for much of the mental aspect of magical training. DO NOT move on from this exercise until you have mastered it thoroughly. Go outside, lie on the grass, and observe the clouds passing over you. It seems so simple and easy doesn't it? When it is just as easy for you to sit in a chair and observe your thoughts for ten minutes, then you have mastered the exercise sufficiently enough to move on.

Before we return to this issue of beginners sitting down to observe their thoughts and then finding they have no thoughts, let's think about why this exercise is so important. The third mental

Chapter 7: Thought-Observation

exercise of Step 1 is to focus on one thought for ten minutes. Imagine if I told you to go outside at night, pick a star above you, and stare at it for ten minutes. This is easy, right? Well what if you were blind? In that case, the exercise would be impossible. Before you have learned to be aware of the individual thoughts passing through your mind and to observe them attentively, trying to hold a single thought in your mind and focus on it is a bit like trying to stare at a single star when you are blind.

The fourth mental exercise of Step 1 is to empty your mind of all thoughts.[33] Imagine that I told you to go into a room filled with cats and to clear all the cats out of there. This is easy. You just go into the room and chase out all of the cats. If you are blind, then this is significantly more difficult. You could be standing in the middle of a room filled with cats and telling me "Ok, I emptied this room of all cats." In reality, the room is still full of cats but you don't know that because you are blind and can't see them. Are you beginning to understand the source of the issue people have with the first mental exercise? The room is your mind. The cats are thoughts. While the fourth mental exercise is to chase all the cats out of the room, the first mental exercise is to just observe the cats in the room. However, this is impossible if you are blind. Before you can observe the cats, you must first learn to see. This is the hard part. Horace, in the message quoted earlier, thinks there are no cats in the room. Really, he is just blind and has not yet learned to see. Once you have learned to see, then it is easy to observe the cats, and to see that there are actually quite a few of them in the room.

The way Bardon explains the exercise is misleading in two ways. The first way is that it makes it seem like observing your thoughts is something everyone can do right off the bat, and that the point of the exercise is to be able to observe them continuously for ten minutes without becoming absent-minded or letting your attention waver. This is not exactly true. To return to the cat analogy, Bardon's wording makes it seem like everyone can see, when in fact, most people need to learn to see before they can begin observing the cats.

Basically what I am saying is this. There are many thoughts that pass through your mind every moment; however, usually people are not aware of them. LEARNING TO BECOME AWARE OF THEM IS A SKILL THAT NEEDS TO BE DEVELOPED!

The Spirit of Magic by Virgil

This is why so many beginners sit down to observe their thoughts and find that they have no thoughts. They do have thoughts; they just haven't learned to become aware of them yet. They are like blind people standing in a room full of cats thinking it is empty, but only because they can't see the cats around them.[34]

This is the first step toward mastering this exercise. Learn to become aware of your thoughts. Once you have done that, then increasing the amount of time that you are able to observe your thoughts without becoming distracted or absent-minded is a relatively simple and straightforward process. It is the first step of learning to become aware of your thoughts that most people struggle with.

The second way that Bardon's description of the exercise is misleading is that he says to "observe" your thoughts. Human language is not perfect, and sometimes you have to do the best you can do. "Observe" is not a bad word, but unfortunately, it gives the impression that the thoughts passing through your mind appear as visual images. This is not true. Thinking the thought "pencil" is not the same as visualizing a pencil. There is no good way to describe what a thought "looks" like when you "observe" it as it passes through your mind.

Instead of "observe," I prefer to say "be aware of." You might have noticed this already, because I've already used "be aware of" instead of "observe" several times in this chapter. If we use this phrase instead of the word "observe," then the first two sentences in that description would read "Take a seat in a comfortable chair or lie down on a settee. Relax the whole body, close your eyes, and be aware of the train of your thoughts for five minutes, trying to retain it." In a book I am currently in the middle of writing, I refer to "thought-observation" as "thought-awareness."

The First Step 1 Mental Exercise: Getting the Hang of It

[Author's note: The following is an old article I wrote that was designed to help students get the hang of thought-observation. Several of the points I bring up in the article are points I have already brought up previously in this chapter, but I don't think it will do you any harm to encounter them again.]

In this article, I hope to provide a clear explanation of the first Step 1 mental exercise, as well as practical guidelines for mastering it smoothly and with as little frustration as possible.

Chapter 7: Thought-Observation

The first thing you should know about this exercise is that there are two stages of mastery. The first stage involves learning to observe your thoughts. The second stage involves extending the length of time you can observe your thoughts continuously without become distracted. When you have extended this length of time to ten minutes, you have mastered this exercise enough to move on to the third mental exercise of Step 1.[35]

It's important to understand why the first stage of mastery precedes the second stage of mastery. You cannot succeed in observing your thoughts for ten minutes if you do not even know what it means to observe a thought. In going through my journal from back when I was working through this exercise, I find that I wrote down quite a few questions that bothered me at the time.

> *"What does it mean to observe your thoughts?"*
> *"What does it feel like to observe your thoughts?"*
> *"How do thoughts appear when you are observing them?"*
> *"Do they appear like images that flash through your mind?"*
> *"Do they appear like words you hear spoken in your head?"*

These are the questions I had and wrote down in my journal, hoping I would be able to answer them at a later date when I had practiced more. They are the same questions I asked other practitioners without ever receiving a satisfactory answer. They are the same questions beginners ask me on Facebook or via email.

Regarding the first two questions about what it is like to observe your thoughts, there is really no way to describe in words what this is like. I'm sorry, but that is the truth of it, and anything you read that tries to explain/describe what it feels like to observe your thoughts will probably only confuse you. It is something you must experience for yourself. The more expectations or preconceived notions you have about what this will be like, the more likely you are to do the exercise incorrectly. Once you "get the hang of it," you will see what I mean. Imagine trying to describe color to a blind person. This is what it's like trying to describe the experience of observing one's thoughts to someone who hasn't yet gotten the hang of observing his thoughts.

I find the phrase "getting the hang of it" to be quite fitting in this case. Once you have gotten the hang of observing your thoughts, extending the period of time you are able to attentively observe your thoughts without becoming distracted is a simple matter. Making progress is just a matter of practice, and you can measure your progress

The Spirit of Magic by Virgil

with a stopwatch or a string of beads. What's potentially tricky is this exercise's first stage of mastery, which is just to get the hang of observing your thoughts. To learn what this is like. To learn what this means.

So, with that said, let me say definitively that observing your thoughts does not mean watching the images that flash before your eyes or listening to words that may be spoken in your mind. Let me give an example that may illustrate the latter point.

Once, while preparing for a children's project, I had to fill many cups with sixty beads each. I would hold a cup with my left hand, reach into a bag of beads with my right hand, and drop bead after bead into the cup. As I did this, I would count in my head so I would know when I had placed sixty beads in the cup. In other words, I would say in my mind "One, two, three, etc." At some point, I realized it was much faster to just think the number instead of saying it mentally. Once I began to do this, the rate at which I worked also became faster. When you say a number in your head, you have to think the number first anyway. Therefore, when I dropped the thirty-seventh bead into the cup, I just thought the number thirty-seven without mentally saying it.

So, I guess the big question right now is how exactly you can get the hang of observing your thoughts. The first and perhaps most important piece of advice I will give is this.

DON'T TRY TOO HARD!!!

Many times, when a student first tries this exercise, he sits down, tries to observe his thoughts, and then cannot because it seems like his mind is empty and he doesn't have thoughts. If this is the case for you, then trust me, you do in fact have many thoughts. The problem is you just aren't aware of them. You haven't learned to notice them. Just as you can be aware of the computer in front of you, or be aware of your emotions if you are sad or angry, you can also be aware of your thoughts. The awareness you are using is the same type of awareness. It is just more refined and sensitive. Thoughts, after all, are more subtle than feelings or computers. So sit down in a chair, close your eyes, relax, and just be aware. That's it. That's all you need to do. Just sit there and be aware. Don't worry if there are no thoughts in your awareness. Do not strain and try too hard to be aware of your thoughts. DO NOT TRY TO CREATE THOUGHTS ON YOUR OWN SO YOU CAN BE AWARE Of (AKA "OBSERVE") THEM! Just sit there and be aware. That's all

Chapter 7: Thought-Observation

there is to it. You are practicing being aware. Do this every day, and as you practice being aware, your awareness will increase. And as your awareness increases, it will encompass more and more things. Eventually it will encompass the thoughts in your mind, and you will realize that they were there after all, and that your mind wasn't as empty as you thought it was when your awareness did not encompass all the thoughts flitting through it. Once you have become aware of your thoughts, you have gotten the hang of it. Being aware of your thoughts is essentially what Bardon means when he says to "observe" them. Once you can remain aware of your thoughts continuously for ten minutes, you have mastered this exercise.[36]

Once you have gotten the hang of observing your thoughts, and once you have practiced a bit more, then you will find that observing your thoughts is actually something you can do throughout your daily life, whether you are getting the mail, or cooking, or walking your dog. In fact, part of being present-minded is being mindful of what is going on in your mind. As you learn to be continually aware of what is going on in your mind as you go about your day, being aware of the thoughts in your mind (AKA "observing" them) will become as natural to you as breathing.

Until you have become proficient at observing your thoughts, you cannot truly practice the third exercise, which is to hold one single thought in your mind for ten minutes without letting any other thoughts enter your mind. A lot of people also ask me about this exercise, and occasionally, their questions lead me to wonder whether they truly completed the first exercise. Let's say I choose to think about a mountain for ten minutes. This is not the same thing as visualizing an image of a mountain for ten minutes or repeating the word "mountain" over and over again in my head for ten minutes. People who have "gotten the hang of it" when it comes to observing their thoughts will know exactly what it means to hold one thought and only one thought in your mind for ten minutes, but once again, it is not something I can describe or explain with words.

It is the same case with the fourth exercise in Step 1. People ask me about that one too. In this exercise, you empty your mind of all thoughts. Sometimes, people will say to me "I think I am good enough at the fourth mental exercise of Step 1 to move on to Step 2, but I'm not certain. The problem is that I'm not sure what exactly it means to empty my mind of all thoughts. Therefore, I'm not sure if my mind is really empty of all thoughts." What do you mean you aren't sure what it means to empty your mind of all thoughts? Observe your mind. If there are thoughts in it, it's not empty of all thoughts. If there are no thoughts in it, then it is empty of all thoughts. There is literally nothing in the world that could be more straightforward. Of course, if you haven't yet mastered the first mental exercise, then nothing about the fourth mental exercise is straightforward at all. Indeed, how can you tell if your mind is empty of all thoughts if you have not yet learned to become aware of your thoughts and observe them?

If you do not understand what Bardon is asking you to do in the third or fourth mental exercise, then it is because you have not yet gotten the hang of thought-observation. Once you've learn to observe the thoughts in your mind, then you should have no difficulty understanding what it means to have only one thought in your mind (third mental exercise) or to have no thoughts in your mind (fourth mental exercise).

Building a Friendship with Your Mind

The first exercise of Step 1, thought-observation, is truly my favorite exercise in all of IIH. At first, you might think that the creation of the soul mirrors is my favorite exercise, after all, I am always talking about it and emphasizing its importance. I definitely believe creating the soul mirrors is the most important exercise in IIH, and one of the key things that separate Bardon's genuine magical system from the many occult systems that are out there. Still, it's not my favorite exercise. Thought-observation is. I am a busy person, but sometimes, I'll go to a quiet place like the local library and practice thought observation for an hour, two hours, or even an entire afternoon. I don't do it because I want to advance along the magical path. I do it simply because I think it's fun.

You will be working with your mind a lot during your magical training. Have you ever worked with a coworker that you did not like and did not understand well? It really sucked, didn't it? Imagine if you could have worked with a friend you understood well instead. The experience would have been much more enjoyable, and you probably would have gotten much more done. Friends don't struggle with each other. Friends cooperate with each other. If your mind is your friend, your mind will cooperate with you. This makes it easier to get your mind into a state of one-pointedness (third mental exercise) or into a state of emptiness (fourth mental exercise).

You should come to think of your mind as your friend. In order to build a friendship with your mind, you need to get to know it. That's

Chapter 7: Thought-Observation

what it's like the first few times you practice thought-observation. You are hanging out with your mind so you can get to know it better in order to become friends with it. Later on, when you continue to practice thought-observation even though you are in the advanced stages of training, you are hanging out with your friend because, well, that's what friends do.

Observing Your Thoughts Doesn't Have to Be Boring

I've heard multiple people say that Bardon's magical training system is good, but the exercises in the system are super boring. Therefore, if you want to succeed in working through the system, you need to have great self-discipline so you can force yourself to practice the exercises every day. Self-discipline is a great thing, and it is an absolutely essential quality for magicians to possess. But self-discipline alone can't carry you through your training. You do need to love the path you choose. In his book *The Esoteric Practice*, Daskalos states that commitment to one's training is necessary, but also asserts that no good will come from forcing yourself to practice esoteric exercises when you are not inclined to. I think there's a lot of truth to that assertion. If you think Bardon's exercises are super boring, you won't ever feel inclined to practice them. Therefore, you won't benefit from them, even if you have enough self-discipline to force yourself to practice them daily.

The thing is, the exercises in Bardon's system aren't super boring, at least not to me. I don't have the room in this one book to explain why I find every exercise fun and exciting, but I do want to share why I find thought-observation fun and exciting. For one thing, thought-observation is basically me hanging out with one of my best friends – my mind. However, there is more to it than that.

Have you ever smelled a flower? It's a very pleasant sensory experience. When I lived in Pittsburgh, I lived within walking distance of Phipps Conservatory and Botanical Gardens. Whenever I was really stressed, I'd walk there and smell a flower. Like I said, it's a pleasant experience. In his book *Eternal Echos: Celtic Reflections on Our Yearning to Belong*, John O'Donohue writes that observing a thought in your mind can be a beautiful, pleasant, and transforming experience like smelling a flower. In his book *Anam Cara: A Book of Celtic Wisdom*, John O'Donohue writes that an empty mind is like a void, and that thoughts are like flashes of light in this void. If you imagine flashes of light in a void, the image is probably beautiful and enchanting. Think

The Spirit of Magic by Virgil

about fireworks. Everything John O'Donohue says reflects my own experiences with thought-observation. Observing your thoughts can be as pleasant as smelling a flower, and as exciting and enchanting as watching flashes of light in a void. This is another reason why I find thought-observation so enjoyable.

Chapter 8: Magical Training Tips and Advice

By means of persevering and graduated athletics, the powers and activity of the body can be developed to an astonishing extent. It is the same with the powers of the soul.

~Eliphas Levi

If you do not get an exercise after repeating it thirty or forty times then don't stop. Try repeating it three or four hundred times. But do not be stupid. Vary your approach and add to your practice anything you can that might assist you in mastering something.

~William Mistele

There are many authors who assert that the reason so few aspiring magicians ever reach the level of genuine adepthood is that they spend too much time reading about magic and not enough time practicing magical exercises. This is only partially true. Practicing the wrong magical exercises is really no better than not practicing at all. There are many individuals who have just collected together random magical exercises from random books to practice, and they never end up better off than those who are too lazy to practice any exercises at all. Practicing magical exercises will only help you advance if you are practicing the right exercises. As I explained in Chapter 6, if you are working through a magical training system, then your magical training system should tell you what the right exercises for you are at any given level of advancement. For example, if you are using the Bardon system and you are on Step 2, then the right exercises to practice are the exercises of Step 2. If you are on Step 5, then the right exercises to practice are the exercises of Step 5.

This chapter won't be of any use to you if you aren't practicing the right exercises. If you are practicing the right exercises, then the tips and

The Spirit of Magic by Virgil

advice I give in this chapter should help you master those exercises faster and more smoothly.

How Long to Spend on an Exercise

People often ask me how long they should spend practicing a magical exercise before moving on to the next exercise. In truth, whether or not you should move on from an exercise does not depend on how long you have practiced the exercise, but on how proficient you are at the exercise. If you are proficient enough at an exercise to be able to move on to the next exercise, then you can move on to the next exercise, even if you haven't been practicing the exercise for that long. If you aren't proficient enough at an exercise to be able to move on to the next exercise, then you should not move on to the next exercise, even if you've been practicing the exercise for a long time.

For example, with the Step 2 visualization exercise, Bardon writes in IIH that you must be able to visualize a simple object for five minutes, keeping it perfectly still and perfectly vivid the whole time. If you can visualize a simple object for five minutes, keeping it perfectly still and perfectly vivid the whole time, then you can move on to the next exercise. If you can't, then you should keep working on this exercise until you meet those standards of mastery. One of the great things about Bardon's system is you never have to wonder whether or not you're proficient enough at an exercise to move on to the next one. Bardon always makes his standards of mastery clear. When you meet the standards for an exercise, you can move on to the next one.

Let's look at another example – the Step 1 concentration exercise. In this exercise, you practice holding a single thought in your mind. Bardon writes that you must be able to hold a single thought in your mind for ten minutes without other thoughts intruding into your mind. Those are the standards of mastery for this exercise. If you can hold a single thought in your mind for ten minutes without other thoughts intruding into your mind, then you can move on to the next exercise (VOM). If you can't, then you should keep practicing the concentration exercise until you can.

Some people might only need to practice an exercise for a week before becoming proficient enough to move on. Others might need a few months, or even a few years. Magical advancement is an individual thing. Do not compare yourself to others. That's one of the biggest traps in magic. If everyone else you know completed Step 1 in a month, that

Chapter 8: Magical Training Tips and Advice

doesn't mean you will be able to complete it in a month. If everyone else you know took five years to complete Step 1, that doesn't mean it will take you that long. How long it takes others to complete a step or master an exercise should not matter to you, and it is really none of your business anyway. Don't worry about what the "average" amount of time others spend mastering a particular exercise or completing a particular step is. Just focus on yourself and on your own training.

Break Exercises Apart

It's often easier to complete a task if you break the task up into smaller tasks and complete the smaller tasks one by one. In IIH, Bardon breaks the task of becoming a magician into ten steps, but he doesn't stop there. He breaks each step into three sections, and he breaks each section into several exercises. If you are having trouble with an exercise, you can break it apart even further into its different aspects or its different stages of mastery.

Let's consider the Step 2 mental exercise of visualizing an object. This exercise has two aspects.

1. Keeping the object perfectly still
2. Keeping the object perfectly vivid

We can try to master aspects at the same time. In other words, you can take an object like a chess piece, study it carefully, and then try to visualize it in front of you so that it is perfectly still and perfectly vivid. Or, you can start by mastering one aspect and then master the second aspect.

Let's say you want to master the stillness aspect first, and that the object you want to visualize is a green pencil sharpener. Study the pencil sharpener and visualize it in front of you. Keep the visualized pencil sharpener perfectly still, but don't worry about making it perfectly vivid. It can be a fuzzy green blob, as long as it is perfectly still. With each practice session, increase the resolution of the image until it goes from a fuzzy green blob to a perfectly vivid solid green pencil sharpener.

You could also master the vividness aspect first. Visualize the green pencil sharpener as vividly and clearly as possible, but don't worry about keeping it still. Allow it to spin and dance around. With each practice session, focus on diminishing its movement until it is perfectly still.

The Spirit of Magic by Virgil

Instead of breaking the visualization exercise into two aspects, as described above, you can also break it into two stages of mastery if you are having trouble with the exercise. This is the approach that worked for me. The two stages of mastery of the visualization exercise are as follows.

1. Get the hang of visualization
2. Extend the length of time you can visualize an object to five minutes

In this case, you first play around with visualization to get the hang of it, and once you have gotten the hang of visualization, then you start the process of visualizing an object for one minute, and then extending this length of time by one minute each day until you can visualize an object for five minutes.

Similarly, the Step 1 thought-observation exercise can be broken down into two stages of mastery.

1. Get the hang of observing your thoughts
2. Extend the length of time you can observe your thoughts to ten minutes

In *A Bardon Companion*, Rawn divides the Step 4 transplantation of consciousness exercise into four stages of mastery. They are as follows.

1. Experience of the object's physical limitations and dimensions
2. Experience of the object's physical sensations
3. Experience of the object's emotions and thoughts
4. Complete unification with the object

When mastering this exercise, you begin by mastering the first stage – transplanting your consciousness into an object to the extent that you are able to experience the object's physical limitations and dimensions. For example, if the object is three feet wide, four feet long, and two feet high, then when you transplant your consciousness into the object, you should experience being three feet wide, four feet long, and two feet high. Once you have mastered this first stage, you move on to the second stage – transplanting your consciousness into an object to the extent that you are able to experience the same physical sensations the object is

Chapter 8: Magical Training Tips and Advice

experiencing. For example, if the object is sitting on a stone table outside on a windy day, then you should feel the cold stone table underneath you and the wind blowing against you when you transplant your consciousness into the object. Once you have mastered this second stage, you move onto the third stage - transplanting your consciousness into an object to the extent that you are able to experience the object's emotions and thoughts. For example, if you transplant your consciousness into a cat, you should be able to experience the cat's emotions and thoughts. Once you have mastered this third stage, you move on to the fourth stage, where you are literally one with the object you have transplanted your consciousness into.

Hopefully after reading the examples in this section, you have some ideas on how to break the task of mastering an exercise into several smaller tasks.

Get the Hang of a Skill First

Each of the exercises in IIH is designed to help you master a specific skill. Sometimes, it may help if you get the hang of a skill first before practicing exercises to master the skill. For example, the Step 2 visual plastic imagination exercise is designed to help you master the skill of visualizing objects. Before practicing this exercise, it might be a good idea to first get the hang of visualization. You could do this by imagining yourself in a scene from your favorite movie or favorite book. Explore this scene, and don't feel compelled to restrict yourself to just using visualization (the visual plastic imagination). Feel free to use the auditory plastic imagination and the tactile plastic imagination to make the experience more enjoyable. For example, you could talk to characters or pick up objects and feel them. When you do something like this, you're not practicing a magical exercise to help you master your plastic imagination. You're just playing around with your plastic imagination, so this activity should be approached in a spirit of play.

Another example is the Step 1 thought-observation exercise. Bardon tells you to begin practicing this exercise by observing your thoughts for five minutes, and then to extend this time by a little bit each day until you can attentively observe your thoughts for ten minutes without becoming distracted or absent-minded. Before you begin practicing this exercise, it might be a good idea to first get the hang of observing your thoughts. If you sit down and try to observe your thoughts for five minutes without first having gotten the hang of observing your thoughts, you're going to have a very frustrating experience.

External Conditions

In the beginning, some people will find it easier to practice their exercises in certain conditions. For example, you might find that meditation is easier when you are in an air-conditioned room, or when it's early in the morning, or when you are sitting in a specific chair. That's perfectly fine. Don't think you are being weak by practicing your exercises when the conditions are the most favorable. Later on in your training, practicing these exercises will become second nature, and you will be able to do them under any conditions.

The second day of my journey through IIH, I got home eager to train. It was warm inside the house and I was about to take my jacket off and practice thought-observation. I stopped myself and wondered if I was being weak by taking off my jacket. I thought maybe I would become a better magician if I always trained in the most unfavorable conditions, such as uncomfortably hot conditions. Now I know that this is silly. At this point, I can sit back and observe my thoughts if I am sitting in an uncomfortably hot room, or an uncomfortably cold room, or a very noisy room. I can observe my thoughts regardless of what my external conditions are. However, when I first began the process of mastering thought-observation, I trained in favorable conditions. I found that the exercise was easier after I took a relaxing shower and if I was in an air-conditioned room, so I usually practiced in an air-conditioned room after showering.

Should You be Doing That Exercise?

I once received an email from someone who was struggling with the Step 5 depth-point exercises. After conversing with him about his struggles, I couldn't figure out why he was having so much trouble with this exercise. A few weeks later, this same individual emailed me, and we had another email conversation about magical training in general. During this conversation, he remarked that he was really bad at visualizing objects.

What?! Visualizing objects is a Step 2 exercise. If this guy had yet to complete Step 2, why was he trying to practice a Step 5 exercise? The reason he was struggling with the depth-point exercises was that he shouldn't have even been practicing them in the first place. He should

Chapter 8: Magical Training Tips and Advice

have been practicing the Step 2 visualization exercise instead. This might seem obvious, but you'd be surprised at how many aspiring magicians think they can learn to run before learning how to walk.

Forming a Plan

Mastering some exercises is just a matter of practicing them every day. However, with other exercises, you can make a broader plan for mastering the exercise. For example, if you want to master the Step 2 visualization exercise, you could create a plan like the following one.

1. Practice visualization for five minutes during your daily practice session.
2. Throughout the day, pay attention to your sense of sight and familiarize yourself with it. Look closely at different textures and at the gradients between light and shadow. You could even take up a hobby like photography or painting that requires you to work with your sense of sight.
3. Every now and then throughout your day, take between five and ten seconds to visualize a simple object. For example, if you are waiting in line, you could close your eyes for a few seconds and visualize a tube of toothpaste. If you are sitting on a bus, you could close your eyes for a few seconds and visualize an eraser. There's no need to do this super often. A couple of times throughout the day is enough.
4. Read and contemplate the chapter about sight in Bill's essay on the five senses.[37]
5. Read any articles about visualization you come across.
6. Use visualization to help you in your day-to-day life. For example, if you play golf, then before each swing, visualize yourself making a perfect swing. If you need to give a presentation, then shortly before the presentation, visualize yourself giving a perfect presentation. Your brain really can't tell the difference between something you are visualizing and something you are seeing, which is why visualizing yourself doing something gives you confidence that you can do it.

The Spirit of Magic by Virgil

As you can see, you are practicing the exercise each day during your daily practice session. However, you are also doing things throughout the day to help you master the exercise.

Prayer

For most magical exercises, you need a calm mind. When you are an advanced practitioner, you should be able to calm your mind instantly at will. However, at the beginning of your training, you probably won't be able to do this. Therefore, I recommend you begin your daily practice session with prayer. Pray for wisdom and understanding. Pray for guidance in becoming more compassionate. Pray for assistance in knowing yourself. Pray for the well-being of your loved ones. Pray for help in becoming a magician. I have found prayer to be a great way to calm one's mind. When I first began my magical training, I noticed that even if my mind was extremely agitated because of my chaotic life, saying a short prayer was enough to calm it. If there are meditation or concentration exercises in your daily practice routine, beginning your daily practice routine with prayer will make those exercises much easier.

Of course, prayer isn't the only way to calm one's mind, but it is one of the easiest and quickest. Plus, there is the fact that you will acquire whatever you pray for, regardless of whether it is wisdom, help in becoming more compassionate, or a blessed life for your loved ones. As one great magician famously said – "Ask and ye shall receive."

Understand the Exercises You Practice

Make sure you understand the instructions for each exercise you practice. If you are training in Bardon's system, note that the way he describes the conscious breathing exercise in Step 1 is kind of confusing. When he says inhale seven times, some people interpret this to mean you inhale once and divide this inhalation into seven segments. This practice, known as viloma pranayama, is not what Bardon meant. He means to inhale fully seven times, with each inhalation followed by a full exhalation.

In addition to understanding the instructions for each exercise, make sure you understand the purpose for each exercise as well. An incorrect understanding of an exercise's purpose can also cause you to practice the exercise incorrectly. For example, some people believe that the purpose of the Step 2 asana exercise is to develop willpower, so instead of

Chapter 8: Magical Training Tips and Advice

mastering the throne posture like Bardon tells you to do, they choose a more difficult asana to master because mastering a difficult asana develops your willpower more than mastering an easy asana does. However, the purpose of the exercise is to provide you with a posture that you can do the rest of your magical exercises in. Therefore, you should not choose a difficult asana, but an asana that would be good for you to practice your magical exercises in. The throne posture described by Bardon is excellent.

Outside Exercises

Outside exercises are exercises that aren't part of the magical training system you are using, but that you practice anyway to supplement your training. If the magical training system you are working through is complete, then there is no need for you to practice outside exercises. This doesn't mean you can't benefit from practicing outside exercises, because you often can. However you shouldn't believe that this is something you have to do. Some people practice too many outside exercises. This reflects a lack of focus and a tendency to become easily distracted. When it comes to outside exercises, you need to make the best decisions when it comes to deciding whether to practice outside exercises, and which outside exercises to practice.

In general, while I was working through IIH, whenever I had extra time that I wanted to devote to my magical training, I preferred to use that time to deepen my mastery over the exercises of IIH, rather than practice outside exercises. However, I did incorporate some outside exercises into my daily practice routine at various points in my training. For example, I prayed regularly. Prayer isn't an exercise found in IIH, so it can be seen as an outside exercise. Furthermore, I made use of Patsy Rodenburg's Second Circle exercises regularly after reading her book. Returning my default state of being to Second Circle with the help of her exercises greatly improved my life and my magic. I was bullied into First Circle on a regular basis throughout my childhood, so this eventually became my default state and remained my default state until I returned it to Second Circle roughly a decade ago. There are also a few spiritual exercises in Frank MacEowen's book *The Mist Filled Path* that I really like and that I practiced periodically throughout my magical training. Finally, Bill developed some great body awareness exercises that I would also practice occasionally.[38] Those are the main outside exercises I practiced throughout my training, and they did do a good job of supplementing my IIH training.

Some students practice outside exercises that don't really supplement their training, and that may even be dangerous. Without exaggeration, many people have literally died practicing Kundalini exercises without knowing what they were doing. In his book *The Esoteric Practice*, Daskalos warns against chakra exercises, stating that he's known many people who have severely damaged themselves messing around with these sorts of exercises. The exercises in Crowley's Liber III vel Jugorum involving cutting yourself with a razor and don't actually help you become free like he claims they do, so I definitely wouldn't recommend using them as outside exercises.

Some outside exercises aren't really dangerous, but are just a waste of time. For example, I once found an exercise in a book that would supposedly help you become balanced. The exercise was basically just to stare at a Yin Yang symbol for ten minutes every day. That's not actually going to do anything to make you balanced, so it's waste of time, but at least it's not dangerous. Needless to say, you should avoid exercises that are a waste of time. Beginning students of magic often have a difficult time discriminating between outside exercises that will help them, and outside exercises that are a waste of time or dangerous. For this reason, it's not a bad idea to restrict yourself to practicing only the exercises of your magical training system at the start of your training. However, as your wisdom and understanding grow, you will eventually reach the point where you can clearly see which outside exercises (if any) will benefit you, and which will not.

Don't Overtrain

Proceed in a safe manner without causing yourself damage through misguided enthusiasm.

~Ikon

The greatest poison to spiritual growth is to be in a hurry. Patience and moderation are the rule.

~Daskalos

Chapter 8: Magical Training Tips and Advice

The Wikipedia page about overtraining states that "People who are overtrained cease making progress, and can even begin to lose strength and fitness." This refers to the physical body, but a well-known Hermetic axiom goes "As above, so below." Therefore, if the physical body can be overtrained, then theoretically, it's possible for the astra-mental body to be overtrained as well.

But to heck with theory! Let's turn to experience instead. The subject of overtraining when practicing magical exercises is one that will hit close to home for many Bardonists, because many Bardonists have experienced the negative effects of overtraining. The reasons for this go back to what I wrote earlier about there being a lot of bad advice out there. In the Bardon community, it is not uncommon to see people telling beginning students to spend hours each day practicing the exercises of IIH. This supposedly shows seriousness, but it doesn't. It shows misguided enthusiasm, a lack of patience, and an unbalanced obsession with magic. Just as overtraining the physical body results in losing physical strength and physical fitness, overtraining the astra-mental body results in losing astra-mental strength and astra-mental fitness.

Don't Get Distracted by Occultism

In Step 2, Bardon asks you to practice visualizing small everyday objects like paperclips, matches, Legos, erasers, chess pieces etc. Some students, when they get to this exercise, instead try visualizing sigils, Tarot cards, astrological symbols, Hebrew letters, etc. Don't do this. Just visualize small everyday objects like Bardon recommends. There are many advantages to doing this. The main one is that visualizing simple objects is easier than visualizing occult symbols.[39] This will allow you to get the hang of visualization faster.

If for some reason visualizing occult symbols is easier for you than visualizing simple everyday objects, then it is certainly appropriate to practice visualizing occult symbols as a stepping stone to being able to visualize small everyday objects. If this isn't the case, then there is no reason to give the exercise an unnecessary occult flavor. Don't get distracted. Stay focused and serious.

Becoming Distracted is a Choice

One of the biggest reasons students of magic make little to no progress in their training is that they keep getting distracted. To prevent

The Spirit of Magic by Virgil

yourself from becoming distracted, you need to understanding a very important truth – becoming distracted is a choice.

If something distracts you from your training, it's because you chose to let it distract you. For example, let's say you are working through Step 1 and you come across a book about Enochian magic. This book is a potential distraction from your training; after all, the work of Step 1 has nothing to do with Enochian magic. However, the book cannot force you to read it. If you read the book, it's because you chose to read it. In other words, you chose to let it distract you. As a result, you have less time to spend reading books that will actually benefit you.[40]

As another example, let's say you are working through Step 1 and you come across a New Age book with a "Druidic Kabbalistic past life chakra exercise." This exercise cannot force you to practice it. If you practice the exercise, it's because you chose to practice it. In other words, you chose to let it distract you. As a result, you have less time to spend practicing the exercises of Step 1, which is the step you are on.

As one final example, let's say you are working through Step 1 and you read a book that mentions Seidr. Seidr cannot force you to study it. If you become so fascinated with Seidr that you spend all your time studying it and neglect to practice the exercises of IIH, then you have chosen to be distracted by Seidr. Of course, this situation could be flipped. If the magical path you walk is Seidr and you come across IIH, then IIH could be a distraction that prevents you from making progress in the path you have chosen.

The occult world is filled with distractions. Some take the form of books. Others take the form of exercises. Regardless of what form a distraction takes, realize that it can only succeed in distracting you if you choose to be distracted by it. You are never at the mercy of these distractions, regardless of how many there are. They have no power over you if you choose not to give them power over you.

Two Passages Regarding Chakra Exercises

I don't know whether the same thing is true for students of other magical training systems, but New Age chakra exercises are one of the most common distractions to affect Bardonists. If a Bardonist has stopped practicing the exercises of IIH because he has become distracted by other exercises, there's a good chance the distracting exercises are chakra exercises of some sort.

Chapter 8: Magical Training Tips and Advice

I think one of the reasons so many people succumb to chakra-themed distractions is that they are unaware of just how drastic the dangers associated with improper chakra work are.[41] I believe an awareness of these dangers and their scope will be a powerful tool that students of magic can use to resist becoming distracted by chakra-themed exercises. For this reason, I want to present two passages that discuss the consequences of these dangers. The passage below comes from the first essay in John Michael Greer's "Foundations of Magical Practice" essay series.[42] He is discussing the negative effects produced by Julius Evola's magical training system and tracing those negative effects to the fact that the system is incomplete and improperly structured.

> *To be fair to Evola, things could have turned out much, much worse. I'm thinking here of the fad for kundalini yoga that flared and burnt itself out in Californian occult circles during the 1920s, in the last years of Theosophy's boomtime. Manly P. Hall, a sympathetic observer as well as a major occult teacher in his own right, described the consequences in one of his books. Young healthy Theosophists launched into practices they thought would make them enlightened masters; one by one, they turned pale, sickened, and died.*

The next passage, which follows, comes from Daskalos's book *The Esoteric Practice*.

> *It is a most dangerous situation when uncontrolled hunger for psychical experience moves a seeker to engage himself in strong exercises without first laying the groundwork within the personality to cope with the ensuing experience. The damage is often irreparable when an emotionally immature student opens certain etheric centers [Sanskrit: chakras] and has neither the means nor the strength to re-collect himself.*

I hope these passages make it clear that chakra exercises are not the best thing to be distracted by. But do be warned, there are plenty of other distractions besides chakra exercises. To increase your chances of recognizing distractions that come your way, you must be aware of all potential sources of distractions. In the next section, we will see that some sources of distractions are ones you never would have suspected to be sources of distractions.

Distractions Can Come From Within

Besides the fact that distractions can only distract you if you let them, another thing you need to know about distractions is that they can come from within. That is to say, from within the communities and circles associated with the system you practice. If you are a practitioner of the Bardon system, then you are probably aware that many books about the Golden Dawn system or the Aurum Solis system are not too relevant to your training. However, many Bardonists assume that all books, resources, and media related to the Bardon system will be relevant to them. This isn't true. Let's examine a simple but common example.

KTQ is a distraction for beginning students of Bardon's system that doesn't just come from within the Bardon community, but from Bardon himself. Students who are working through the first steps of IIH don't really have a good reason to study KTQ, yet many of them are fascinated by this book and spend more time studying this book than they do practicing the exercises of IIH. This really isn't a good way to use one's time.

As time goes by, there are going to be more and more books written about the Bardon system. There are always going to be Bardonists who think they must have the latest Bardon-related book or they have no hope of completing IIH. These are the Bardonists who spend more time reading books about the Bardon system than they do practicing the exercises of the Bardon system. Bardon-related books are meant to help you with your training, not distract you from your training. There are indeed many books, such as Rawn's *A Bardon Companion*, that are undoubtedly helpful, but at the end of the day, you have to remember that none of them are necessary. Only IIH is necessary, and before all those other supplementary books and commentaries were written, IIH was all Bardonists had and many Bardonists got along just fine with nothing other than IIH. If anyone ever claims that IIH isn't enough and that you need other books, they are trying to make money off of you.

Chapter 8: Magical Training Tips and Advice

Don't Get Distracted by Earlier Versions of Your System

Magic is a form of engineering, a form of science, a form of art, and a form of spirituality. Having a background in engineering, science, art, or spirituality will provide you with certain advantages in magic, but the advantages will be different depending on what the specific background you have is. For example, if you have a scientific background, you will be great at observing things objectively and drawing conclusions without letting biases or emotions get in the way of rational thought. This is something scientists have to do all the time. If you have an artistic background, you are probably in touch with your inner life, and this is indeed a huge advantage for a student of magic to have.

A background in engineering will also provide the student of magic with many advantages, and one of those advantages is an understanding of iterative design. The process of iterative design pops up all the time in engineering. For example, let's say I am a geotechnical engineer trying to design a driven pile foundation for a building. I would design the foundation, test it out via a simulation, improve the design, test the improved design again, and continue this process of improving the design and testing the new improved version until I arrived at a design that is satisfactory. Each iteration produces a new and better design.

The process of creating a magical training system is similar. You create an initial version of the system and then test it by guiding students through the system. Then, based on the results, you improve the system, creating a new and better version of the system. You then test the new version of the system by guiding students through it. You then improve the system even more based on those results. This iterative process continues until you arrive at a version of the system that is satisfactory.

Memories of Franz Bardon was written by two direct students of Bardon. The book contains some glimpses of earlier versions of the Bardon system generated during iterations that occurred before the final iteration produced the final version of the system found in IIH. For example, in an earlier version of the system, there was a color visualization exercise that came before the thought-observation exercise in Step 1. This was the version that Bardon guided Dr. M.K. through. When the book came out, some people found these earlier versions interesting and tried to practice these earlier versions of the system instead of the final version found in IIH. This is not a good idea. The whole point of iterative design is to improve a product. Each iteration of the process generates a better version of the product. If you use an earlier version of the product, you are using a version that isn't as good as the final version, so in cases like these, use the final version.[43]

Sometimes, people who don't know what they are doing will modify a system in ways that make it worse. In that case, you obviously should not use the newer but corrupted version of the system. However, in the case of a system like Bardon's where Bardon himself passed the system through various iterations to generate new and improved versions, we can be sure that the final version that he published in IIH was what he considered the best version.

Don't Force Truths Upon Those Not Ready For Them

No sincere adept will impose his truth to anyone who is not yet ripe for it.

~Franz Bardon

In the course of your training, you will learn many profound truths about magic, the four elements, spiritual evolution, maturity, and power. When you travel to the Sphere of the Sun, you will learn many profound truths about the process of uniting with Divinity. When you travel to the Sphere of Jupiter, you will learn many profound truths about loving-kindness, communities, and fortune. When you travel to the Sphere of Saturn, you will learn many profound truths about taking responsibility for yourself and taking responsibility for the world. It is a beautiful form of service to share these truths with those who are ready to receive them and who could benefit from receiving them. However, you should never force these truths upon those who are not ready to receive them.

This is common sense. No good ever comes from receiving something before you are ready to receive it. This is why you don't see many arguments in the Bardon community. You'll see conversations, discussions, and respectful debates, but arguments are rare. When you argue with someone, you try to force a truth (or at least what you perceive to be a truth) onto the person you are arguing with. There is just no point in doing this.

Chapter 9: The Magician's Life

The great disadvantage of working with Divine Providence is that you have to upgrade and change yourself many times as if you living three or four lifetimes in one life. You do not have the luxury of clinging to one identity. Your personality is under constant assault because you are developing both as a spirit and as a human being.

~William Mistele

Whoever is willing to enter the magic path should regard it as his sacred duty to practice regular exercises. He ought to be kind, generous, and tolerant with his fellow men, but relentless and hard with himself.

~Franz Bardon

The way students of magic approach life is quite different from the way those who are not students of magic do.[44] In this chapter, I hope to provide useful guidelines regarding how to live in a way that supports one's magical advancement.

Make Necessary Sacrifices

If you want to advance along the magical path, you're going to have to make a few sacrifices. For example, I used listen to music a lot. The thing is, songs get stuck in my head easily. When I began training in the Bardon system, I found that some exercises were harder for me to practice if there was a song stuck in my head. For example, it was difficult to impregnate my food while there was a song stuck in my head. Therefore, I decided to stop listening to music. That was a sacrifice I made.

A question many aspiring magicians have is how much sacrifice is needed to undergo magical training? There's no good answer to this question. My advice is to sacrifice whatever is needed so that you can practice at least once a day.

Some sacrifices are avoidable if you are good at planning and looking ahead. Let's say you want to go to a party in the evening but you have not practiced that day. You have two options.

1. Sacrifice going to the party so you can practice.
2. Sacrifice some of your sleep so you can practice when you get back from the party.

Of course if you had just practiced in the morning or found some time in the early afternoon to practice (maybe during your lunch break), you wouldn't be facing this dilemma. If you know that there is an event you want to go to at your usual practice time, then you should plan ahead so that you can practice at another convenient time. As you can see, if you are good at planning, you might be able to plan things so that you can practice daily while still going to all the events you want to go to without sacrificing sleep. But if you aren't good at planning, then you may find yourself having to sacrifice going to some events or sacrificing some sleep so you can have time to practice.

There is this idea going around that once you start to pursue any form of spiritual training, everything will fall in place and Divine Providence will change your life for you so you can devote as much time as possible to your training. This is completely false. If you want to devote more time to your training, then it is entirely your responsibility to make the sacrifices and schedule changes necessary to do so. No entity or deity, divine or otherwise, will do this for you.

Strive to Become More Mature

Magical training isn't just a process of acquiring magical skills and abilities by practicing magical exercises. Magical training is also a process of becoming more mature. Divine Providence is not an idiot. She will not give genuine magical power to people who are immature for the obvious reason that they will use it immaturely. With each step of IIH you complete, your genuine magical power grows. Therefore, you will not be able to complete a step of IIH until you have acquired the level of maturity needed to move on to the next step. For example, if you do not have the maturity needed to move on to Step 2, you will never advance to Step 2, even if you spend ten hours a day every day practicing the exercises of Step 1. There are just certain inner blocks that will prevent

Chapter 9: The Magician's Life

you from mastering the exercises no matter what you do – a fact that many people who have spent years stuck on a step can attest to.

This is one reason magic isn't like other arts. The more you practice ballet, the better you will become. The more you practice playing the piano, the better you will become. This is true of magic if you have the maturity to practice magic. But if you don't, then you won't make progress, no matter how much you practice. For this reason, the magician should never pass up an opportunity to become more mature. Life is constantly providing us with opportunities to become more mature, so when we hide from life, we hide from opportunities to become more mature. Unfortunately, many students do that by locking themselves in their room for ten hours a day practicing magical exercises. These same students then wonder why they aren't making any progress.

We should not hide from life, but embrace life and welcome its various experiences because those experiences are great teachers. This subject is covered in more detail in my book The Covert Side of Initiation.

Discriminate

Learn to discriminate. Draw proper conclusions.

~Daskalos

It is absolutely imperative that the student of magic acquire the virtue of discrimination at the beginning of his training. In modern Qabalah, discrimination is the virtue associated with Malkuth, the sephirah representing the first stage of the student's journey toward self-realization and full adepthood. Consider all the ways the student must discriminate if he is to make any progress in his training.

He must discriminate between effective magical training systems and ineffective magical training systems.

He must discriminate between those books that are worth reading and those books that aren't worth reading.

He must discriminate between the good advice he receives and the bad advice he receives. Otherwise, he may destroy himself by following the bad advice.

He must discriminate between activities that are a good use of his time and activities that are a bad use of his time.

The Spirit of Magic by Virgil

If he wants to study with a teacher/order, he must discriminate between the teachers/orders that will benefit him and the teachers/orders that are fraudulent.

Many students of magic never bother learning to discriminate. Therefore, they work through ineffective magical training systems, read books that aren't worth reading, follow bad advice, waste their short lives engaging in practices that are a waste of time, and learn from charlatans pretending to be great adepts. This is why there are so many students of magic walking in circles or walking in the wrong direction.

Have a Stable Ship

Your life is like a sea voyage. Your elemental equilibrium is your ship. Those who sail must endure storms. Sometimes, you can avoid storms by sailing around them or sailing out of their way if they are coming towards you. Other times, you can dissolve storms using magical or non-magical methods. However, there are many storms you should pass through because many storms are good teachers. The magician relies on his wisdom to tell him which storms he should sail around, which storms he should dissolve if he can't sail around them, and which storms he should pass through. The sorcerer, on the other hand, tries to dissolve or banish away every storm with his spells, and therefore never learns anything.

A bad ship will rock violently during a storm. A really bad ship will be overturned by the storm, representing a breakdown of some sort. A good ship will hardly rock during a storm. The passengers in the ship may not even notice they are passing through a storm. Because of the way the ship is designed, the passengers experience smooth sailing, even in the midst of a storm. Unstable boats rock a lot and are easy to overturn. Stable boats barely rock, even in the middle of storms. You must have a stable boat – a solid elemental equilibrium. In this way you will be fine, even if your life is stormy.

Stable and unstable ships both sail well in calm seas. It's when the stormy weather comes that it become clear which ships are the stable ones and which are not. The adepts all say that life is the ultimate test of how good your elemental equilibrium is. If you can pass through the storms of life without being rocked and overturned, then you have a good elemental equilibrium. The personality that carries you through life is stable, and therefore strong and balanced. You cannot avoid storms forever. Even the best sorcerers eventually must face them when the

Chapter 9: The Magician's Life

universe forces them to learn. Therefore, it is wiser to work on making your boat more stable than to worry about dissolving or sailing around every storm you see on the horizon.

Do Not Neglect the Mundane Aspects of Life

Those who walk the path of magic must understand that balance is key. You cannot spend all your time practicing magical exercises and neglect other more "mundane" aspects of your life, such as your family, your job, and your social life. Those mundane aspects are just as magical as the exercises of IIH because magic is comprehensive and balanced. To be a magician requires that you have a balanced and well-developed personality. If the "mundane" aspects of your life are in a bad state, this is indicative of some major defects in your personality. An inability to hold a job could be indicative of laziness. An inability to make friends could be indicative of poor interpersonal skills or a lack of charisma. An inability to have a healthy romantic relationship could be indicative of poor listening skills. Problems in all aspects of our lives, including both the "magical" and the "mundane" aspects of our lives, often arise from negative personality traits. You must discover what those negative personality traits are through introspection and record them in your black soul mirror so you don't forget them. Then, you must root them out one by one using the six-pronged attack. When you do this, the problems should disappear.

The idea that balance is important in magic, and that a balanced life must involve being attentive to the mundane, can be found in the following passage from Bill's essay on the spirit Emrudue. Recall that after the student works through IIH, he travels to the Earthzone and then to each planetary sphere to learn from their ruling genii. Emrudue is one of the ruling genii of the Sphere of the Moon.

> *But if this distinction between higher and lower somehow implies that material desires are somehow of lessor importance in life, some of the lunar spirits would immediately stand up and object. From their point of view, the material universe has been created in order to celebrate love. You are going against the laws of the universe and generating karma if you leave physical happiness and gratification out of your equation for the meaning and purpose of life. If you seek the physical and ignore the spirit, you generate horrible karma. If*

The Spirit of Magic by Virgil

you seek the spirit and ignore the physical, you generate horrible karma. This is because the two are a part of the same design.

For example, in the scheme of things, enjoying sex is just as important as communing with God. If you do the "higher" at the expense of the "lower" you have a demon waiting for you behind a door and he is slowing prying out the hinges and picking the lock in order to get to you. This is because God created that demon to remind you of the importance of sexuality as a key to discovering who you are. The demon's authority and commission are activated by your act of repression. The demon represents your blind spot--an essential area of life which you have written off as unworthy of your attention.

If you pursue sex at the expense of communing with God, there is another demon waiting for you. His power derives from the creativity in life you have left behind because if anything God is creative and that power is the essence of your being. This demon haunts an abyss of chaos. He is authorized to bring that chaos into your life. The reason is that divine creativity is unafraid of emptiness and any abyss. It seeks them out because that is the space of the imagination which it requires to create. The creator is unafraid and freely and willingly enters the unknown in order to make something new.

This is real magic here. It's not practicing random exercises because you want to move a candle flame with your mind. It's not dabbling in different systems because you don't have the discipline to stick to one and master it. It's not studying tables of correspondences all day or performing inert theatrics disguised as rituals. It's not feuding between orders or boasting about ranks and lineages. It's a lifelong discipline in which you develop all aspects of your personality so that it becomes balanced and strong enough to engage potent inner forces and wield them to recreate the world. So yes, your sex life, your finances, your social life – all these "mundane" aspects of your life and more are worth just as much of your attention as the magical exercises of the magical training system you are working through.

Chapter 9: The Magician's Life

Be Present-Minded

You make your mind completely empty of thoughts so it is reflective like a mirror, receptive like the ocean, empty like a void, open like the sky, intense like air the moment before lightning strikes, serene like moonlight, fragile and responsive to suggestion like a dream, and solid and enduring like a mountain.

~William Mistele

The magician's mind is one of his greatest tools, and magical training involves a long process of refining this tool and learning to use it. By the time the aspiring magician has completed his training, he will have achieved a high level of mental maturity and mental discipline.

The level of mental maturity and mental discipline required to stay continually present-minded is relatively low compared to the level of mental maturity and mental discipline the magician will have acquired at the end of his training. However, learning to be continually present-minded is an important beginning step on the road to mental mastery. Those who have not taken this beginning step are not very far along in their mental training, and therefore not very far along in their magical training in general.

So, what does it mean to be present-minded? Have you ever gotten into a car to drive to a location and found yourself at that location with no recollection of how you got there? Clearly, you weren't present-minded while you were driving. You were absent-minded or distracted. When you first begin the practice of present-mindedness, you have to try to be present-minded. Later, you no longer have to try because present-mindedness becomes your default state of being.

There are many benefits to be gained from being present-minded. It improves your ability to focus. It helps you learn more from your life experiences; after all, you can't learn anything from your life experiences if you are absent-minded while going through them. It makes it possible for you to "carefully observe your routines and seize opportunities as they occur to improve on what you are doing." Finally, being present-minded will improve your life because the present-moment is the only moment that truly exists, and therefore the only moment when you can consciously make changes that will transform your life. This isn't possible if you are absent-minded and running on autopilot.

Listen to Your Conscience

The problem of morals and ethics is difficult to tackle in the world of philosophy, but not in the world of magic. Your intuition is the voice of Divinity speaking to you to give you guidance. When your intuition gives you guidance in moral issues, it is often called your "conscience" or "moral compass." When you are faced with moral issues and ethical dilemmas, just listen to your conscience and you will know what to do.

There is a big trap that some people fall into called the "rationalization trap." This is when you don't like what your conscience is telling you, so you use logic to convince yourself that your conscience is wrong. For example, let's say you are really tempted to cast a love spell on a woman you desire and your conscience tells you this is wrong. You could use logic to convince yourself that your conscience is wrong and then cast the love spell. This is a common example. Another common example involves curses. A person will be tempted to curse someone he doesn't like. His conscience will tell him this is wrong, but he will use logic to convince himself that his conscience is wrong and send the curse anyway.

Logic uses deductive reasoning to draw conclusions from what we know. However, we don't know everything, and oftentimes, what we think we know is false. Therefore, logic is fallible. Divinity, however, is omniscient and infallible. When Divinity speaks to you through your intuition, you should listen. Oftentimes, our intuitions can tell us things that logic can't tell us. If your intuition has ever warned you against going to a seemingly safe place or dating a seemingly ok person, then you already know this.

Another common trap is confusing one's emotions with one's conscience. If you are angry at someone and this anger is compelling you to curse that person, this doesn't mean your conscience is telling you to curse that person.

Be Open-Minded

When you finish your training and magician, you will often find yourself working with energies, powers, and entities that the human mind

Chapter 9: The Magician's Life

really wasn't designed to comprehend. This might seem like a problem, after all, it is difficult to grasp or engage with an energy/power/entity if you have no understanding of it, and even if you do, you will be working with it from a position of ignorance, which is dangerous.

The human mind, however, can evolve/adapt to understand these energies, powers, and entities, but only if it is flexible. A rigid mind cannot bend, and therefore cannot change, develop, or evolve in any way. Narrow-mindedness is a sign of a rigid mind, while open-mindedness is a sign of a flexible mind. When you come across an aspiring magician who is narrow-minded, you can be sure that he is a long way from adepthood.

Open-mindedness is not a quality you cultivate when you are an adept and need to have a flexible mind to comprehend the strange forces you are working with. It is a quality that we begin developing at the very beginning of our training, and that we cultivate with each step we take as we walk the path of magical training. In fact, when it comes to magic, open-mindedness is not just a quality that allows our minds to be more flexible, and therefore more versatile and useful tools. It is also a quality that is imperative for survival. When you are narrow-minded, you see little and you see from one angle only. Therefore, you miss seeing dangers and warnings. When you are open-minded, you see much and you see from many angles. Therefore, you are more likely to dangers and warnings. You are also more likely to see solutions and opportunities.

Strive to Constantly Improve Yourself

I used to be a really snarky person. I remember one day in college, I was chatting with a friend of mine named Sarah right before spring break. Sarah was a devout Christian. When I asked her what she was doing over spring break, she told me she was travelling to developing nations with a Christian organization she was a member of to convert people to Christianity. Later during our chat, our friend Mike passed by us and sat down to join our chat. He asked me what I was doing over spring break, and I told him I was driving to Minnesota to visit a high school friend of mine. He then asked Sarah what she was doing. Before she could answer, I said something like "She's travelling around the world to brainwash people." That was a mean thing to say. I thought it was a harmless joke, but Sarah was hurt. She didn't tell me she was hurt by the remark, but a momentary look of hurt flashed across her face. I noticed it, and realized that the cutting sarcastic remarks I often made when I was trying to tease others could be hurtful. Later that night, I described this incident in my journal and made a note to stop making such remarks.

A few days later in a creative writing course, a classmate was reading a story I wrote and was giving me constructive criticism so I could improve it. Although she was giving me good constructive criticism and her only intent was to help me improve my story, I got defensive and began arguing with her. Later that night, I described this incident in my journal and made a note to stop getting defensive when people were giving me constructive criticism.

A few days later, I was on a date with a girl. Since I was a shy person back then, I had trouble making eye contact with her. While the date still went well, I think we would have connected even better if I had been better at making eye contact. Later that night, I described how I was uncomfortable making eye contact in my journal, and made a note to practice making better eye contact whenever I had a conversation with anyone.

You should constantly work to improve yourself. That means making a mental, and perhaps physical, note of everything you do that is bad, and then thinking about how you can avoid making the same mistakes in the future. I did become less snarky; I did learn to accept constructive criticism without getting defensive; and I did become more comfortable making good eye contact. To this day, my efforts to improve myself continue.

Regulate Your Thoughts

Thoughts aren't just illusions that exist only "in our heads." Thoughts are real, and therefore they can affect the real world. The mental plane is just as real as the physical plane. The thoughts you generate affect the mental plane. Changes on the mental plane are reflected on the astral plane and on the physical plane, as stated in the magical axiom "As above, so below." A malicious thought will not only have a direct negative impact on someone's mental body; it will also have an indirect negative impact on his astral body and on his physical body. Just as a malicious physical action harms other people, a malicious thought also harms other people. Since thoughts are more subtle than physical actions, the harm wrought by a malicious thought is usually more subtle than the harm wrought by a physical action. For example, shooting a person may kill him. Thinking malicious thoughts about a

Chapter 9: The Magician's Life

person probably won't kill him, but it may cause him to fall ill. The stronger your mind is, the more severe the harm wrought by your malicious thoughts will be. Magical training will strengthen your mind, so it is imperative that you refrain from thinking malicious thoughts towards others. Developing compassion is really the only sure way to do this because compassionate people never think malicious thoughts towards others. It's not in their nature to do so.

This isn't just me moralizing or feeding you religious dogmas. At various points in my magical training, I found myself butting my head against a wall and unable to move forward. I wasn't mature enough to reach the next stage of training, so Divine Providence put these inner blocks in my way to protect me from myself and to protect others from the possibility of me using magic immaturely. I remember one of the biggest blocks I encountered was caused by my tendency to think malicious thoughts about others. It took me almost three years to eliminate enough of this tendency for the inner blocks to be removed. After that, I found myself making progress once more.

Seize Opportunities to Face and Understand Your Ego

Many adepts have stated that the ego generates some of the biggest traps that ensnare aspiring magicians and prevent them from making progress in their training. These adepts, however, usually don't explain what the ego is, and so these warnings about the ego are of limited use. They let people know that there is something called an "ego" that can create traps, but these people might not know what an "ego" is, and therefore, all the warnings against ego-generated traps aren't very helpful.

The fact of the matter is, it's really hard to explain using words what exactly the ego is, and this is why few magical writers have tried defining it. Understanding the ego isn't a matter of reading dictionary definitions of the word "ego," but of facing the ego and observing it. Daily life often provides us with opportunities to do this. This yet another reason to not hide from daily life by sitting in your oratory all day reading books about magic and practicing magical exercises.

One time I was at a Christmas party and I met someone I didn't know. We introduced ourselves to each other and shook hands. As soon as we were finished shaking hands, he said to me "Man your handshake sucks. It's so weak. You really need to work on it." I was upset by this statement of his. When I used my mind to trace this feeling of being upset back to its source, I found myself face to face with my ego. This experience helped me see quite clearly what an ego is, but again, it's difficult to explain using words.

Another time, I was at a Christmas party (different Christmas party, lol) and a group of people, including me, were having a casual conversation. Somehow we started talking about our salaries. I mentioned what my salary was and another person in the group started making fun of how low it was compared to that of the others. I found myself getting upset at his comments, but when I used my mind to trace this feeling of being upset back to its source, I once again found myself face to face with my ego, which again gave me the opportunity to observe my ego, get to know it, and understand it.

I will give one more example. One time, I met a woman who practiced witchcraft. She had read a few books about witchcraft and Wicca and liked to practice spells. We began talking about magical subjects and it became clear to me that I knew a lot more than she did and understood a lot more than she did. As a result, I felt superior to her. However, when I used my mind to trace this feeling of being superior to her back to its source, I found myself face to face with my ego and was able to observe it and learn about it.

The better we understand our egos, the easier it is to free ourselves from the influence of our egos. The student of magic should not seek to destroy his ego or repress his ego. Such goals are not healthy and may prove disastrous. The student of magic only seeks to free himself of his ego, meaning to ensure that he is not enslaved by his ego. In other words, instead of ego, it is wisdom, intuition, reason, and logic that determine our choices and actions. Anytime you find yourself feeling upset after being criticized or feeling superior to others, you should trace the feeling back to its source. There's a good chance you will find yourself face to face with your ego.

Keep Silence

Keep silent about your interest in magic, your magical practices, and your magical training. The better you are at keeping silence, the more quickly you will advance. This is because the more mature you are, the more quickly you will advance, and being good at keeping silence is a part of being mature. When those who are advanced write about magic or talk about magic, they do it because they are compassionate and want to help others by sharing their knowledge. When beginning students of

Chapter 9: The Magician's Life

magic desire to tell others about their interest in magic and their magical training, they do it because it feeds their egos. When you talk about a subject in order to feed your ego, you profane that subject. The mysteries of magic are very sacred, and will not be profaned. Those who tout themselves about as mages well-versed in occult knowledge because such behavior feeds their ego will never penetrate into the mysteries of magic, regardless of how many books they read or how long they practice magical exercises.

As you make more progress in magic, your ego will go from being your master to being your friend and servant. You will also acquire more insights into the magical mysteries that are worth sharing with those who could benefit from those insights. Furthermore, you will acquire wisdom, and thus know who to share what insights with.

Learn About Your Flaws from Your Mistakes

You must learn to overcome all passions, and conquer all tendencies to folly. But let there be no misunderstanding. To vanquish an enemy there must be no running away: true victory can only follow meeting him face to face, joining in a struggle, and so showing your command over him.

~ Eliphas Levi

The genuine magician takes life such as it is; he enjoys the good things and learns something from the bad ones, but he will never hang his head. He is aware of his own weaknesses and tries to overcome them. But he ignores any thoughts of repentance, since they are negative thoughts that are to be avoided. It is sufficient to recognize his own faults and never to relapse into them again.

~Franz Bardon

In *Memories of Franz Bardon*, Dr. M.K. writes about the time he first asked Bardon to teach him Hermetics. According to Dr. M.K., "He (Bardon) told me that at this time there were no openings and since I was only 16 years old, he said that I was too young, that I had committed no sins, and that I had no passions."

The Spirit of Magic by Virgil

When I first read this passage, I was baffled. Bardon said that Dr. M.K. was not ready to study Hermetics because he had never sinned! Isn't that a good thing? Well, sometimes it is, and sometimes it isn't. If you haven't sinned because you are truly a righteous person, then that's a good thing. If you haven't sinned because you have been sheltered your whole life from the temptations and stimuli that would cause you to sin, then that's a bad thing because it means you don't know yourself.

In his book *Conquest of Anger*, Swami Sivananda states that it is very difficult to master one's anger. He tells the story of a man who has isolated himself from society by sitting in a remote cave. This man believes he has mastered his anger because he never gets angry. Because he never gets angry, he has never murdered anyone out of anger, hit anyone out of anger, yelled at anyone out of anger, or "sinned" in any way out of anger. However, although he has never sinned out of anger because he has never become angry, he is actually very far from mastering his anger. The only reason he never gets angry is because there is no one around him to make him angry. Because there is no one around him to make him angry, he does not know how easily he can become angry, and has never had the opportunity to overcome his anger.

Often times, the person who has never sinned is like the man in the cave who thinks he has overcome anger. Human beings are not perfect. We all make mistakes ("sins), but that's ok because our mistakes are valuable teachers. When we murder others out of anger, we learn that we are irascible. When we steal peoples' jewelry, we learn that we are greedy. When we intentionally break up our friends' perfect marriages by sleeping with their wives or husbands, we learn that we are envious. When we eat an entire pizza for lunch, we learn that we are gluttonous. Each time we "sin," we learn that we possess a vice – the vice that caused us to sin. Once we are aware that we possess that vice, we can write it in our black soul mirrors and root it out with the six-pronged attack. We can overcome the vice by resisting its influence on us each time in the future that it pressures us to sin again. In this way, we root out the vice and return to a state of righteousness.

So basically, our sins/mistakes are vital learning experiences that provide us with important self-knowledge. When I look at my black soul mirror, I see that rudeness was a negative personality trait of mine. How did I know that rudeness was a negative personality trait of mine when I was making my black soul mirror? It's because I remembered that I had "sinned" many times by treating others rudely. Also when I look at my black soul mirror, I see that passive-aggressiveness was a negative

Chapter 9: The Magician's Life

personality trait of mine. How did I know that passive-aggressive ness was a negative personality trait of mine when I was making my black soul mirror? It's because I remembered that I had "sinned" many times by treating others passive-aggressively. When Dr. M.K. was 16, he had not sinned enough, and therefore, Bardon did not feel he had the self-knowledge needed to practice magic.

Strengthen Your Will By Exercising it Regularly

Self-discipline is an absolutely essential trait to have. It can be roughly defined as how good you are at using your will to force yourself to do things you don't want to do. The stronger your will is, the better your self-discipline will be. In one of his books, Levi writes that the method of strengthening the will was closely guarded by magical schools in the past, and that those who tried to learn the method put themselves in great danger. He then goes on to write that the method of strengthening the will is to exercise it regularly. I always thought that was kind of funny. Of course there is the question of how exactly we exercise the will. This is a simple matter. Whenever we have a chance to give ourselves immediate pleasure, we should practice temporarily refraining from giving ourselves that pleasure. I'll give three examples.

Let's say there is an annoying coworker who is being particularly frustrating and you really want to punch him. Also, let's just say that in this hypothetical situation, you know you would not be punished for punching him.[45] Obviously, punching him would give you immediate pleasure. However, you can will yourself not to punch him and deny yourself that immediate pleasure. In this way, you exercise your will and it grows stronger.

Let's say it is a weekend and you wake up early. It's cold, and you want to just remain in your bed for a little while longer. Remaining in bed would give you immediate pleasure. However, you can deny yourself that pleasure. Instead, you can will yourself to get out of bed, get dressed, and start your day. In this way, you exercise your will and it grows stronger.

The practice of asana strengthens the will in that same way. When you have been sitting perfectly still for a long time, your body really wants to move. It wants to squirm around a little and relieve itself of its cramps and itches. Doing that would give you immediate pleasure. However, when you deny yourself that pleasure and will yourself to continue remaining still until your timer goes off, you exercise your will and strengthen it.

Most humans impulsively do whatever gives them immediate pleasure. Anytime you exercise a muscle, there is some weight you are using. When you lift a dumbbell, the weight of the dumbbell fights against the strength of your bicep. Your bicep gets stronger as a result. When you exercise your will, it is your impulses you are fighting against. You impulsively want to punch your coworker, remain in bed, or squirm while practicing asana. However, despite these impulses, you will yourself not to do those things. This is the method of exercising your will. Your daily life will provide you with many opportunities to strengthen your will. You can keep yourself from putting your hands in your pocket when it is chilly outside. You can force yourself to shower in water that is slightly colder than what you are comfortable with. Always look for small opportunities like these to strengthen your will by exercising it. Over time, it will become quite formidable.

Be Open to Learning from Everything

I've never actually stated my age in any of my writings, but I've often implied that I'm an adult. That's not true. I'm actually just a kid, and I'm not even in middle school yet. During recess, I used to play kickball with my friends, but I was never very good at it, so I stopped doing that. I also liked playing on the swings, but all the swings are usually occupied, so I rarely got the chance to. The monkey bars were kind of fun, but those got old after a while, and the slides and the rest of the jungle gym on the playground bored me. As a result, I didn't have anything enjoyable to do during recess, which is why I started writing books about magic during that time. I carry my laptop with me everywhere, so I'm also able to do some writing on the bus to school, and in my mom's car on those days when I miss the bus and she has to drive me to school. So, why do I periodically imply that I'm an adult when I'm just in fifth grade?

There is a saying that is commonly passed around in esoteric circles – "When the student is ready, the teacher will appear." In his correspondence excerpts, Rawn makes the following remark about this saying.

> *"Ready" does not mean just that you desire a teacher. That is not readiness; that is only desire. True readiness is when a*

Chapter 9: The Magician's Life

student realizes that EVERY thing is their teacher and when the student is prepared to *learn* from EVERY thing. If the student has realized that initiation is not a matter of finding *a* teacher, but rather a matter of cultivating the ability to *learn from EVERY thing*, that is when they are "ready/

In his essay *Teaching Methods, Initiation, and Esoteric Traditions*, Bill writes the following.

The student's experience is always new. It is full of incomprehensible possibilities and experiences which the teacher may never in this life time have the resources to fathom. From my point of view, the only way to tell a teacher in any group of people is by observing the individual who is learning the most. That is the one with the most open and receptive heart.

Rawn's remark states that the student who is truly ready to learn magic is the student who realizes that everything is their teacher and is prepared to learn from everything. Bill's statement implies that the magician who has reached a high level of advancement in his training can be identified by his ability to learn from everyone because of his open and receptive mind and heart. The people who do not have this open and receptive mind and heart are the people who are too narrow-minded to believe that they can learn from someone who is younger than them, less experienced than them, of a lower grade than them, or who wears less fancy robes than they do.

In the magical community, you see many people taking pride in how many years they have been studying magic, or in how expensive their ritual tools are, or in how many orders they have joined. You rarely see people taking pride in their preparedness to learn from everything and in their ability to do so because of their open hearts and minds. That's because there just aren't that many people who have cultivated the ability to learn from everything. This is why I must regularly imply that I'm an adult. That way, more people will buy my books. If I didn't do that, then the only people who would buy my books would be the people who had cultivated the ability to learn from everything, and therefore would consider the possibility of learning new things from a book written by a fifth grader. Perhaps in a future time when more students of

The Spirit of Magic by Virgil

magic have open and receptive minds and hearts, all the elementary school students who write books about magic, including me, won't have to keep pretending we're adults in order to get people to read our books. That time has not yet come.

Live Consciously

Conscious living is one of the pillars of self-esteem listed in Nathaniel Branden's book *The Six Pillars of Self-Esteem*. Self-esteem is an important quality for magicians to have because a lack of self-esteem is a weakness that darkness can use to enter you and gain control of you. While I could have included a section on each of Branden's six pillars, I wanted to single out the pillar of conscious living because I think it is especially important. Bardon tells us that the student of magic must possess knowledge, courage, volition, and silence. Conscious living is the way courage primarily expresses itself. There are many unpleasant facts about ourselves and about our lives. It takes courage to face those facts. In other words, it takes courage to be conscious of those facts. The decision to be in denial of them instead is driven by cowardice.

Conscious living isn't quite the same as the present-mindedness that was discussed earlier. Present-mindedness is being attentive to what you are doing. Conscious living is being conscious of all aspects of yourself and your life, and all facts about yourself and your life that are important. Another way to describe it is acknowledging all aspects of yourself and your life, and all facts about yourself and your life that are important. Yet another way to describe it is not being in denial about any aspects of yourself and your life or facts about yourself and your life that are important. This third description is the one I think is easiest to understand. There are many facts that are unpleasant and that we would like to remain in denial about. Conscious living is choosing to be conscious of those facts instead of in denial about them. Actually, conscious living isn't just choosing to be conscious of those facts. It's also allowing those facts to factor into the choices you make. This allows you to make more informed, and therefore better, choices. If you're confused, I have two examples from my own life that illustrate what conscious living is and why it will improve your life.

When I was in my junior year of college, my friend Eric and I both applied for a number of engineering internships over spring break. A few weeks later, we were eating lunch together. Neither of us had heard back from any of the companies we applied to, and we were discussing our

Chapter 9: The Magician's Life

summer plans. Eric simply remarked that he would probably hear back from one of the companies eventually. He chose to remain in denial about the fact that he probably wouldn't hear back from any of them at this point.

I, on the other hand, chose to be conscious of the fact that I probably wouldn't hear back from any of the companies. As a result, later that afternoon, I searched for more engineering internships in my area and applied for them. I ended up getting one that proved very beneficial for my profession development (I was an engineering major). Eric, on the other hand, didn't really have anything to do that summer. If he had chosen to be conscious of the fact that he probably wouldn't hear back from any of the companies he applied to during spring break, he would have applied for more internships and perhaps gotten one. However, because he chose to be in denial about that unpleasant fact, he didn't feel the need to apply for any more internships.

Another example is this. My interpersonal skills used to be really bad. However, admitting to myself that my interpersonal skills were bad would obligate me to improve my interpersonal skills, and that seemed like a lot of hard work. Because I was lazy, I chose instead to be in denial about the fact that my interpersonal skills were bad. As a result, the quality of my life suffered. Eventually, when I began to make conscious living a way of life, I finally chose to become conscious of the fact that my interpersonal skills were bad. I embarked on a quest to improve them. My quest started with reading Olivia Fox Cabane's book *The Charisma Myth: How Anyone Can Master the Art and Science of Personal Magnetism* and doing the exercises in that book. I continued to read books on the subject and practice the exercises in them. Eventually, when I discovered Bardon's system, I was able to use conscious eating, conscious breathing, magical washing, and autosuggestion to improve my interpersonal skills. I've benefited a lot from improving my interpersonal skills, and to this day, the quest continues.

Learn What Projection Is

The magical community is filled with egotistical people accusing others of being egotistical, immature people accusing others of being immature, and ignorant people accusing others of being ignorant. I was always curious about this strange phenomenon. One day, I learned that it had a name – "projection." It turns out that when we are in denial about an unsavory aspect of ourselves, we sometimes "project" this aspect onto

The Spirit of Magic by Virgil

others as a way of telling ourselves that it is others, as opposed to ourselves, who possess this aspect. In other words, we project onto others unsavory qualities that we possess but that we are in denial about possessing. When I learned more about projection, I was able to catch myself each time I projected my own unsavory qualities onto others. This helped me realize that I was the one who possessed those unsavory qualities, which in turn allowed me to be conscious of those qualities, put them in my black soul mirror, and root them out with the six-pronged attack.

The next time you feel tempted to criticize others, check to make sure that the quality you are criticizing is not actually a quality you yourself possess and that you are merely projecting onto others. You might not be projecting, but you also might be. Only by observing yourself and the situation objectively will you be able to tell.

Learn from "Instructive" People

Writing is a craft. When I wrote my first three books, I didn't really have any formal training in this craft. This is why my writing in those books was a bit rambly and unpolished. Realizing I could become a lot better at this craft if I received formal training, I enrolled in a professional and technical writing night class at a local community college.

I learned a lot in the class. I learned how to write feature stories, cover letters, and proposals. The unit on writing proposals was especially interesting. Before we wrote our own proposals, the professor had us analyze two proposals so we could learn from them.

One of the proposals was good. Needless to say, we learned a lot by analyzing that proposal.

The other proposal was one the professor called "instructive." This adjective did in fact accurately describe the proposal, because it was indeed instructive. By analyzing this proposal, we learned a lot about what *not* to do when writing a proposal.

Just as proposals can be either good or "instructive," people can be either mature or "instructive." We all know that if we want to become more mature, it is a good idea to observe mature people, because doing so will tell us how we should be. However, it's important to remember that we should also observe immature people, because these people are truly "instructive." Please realize that when I describe these people as "instructive," I am not being sarcastic. They tell us how NOT to be if we

Chapter 9: The Magician's Life

want to be mature, and this is very important to learn. In fact, I'd even go so far as to say you can probably learn more about what it take to become mature by observing and interacting with "instructive" people than by observing and interacting with mature people.

Don't Become Involved in Drama in Magical Communities

Communities often spring up around magical training systems. For example, there is the Bardon community, which is the community of people who have worked through or are in the middle of working through Bardon's magical training system. Members of the Bardon community interact with each other through various online forums, email groups, blogs, and chatrooms. Not every Bardonist is a member of the Bardon community. There are many Bardonists who work through IIH without interacting with other Bardonists because they have no need to or reason to. The more you interact with other Bardonists, the more you are a part of the Bardon community.

Drama is pretty rare in the Bardon community, but it does happen sometimes. When new Bardonists see drama in the Bardon community, they are often disheartened, after all, the Bardon system is supposed to produce genuine magicians, and genuine magicians are above drama, right? They are, but not every member of the Bardon community is a genuine magician because that requires one to have finished working through IIH, and many of them are still in the middle of working through IIH, and therefore don't yet have the level of maturity one would expect a genuine magician to possess. Even many of the very active members of the Bardon community who are extremely passionate about all things Bardon-related have not yet finished working through IIH and do not have the maturity of a genuine magician.

Drama usually arises from ego. Magical training frees us from our egos. Again, this doesn't mean we destroy our egos during our magical training. It just means we change our relationship with our egos so that we are no longer enslaved by our egos. When you have finished working through a magical training system, you should be free from your ego, so your ego cannot compel you to do things like start drama or get involved with drama. If you observe people like Rawn and Bill who have finished working through IIH, you'll see that they don't start drama or get involved in drama. The more advanced of a magician you are, the wiser you are, and the wiser you are, the more you realize that life is too short for that sort of thing.

The Spirit of Magic by Virgil

But since magical training is a gradual process of freeing oneself from one's ego, those Bardonists who are in the middle of their magical training or at the very beginning of their magical training (e.g. on Step 1 or Step 2) are not fully free from their egos. This is why you sometimes see Bardonists starting drama in the Bardon community.

Although the Bardon community is the primary magical community I have been a part of for the past couple of years, I'm sure other magical communities, including communities that have developed around other magical training systems, also experience similar problems. Here's my advice. The people who start drama and engage in drama are often very "instructive." So when you see drama, observe the people involved in the drama so you can learn from them. Once you have learned from them, ignore the drama and turn your attention to more important things like your magical training, caring for your loved ones, and pursuing your dreams.

Pursue Your Dreams

In the magical world, you often hear people talk about the inner life and the outer life. You do have both an inner life and an outer life. You probably know a few people who focus exclusively on their outer lives and completely neglect their inner lives. You might even know a few people who focus exclusively on their inner lives and completely neglect their outer lives. Magic is a path of balance. The magician needs to focus on both his inner and outer lives so that both are nourished and healthy. Someone with no dreams hardly has an inner life because dreams are the main components supporting one's inner life. Without dreams, one's inner life is like a desolate and bleak landscape. So have dreams. They don't necessarily have to be "big" dreams. Some people dream of winning a Nobel prize in literature, while other people dream only of writing just one novel and managing to get it published. Neither dream is "better" than the other. All dreams are equally sacred and equally valid, so don't belittle another's dreams. Just because your dream is to become a famous rock star doesn't mean you are better than a person whose dream is to start a harmonious family and live a peaceful life.

In the magical world, you'll come across a lot of people making their magical training unnecessarily inefficient. I see this happen all the time in the Bardon community. You have a certain amount of time each day. You need to use some of that time to eat, sleep, and go to work to make money. The rest of your time is free time. If the magical training

Chapter 9: The Magician's Life

system you are using is very inefficient, it may require you to devote all of your free time to your training. If the magical training system you are using is very efficient, it won't require you to devote all of your free time to your training. You'll have plenty of free time left to pursue your dreams.

There are many students of magic who don't have any dreams. If they use inefficient magical training systems, then their magical training takes up all of their free time, so they don't have any free time left with which to pursue their dreams anyway. However, some students of magic don't have any dreams but use efficient magical training systems. They don't know what to do with the rest of their free time. The right solution to this dilemma is to develop some dreams to pursue, or to remember the dreams you had as a child.[46] Unfortunately, the solution most of these students pick is to mix things into their magical training in order to make it inefficient. This causes their magical training to consume all of their free time.

You see this sort of thing frequently in the Bardon community. The Bardon system is a very efficient magical training system, but many Bardonists are training in a very inefficient manner because they mix a bunch of random crap into the Bardon system that makes their training less efficient and unnecessarily time-consuming.[47] Many people are afraid to pursue their dreams because they are afraid of failure and don't have the courage needed to overcome this fear.[48] If they make their training inefficient so that it consumes all of their free time, then they have an excuse to refrain from pursuing their dreams, after all, they no longer have any free time they can use to pursue their dreams. If you spend time in the Bardon community, you'll see some Bardonists claiming that a certain spiritual system should be practiced alongside the Bardon system, and some Bardonists claiming that a particular form of mystical philosophy should be studied alongside the Bardon system. That's all nonsense, but it's very popular nonsense, so you see many Bardonists mixing random chakra exercises, past life exercises, ritual magic exercises, "alchemical" exercises, Kabbalistic texts, yogic texts, and God knows what else into their magical training in order to make it unnecessarily complicated, unnecessarily time-consuming, and therefore less efficient. As I discussed in the last chapter, bringing outside exercises into your training can be helpful if it is done intelligently and for the purpose of supplementing your training, but oftentimes, people do it unintelligently and for the purpose of making their training more time-consuming because they have no dreams to pursue and therefore nothing to do with the rest of their free time.

Of all the things you can do to supplement your magical training and facilitate your magical advancement, pursuing your dreams is one of the best. The home of your dreams is in your inner life, but the realization of your dreams (getting that novel published, starting that family, winning that Oscar, climbing Everest, etc.) occurs in your outer life. Thus, it is in the process of pursuing your dreams that your inner and outer lives come into harmony and healthy channels of communication are formed between them. Furthermore, magical training helps you realize your highest potential, and pursuing your dreams often requires you to tap into your highest potential. Since the process of magical training and the process of pursuing your dreams both require you to move closer to the person you could be if you fulfilled your highest potential, the two processes complement each other.

Use the "Color-Based Reminder Technique"

To become a magician, the student must live his life in a way that facilitates his magical advancement. A life lived in this way would include doing the following things.

- Periodically studying the writings of genuine adepts to extract useful knowledge and understanding of magic from those writings
- Practicing magical washing every time you shower or wash your hands
- Practicing conscious eating at every meal and while eating snacks between meals
- Practicing autosuggestion immediately before falling asleep and immediately after waking up, as well as during the day whenever you have the opportunity to
- Using conscious breathing throughout the day whenever you have the opportunity to
- Practicing the exercises of your current step at least once a day
- Remaining patient when you find yourself in frustrating situations

Chapter 9: The Magician's Life

- Treating everyone with compassion, including those who are nasty to you
- Maintaining your health through physical exercises, eating a healthy diet, and getting adequate sleep each night
- Remaining present-minded every waking moment
- Everything else I've discussed in the previous sections of this chapter

At some point in time, you will do all of these things naturally. You will easily live your life in a way that facilitates your magical advancement because it will be your nature to live your life in such a way. That point usually comes when you're on the intermediate and advanced steps of IIH. When you're on the beginning steps of IIH, however, living your life in a way that facilitates your magical advancement will take some effort because you have not yet reprogrammed yourself into the kind of person who naturally lives in a way that facilitates his magical advancement. Unfortunately, people are lazy. At times, you might find yourself too lazy to make the effort to practice magical washing while showering in the morning because it's a cold day and you want to keep the water warm, or too lazy to make the effort to practice conscious eating while eating a sandwich during your lunch break, or too lazy to make the effort to practice visualization exercises after getting home from work because the traffic was bad and you just want to plop yourself down in front of the television instead. In these cases, it is helpful to think of something that inspires you to train, because that source of inspiration will motivate you to make the effort.

The technique I'm about to describe is one that is often used by beginning students of the Bardon system. This technique has several names, but the most common one is probably the "color-based reminder technique." While it is one of several techniques Bardonists have developed to solve the issue of being too lazy to make the effort to do the various things living in a way that facilitates your magical advancement entails, it is the one I have chosen to share because I believe it to be the most versatile and effective. The idea behind the technique is pretty simple. Colors are all that you see. When you look at a chair, you see a bunch of colors that your brain interprets as a chair. When you look at a person, you see a bunch of colors that your brain interprets as a person. When you look at a building, you see a bunch of colors that your brain interprets as a building. If every color reminds you of something that

The Spirit of Magic by Virgil

inspires you to train, then because you are always looking at at least one color (even when your eyes are closed you're looking at the color black), you'll always be looking at something that reminds you of a powerful source of inspiration that motivates you to make the effort. Make a list of colors and next to each color, write down a powerful source of inspiration that the color reminds you of. For example...

Red: The red stone depicted inside the lotus in Bardon's rendition of the first Tarot card is the philosopher's stone. The color red reminds me of this stone, which inspires me to keep training and living in a way conducive to my magical advancement.

White: Some types of coral are white. A friend of mine who is also a magician once showed me a magic ring made of white coral that had incredible properties that gave its wearer immense control over the water element. This ring was created using highly advanced forms of magic. I think it's a cool ring, and hints some of the amazing things you come across once you finish your training/initiation and start getting your hands dirty in the magical world. The color white reminds me of this ring, which inspires me to keep training and living in a way conducive to my magical advancement.

Blue: When I was a kid, I had a copy of *The Arabian Nights* with a blue cover. I was fascinated by the stories of magicians, flying carpets, enchantments, jinn, and fantastical creatures. I didn't just want to read about this magical world depicted in the stories. I also wanted to experience it for myself. Being a magician allows me to enter this magical world. The color blue reminds me of this book, which inspires me to keep training and living in a way conducive to my magical advancement.

Yellow: This color reminds me of the golden key, of the country whence the shadows fall, and of Tangle and Mossy's journey to the country whence the shadows fall.

Green: Someone close to me whom I love dearly has a favorite ring she likes to wear. It has an emerald on it. Each time I advance along the magical path, I gain some power and wisdom that I can use to make her life more blessed. This inspires me to continue training and living in a way that is conducive to my magical advancement. The color green reminds me of her because of her ring.

Black: This color reminds me of Bill's essay "The Shadow in Psychology and Magick." There are many passages in this essay that I find inspiring. When I see the color black, it reminds me of those

Chapter 9: The Magician's Life

passages, and I am inspired to keep training and living in a way conducive to my magical advancement.

Brown: This is the color of wood. The wizards of Earthsea carried wooden staffs and used their magic to uphold justice, heal others, and protect others. Whenever I see the color brown, I am reminded of these wizards and inspired to keep training and living in a way conducive to my magical advancement so that I too can use magic to help others the way the wizards of Earthsea did.

Let's say that you are about to eat spaghetti for lunch but are too lazy to make the effort to impregnate the spaghetti and practice conscious eating with it. You might notice that the spaghetti sauce is red, or that the plate is white, or that the table the plate is sitting on is grey. Any of these colors could remind you of something that inspires you and motivates you to make the effort.

Or, let's say that you get home from work and are tired and therefore don't want to make the effort to practice thought-observation, or visualization, or whatever. As you walk through your home, you might notice the green paperweight on your table, or the yellow flowers on the wallpaper, or the pink cover of a book sitting on a table. Again, any of these colors could remind you of something that inspires you and motivates you to make the effort.

As I've stated before, there will come a time when you won't have any use for this technique. You will enjoy your magical exercises, and you will naturally live in a way that is conducive to your magical advancement without needing to struggle to make an effort to do so. However, before that time has come, it is useful to use techniques like the color-based reminder technique when you do find yourself struggling to make the effort.

Chapter 10: Working Magic

Hold the world within your heart, or, at least a small area of the world in which you can play a part. See it as it is and also as it can be. And then connect the two through your art.

~William Mistele

Let's get something done. Let's accomplish something.

~The Voice of Akasha in the Earthzone

During the course of his magical training, the magician will have acquired wisdom, understanding, and compassion. These are the three qualities at the heart of his art and that differentiate his art from other disciplines like sorcery and occultism. There wouldn't be any point in developing these qualities if the magician never used them, but as you can imagine, the magician does use them, and they are woven into every aspect of his work. In the following sections, I show examples of how this is the case.

The Future is Not Set in Stone

The future is not something that is predetermined. There are always an infinite number of possible futures. Some possible futures are more likely to happen than others. Those are the futures you see when you try to use divination to foresee the future. But no future is ever set in stone. I want to present three stories to illustrate this.

The first story comes from Melita Denning and Osborne Phillips's book *The Sword and the Serpent*. There was a mother whose son's hobby was rock climbing. One night, she had "a particularly vivid and horrifying dream in which she saw him struggling to regain his balance upon a narrow ledge, from which he eventually fell." The mother felt that this was no mere nightmare, but a premonition of something that was about to happen very soon. She couldn't get the horrifying scene she saw in her dream out of her mind, so it kept replaying itself in her imagination. She eventually decided that whenever the dream replayed itself in her imagination, instead of passively watching it happen, she would take control of the scene and imagine her son regaining his balance. She did this each time the dream played itself in her imagination. A short time later, her son visited her and told her a recent incident where he was about to fall off a precipice while rock climbing because he had mistakenly believed a certain rock to be more secure than it actually was. He lost his balance and "believed himself to be irrevocably falling over the precipice" when "a powerful gust of wind had suddenly risen to meet him, giving him just the help that he needed to regain mastery of the situation." So we can see here that the mother foresaw the future but was able to change the future and save her son.

The second story comes from José Luis Stevens's book *Awaken the Inner Shaman*. Stevens writes that when he was in India, he met a master of divination who told him some of the things that would happen to him in the future, including his early death. Stevens writes that "fortunately, I was to learn that I could change these seemingly fixed plans, and now I have outlived the date of my foretold demise by many years. Through my shamanic practice, I recovered my freedom to choose my future."

The third story comes from Bill (William Mistele), who regularly speaks with the Earthzone spirits. One day, the Earthzone spirit Cigila told Bill that a nuclear explosion was going to happen in the near future. He also explained to Bill what kind of magical work he could do to prevent the nuclear explosion from happening. Bill did the work and the nuclear explosion did not happen.

The individuals in the three stories above all saw an ominous future and then worked magic to recreate the future into a future that was less ominous and more joyful. To do this, you must first understand that it is possible.

The Masculine Mysteries

The magical path is a balanced path. The magician must penetrate into both the masculine and feminine mysteries to the same depth, never focusing only on one and neglecting the other. In alchemical drawings, the synthesis of the masculine and the feminine mysteries is represented by the alchemical marriage and by the hermaphrodite. Mastery of both mysteries is required for balanced development.

Chapter 10: Working Magic

The masculine mysteries are the subject of Bill's essay on the salamander Amtophul, who teaches the magician about these mysteries and leads him to greater understanding in these mysteries. In his essay, Bill writes the following.

> *This is the masculine mystery. It is not about ego or abusing power or dominating others. There is no patriarchal abuse present since this power is not derived from or found within human civilization. It is about recreating the world, even when you have to become absolutely nothing, unknown, and unappreciated and without support during the process.*

Elsewhere in this essay, Bill presents an exercise that involves imagining a lake of fiery energy that embodies the power underlying the masculine mystery. He explains that "this is a place where you go to meditate, not on how to see the future; rather, the meditation is about how to create what is to be."

In the previous section, I explained that it is possible to recreate the future. In this section, I have shown why this is not just possible for the magician to do, but also necessary for the magician to learn how to do. However, it is one thing to approach recreating the future ignorantly, and it is another thing to approach recreating the future wisely. Proper magical training should teach you to do the latter and prevent you from doing the former. A good way to begin learning is to examine the story of Anakin Skywalker. Anakin saw an ominous future, tried to recreate the future into a more joyful one, and failed miserably. Let's see why this happened.

The Story of Anakin

Magicians can learn a lot from the story of the Star Wars character Anakin Skywalker. Anakin was married to his wife Padmé, whom he loved dearly. In his dreams, Anakin saw frightening visions of Padmé's death (oneiromancy) and tried to save her life. He thought acquiring more power was the key to being able to save Padmé, so he began to reach for more power. In the process of reaching for power and gaining it, he ended up killing Padmé himself.

The Spirit of Magic by Virgil

Anakin was filled with rage, hatred, confusion, despair, and sorrow. These negative emotions are what drove him to kill his wife. Anakin did not understand himself very well. If he did, he would have realized that his inner state was dark and disturbed. This understanding of himself would have caused him to make the wise choice of reforming himself into a more stable and secure individual. If he had done this, he wouldn't have impulsively killed his wife.

Anakin's mistake is very understandable. Power is needed to change anything, including the future. The more power we have, the easier it is for us to change the future. However, power will only change the future for the better if it is used wisely. If it is used unwisely, it will make the future worse. This is why if we want our futures to be pleasant, joyful, wonderful, and enriching, then we should seek wisdom first. Without wisdom, whatever power we have will only bring us sorrow and despair. In Chapter 14, I'll explain that understanding leads to wisdom, and that acquiring understanding begins with understanding yourself. Anakin did not understand himself, which is why he wasn't wise, which is why he didn't make the best choices when he tried to change the future.

Serving the Id

Many people study sorcery so they can cast spells to fulfill all their petty desires. They are like children, and Divine Providence will let them have their fun for a bit before forcing them to grow up. Genuine magic is for those who are already grown and desire to grow more. It is for those who are responsible enough to handle the vast power it gives.

The Hermetic idea of a lower animal nature has its parallel in Freud's concept of the id. The id wants food, warmth, sex, and whatever else makes it feel comfortable. Furthermore, it wants it immediately, and if it doesn't get it immediately, it gets angry. When I was in high school, one of my teachers referred to little children as "creatures of id." That phrase always stuck with me, so I use it here. There is nothing wrong with children being "creatures of id," after all they are just children, and most of them will become more mature as they grow older. Unfortunately, some of them grow up without becoming mature and remain "creatures of id" as adults. When these people get tangled up in occultism and apply their occult knowledge in the form of sorcery to serve their ids, things get really problematic. When you constantly serve your id, you constantly acknowledge and reinforce the power and authority your id has over you. This strengthens the power and authority

Chapter 10: Working Magic

your id has over you, resulting in spiritual regression instead of spiritual evolution. Magicians are reluctant to become servants of their ids, choosing to serve Divine Providence instead. Living harmoniously with one's id, which magic can certainly help you do, is a wiser way of life than living subservient to one's id.

Mastery of Practical Magic

In Chris Bradford's novel The Way of the Sword, one of the characters, the swordsman Sensei Hosokawa, demonstrates his mastery of the katana. He calls his student Yamato to sit in front of him and places a grain of rice on Yamato's head. He then pulls out his katana and slices the grain of rice in half. Yamato is not even touched by the sword and remains completely unharmed. Sensei Hosokawa was a true master of the katana, and he demonstrated his mastery by using the weapon with great precision.

Anyone can paint a tree. All you have to do is paint a green blob and then a brown line under it. Only a master painter can paint a tree so realistic that the painting looks like a photograph. The master can do this because each stroke of his brush is very precise. When you examine other arts like dance, you will find that the novice dancer's movements are sloppy while the master dancer's movements are precise. In many arts, precision is the sign of mastery.

Imagine if someone said "I'm going to build up my muscles so that they are really strong. Then, I'll be able to swing my katana around with a lot of strength and master the weapon." This is silly. Any fool off the street can do pushups until his biceps are as thick as tree trunks and he can swing a katana around with great strength, but that doesn't make him a master swordsman. A real master swordsman like Sensei Hosokawa would defeat him in less than a fraction of a second.

Yet some people take that approach to mastering magic. They believe that if they can move large amounts of astra-mental energy around, then they have mastered magic. They take drugs, deprive themselves of sleep, subject themselves to extreme pain, make themselves dizzy, or stir themselves up in a frenzy of emotion in hopes entering an altered state of consciousness that will allow them to more easily influence the inner planes and move astra-mental energy around. Regardless if these tricks work, they always impede their user's ability to concentrate. Thus, whatever currents they send forth during their workings have a chaotic and unpredictable nature that may result in many negative side effects.

Precision in practical magic comes from concentration. Therefore, familiarize yourself with your mind and learn to discipline it. Crowley says the majority of people "cannot coordinate their mental muscles to make a purposed movement." Close your eyes and visualize Sensei Hosokawa practicing a sword kata. Note the precision and deliberateness of every cut and parry. As a magician, you must have as much control over your mental muscles as Sensei Hosokawa does over his physical muscles.

Memorizing Elemental Correspondences vs. Understanding the Elements

A fluid condenser is a physical substance that has a very high capacity when it comes to storing astra-mental energies. In IIH, Bardon gives some recipes for general fluid condensers, as well as four recipes for fluid condensers that are specific to an element. These fluid condensers are often used to coat mirrors, tools, and talismans to increase the amount of energy the magician is able to condense into them. They can also be used by themselves in more direct practical magic operations.

When Lumir Bardon was suffering from poor eyesight, he asked his father's student Dr. M.K. to help him. Dr. M.K. filled a potato with an earth fluid condenser, condensed the earth element into it, impressed upon the condensed energy the idea that Lumir's eyesight would improve, and then buried the potato as a way of releasing the condensed earth element into the world to manifest the idea impressed upon it. Lumir's eyesight grew better.

If you look at an elemental table of correspondences, you will find that the sense of sight corresponds to fire, and that the senses of taste and smell correspond to earth. At first, it might seem like a fire fluid condenser and the fire element would have been the most appropriate choice to use because Dr. M.K. was trying to fix Lumir's sense of sight, but this is simplistic thinking. Fire manifests things quickly, suddenly, and even violently. Earth manifests things slowly, naturally, and organically. When trying to magically change something as sensitive and fragile as the human eye, earth is obviously the better and safer element to use. Dr. M.K. did not turn to a table of correspondences. His years of training gave him a very intimate understanding of the elements and their

Chapter 10: Working Magic

functions. As a result, he was able to choose the best elemental energy to use.

One key lesson to take away from this story is that knowing the things that correspond to an element because you have memorized a table of correspondences is not the same as actually understanding an element. Real understanding of an element comes from interacting with it when practicing magical exercises and doing magical workings. It comes from experience, not reading or studying tables.

Place and Time

Some magical systems provide complicated rules regarding the place and time to conduct a magical working. People worry about things like whether the working should be done in a temple or in a graveyard, and at what planetary hour the working should take place. I myself have never worried too much about the location and time of the magical workings I plan because I know that in the end, all magical workings are conducted in the same location and at the same time anyway. What I mean is that all magical workings, whether they are simple spells or elaborate rituals, are conducted "here" and "now." Seriously, the next time you step up to an altar to cast a spell or step into a circle to conduct a ritual, think about the time and place you are working magic in. You will always find that you are working "here" and working "now." A magical working won't succeed if you aren't comfortable with the time and location of the working, so get comfortable doing things "here" and "now." In magical jargon, this is called doing things in a state of "presence" or simply "being present." You cannot tell how far a magician has advanced in his training by his knowledge of magic because there are quite a few armchair magicians who know a lot about magic from hundreds of hours of reading. However, you can tell how far a magician has advanced in his training by how deep his understanding is of certain key concepts. One of those key concepts is the concept of presence.[49] The more you advance along the magical path, the more you will understand what it means to be present. The art of magic involves changing the world, but you can't change a world you are not present in.

What's Important?

Bill writes that when you begin learning about divine wisdom, which is a part of magical training, you begin "training as an engineer,

The Spirit of Magic by Virgil

workman, architect, and builder in the divine workshop." For this reason, I want to share an old Russian folktale that may be of interest to those who plan to one day work in the divine workshop.

In Russian folklore, St. Nicholas is one of the most important figures. He is protective, fatherly, kind, compassionate, and merciful. He is a blessing to society and everyone loves him. St. Nicholas has two feast days a year.

St. Cassian is a different story. Despite his title of "saint," he is generally viewed as a malevolent figure who is the cause of misfortune and suffering. St. Cassian only has a feast day on leap years.

There is a well-known Russian folktale about why St. Nicholas has two feast days a year and St. Cassian has only one feast day every four years. In this folktale, there is a peasant who is stuck in the mud along with his cart and horse. St. Cassian passes by and the peasant begs him to help him. Cassian says "Are you crazy? I would get my robes all dirty. Surely I can't appear in heaven before God with dirty robes." He then goes away. A short time later, St. Nicholas passes by and the peasant begs him for help. Nicholas, being a compassionate individual, gets into the mud, helps the peasant climb out, and then pulls the horse and cart out. The peasant thanks him. A short while later, both Cassian and Nicholas appear before God. God asks Nicholas why his robes are all dirty and Nicholas explains that he helped a peasant escape from the mud he was stuck in. God then asks St. Cassian why his robes are not dirty, and he explains that he did not think it was proper to appear in heaven before God with dirty robes on so he didn't help the peasant. God rewards St. Nicholas with two feast days a year and punishes St. Cassian by giving him only one feast day every four years.

IIH comes before PME for a reason. I know I've written that before but it bears repeating. The evocation work of PME is ritual work, and Bardon goes to great lengths to describe tools like the robe, the wand, the sword, and the lamps. Some people have the money to afford silk robes and tools made of the rarest wood and etched with gold. That is all great, but that is not what makes a magician. The first step along the magical path is acquiring the golden key, which is compassion. Once you have it, all of the doors will open. If you do not have it, then despite how fancy and expensive your tools and robes are, you will never advance past even the lowest neophyte. In IIH, you balance and purify your personality, in the process developing positive traits like compassion. After you work through IIH, you can worry about things like robes and wands when you begin working in the divine workshop as a practicing magician recreating

Chapter 10: Working Magic

the world into a better place. But if you are not sufficiently pure and balanced, you will not be welcome in the divine workshop and its doors will remain closed to you.

Invoking and Calling Upon Powers

The man who addresses to a power unknown to him words which he does not fully comprehend makes a tenebrous prayer to the spirit of darkness; in other words, he invokes the devil.

~ Eliphas Levi

Every magician and student of magic should make wisdom, understanding, and compassion his highest ideals. They are the trinity which guides him. They are what distinguish him from sorcerers and occultists. The idea of understanding is particularly relevant to this section.

In Python, there is something called the eval() function. This function takes a string and evaluates it as Python code. It is also a major security hazard. If eval() is used indiscriminately, than it could end up evaluating a string encoding a program designed to destroy the computer you are using. To say that another way, the program is taking in a random set of instructions without knowing anything about it and then running the instructions.

In magic, a similar thing happens when people put themselves at risk by invoking powers they don't know the nature of. Take the following section from the Golden Dawn's Adeptus Minor ritual for example.

I furthermore solemnly pledge myself never to work at any important symbol without first invocating the highest Divine Names connected therewith, and especially not to debase my knowledge of Practical Magic to purposes of evil and self-seeking, and low material gain or pleasure, and if I do this, notwithstanding this my oath, I invoke the Avenging Angel HUA, that the evil and material may react on me.

The Spirit of Magic by Virgil

This is a very noble statement to make. It shows the magician is determined not to use his abilities for evil purposes. However, who/what is HUA? No one knows... Thus, the magician invoking HUA could be putting himself in danger because HUA could be anything.

Anytime a magician calls upon a power, there is a very specific power he has in mind and he understands its nature. This allows him to pinpoint that power with his focused intent and call it into his circle or into a triangle. Sometimes, giving the power a name can make things easier. However, if you have a name but do not know anything about the power the name is supposed to represent, then you cannot pinpoint that power with your focused intent when you invoke it into your circle or evoke it into a triangle. Thus, when you try to call down the power associated with the name, you are really sending out a general call that any spirit can answer. Often, it is a negative parasitical spirit that answers, pretending to be the spirit you are actually looking for.

I had the chance to examine a correspondence course offered by a certain occult group. In an early lesson in the course, the student was taught the LBRP and told to practice it. In a later lesson, all of the names and Hebrew words used in the ritual were explained. This is backwards thinking. If you invoke Eheieh without understanding what that name means and without understanding what it refers to, then as Levi points out, you are invoking the devil.

Ritual Tools

There is a parable in the Bardon system that goes as follows.

When Lumir Bardon was in middle school, he wanted to become class president. Since he was not the most popular kid at school, he was afraid that another candidate would get more votes than him. He went to his father, Franz Bardon, and asked him what he should do. His father told him that anyone who had a true magic wand would be successful in everything and could do anything he wanted.

Lumir immediately went to his father's bookshelf, read the instructions in some old grimoires for making a magic wand, and then made one. The wand was made of virgin hazel wood

Chapter 10: Working Magic

and etched with various divine names and symbols. He carried the magic wand around with him everywhere he went, confident that he would succeed in becoming class president.

The day of the election came and Lumir did not receive the most votes. Therefore, he was not class president. He angrily went to his father and said "You said that if I had a magic wand, I would be successful in everything I did, but I made a magic wand and was not successful in becoming class president.

His father replied "No, you misunderstood me. I was not talking about the external magic wand, but the inner magic wand, which is the human will."

This parable is probably not true, since I just made it up, but it serves to teach Bardonists a very important lesson. In modern times, ceremonial magic is viewed as a path of initiation, but in Bardon's system, this is considered backwards thinking. If you do not possess the inner magic wand, then the external magic wand remains a powerless toy in your hands. Crafting the inner magic wand is the work of initiation. It is the work of IIH. Using physical wands is an optional subset of the work of PME.

There are a number of parallels between the art of magic and the art of writing, and it is a well-known fact that many deities of magic, like Thoth, were also deities of writing. Magic gives the magician the ability to write his life the way an author writes the plot of a novel. Aleister Crowley speculated that the wand, cup, knife, and pentacle evolved from the stylus, ink holder, sharpening blade, and paperweight of the first scribes. Regardless of whether this is factually accurate, I like the idea.

No one wants to read a boring book, and likewise, no one wants to live a boring life. The study of magic helps a person live a more interesting and meaningful life. If you find life boring and want to rewrite it so that it is more interesting, then acquire the inner wand, dagger, cup, and pentacle. Do you want your story to end "And they lived happily ever after"? Forget what the position of the stars in your natal chart or the lines on your palm say your life will be like. Write your story so it ends in this way.

The Spirit of Magic by Virgil

Two Questions

In *Problems in the Study of Magic: Part IV*, Bill points out that the electric and magnetic fluids are the two primordial forces with which magicians work, and that they flow through our lives and all of our endeavors. The magical path, unlike some occult paths, is not a path of spiritual regression, but a path of spiritual evolution. Therefore, any time you work magic, you must do so in a way that works for your personal development instead of against it. Magic requires that we be mature and responsible. Mature people do not want instant fixes to all the challenges they face. They recognize that dealing with challenges is the way they grow stronger and develop their personalities. The electric fluid reminds us of this fact by asking us a question each time we use it. This question, as presented by Bill in his essay, is as follows.

> *The question the electrical fluid will ask you in terms of your faith and conviction is 'Are you willing to work without using magic to attain what you want if we set a clear path before you?' You want money? Are you willing to work for it? Here is a job. Do you want love? Are you willing to first give the love you want to others? You want to succeed in life? Are you willing to prepare yourself so that you will be ready to seize the opportunity when it comes to you? The electrical likes to check up on just how much you really want what you are asking for.*

Since magic is not a frivolous matter but a serious one, we must take responsibility for the changes we effect using this art. The magnetic fluid reminds us of this fact by asking us a question each time we use it. This question, as presented by Bill in his essay, is as follows.

> *The question the magnetic will ask you about your request is 'Once you have what you want, do you really want it enough that you will go on putting good energy and thought and vision into it?' The feminine nurtures. A mother goes on loving her children all their lives. They always remain her children. If you bring a magical work into being, do you really care enough for*

Chapter 10: Working Magic

it that you will continue nurturing and sustaining it if that is what is required?

You can't get around answering these two questions whenever you work practical magic because all magical energies are rooted in the electric and magnetic fluids, and they will always confront you with these questions whenever you use them. As a meditation, you can contemplate your answer to these questions, but it is even better to contemplate the reasons these questions are being asked in the first place. Your insights will help you understand how to approach magical work wisely.

Elemental Magic

The salamanders are the elemental spirits who are proficient at controlling and working with the fire element. In the Bardon system, we are taught that if we want to become proficient at controlling and working with the fire element, we must become salamanders ourselves. This means we must develop the (positive) qualities/traits that salamanders possess. These traits are indicative of a level of personal and spiritual development that allows us to safely and easily interact with the fire element and weave it into our magical workings. In addition to this, becoming a salamander in this way will cause the salamanders to think of us as one of their own, which will make it easier to befriend them, earn their respect, and get them to cooperate with us when we wish to work with them.

I once came across a rather lengthy online argument between two people over what the correct divine name to paint on a Golden Dawn fire wand is. Does this even matter if the user of the wand does not possess a strong will that operates with the precision and strength of a laser, act with the intensity of lightening, advance toward his goals in life with the force of a pyroclastic flow, or radiate joy as strong as the light of the sun?

Can you raise within yourself the passion of a raging forest fire whenever you want and then calm it at will without losing control? Does your personality reflect the power and transformative properties of nuclear fission, and can you channel this power to bless the world? Or, even better, does your personality reflect the power of nuclear fusion and its ability to join separate substances into one, and can you use this

The Spirit of Magic by Virgil

power to overcome the dark forces that divide and separate where there should be unity and oneness? Is part of your life a quest to achieve independence and the genuine freedom that comes with it? Have you learned to set your ego aside so you can take on true power? Have you acquired power over yourself? Do you now seek to extend your power to the external world so you can be a better, stronger, and more effective servant of Divine Providence? If not, go back to Step 2 and work on developing an elemental equilibrium. Establish the positive traits and qualities of the elements within you, because if you do not establish the positive traits and qualities associated with the fire element, then the fire element will not cooperate with you, no salamander will befriend you, and any "fire wand" will remain nothing but a mere toy in your hands, regardless of what divine names are painted upon it. This is why, in the Bardon system, the work of IIH must come before the work of PME.[50] As Bardon writes in PME, "The person who thinks it suffices to hold a magic wand in his hand in order to fulfil wonders is led astray." That is superstition, not magic. If you wish to befriend the salamanders, gain their respect, and work with their element safely, then show that you are determined to become independent and self-reliant. Show that you have understood, embodied, and assimilated the best of their essential nature. Otherwise, to use Bill's term again, you are doing "pretend magic." Of course, "pretend magic" is fun, which is why so many people do it, but it is very far removed from genuine magic.

The Sons of Sceva

The Biblical story found in Acts 19.13-20 contains a lesson that all aspiring magicians should take to heart. The following story is a variation of the story of the sons of Sceva that was written to illustrate why that story's lesson is an important one for magicians to learn.

One day, it came to pass that a certain occultist wished to evoke the salamander king Pyrhum. He drew a circle and a triangle, placed Pyrhum's sigil in the triangle, and proceeded to recite a long series of conjurations. The salamander king appeared, very angry, and began to berate the occultist for bothering him. The occultist, in reply, said 'In the name of Elohim and by the power of the archangel Michael, I order you to obey me.' Pyrhum, in response, said 'I respect Elohim, and I

Chapter 10: Working Magic

know Michael, but who are you?' He then incinerated the occultist and returned to the elemental realm of fire.

The work of IIH precedes the work of PME for a reason. Are you tired of me saying that yet? My apologies, but my experience has shown me that I cannot say this enough. Bardon himself frequently warns that the student must complete the first eight steps of IIH before beginning the work of PME, yet the people who ignore his warnings significantly outnumber the people who heed them.[51]

Emily

[Author's note: This is a true story. It totally happened exactly as related below.]

Once upon a time, there was an occultist named Bob who lived in Nicosia. Bob really wanted to be an adept magician. He had read numerous books about occult and magical subjects, and was constantly practicing random exercises in hopes of advancing. One day, he heard about a great magician named Emily who lived in Dallas.

"Hmmm," said Bob to himself, "I think I'm going to visit this magician. I could learn a lot from her."

Bob bought an airplane ticket, packed his luggage, and prepared to leave for Dallas. He rode in a taxi to the airport, checked in his luggage, and boarded the plane.

The flight to Dallas was relatively uneventful. The plane he rode in was a Boeing 777. There was a small TV screen in front of every chair. This was nice. Bob was able to watch all three parts of *The Hobbit* before the plane landed at Dallas/Fort Worth International Airport. Bob got off the plane, grabbed his luggage, and went to his hotel. It was late in the evening so he went to bed, planning to search for Emily the next day.

The next morning, Bob got up early. He ate a big breakfast consisting of kumquats, artichokes, and thyme. He then had an omelet for dessert. "Hey waitress," he said to the waitress. "Do you know where Emily lives?"

The waitress told Bob that Emily could be found in the mountains just outside of the city. Bob took a taxi to the border of the city and began walking into the mountains, searching for Emily's hut. After five

The Spirit of Magic by Virgil

hours and twenty-two minutes, he found it at last and knocked on the door.

Emily opened the door. "Hi..." she said.

"Hi, I'm Bob," said Bob. "I wanted to visit you because I think there is a lot you can teach me."

"Oh, ok, come on in," said Emily.

Bob walked in through the door and looked around. It was a modest hut. There was a rack filled with lightsabers in one corner next to a painting of the sun rising behind Mt. Fuji. In the center of the hut was an enormous septagonal contraption.

"Is that a vault?" asked Bob excitedly.

"No, it's a water purification device I designed and built myself. Well, actually, I had quite a bit of help from my friend Lanoiah too. It's completely solar powered and removes all impurities from the water you put in it. I think it's my finest invention. I've sent many to various countries throughout the world that are afflicted by droughts."

"Oh," said Bob, somewhat disappointed. He hoped it would be a vault. So far, he had seen nothing in the hut suggesting that Emily really was the great magician people said she was.

"Have you had lunch yet?"

"No."

"Eat with me then."

Emily sat Bob down at a table and placed a bowl of Starbursts in front of him. Bob was hungry from his morning hiking, so he ate quickly. He didn't even unwrap the Starbursts before eating them. The two of them ate in silence. When they had finished eating, Emily began speaking.

"So, you said you wanted to learn from me. What exactly is it you want to learn."

"Why I want to learn magic, of course. What else?"

"Oh, magic. Well, some people also come to me to learn electrical engineering, but I teach magic too. I also confuse the two a lot. Hmmm, let's start with some introspection."

"What's that?" asked Bob.

"One of the most basic and important exercises in magic," said Emily. "Tell me. If your life were a movie, what would its title be?"

"Ummm, I don't know."

"Well, spend a few hours thinking about the answer," said Emily. "It'll be the first magical exercise you do. How exciting!"

Chapter 10: Working Magic

"You've got to be kidding me," said Bob. "That's the dumbest thing I've ever heard. Give me a real magical exercise."

Emily looked baffled. "What do you mean?" she asked.

"I'm interested in elemental magic."

"Oh, wonderful, that's what I specialize in," said Emily.

"Great, can you give me an exercise to help me learn it?"

Emily handed Bob a small yellow dagger with purple words and symbols written on it. "Hold this, close your eyes, empty your mind, and tell me what thoughts and sensations pass through you."

Bob was about to do that when he gasped. The dagger he was holding was obviously Emily's air dagger, but he noticed a mistake.

"Ummm, there's a mistake on your air dagger," he said.

"Really?" asked Emily, genuinely surprised.

"Yeah," said Bob. "You got the archangel, angel, spirit, and river of Eden right, however, you wrote the wrong divine name. The colors are also right, but the divine name associated with air is not נטע-לי הרשלג; it's יהוה."

"Oh, wow, I never knew that," said Emily. "My own teacher told me it was נטע-לי הרשלג, but I guess she was wrong."

"Yeah, it's definitely יהוה," said Bob. "Some people think it's שדי אל חי but they're wrong. Your air dagger is defective and will not possess any power over the air element and the spirits of the air. I'm really sorry about that. You should get it fixed as soon as possible."

"I agree," said Emily. "I am going to have to do this immediately because I don't want to wait. Unfortunately, that means I must ask you to leave so I can get started on fixing this dagger right away."

"Of course," said Bob. "I completely understand."

Bob left Emily's house and returned to his hotel. He felt very bad for Emily. "Gee, I wonder how she messed up that much," he thought to himself. In any case, it didn't matter. Surely there was not much he could learn from someone who didn't even know the correct divine name associated with air.

The next day, Bob left for the airport. He checked in his luggage and boarded another Boeing 777 in order to head back to Nicosia. It was going to be another long fourteen hour flight and he wasn't look forward to it.

Three hours into the flight, the airliner was over the Atlantic Ocean. Bob closed his eyes and began to doze off. Suddenly, he was startled by a knocking sound on the window. He opened his eyes, looked out the

The Spirit of Magic by Virgil

window, and was astounded when he saw Emily flying alongside the airplane. Bob rolled down the window. "Hey," he said.

"Hey Bob," said Emily. "So, yesterday I went to the grocery store to buy some yellow and violet paint so I could fix the mistake on the air dagger. I didn't get home until late in the evening, so I decided to wait until this morning to start the process. When I woke up this morning, I realized I had forgotten what the right divine name should be. Can you teach it to me?"

Bob was completely bewildered. "Um, yeah. The right divine name is יהוה," he said.

"Oh, that's right, silly me," said Emily.

"Uh, how are you flying?" asked Bob.

"The sylphs are carrying me," said Emily. "They're my best friends and are always doing me favors. Like them, my mind is open and embodies the clarity of the sky. I can easily focus my mind onto any problem and perceive its solution. I value freedom and beauty. When I inhale and exhale, I can sense the connection my breath has with the wind. I can detach myself from any situation and observe it objectively. It's kind of like identifying with the sky. You are free and detached from the mess of the world below, and therefore able to observe it from a balanced and objective point of view. I value harmony, and am able to form a balance between conflicting ideas and opposing forces by finding their common ground. For some reason, the sylphs are impressed by that, and therefore, they chose to befriend me and teach me the secrets of their element."

"Umm, well, in that case why the heck do you care what the divine name corresponding with air is?" asked Bob. "You obviously don't need it."

"Hmmm," said Emily frowning. "Hey, yeah, I guess you're right. I never even use that dagger thing anyway. Well, have a safe trip. Good luck with your path."

Emily did a barrel roll and then flew back to Dallas.

Joe the Sorcerer

[Author's note: Unlike the previous story, the following two stories are fictional. However, they do contain important lessons about the nature of genuine magical training. Therefore, you should still read them.]

Chapter 10: Working Magic

Once upon a time, there was a boy named Joe who lived in a small suburb outside of Frankfort. Not many people liked Joe. He was quite an interesting person in many ways, but he was also very irritable, argumentative, selfish, and lazy.

One Sunday morning, Joe decided to visit the local bookstore. He had finished all of his homework the previous day and had nothing better to do. Being a bookworm, he thought he'd look for a good fantasy or science fiction novel. As he walked around the store, he happened to pass a book on palmistry. It was a small book, but had a very pretty cover depicting a shiny silver outline of a palm with a deep midnight blue background. Since Joe also happened to have an interest in occult subjects, he grabbed it off the shelf and began to flip through it.

It was an interesting book. It described the different mounts of the hand and their planetary associations, as well as the different shapes one's fingers could take and their respective meanings. One chapter in the book was about the love line. According to this chapter, if a person's love line splits into two lines and comes back together, this symbolizes a divorce. Curious, Joe looked at the love line on his own palm and saw that it split and merged together three separate times. His heart fell, since according to the book, this meant that he would divorce three times. "Wow, it looks like my love life is going to be very turbulent and rocky" he thought to himself.

Joe flipped to another chapter about the head line. According to this chapter, if your head line did not extend past your life line, then this meant that you were not smart enough to get the job you want. Joe looked at the palm of his hand and saw that his head line did not extend past his life line. He put the book down on the table and slid it away from him. He did not want to know anything more about his future since everything he had learned so far had been terrible and disappointing. As he sat there, tears came into his eyes.

Several years passed. During this time, Joe continued to maintain an interest in occultism. One day, he was looking through the bookstore again when he found a book about sorcery. According to the book, anyone who learned the spells and rituals inside of it could fulfill all their fantasies. Joe's mind wandered back in time to the day he came across the palmistry book and to how helpless he felt after examining his palm. He looked again at his palm and saw that his love line still had three islands, and that his head line still did not extend past his life line. He then looked at the book of sorcery he held in his hands. "Hmmm, maybe this is the solution to all of my problems," he thought to himself.

The Spirit of Magic by Virgil

At this time, Joe was in high school. He didn't do well in school because he was lazy and rarely did his homework. He never studied for tests. Instead, he spent most of his free time reading about sorcery and practicing it, since he found the subject fascinating and soon became obsessed with it. He started off by performing simple spells, and when he was proficient with them, he moved on to more complex rituals.

One day, shortly after Joe graduated from college, he met a girl named Sarah at a concert and fell in love with her. After the concert, he went home and cast a love spell on Sarah so that she would fall in love with him. The very next day, Joe proposed to Sarah and she agreed to marry him, despite having met him for the first time only the day before. Joe was a really powerful sorcerer!

Sarah was unemployed, and so was Joe. Joe realized he needed to get a job so that he could support the two of them. He had always dreamed of being a calculus teacher. By some odd coincidence, there just happened to be a high school nearby whose calculus teacher had been fired for making racist jokes during class. Joe applied for the job. The interview went really poorly. The person interviewing him was clearly not impressed with his qualifications or with his knowledge of calculus.

Because of this, Joe went home and decided to perform a ritual to help him get the job. He drew a circle, invoked the elements at the quarters, and sent forth a blast of energy into the astral plane to manifest his desire of getting the job. A few days later, Joe received a call from the school's principle telling him he was hired.

"Alright!" thought Joe. Because of his spells and rituals, he had married the girl of his dreams and had gotten his dream job. From that point onward, things started to go downhill. Sarah and Joe began to argue and fight with each other more and more. Soon, there was never a moment of peace in the house. One day, Sarah decided she had had enough.

"You know what? I'm done with you!" she screamed. "You're so irritable, argumentative, selfish, and lazy. I don't even know why I married you. I didn't really know you at the time but you seemed nice. Now I see the kind of person you really are. Now I know that you are a despicable human being, and the last person I'd want to spend my life with." She left the house, slamming the door behind her, and filed for divorce.

At the school where he worked, things weren't going well for Joe either. He really had no idea what he was doing. Soon, the principle began to receive phone calls from parents complaining that their children

Chapter 10: Working Magic

weren't learning anything. The principle became angry with Joe and fired him. Joe did not even attempt to use sorcery to keep his job. He knew that he wasn't strong enough to counter all of the angry parents, and that he couldn't keep up the façade of being a qualified teacher forever, since he really didn't have any idea what he was doing.

The rest of Joe's life consisted of him hopping around between various odd jobs. And yes, he did marry and divorce two more times before finally dying after he was mauled by a bear.

Ivan the Magician

Once upon a time, there was a boy named Ivan who lived in a small suburb outside of Frankfort. Not many people liked Ivan. He was quite an interesting person in many ways, but he was also very irritable, argumentative, selfish, and lazy.

One Sunday morning, Ivan decided to visit the local bookstore. He had finished all of his homework the previous day and had nothing better to do. Being a bookworm, he thought he'd look for a good fantasy or science fiction novel. As he walked around the store, he happened to pass a book on palmistry. It was a small book, but had a very pretty cover depicting a shiny silver outline of a palm with a deep midnight blue background. Since Ivan also happened to have an interest in occult subjects, he grabbed it off the shelf and began to flip through it.

It was an interesting book. It described the different mounts of the hand and their planetary associations, as well as the different shapes one's fingers could take and their respective meanings. One chapter in the book was about the love line. According to this chapter, if a person's love line splits into two lines and comes back together, this symbolizes a divorce. Curious, Ivan looked at the love line on his own palm and saw that it split and merged together three separate times. His heart fell, since according to the book, this meant that he would divorce three times. "Wow, it looks like my love life is going to be very turbulent and rocky" he thought to himself.

Ivan flipped to another chapter about the head line. According to this chapter, if your head line did not extend past your life line, then this meant that you were not smart enough to get the job you want. Ivan looked at the palm of his hand and saw that his head line did not extend past his life line. He put the book down on the table and slid it away from him. He did not want to know anything more about his future, since

The Spirit of Magic by Virgil

everything he had learned so far had been terrible and disappointing. As he sat there, tears came into his eyes.

Several years passed. During this time, Ivan continued to maintain an interest in occultism. One day, he was looking through the bookstore again when he found a copy of a book called Initiation into Hermetics. It was written by a magician named Franz Bardon. It didn't have a flashy title or cover, but for some reason it still managed to catch Ivan's eye. He felt drawn toward it and opened it up. Inside, he found instructions for magical training.

"Huh, interesting" he thought to himself. "Maybe I'll give this a try." And so Ivan began his magical training.

The training did wonders for him. Creating the soul mirrors helped him understand himself better. Through introspection, he realized he was very irritable, argumentative, selfish, and lazy. "Hmmm, I wonder if that's why no one likes me," he said to himself. He had always assumed he was just cursed from birth or had been born under an unlucky star. As an experiment, he decided to use the six-pronged attack to eliminate these negative personality traits from himself.

Sure enough, people started to actually like him once he stopped being irritable, argumentative, selfish, and lazy. Soon, a miracle happened; he made friends! Furthermore, his magical training caused him to be much more disciplined and hard working. He was able to will himself to do his homework and study for tests. He understood the material in all of his subjects, he aced all of his tests, and during his senior year of high school, he was accepted into one of the best universities in the country.

One day, shortly after Ivan graduated from college, he met a girl named Lily at a concert and fell in love with her. He asked her out to dinner, and soon afterwards, they were dating regularly. Before long, Lily fell in love with him too because he was compassionate and mature. When he eventually proposed to her, she gladly accepted.

Lily was unemployed, and so was Ivan. Ivan realized he needed to get a job so that he could support the two of them. He had always dreamed of being a biology teacher. By some odd coincidence, there just happened to be a high school nearby whose biology teacher had been arrested for arson after she was caught trying to set the building on fire. Ivan applied for the job. The interview went really well. The person interviewing him was clearly impressed with his qualifications and with his knowledge of biology.

Chapter 10: Working Magic

Ivan thought he had a pretty good chance of getting the job, so he didn't worry about it. Sure enough, two days later, the principle called him and told him he was hired.

"Alright!" thought Ivan. Somehow, he had married the girl of his dreams and had gotten his dream job.

Life continued to stay great for Ivan. He was always patient with his wife and kind to her. She considered herself blessed to have met him. His students loved him too because he was great at explaining the subject material. He was always helpful, and his lectures were very interesting.

One day, Ivan and his family were camping in the woods. He woke up early in the morning, and since his wife and children were still asleep, he decided to take a walk on his own. He walked through the paths of the forest humming to himself when suddenly, an angry bear stepped onto his path and charged toward him. Immediately, Ivan used certain magical techniques taught to him by the Earthzone spirit Kiliosa to paralyze the bear. He ran back to his family, woke them up, and told them what had happened (leaving out the magic, since they didn't know he was a magician). They got into the car and drove home before any other bears came along.

Many years later, when his children had long since graduated from college and had families of their own, Ivan sat on a rocking chair on the porch watching the bustling street in front of him. Lily was inside making dinner, since it was her turn to do so that day. It was the middle of summer break, so Ivan had no tests or homework he needed to grade, or lessons plans to design. The upcoming school year would be his last year of teaching before he retired. Although he loved teaching, he was still looking forward to retiring. It would allow him to spend more time with Lily, and also focus more on his magical work, which consisted of various inner plane tasks designed to dissolve the hostility and distrust between the Israeli and Palestinian governments. After completing his training via IIH, a large portion of his magical path had centered on making the world more peaceful, and he had often worked with spirits like Erimites and Achaiah to do this.

As he sat on the rocking chair, his mind wandered back, reviewing his career and his life. He had accomplished a lot and was satisfied with what he had done. His mind went all the way back to that day, many decades ago when he was still a little boy, when he wandered into a bookstore and came across a book on palmistry. He laughed at its dire predictions. "I ended up staying happily married, and I did get the job I wanted," he thought to himself. He turned over his palm to examine it again. To his surprise, he found that at some point his palm had changed. His love line no longer had any islands in it, and his head line did reach past his life line

Chapter 11: Talismans

Creating talismans are one of the most straightforward examples of working magic. Therefore, I will use the talisman creation process to concisely illustrate the differences between magic, occultism, and sorcery. First, let's try to gain a basic understanding of what talismans are and how they work. Talismans are similar to magnets and the astra-mental body of humans, so let's begin by examining those.

Think of a magnet. There is the magnet itself, and then there is the magnetic field surrounding the magnet. Whenever you place a small metal object near the magnet, it is pulled towards the magnet. The stronger the magnetic field is, the more strongly the object is pulled towards the magnet.

Many people confuse the astra-mental body with the aura, but this is a mistake. Just as a magnet and the magnetic field around it are not the same, the astra-mental body and the astra-mental field around it, which is the aura, are not the same. Magnets attract certain types of objects – namely metal objects. Similarly, an individual attracts certain types of people. He attracts the people whose auras resonate well with his. The stronger the individual's aura is, the more strongly he will attract those people. Some individuals have strong auras that resonate well with the auras of many other people. These individuals are always attracting friends, lovers, followers, fans, etc. They are said to possess charisma, also known as "personal magnetism."

So, magnets attract objects and charismatic individuals attract other people. Talismans also attract things. You make a talisman by condensing astra-mental energy into an object. You then program this energy to attract something like wealth, romance, or friends. The condensed energy creates an attractive field around it. Just as a magnet pulls metal objects to the magnet and a charismatic individual's aura pulls other people to the charismatic individual, the field around a talisman pulls wealth, romance, friends, or whatever towards whoever is wearing the talisman. The more energy you condense into the talisman, the stronger the field around the talisman will be.

From our brief analysis of talismans so far, we can see that the effectiveness of a talisman depends on two things.

1. The amount of astra-mental energy it contains
2. How precisely the astra-mental energy is programmed to attract what you want

The Spirit of Magic by Virgil

The more astra-mental energy an object contains, the stronger and farther reaching the field around it will be. If you are making the talisman for yourself, then you should accumulate the energy into yourself via pore breathing, condense it into your hand, and then transfer the energy from your hand to the object. If you are making the talisman for another person, then you should condense the energy from the environment to the object directly without letting it pass through your body first. This can be done through a combination of will and plastic imagination. The magician who wishes to make talismanic magic a regular part of his practice should practice both of these techniques for condensing energy into objects. The more proficient he is at using these techniques, the more energy he can condense into objects with them.

A large accumulation of astra-mental energy does nothing useful by itself. The energy must be programmed. You must program the condensed solar energy to attract friends. You must program the condensed Venusian energy to attract a suitable romantic partner. You must program the condensed Mercurian energy to attract the right books to you. How well you can program the condensed energy to attract what you want it to attract depends entirely on how well you can concentrate. Through the power of concentration, you hold the talisman's purpose in your mind and then impress this purpose onto the talisman. If you are trying to program the energy but random distracting thoughts are flitting through your mind and preventing you from focusing, then those thoughts will also become impressed onto the condensed energy and muddle its programming. Therefore, the magician who wishes to create effective talismans should learn to discipline his mind and concentrate.

In addition to the magician's ability to condense and program energy, the material the object is made of also matters. Certain materials store large amounts of astra-mental energy better than others. When you pick an object to turn into a talisman, you should choose an object made from one of those materials.

So we see here that the magician's ability to condense astra-mental energy into objects, the magician's ability to program that energy, and the material the object is made of are the main factors determining how effective the talisman will be. These are the essential components of the talisman creation process. Everything else is just non-essential details. All the symbols, names, glyphs, etc. that one can draw on a talisman – none of those are essential, and the magician is free to use or ignore them based on his own personal style. Some people find squares filled with numbers to be aesthetically pleasing, so they draw them on their talismans. Others don't find squares filled with numbers to be aesthetically pleasing, so they draw other things instead. Maybe they

Chapter 11: Talismans

draw an alchemical symbol here and write a Bible verse there, or maybe they draw a Hebrew letter there and an astrological symbol here. In the occult community, you often see people arguing about what the "correct" non-essential details to add to a talisman are, and many occultists lose plenty of sleep thinking about which non-essential details they should add to their talismans. If they want to make better talismans, they should instead focus their efforts on mastering the essential skills of condensing and programming energy, instead of on worrying about the non-essential details.

Let's briefly consider the concept of chaos magic. What exactly is chaos magic? Recall my comment in the tenth chapter that it is possible to accomplish things through low magic by sitting down and willing something to happen. You can also add things like chants and ritual gestures to the process, but that's all just extra. If the extra stuff you add is conventional, then you're seen as a normal magician. If the extra stuff you add is wacky and weird, then you're a chaos magician.

The conventional way to design a talisman in Western magic is to write a sentence between two concentric circles and draw a symbol in the middle. The sentence usually comes from scripture that is meaningful to the magician. Some take sentences from the Bible; others the Orphic hymns or the Vedas. However, isn't it just as valid to use sentences taken from more contemporary sources instead of the scriptures that are traditionally used for this purpose? If I want to use the two concentric circles design to create a friendship talisman, isn't "The spark ignited inside me when I realized that you all are my friends" just as valid of a line to use as the Bible's "A friend loves at all times, and a brother is born for adversity"?

Chaos magic is not a system of low magic. It is a liberal attitude toward low magic that allows the magician to personalize his workings to such an extent that it makes traditionalists queasy. It works because the bulk of low magic is in the essentials, not the details. When you consider other forms of magic like ritual magic, high magic, etc. the same principles apply. The essentials may be more complex or more profound, but they are still the crux of the magic and tower in importance over the non-essential details. If you survey the occult community, you will find a major fixation with the non-essential details, but if you examine any good magical training system, you will see a path toward mastery of the essentials.

I wish to talk a little more about the theme of understanding, which, as I have already mentioned, is central to magic. True mastery over any subject can never happen without understanding. Let's say you are asked to find the sum of the numbers from 1 to an arbitrary number, which we

The Spirit of Magic by Virgil

will call n. Most math classes here in America would teach their students the following formula,

$$S = (n / 2) * (n + 1)$$

In this formula, S is the sum. So, for example, if we want to find the sum of the numbers from 1 to 6, then we use the formula as follows,

$$S = (6 / 2) * (6 + 1) = (3) * (7) = 21$$

This formula gives us the correct answer, after all,

$$1 + 2 + 3 + 4 + 5 + 6 = 21$$

And so the student memorizes the formula and the teacher has done his job of teaching the student how to find the sum of all the numbers from 1 to n. All you have to do is plug some values into a formula, and through some sorcery you don't understand, the formula spits out the right answer. Brilliant!

The problem here is that the student isn't learning math. The student is just learning to plug values into formulas. Really, any idiot off the street can do that. It's clear that to pass such a math class, you don't have to understand math at all. You just need to be able to memorize formulas and plug values into them. Physics is taught in a similar manner. Let's say you have two resistors – R1 and R2. Most people taking high school physics are taught that when these two resistors are in series, their equivalent resistance can be found using the following formula,

$$Req = R1 + R2$$

And that when they are in parallel, their equivalent resistance can be found using the following formula,

$$Req = (R1 * R2) / (R1 + R2)$$

Most physics students just memorize these formulas and use them. Of course, these physics students will be the first to deny the existence of sorcery, but this sort of plugging values into formulas without understanding them in hopes of getting the right answer is a very real example of sorcery.

Let's return to the formula for summing the numbers from 1 to n. If you simply remember this formula without understanding it, your

Chapter 11: Talismans

mastery over mathematics will not increase. Now let's look at why this formula actually works. Consider the following equation.

$1 + 2 + 3 + 4 + 5 + 6 = 21$

This can be rewritten as follows.

$(1 + 6) + (2 + 5) + (3 + 4) = 21$

Within each pair of parentheses is a pair of numbers added together. If you examine them, you'll notice the following.

$(1 + 6) = (2 + 5) = (3 + 4) = 7 = (n + 1)$

So this is where the (n + 1) part of the formula comes from. The number of pairs is half of n, or (n / 2). Thus, the complete formula for the sum of all the pairs is (n / 2) * (n + 1). Once you really understand this formula, then your mastery over mathematics has increased a little bit.

Math devoid of understanding is no longer math, but simply the ability to mindlessly plug values into formulas. Magic devoid of understanding is sorcery and superstition. These have no place in genuine magic. However, there are many sorcerous and superstitious practices that are widely and mistakenly considered to be magical.

One of these practices is the usage of the mysterious symbols scattered through the pages of medieval grimoires. For example, in the sixth chapter of the second book of *The Key of Solomon*, there are instructions for creating robes. The instructions tell you to embroider some mysterious symbols on the robes with red silk. Does anyone know what those symbols mean? I definitely don't. Consider the following two scenarios.

Scenario 1:

A long time ago, there was a genuine magician who practiced evocation. One day, he asked a spirit for methods of strengthening his robe so that they would protect him even better from the intense energies radiating from the powerful entities he worked with. The spirit taught the magician some sigils to draw on his robes. These sigils had protective and shielding properties. The magician copied the sigils down in his magical notebook. Many years after the magician's death, some random person stumbled across the magician's notebook by chance. In order to make some extra money, this person decided to make copies of the

The Spirit of Magic by Virgil

notebook and sell them to people interested in occultism and magic. Other people got ahold of the copies and made copies of the copies so they could sell them. Later, people made copies of the copies of the copies. Over a long period of time, the original notebook, the copies, and the copies of the copies became lost, destroyed, or worn out. Eventually, all that existed were copies of copies of copies of copies of copies of the original notebook. The sigils, as a result of all the copying, became distorted and corrupted. In this way, they transformed over time into meaningless and powerless scribbles.

Scenario 2:

A long time ago, some clever con artist realized he could make a lot of money selling grimoires to all the people interested in occultism and magic, as well as to all the people desperate for some easy way to acquire riches, power, and fame. Therefore, he made his own grimoire, and in the process, added in a bunch of mystical looking symbols that he made up off the top of his head. He then proceeded to sell copies of his grimoire while claiming that it was written by Solomon.

One of these scenarios is factual. Either the symbols are descended from real magical and meaningful symbols, or they are not. The manuscripts that most published grimoires like *The Key of Solomon* were based off of were copies of older manuscripts, which in turn were copies of even older manuscripts. The originals are lost to the mists of time, and the sigils those originals contained become distorted over years of copying into the mysterious-looking but powerless scribbles you see in the most recent copies that become the published versions of the grimoires. If you are making robes or talismans and want to draw some sigils on them that do embody some type of magical power, the Earthzone spirit Jugula (28° Aries) can provide you with whatever sigils you need. There is no point using the symbols you see in the grimoires. If you were to evoke a spirit while wearing a robe with those symbols embroidered on it, the symbols would do nothing but announce your ignorance to the spirit. The same goes for the symbols meant to be drawn on the virgin parchment, the black and white handled knives, the silken cloth etc. If you don't know what a symbol means, don't use it. If it came from a grimoire, it probably doesn't mean anything anyway.

In this chapter, we have seen the difference between magic, occultism, and sorcery. The magician who wants to make talismans understands the importance of the two essentials of condensing and programming astra-mental energy, and will work to master these two

Chapter 11: Talismans

essentials. The occultist will focus most of his attention on non-essential details like the symbols, names, glyphs, and colors to paint on the talisman. The sorcerer will make use of symbols and names he doesn't even understand.

Chapter 12: Lessons from the Tarot

The Chariot

This card depicts a prince sitting in a chariot. The chariot contains four pillars which hold up its roof. The prince is wearing two shoulder plates. One shoulder plate is shaped like a waxing moon, and the other is shaped like a waning moon. The chariot is pulled by two sphinxes; one is black and the other is white. The prince holds the reigns of these sphinxes.

The prince sitting in the chariot is often described as "victorious," which hints that the theme of "victory" is an important part of this card's message. If we examine IIH, we can see that it consists of ten steps, and that each step contains a collection of exercises. Every exercise the student masters is a small victory. Every step he completes is a larger victory. Thus, we can see that his journey from Step 1 to Step 10 is a series of victories. Any student of magic who makes steady progress through a magical training system will eventually complete that system. This is a big victory indeed.

The Chariot teaches us that these victories are only possible through balanced progress. The card is filled with symbols that allude to the concept of balance. The black and white sphinxes pulling the chariot balance each other. The waxing and waning moons on the prince's shoulders balance each other. The four pillars that make up the chariot also balance each other. The prince, his chariot, and the sphinxes pulling it are all balanced. This is why he can make progress. This is why he stays on track, and does not stray from the path onto other paths that don't lead to adepthood.

Each of the four pillars that make up the prince's chariot corresponds to one of the elements. These four pillars are with the prince at every point in his journey; after all, they are a part of his chariot. If we examine IIH, we can see that in Step 3, the student doesn't just learn how to accumulate one element. He learns how to accumulate all four elements. When he moves on to Step 4, he doesn't just learn how to condense one element. He learns how to condense all four elements. When he moves on to Step 5, he doesn't just learn how to project one element. He learns how to project all four elements. During each step, the student is working with all four elements. They must be mastered simultaneously, and not successively. The prince's right shoulder plate,

The Spirit of Magic by Virgil

which is shaped like a waxing moon, symbolizes his ability to control the electric fluid. The prince's left shoulder plate, which is shaped like a waning moon, symbolizes his ability to control the magnetic fluid. As discussed in Chapter 2, only a very balanced person can work with the electric and magnetic fluids. Therefore, the fact that the prince is able to control these fluids implies that he is very balanced.

The white sphinx represents the electric fluid. The black sphinx represents the magnetic fluid. Both sphinxes pull the chariot, which means throughout his training, the student must work with both forces. If only one sphinx were pulling the chariot, the chariot would go out of control. All forces/energies/powers have their roots in the electric and magnetic fluids. For example, the fire element is rooted in the electric fluid, the water element is rooted in the magnetic fluid, and the air and earth elements are rooted in both fluids. The presence of both the black and white sphinxes shows that regardless of what forces you are working with, no matter if they are elemental, planetary, zodiacal, or the pure electric and magnetic fluids themselves, you must work with them in a balanced manner, which means you cannot work exclusively with just one of them. Those magical training system that focus exclusively on mastering and working with one elemental energy or one planetary force are not balanced, and unbalanced training leads to an unbalanced mind and an unbalanced personality.

The student's training does not end once he completes the work of IIH. Once the student has steadily progressed through the work of IIH, he is now ready to steadily progress through the work of PME. This process involves using mental wandering to travel to the Earthzone, the Sphere of the Moon, and all the planetary spheres above it. In modern occultism, there are certain exercises called "pathworkings" that allegedly allow people to travel to these realms. To really travel to these realms requires one to have mastered the technique of exteriorization, and to have the maturity and elemental equilibrium necessary to reach them. Bardon gives many warnings in PME about attempting to reach spheres you do not have the maturity to handle. For example, in the warning quote dbelow, Bardon explains what will happen to the initiate if he tries to enter the Sphere of the Sun before he is ready to do so.

> *The same naturally also applies to the next sphere, the Sun sphere, which is the sphere that is most difficult to reach as the beings of that sphere all have such a strong accumulation of light that the magician who has not provided for a sufficient accumulation of the light power of the Sun, i.e. an*

Chapter 12: Lessons from the Tarot

accumulation equivalent to the glowing Sun, cannot resist the vibrations of the Sun genii. If the magician got into touch with a genius of the Sun without having sufficiently prepared himself by an appropriate light impregnation of his mental body, the glowing power of light rays would throw him back into his physical body and his mental matrix would, as a consequence, loose its equilibrium; and disharmonies would be the inevitable result. Such disharmonies would soon become obvious by various accompanying effects in the astral body, sometimes even in the physical body. Under certain circumstances a nervous breakdown would be the result. But also other psychic disadvantages might show up. Therefore the magician will consider my warning absolutely necessary and realize that it is not possible to betake oneself into other spheres without knowing their laws of analogy and their application and without having a sound knowledge of the magic of evocation.

A certain level of maturity and inner strength is needed in order to enter the Earthzone. A higher level of maturity and inner strength is needed in order to enter the Sphere of the Moon. An even higher level of maturity and inner strength is needed in order to enter the Sphere of Mercury. This pattern repeats itself, up to the Sphere of the Sun and beyond. This is a process of steady advancement through the spheres. Steady does not mean rushed. Rushed progress is what happens when you try to enter a certain planetary sphere before you are ready to do so. You strain your mental body and mental matrix, and this strain permeates down into your astral body, astral matrix, and physical body in the form of disharmonies, disturbed equilibrium, and even a nervous breakdown, as Bardon described in the warning quoted above.

So be like the prince in the chariot and make steady progress through the planetary spheres once you have made steady progress through IIH. Do not impatiently rush through the process and get blasted back and injured as a result of trying to travel to inner realms you do not have the maturity needed to enter safely.

The Devil

This card teaches us about astral currents and the ways we may become enchained by them. The imagery of the card shows a devil, who

The Spirit of Magic by Virgil

represents an astral current, as well as two humans who have been successfully captured, enchained, and enslaved by this current.

In the context of everyday life, the concept of an astral current can be seen in the phenomenon of mob psychology. Long ago, psychologists discovered that when people are part of mobs, they often act differently than they do when they're alone. This is referred to as "mob psychology." Simply, put, people are not themselves when they are part of a mob. The mob stirs up an emotional current that then runs through the mob. The members of the mob feel compelled to act in accordance with this current. This current isn't visible to those who can only see on the level of the physical, but those who are clairvoyant and can see on the level of the astral can easily observe this current as it flows through the mob. People who are normally peaceful may act violently if the current passes close to them and they become pulled into it and ensnared by it. Later on, they may look back and ask themselves "What the hell was I thinking?" They weren't thinking. They were blindly following the impulses generated within them by the current flowing through them. The force of the current that flows through a mob gives the mob the energy it uses to wreak havoc and cause massive damage.

The idea of astral currents is a prominent part of magic. For example, some lineages and traditions advertise themselves by saying "Our lineage/tradition has a powerful and ancient current empowering it. If you join us, then you will become connected to this current. You can tap into it and it will make you more powerful." To those seeking power, this is an attractive offer. To the perceptive, such a claim is tantamount to saying "Chain yourself to the devil of our tradition and you will become more powerful." Viewed this way, the claim becomes quite amusing. What is gained by the new recruit is not true power, but the illusion of power. He believes he has grown more powerful, and perhaps his rituals, spells, and other workings will become stronger once he has enchained himself to the current of a tradition so he can tap into the current's power. At the same time, however, he develops a dependence upon that devil. He begins to lose his individuality as his mind and will are absorbed into the tradition's current. In the worst-case scenario, he becomes fully absorbed into the current. When this happens, his body is basically a shell for the current. Look past this shell and you do not see a unique individual, but the devil that has assimilated the individual. True power is not gained by enchaining oneself, but by liberating oneself.

In modern magic, the word "initiation" usually refers to the process of becoming connected to the current of a magical tradition. Groups that belong to a magical tradition often have initiation rituals to connect new members to their tradition's current. One of the more popular debates in

Chapter 12: Lessons from the Tarot

the modern esoteric world is whether "self-initiation" is possible. In other words, whether it is possible for an individual to connect himself to a group's current without undergoing an initiation ceremony conducted by the group's members. Because IIH has the word "initiation" in it, and because IIH is meant to be worked through alone, some people interpret the book as a set of instructions for self-initiation and want to know which current students of the Bardon system are self-initiating themselves into when they work through IIH. For this reason, I want to clear up a very important matter.

Although the word "initiation" is part of the title of Bardon's first book, Bardon is not trying to teach students how to connect themselves to the current of some tradition or lineage. Think about the word "gum." "Gum" can mean the pink fleshy area that surrounds your teeth. "Gum" can also mean a type of chewy candy. These are two completely different things, but they are both called "gum." My point is, one word can have two different definitions. When the word "initiation" is found in Bardon's books, a different definition is being used. In the context of the Bardon system, initiation does not mean connecting yourself with a current. It means liberating yourself from the currents that have already taken ahold of you by developing a high enough level of inner strength that you are no longer affected by them and are resilient to their influence. As I have shown in Chapter 3, each step of IIH is designed to make the student more balanced. With balance comes strength, and with strength comes freedom. When you eventually learn to exteriorize your mental body and wander through the inner planes in this body (mental wandering), then you will find that the inner planes are like an ocean with many currents. If you are balanced and strong enough to not be at the mercy of these currents, then you will not drown.

In the chapter of MRSR about The Devil, Levi presents the following story, which conceals some of the esoteric teachings contained in this card.

The Devil, one day, desiring to stop the progress of an adept, broke one wheel of his chariot; but this true adept compelled the Devil to curl himself up on the wheel and act for the time as its tire, and so drove on, reaching his destination even sooner than he would have done if the Devil had let him alone. Meditate deeply on this old allegorical epigram, Aude et Tace, and when you have seized its occult sense, tell no other of your success.

The Spirit of Magic by Virgil

Various astral currents are constantly flowing in and out of our lives. According to astrologers, the natures of the currents that flow through our lives at a certain point in time are mirrored in the position of the stars at that point in time. Sometimes, these currents will affect our lives in ways that help us. Other times, these currents will affect our lives in ways that inconvenience us. Adepts have reached a high level of magical mastery, and therefore have a high amount of control over astral currents. In the story, a current (represented by the devil) has inconvenienced the adept by knocking a wheel off of his chariot, thus halting his progress. The adept, however, compels the devil to become a new wheel. This means that whenever astral currents flow through the adept's life in ways that inconvenience him, the adept can redirect those currents so that the currents serve him instead of inconveniencing him. While sorcery is a collection of tricks people use to try to nudge the currents of the astral plane in ways that are advantageous to them, magic is a rigorous discipline that allows a person to command these currents so that they conform perfectly to his will.

One example of an adept redirecting currents can be seen in the novel *Frabato the Magician*. In one chapter, Frabato is being attacked by a group of black magicians who try to kill him by sending a powerful astral current of the fire element to destroy him. Frabato, because he is an adept, is able to redirect the current of astral fire energy into a bucket of water.

Consider the following three statements by Levi,

> *In Black Magic, the Devil means the employment of the Grand Magical Agent (astral light) for a wicked purpose by a perverted Will.*

> *Absolute will power unguided by a right Reason is the quintessence of the Devil; and here is the explanation of the secrets of Black Magic, which leads to madness of mind and poisoning of body.*

> *All that happens in the world that is devoid of justice and right has the devil for its author.*

So we see that in the context of general magic, the Devil represents an astral current; but in the context of black magic, the Devil refers

Chapter 12: Lessons from the Tarot

specifically to a current directed "for a wicked purpose by a perverted will." We also see that such Devils are responsible for much of what is "devoid of justice and right" in the world.

These ideas provide us with many useful insights when it comes to understanding the Bardon system. In one of his essays, Bill Mistele writes about a time he used clairsentience and akasha (which transcends time) to study Bardon's aura. Bill found Bardon's aura downright frightening because it embodied a completely superhuman level of willpower. In PME, Bardon writes about an incident where he used his will to accumulate so much energy into a magic mirror that it physically shattered. Yes, such a high level of willpower is indeed frightening. It can move the astral light in drastic ways to stir up extraordinarily powerful currents.

This makes it clear why any aspiring magician must always make it his first priority to cultivate virtues and morals. He must develop compassion and acquire wisdom. He must hold himself up to high ethical standards and must not allow himself to stray from those standards. For Bardonists, all of this begins with the astral work of Steps 1 and 2 where Bardon teaches his students introspection and the six-pronged attack. Without this work of constantly analyzing and improving one's character, IIH becomes the world's most potent training manual for black magicians. It becomes the most dangerous book in existence. In fact, some would say that right now, it is already the most dangerous book in existence because although Bardon does stress the importance of becoming mature, balanced, and self-aware, too many rash beginners ignore him. They find all the exercises of accumulating and projecting the elements much more interesting than trying to eliminate their vices and strengthen their virtues. This is the wrong attitude with which to approach the Bardon system, and will lead to "madness of mind and poisoning of body."

In the chapter of D&R about the card The Star, Levi writes the following.

> *For our souls, when separated from our bodies, resemble revolving stars; they are globules of animated light which always seek their centre for the recovery of their equilibrium and their true movement. Before all things, however, they must liberate themselves from the folds of the serpent, that is, the unpurified Astral Light which envelops and imprisons them, unless the strength of their will can lift them beyond its reach.*

The Spirit of Magic by Virgil

The immersion of the living star in the dead light is a frightful torment, comparable to that of Mezentius.

In this passage, we see many of the same themes discussed previously in this book. Nahash is the great astral serpent formed from many smaller serpents, which are the currents of the astral plane. The man who has a weak will is at the mercy of these currents. The imagery of The Star shows a woman with a bright star above her head who is pouring two fluids into a river from jars in her hands. The bright star above the woman's head symbolizes the woman's strong will. Its bright white color alludes to the sephirah Kether, which represents the concept of Divine Will in traditional Kabbalah. She pours the electric and magnetic fluids downward, so that they can manifest her will on the physical plane. These fluids fall into the energetic river that flows from the void into the physical plane to nourish, sustain, and continuously recreate it. She is only able to use the fluids to manifest her will on the physical plane in this manner because she has "freed herself from the folds of the serpent."

Those stars that are not in equilibrium (AKA those humans without an elemental equilibrium) live as if they were dead. Undines are very empathic and sensitive to the feelings and life energies of those around them. They possess clairsentience in abundance, and one of the things incarnated undines unanimously agree on is that the vast majority of the human race seems dead. They are walking, talking, and moving, but it is as if they are zombies. They are more a mockery of life than actual life. This is reflected in Gustav Meyrink's assertion that "Man is firmly convinced that he is awake; in reality he is caught in a net of sleep and dreams which he has unconsciously woven himself." This same observation is the reason most incarnated undines first begin to suspect that they are not human. They say to themselves "I am not like those around me. Everyone seems so lifeless." Due to their increased psychic sensitivity, this net of sleep and dreams made from the folds of the serpent that the uninitiated are ensnared in is quite real and tangible to them. They don't understand why people do not actively seek to free themselves from it. It's because most people are not aware that they are trapped in this net, so they continue to live like zombies.

One difference between a living person and a dead person is that a living person can will. To will is to act. Think back to the Death card. Those doomed to die are stuck in the ground. They are not moving. They are not acting, which implies that they are not willing. Their lives are stagnant because they do not act. It seems like they are actively moving,

Chapter 12: Lessons from the Tarot

but really, they are just carried along. Sometimes they are carried along by the wheel of routine and habit. Other times, they are carried along by the astral currents flowing through their lives, and that they are at the mercy of. The devil enchains people. The woman enchains the devil; she is able to do so because she has a strong will and has recovered her equilibrium. She bottles up astral energies and releases them downward to manifest her will on the physical plane. And, as the imagery of the card shows, her will reflects Divine Will.

The Hermit

He will no more wander in darkness and uncertainty, but he will carry a torch in his hand, the light of which will penetrate the night of ignorance.

~ Franz Bardon

In Western magical lore, The Hermit is said to embody the concept of an "initiation," and since this concept is a recurring theme in this field, many authors who have written about the Tarot have paid particular attention to this card. The imagery of this card shows an old man wearing a mantle, and holding a staff and a lamp.

In a previous section, I stated that The Chariot represents the idea of balanced progress. The Hermit also represents this idea, with one difference. In The Chariot, the emphasis is on a balance between the four elements. In The Hermit, the emphasis is on a balance between the three planes. The figure in the card carries a lamp, wears a mantle, and carries a staff. According to Levi, "the lamp burns with a triple flame, the mantle is thrice-folded, and the staff is divided into three parts." This symbolizes the fact that the process of initiation must have three aspects – mental, astral, and physical – and that these three aspects must be balanced. The mantle represents the initiate's mastery over his physical, astral, and mental bodies. The staff represents the initiate's mastery over the physical, astral, and mental planes. The lamp represents the initiate's knowledge of the physical, astral, and mental planes. Let's explore each of these three symbols in more detail.

The mantle of the figure represents the idea of self-mastery; in other words, mastery of one's mental, astral, and physical bodies. According to some esoteric authors, it also represents the idea of "insulation," which is

The Spirit of Magic by Virgil

a closely related concept. If you are the master of your three bodies, then you and you alone are in control of your bodies. In other words, outside influences do not control or affect your bodies. Thus, your bodies are "insulated" from those outside influences. For example, let's consider the astral body, which is the home of one's emotional life. When someone insults you, the insult does not cause anger to flare up in your astral body. Anger would never flare up in your astral body unless you consciously allowed it to or willed it to, because the state of your astral body is subject to your will alone, and it is not affected by outside influences such as the insults of other people. Your astral body is "insulated" from those insults. Compare this to people who are "thin-skinned." These people are easily affected by outside influences. They lack the thick insulating mantle of The Hermit. Acquiring the insulating mantle of The Hermit isn't about cutting yourself off from the world. It's about not letting the world affect you negatively unless you allow it to.

The staff of the figure represents mastery over the three planes – physical, astral, and mental. The student acquires this mastery by practicing exercises that will increase his mastery over these three planes. These exercises can be found in whatever magical training system the student has chosen to work through.

The lamp of the figure represents knowledge of the three planes. This is not mere intellectual knowledge, which can be gained from reading books, but genuine knowledge obtained from experience. Those who attempt to acquire knowledge through books alone will never obtain the lamp of The Hermit. Note that in IIH, Bardon spends a few paragraphs describing the physical, astral, and mental planes so that students will have some basic information about them. However, he does not spend pages and pages describing these planes. Instead, he provides the student with ten steps containing physical, astral, and mental exercises so students can learn about the planes through their experiences practicing those exercises.

In IIH, Bardon writes the following.

> *We must always be aware of the fact that the body, soul and mind are to be trained simultaneously, for otherwise it would be impossible to gain and maintain the magic equipoise. In the theoretic part I already called attention to the dangers possibly rising from one-sided training. It is not advisable to hasten development, because everything needs time.*

Chapter 12: Lessons from the Tarot

This idea of the three planes is an important one to grasp. The students should understand that his training should be balanced between these planes, and that these planes should be mastered simultaneously, as opposed to successively.[52] The soundness of a magical training system depends in large part on how well its exercises are balanced between these three planes.

There are many people who use unbalanced magical training systems. Most of these people end up just fine. They approach their training in a lazy and unserious manner. They don't practice their exercises every day. When they do practice their exercises, they do so in an absent-minded manner. This lazy and unserious attitude protects them from great injury. When it comes to unbalanced training systems, the harder and more seriously you train, the more you injure yourself. Bardon realized that in order for students to become adepts, they needed to train hard and train seriously. For this reason, he put a lot of focus on weaving a balance between the three planes into his system.

However, although Bardon's system, when practiced correctly, is perfectly safe, there are many Bardonists who suffer from the effects of unbalanced training. I am not referring to people who cherry pick random exercises from IIH to practice, because they are not real Bardonists. I am referring to people who make a serious effort to work through IIH, but who suffer from the effects of unbalanced training anyway. Usually, they have unknowingly moved on from an exercise before they were ready to, or made some other similar mistake.

For example, many Bardonists get headaches and migraines because they spend a lot of time on the mental exercises and not enough time on the astral and physical exercises. These Bardonists usually moved on from the thought-observation exercise before they were ready to. Instead of taking the time they should have to master this exercise, they were too eager to move on to the famed VOM exercise, or to the fun plastic imagination exercises of Step 2. They made an honest mistake, but a costly one. As discussed in Chapter 7, you become friends with your mind when you practice the thought-observation exercise. When you are friends with your mind, your mind cooperates with you. You can get it to do whatever you want, and the mental exercises of IIH become easy. If you aren't friends with your mind, then the mental exercises become unnecessarily difficult. You spend more time on the mental exercises and neglect the astral and physical exercises. Your training becomes unbalanced, and you suffer the same sorts of negative effects as those students who train using inherently unbalanced systems.

While one major theme of The Hermit is that genuine initiation is a process that is balanced between the three planes, there are other lessons contained in the card as well. The figure in the card is old, and this old age symbolizes maturity, implying that initiates are very mature. When we examine George MacDonald's fairy tale *The Golden Key* in Chapter 17, we will see that this story also uses old age as a symbol for maturity.

Some esoteric authors have asserted that the real name of this card is Prudence, which I will call "caution" since this synonym is probably more familiar to most readers.[53] I find this assertion intriguing because caution is indeed an important quality for would-be initiates. Some magicians have described magic as the study of life. Magic can teach you a lot about life, and life can teach you a lot about magic. There are many people who have died or become permanently paralyzed and maimed because they lacked caution. In magic, you work with many dangerous forces and entities. If you work with them only when you are ready to, then you should be fine, but accidents can happen and life is always unpredictable. You must always be cautious. Most magical teachers have a few good stories about students who lacked caution and ended up burning themselves with the powerful energies they were working with. Although I don't take on students, I frequently get messages and emails from people who have burned themselves and want help returning themselves to their pre-magic status quo. Without being in their vicinity, the best I can offer them is general advice.

In Western magic, four personality traits are said to be especially useful for aspiring magicians. Sometimes they are expressed as the four powers of the sphinx – to know, to dare, to will, and to keep silence. Other times, they are expressed as the four pillars of Solomon's temple – knowledge, courage, volition, and silence. Since students are told to have courage and to dare, some may wonder how they can be cautious at the same time. Caution is not the opposite of courage. During the twentieth century, many European esoteric circles were immersed in a culture that often promoted toxic masculinity, and this influenced the way some esoteric authors interpreted the power of daring and the pillar of courage.[54] Courage is not synonymous with stupidity, and it does not mean recklessly jumping into danger. It does not mean you are willing to enter a very dark part of the forest when your lamp is dim and your staff is weak.

Imagine that you are about to embark on a journey that is filled with uncertainties and obstacles. Courage is a willingness to take this journey anyway, trusting that whenever you come across an obstacle or uncertainty, you will be able to work through it by adapting. Since you don't know everything about the journey, you have to be able to adapt, and you have to trust in your ability to adapt.

Chapter 12: Lessons from the Tarot

When I first started working through IIH, I knew the path would require daily practice, and I knew I would be in for a long ride. I didn't know if I'd always have the time to practice daily. I didn't know if I'd always have the energy to do so either. I was moving around a lot, and didn't know if the circumstances of my life in the future would prevent me from training. But I decided to begin the work anyway. That's courage. It's not the absence of caution. It's willing to walk into uncertainty because you are confident in your ability to adapt and to find solutions to problems.

Each of the four pillars/commands corresponds to one of the four elements. Knowledge corresponds to air. Volition corresponds to fire. Silence corresponds to earth. Courage corresponds to the water element. Water is the master of adaptation. When water flows and then encounters an obstacle like a stone, it doesn't freak out or start complaining. It simply adapts by changing its path so that it goes around the obstacle and continues on its journey.

Chapter 13: Becoming a Guardian Angel

Blessed are those who meet another in his darkest place and walk beside him back into the light. There is no greater or more sacred celebration of life.

~ William Mistele

This is a chapter about blessing other individuals. Since the job of a guardian angel is to bless its ward, this is like becoming a guardian angel for other individuals.

The microcosm is reflected in the macrocosm, and vice versa. The individual is the microcosm. The world is the macrocosm. In Chapter 16, we will discuss blessing the world, or becoming a guardian angel for the world if you will. When you read that chapter, you will see that many of the principles I present in this chapter also appear in that chapter.

What is a Blessing?

A blessing is something that reduces suffering and increases joy. When you bless a person, you reduce the amount of suffering in that person's life and increase the amount of joy in that person's life. When you bless a community, you reduce the amount of suffering in that community and increase the amount of joy in that community. When you bless the world, you reduce the amount of suffering in the world and increase the amount of joy in the world. Magic is the art of blessing.

The Two Types of Suffering

There are two types of suffering. The first type of suffering serves no purpose. The second type of suffering serves a teaching purpose, and is usually created by karma.

When suffering is present in a person's life to teach him important lessons, you must first find an alternate way for that person to learn those lessons before eliminating the suffering. Otherwise, you deprive that person of important lessons he needs in order to grow and mature.

The Spirit of Magic by Virgil

The magician must always distinguish between purposeless suffering and suffering that does serve a teaching purpose. Franz Bardon was a great healer. Sometimes, he would be able to heal an ill person very easily because the illness didn't serve any purpose and was the result of bad luck. Other times, he wasn't able to heal an ill person easily becausee the illness did serve a purpose. In other words, it was caused by karma, which is our teacher. If Bardon simply healed these people, the illness would keep coming back until they had worked through their karma. In one instance, a girl came to Bardon so he could heal her tuberculosis. Bardon realized that her tuberculosis was caused by her karma, so to heal her, he took her karma upon himself. However, the suffering caused by the karma was so bad that it was preventing him from accomplishing his life's work. Therefore, he had to give her karma back to her.

Daskalos was also a great healer, and many of his healing feats are described in Kyriacos Markides's book *The Magus of Strovolos*. Like Bardon, Daskalos was often able to heal people easily. However, in those instances where an illness was caused by karma, he too needed to deal with the karma first before getting rid of the illness. Sometimes, this required him to take the karma upon himself. For example, in one instance, his nephew's son was born with a very bad leg disease that was caused by some karma the baby had accumulated in his previous lives. To heal his nephew's son, Daskalos took the baby's karma upon himself. The baby's leg healed, but Daskalos's own leg became diseased.

Bardon and Daskalos had no trouble discriminating between purposeless suffering and suffering created by karma to serve a teaching purpose. This ability to discriminate isn't a matter of magical power, but a matter of wisdom and understanding. Here we see again the error in reaching only for power without also reaching for wisdom and understanding. A genuine magical training system does not just provide the student with power, but also with wisdom and understanding.

In this chapter, I teach some principles that can be used to reduce the suffering of others. These principles can be applied without worrying about karmic issues because they are designed to eliminate purposeless suffering caused by ignorance, as opposed to suffering caused by karma to serve a teaching purpose. These principles include helping others learn the truth about themselves, helping them find wisdom, and helping them see clearly. I also teach principles that can be used to increase the amount of joy in peoples' lives.

Chapter 13: Becoming a Guardian Angel

This Chapter's Backstory

I once had a friend who was undergoing a lot of suffering. This was long before I had completed Step 8, so I did not have access to the guidance of the Earthzone spirits. I asked Bill, who I was in frequent correspondence with at the time, for advice. He told me to reflect on the sixth card in the Major Arcana – The Lovers – and to "become the angel in the card." As a result, I spent a few weeks doing an in-depth study of this card. In the process, I learned a lot about what it means to bless others, and what it means to be a guardian angel for others. In this chapter, I share some of the things I learned.

The Imagery of The Lovers

This card shows a young man standing at a fork in the road. In other word, the road he is travelling on splits into two roads. One road goes right and represents the path of righteousness. The other road goes left and represents the path of vice. A woman (the personification of wisdom) stands on the man's right side and tries to convince him to choose the path of righteousness. Another woman (a temptress) stands on the man's left side and tries to convince him to choose the path of vice. The man's guardian angel hovers over him holding a bow and arrow.

In some versions of the card, the angel's arrow is pointing toward the temptress to drive her off if she goes too far. Exposure to temptation is important for our spiritual evolution because overcoming temptation makes us stronger and succumbing to temptation can teach us valuable lessons. However, some temptations are too much. They are too dangerous, and put the man at risk of drastically ruining himself. For example, using akashic magic for evil purposes can result in colossal karmic consequences, so the temptation to use akashic magic for evil purposes is very dangerous indeed.[55]

In other versions of the card, the man is looking at the woman personifying wisdom. In these versions, the man's guardian angel resembles Cupid and the angel's arrow is pointing at the man. When a person is struck by Cupid's arrow, he falls in love with the first person he sees. The guardian angel is getting ready to shoot the man so that he falls in love with wisdom. The guardian angel wants the man to live a blessed life, and the guardian angel knows that if the man falls in love with wisdom, he will constantly seek wisdom, which will result in him constantly becoming wiser. Wisdom allows the man to make the best choices in his life, which in turn will result in him living a blessed life (a life with little purposeless suffering and with much joy and wonder).

According to Eliphas Levi, this card as a whole represents idealism and beauty. Levi also states that the angel in the card is reminiscent of the sun and represents a source of truth and love.

A Guardian Angel Protects Its Ward

The temptress is the woman trying to persuade the man to choose the path of vice. People develop inner strength and grow spiritually by overcoming temptations. To overcome temptations, one must be exposed to temptations. The temptress provides the man with the temptations he needs in order to spiritually evolve, which is why his guardian angel does not shoot her. However, the angel's arrow is pointing at the temptress because he is prepared to shoot her if she goes too far. Going too far means putting the man in serious spiritual danger by exposing him to temptations that will truly ruin him if he succumbs to them. The most extreme example of such danger is described by Bardon in Step X of IIH.

> *If he (the magician) misused his knowledge for evil deeds, it would be Divine Providence that would punish him, instead of fate. Divine Providence would give him, as it were, the cold shoulder and he would have to live on as a lonely individual forsaken in the universe. The only possibility of relying on Divine Providence would be lost forever, which surely would be worse than any curse. Such a magician would be doomed to destruction, and he can easily realize what that would mean from the magical point of view.*

Bardon gives this warning after teaching the student how to use akasha to become invisible. Since this invisibility technique uses akasha, to abuse this technique is to abuse akasha, which has serious negative consequences. Luckily, instances of people abusing akasha are rare. Most magicians who are able to work with akasha are mature enough to never abuse it. However, in the event that a magician does learn to work with akasha and then uses it for evil purposes, he would be given the cold shoulder by Divine Providence.

The bottom line is this. When you are a guardian angel for someone, you protect that person from serious danger, but you don't prevent the

Chapter 13: Becoming a Guardian Angel

person from experiencing the challenges that will make him stronger or from facing the problems that will teach him important problems solving skills.[56]

A Guardian Angel Helps Its Ward Acquire Wisdom and Live an Ideal Life

Think about an important moment in your past when you had to make a choice. Which choice was the wise choice? Which choice was the best choice?

Now think about another important moment in your past when you had to make a choice. Which choice was the wise choice? Which choice was the best choice?

You might have noticed that the wise choice also happened to be the best choice in both of those instances. This isn't a coincidence. Wisdom is, by definition, the ability to make the best choices. When faced with a decision, the wise person knows what the best choice is. The unwise person does not. The wiser you are, the easier it will be to see what the best choice to make is whenever you have to make a choice in life.[57]

Your life is built entirely out of choices. They're literally the building blocks of your life. Making the worst possible choices leads to you living the worst possible life. Making the best possible choices leads to you living the best possible life, meaning an ideal life. This is why Levi says that this card represents the concept of idealism. When you help someone find wisdom, you help that person gain the capacity to make the best choices in life.

A guardian angel tries to make its ward's life an ideal one. Note that I say "an idea one" and not "the ideal one." There is no single ideal life for anyone. Each time we make a decision, we are faced with a set of multiple choices, and it could be that a subset of several choices ties for the position of the best choice. When it comes to providing guardian angel guidance for those you love, the idea is to help them make a choice that is in that subset of best choices.

A Guardian Angel Helps Its Ward See Unpleasant Truths

According to Levi, the angel in the card is a source of truth. Since the angel's job is to bless its ward, this implies that helping people see the truth is a way of blessing them.

The Spirit of Magic by Virgil

In the first edition of this book, I frequently made references to Arthur Miller's play *Death of a Salesman*. Unfortunately, it seems many of my readers were unfamiliar with this play, so I took out most references to this play when creating this book's second edition. However, in this section, I do wish to discuss this play a little. Let me begin with a highly simplified summary of what happens in this play.

In *Death of a Salesman*, there is a character named Willy Loman who is really pathetic. This isn't a problem in and of itself. If you are pathetic and aware that you are pathetic, then you can begin taking steps to become less pathetic. However, the fact that he is pathetic is a truth that is too hard for Willy Loman to swallow. Therefore, he is in denial about the fact that he is pathetic. Being in denial disconnects him from reality and forces him to live in a fantasy world of his own self-delusions. Because he is so disconnected from reality, he is unable to do anything productive with his life. Eventually, near the end of his life, he awakens to the truth that he is pathetic, and that he has not done anything productive his whole life because he was in denial about this the whole time. He desperately tries to plant a garden so that he'll have done at least one productive thing before he dies.

So, what does this play have to do with magic? Clearly, Willy Loman did not live a blessed life. It's a good exercise to think about why he did not live a blessed life, and what you could do to make his life more blessed if you were his guardian angel. The master Jesus Christ once told his followers "And ye shall know the truth, and the truth shall set you free." Willy Loman did not see the truth about himself. Being in denial about the kind of person he was kept him enslaved to the same problems that plagued him until the end of his life. A life in chains is no life at all. Someone acting as his guardian angel could have helped him see the truth about himself.

Not all truths are pleasant. Many truths are unpleasant, which is why we prefer to remain in denial about them rather than face them. When it comes to awakening our wards to unpleasant truths, we must do so in a kind and gentle manner to avoid making the awakening process more unpleasant than it needs to be.

A Guardian Angel Loves Its Ward and Treats Its Ward with Love

There are many different types of love. One type of love is compassion. When Levi wrote that the guardian angel represents a

Chapter 13: Becoming a Guardian Angel

source of love, he was referring specifically to compassion. Compassion is not just the type of love guardian angels show their wards. It is also the type of love schoolteachers should show their students and parents should show their children.

What is Compassion?

Like wisdom, there is no single correct way to define compassion. There are multiple valid ways that are essentially the same but appear different. Each different way of defining compassion allows us to view this concept from a different angle. The more valid definitions we contemplate, the more comprehensive our understanding of compassion becomes. One way of defining compassion is that it is a desire to relieve the suffering of others. Another way of defining compassion is that it is a desire to bless others. Yet another way of defining compassion is that it is the perfect balance between loving-kindness and severity. In Kabbalah, loving-kindness corresponds to Chesed and severity corresponds to Geburah. Compassion corresponds to Tiphereth, which is between Chesed and Geburah. These three definitions don't contradict each other. A blessing relieves others of purposeless suffering, and blessing others requires showing them a perfect balance between loving-kindness and severity.

Good Teachers Show Their Students Compassion

In 1939, a psychologist named Wendell Johnson and a graduate student named Mary Tudor performed an experiment that involved teaching children to speak better. Half of the children were taught using teaching methods reflecting pure severity and no loving-kindness. They were basically harshly criticized for every little mistake they made when speaking, and never given praise or encouragement. Many of these children developed major speech issues and other psychological disorders that lasted their entire lives. The message for magicians is clear. A teaching approach that reflects just severity and no loving-kindness will make people regress and damage them irreparably. It will only hurt them, and will not benefit them in any way.

If you think back to your school days, you probably remember a few teachers whose approach to teaching may not have reflected pure severity, but was definitely unbalanced toward the severity direction. You probably disliked those teachers immensely, and therefore were

The Spirit of Magic by Virgil

unwilling to learn from them. A teaching approach unbalanced toward the severity direction is not effective.

If you think back to your school days, you probably also remember a few teachers whose approach to teaching was unbalanced toward the loving-kindness direction. These teachers were really nice and let you do whatever you wanted without ever punishing you. You probably didn't have much respect for these teachers, and spent most of your time goofing off in class instead of learning. These teachers often have trouble getting their students to behave because they are too nice to command respect from their students. A teaching approach unbalanced toward the loving-kindness direction is not effective.

The good teachers were the teachers whose approach to teaching had the perfect balance between loving-kindness and severity. These teachers showed their students genuine compassion because they did what was truly in the best interest of their students. Their students actually learned. Their students actually received an education, and therefore, their students were more likely to succeed in life than the students of other teachers who showed too much loving-kindness or too much severity.

If you have had such a teacher in your life, then you have been blessed. If you are such a teacher, then you are a blessing to your students.

Good Parents Show Their Children Compassion

A study conducted by researchers at the University of Manitoba and McMaster University, titled "Physical Punishment and Mental Disorders: Results from a Nationally Representative US Sample," shows that hitting children results in an increase in the probability that they will develop a wide variety of mental illnesses. This is the case even if the child is hit only once. Just try to imagine the negative effects children suffer from if they are hit regularly. Children going through that kind of abuse often develop deep psychological issues that affect them negatively the rest of their lives. Clearly, an approach to parenting that is unbalanced toward the severity direction is ineffective because it can cripple children for the rest of their lives by causing them to develop mental illnesses.

An approach to parenting that is unbalanced toward the loving-kindness direction is ineffective as well. It results in children who are spoiled brats. They are used to being pampered, so they never learn to earn things through their own work.

Chapter 13: Becoming a Guardian Angel

The only effective approaches to parenting are the ones that reflect a perfect balance between loving-kindness and severity. The parents who adopt such an approach to parenting show their children genuine compassion because they are doing what's best for their children. Their children will not grow up with the psychological issues that come from abuse, nor will they grow up to become spoiled brats.

If you have such parents, then you have been blessed. If you are a parent and your parenting approach reflects compassion, then you are a blessing to your children.

Non-Magical Blessings

It is God's nature to bless. The magician, who is a divine being himself, has the same nature. Therefore, it is also the magician's nature to bless.

Some people regularly bless others through their magical acts. They cast spells and perform rituals to reduce the amount of purposeless suffering in the world and to increase the amount of joy in the world. However, if they don't bless others through their non-magical acts as well, then they don't have the nature of a magician, and therefore aren't magicians. When it is your nature to bless, you bless. There is no fundamental distinction between magical and non-magical. We have created this distinction in our minds for our own benefit because sometimes it is easier to think in terms of the "magical" and the "non-magical." However, if your nature is to bless, then you bless using whatever means and methods are at your disposal, regardless of whether they are "magical" or "non-magical."

There is a story about a guy who committed suicide by jumping off the Golden Gate Bridge. Before he left his apartment, he wrote a note that said "I'm going to walk to the bridge. If one person smiles at me on the way, I won't jump." Apparently no one smiled at him, because he did jump and he did die. How would you have saved him? Would you cast a spell designed to make someone smile at him, or would you go to him yourself and smile at him? Which approach to saving him would have had a greater chance of succeeding?

I know quite a few people whose nature it is to bless. This does include the magicians I know who underwent a proper magical training, but it also includes many people who never underwent magical training of any sort. It includes many people who have never done an LBRP, who don't know a thing about the Tree of Life, who have never heard of the

The Spirit of Magic by Virgil

Goetia, who don't know what Tarot card corresponds to what Hebrew letter, and who don't believe in spirits. Despite this, they show compassion to those around them, reduce the suffering of others, and fill others' lives with joy.

It's not just about using spells, rituals, sigils, and servitors to bless others. You can make your very presence a blessing to those around you by changing the way you live your life. This is what magical training teaches you how to do. It might not look like it the first time you read through IIH, but once you begin practicing the exercises and making progress through the book step by step, you will see that this is true.

A Guardian Angel Helps Its Ward be Alive

Levi says that the angel in the card is reminiscent of the sun. The sun is seen by many cultures as a provider of life. For example, in some yogic traditions, the sun is the symbolic source of prana – the vital force. To become the solar angel of The Lovers and bless others is to give them life. One archangel corresponding to the sun is Raphael. In the Rider-Waite-Smith version of the Tarot, The Lovers does not show a guardian angel blessing its ward. It shows Raphael sending vitalizing energy to two people. The poet E.E. Cummings wrote that "Unbeing dead isn't being alive." When you are a guardian angel for someone, you help him stop unbeing dead and start being alive.

A Guardian Angel Helps Its Ward See

The sun is a source of light that drives away darkness and helps people see. Raphael cured Tobit of his blindness. In the Book of Enoch, Azazel teaches humanity how to war against each other and how to obsess over makeup. These might seem like they have nothing to do with each other, but both practices arise from blindness. When people cannot see the unity underlying humanity, they wage war against each other. When people cannot see that their value has nothing to do with how well they conform to society's current arbitrary beauty standards, they obsess over makeup. Raphael was the angel sent by God to bind Azazel and cast him into darkness until the end of time. To be able to see is to be blessed. By learning to see, we overcome the curses Azazel placed upon our race.

To bless another person is to help that person see. Bless those who lack self-esteem by helping them see that they have a great deal of potential. Bless those who are insecure about their looks by helping them

Chapter 13: Becoming a Guardian Angel

see that they are beautiful. Bless those who are irritable by helping them see the negative effects of anger. Bless those who aspire to be magicians by helping them see the difference between good magical training systems and bad magical training systems.

The Youth of the Man

He man who stands between the two women is young. Regarding the man's youth, Mouni Sadhu writes that since he is young, "this gives us a hint on the necessity of making fateful decisions while there is still time to put them into practice." When you make a good decision/choice, you often reap the benefits of that choice for the rest of your life. For example, a long time ago, I chose to use the six-pronged attack to become patient. I have been reaping the benefits of that choice ever since the day I made it. This is why it's important to acquire wisdom as early in your life as possible. It allows you to begin making the best choices as early in your life as possible.

To become wise is one example of a blessing. When it comes to blessing others, people usually benefit more from a blessing the earlier they receive it in their lives. People who receive blessings late in their lives don't have time to do much with those blessings.

The School Analogy

This is one of my favorite analogies, and the one that I think best illustrates what it means to bless someone.

In IIH, Bardon writes "Life is a school, not a playground." Some schools are bad. The infrastructure is collapsing, the cafeteria food is terrible, the bathrooms are dirty, the teachers are incompetent and don't care about their students, the examinations are poorly designed, overly harsh grading criteria is used for all assignments, and there are no extracurricular activities to provide the students with enrichment outside of their classes. Other schools are great. They are lively, clean, and well-built. The teachers care about their students, and all their lessons are fun and interesting, but still very informative. They enjoy teaching and the students enjoy learning. The material in each class is challenging, but the teachers inspire the students to push themselves and succeed. They show their students guardian angel love. Outside of academics, there are plenty of extracurricular activities to accommodate the students' wide range of interests. The cafeteria food is good and the bathrooms are clean.

The Spirit of Magic by Virgil

One school is filled with suffering and restriction. The other is filled with joy, wonder, and opportunity. You can take a class in either school and learn the same lessons, but the learning process will be much more pleasant if you attend the second school. Saturn does not care how you learn your lessons, as long as you learn them. To bless someone is to make their life like the second school. This is what it means to be a guardian angel for someone else.

Chapter 14: Wisdom

In a land where sorcerers come thick, like Gont or the Enlades, you may see a raincloud blundering slowly from side to side and place to place as one spell shunts it onto the next, till at last it is buffeted out over the sea where it can rain in peace. But Ogion let the rain fall where it would.

~Ursuala Le Guin (A Wizard of Earthsea)

One of the most well-known stories in magical lore is the story of King Solomon. The story goes that God once asked Solomon what he wanted. Instead of asking for riches, women, or power over his enemies, Solomon asked for wisdom. God was so impressed with this response from Solomon that he not only gave Solomon wisdom, he also made Solomon the greatest magician on Earth.

Solomon is an important figure in magic. There are numerous grimoires, pentacles, and magical teachings attributed to him. The fact that Solomon, one of the greatest magicians in magical lore, was known for his immense wisdom should alert students that there is a profound connection between magic and wisdom, and that these two subjects are deeply intertwined. The student who notices this will likely begin asking questions about the nature of wisdom in order to understand it better. What is wisdom? Why is wisdom so important in magic? How does one acquire wisdom? These are questions we will begin to answer in later sections of this chapter, and in later chapters of this book.

Paracelsus wrote that "Magic is not sorcery, but Supreme Wisdom." Paracelsus pretty much equates magic with wisdom. Abraham also uses the terms "wisdom" and "magic" interchangeably numerous times throughout his three books of the sacred magic of Abramelin. In the Middle East, the Arabic tradition of magic is called al-Hikmah, meaning "the Wisdom." Bardon also agrees that wisdom is extremely important in magic. In PME, he writes,

Thus every reader, every theorist, and foremost, everyone interested in the secret knowledge, will come to the conviction that magic and especially, sphere magic, is no witchcraft or

The Spirit of Magic by Virgil

sorcery but the peak of attainable knowledge, surmounting all other intellectual sciences and being the very crown of wisdom.

The word "wisdom" appears thirty times in IIH, and each sentence the word appears in is worthy of contemplation. Bardon calls magic a "sacred wisdom," a "sublime wisdom," an "ancient wisdom," and the "crown of wisdom." He also refers to the set of Tarot cards as the "Book of Wisdom." Like Paracelsus, Bardon also asserts that wisdom is what distinguishes magic from sorcery. The sorcerer lacks wisdom.

Defining Wisdom

In Chapter 12, I defined wisdom as the ability to recognize what the best choices are. Presidents need to make the best choices when deciding how to handle international relations. Everyday citizens need to make the best choices when deciding which job offer to accept after being interviewed for several different positions. College students need to make the best choices when deciding which courses to take. Teachers need to make the best choices when deciding what assignments to give their students to help them learn better. Novelists need to make the best choices when it comes to how to develop their characters and form plots. Doctors need to make the best choices when it comes to which medicines to prescribe to their patients. Magicians need to make the best choices when it comes to whether to use magic, and how to use magic. Regardless of who you are, you can benefit from improving your ability to recognize what the best choices are. In other words, regardless of who you are, you can benefit from wisdom. "The ability to recognize the best choices" is a very useful, very practical, and very accurate way of defining wisdom. However, it is not the only valid way to define wisdom. To broaden our understanding of wisdom, let's examine another way of defining wisdom.

In traditional Kabbalah, the sephirah Kether represents God's will, and the sephirah Chockmah is the means of accessing and perceiving God's will. Chockmah translates to Wisdom. This means that through wisdom, we know the will of God. In other words, wisdom is the ability to know the will of God. This definition doesn't contradict the definition

Chapter 14: Wisdom

of wisdom presented in the previous paragraph. God is compassionate, supportive, and wants us to make the best choices. Therefore, to know the choice God wants us to make is to know the best choice, and to know the best choice is to know the choice God wants us to make. This second definition of wisdom should not muddle our understanding of wisdom, but deepen our understanding of wisdom.

Righteousness

Wisdom is knowing what the best choices – the choices God wants us to make – are. We may know what the best choice is, but temptation or emotion may compel us to make a bad choice anyway. For example, let's say your boss is rude to you. You have many choices when it comes to how you will deal with a situation like this. The best choice is to deal with it patiently and assertively. Dealing with this situation aggressively, on the other hand, is definitely not the best choice. However, even if you know what the best choice is, your anger may compel you to deal with this situation aggressively. Clearly, knowing what the best choice is does not guarantee you will make it.

Wisdom is knowing what the best choices are. Righteousness is actually making those choices.

God's Will

Magicians serve God by carrying out God's will on Earth. Clearly, we cannot do that if we don't know what God's will is. While a single book can't address what God's will is in any specific situation an individual may encounter in life, we can address what God's will is in a general sense.

The Kabbalists noticed long ago that the Hebrew letter Beth is the first letter in the words *baruch* (blessing) and *bereshit* (in the beginning). *Bereshit* is also the first word of the Torah, which begins with a description of how the universe was created. This was interpreted to mean that God intended for the universe to be blessed from its inception.

The enormous value of stories as teaching tools has long been recognized in the Bardon community. In Appendix C, I present a story written by Bill containing many useful insights about magic, evolution, and the universe. Note the theme of blessings that runs throughout this story.

The Spirit of Magic by Virgil

So in general, it can be said that the will of Divine Providence is that the universe be blessed, and that it continually become more blessed. When we act wisely, we make the universe more blessed. When we serve Divine Providence, we make the universe more blessed. We reduce the amount of suffering in the universe and increase the amount of joy and wonder.

Why Wisdom is Important

There is a well-known saying – "The road to hell is paved with good intentions." This means that people often create a lot of suffering by doing things with good intentions. In the mundane world, this happens all the time. For example, when I was an undergraduate, I worked in a lab. One day, I noticed that the lab was very messy, so I decided to do everyone a favor by cleaning it up. In the process of cleaning it up, I threw out a bunch of things I thought were garbage. Well, it turns out that some of the things I threw out were important samples that the researchers working in the lab needed. So, although I had good intentions when I cleaned up the lab, I only succeeded in causing a lot of people suffering.

When it comes to magic, you often see people perform rituals or cast spells to improve the world, but only succeed in creating chaos in the world, or as a student of Roke Island would put it, disturbing "the Balance and the Pattern" of the world, instead.[58] While they had good intentions, they did not understand enough to foresee the harmful effects of their magical work. My point isn't that you should avoid using magic to improve the world; after all, that's kind of the purpose of magic (from a high level perspective). My point is that you should strive for wisdom and understanding so that when you do eventually acquire magical power use it with good intentions, you can use it with good intentions wisely.

Wisdom and Understanding

Wisdom is knowing the best choices to make. In Kabbalah, it is taught that Chockmah and Binah cannot exist without each other. It's kind of like how the concept of "high" cannot exist without the concept of "low," or how the concept of "big" cannot exist without the concept of "small." Where there is wisdom, there is understanding. Where there is understanding, there is wisdom. Wisdom leads to understanding and understanding leads to wisdom.

Chapter 14: Wisdom

When I was cleaning up the lab, the wise choice would have been to leave the samples alone. However, I did not understand that they were samples, and I did not understand their importance. Because I lacked understanding, I acted unwisely by throwing them out.

Dumbledore's Lack of Wisdom led to Many Atrocities

In *Harry Potter and the Deathly Hallows*, we learn a lot about the great wizard Albus Dumbledore. When Dumbledore was young, he and his friend Gellert Grindelwald wanted to make the world a better place. They decided that the world would be a better place if wizards took over the world and ruled over those who weren't wizards. They knew that the muggles (non-wizards) would not want this, and would wage war against the wizards if the wizards tried to take over the muggle world. They also knew that many people would die in this war, but decided that this was ok because in the end, it would all be worth it because the world would be a better place. In a letter to Grindelwald, Dumbledore writes the following

> *Your point about Wizard dominance being FOR THE MUGGLES' OWN GOOD – this, I think, is the crucial point. Yes, we have been given power and yes, that power gives us the right to rule, but it also gives us responsibilities over the ruled. We must stress this point, it will be the foundation stone upon which we build. Where we are opposed, as we surely will be, this must be the basis of all our counterarguments. We seize control FOR THE GREATER GOOD.*

Dumbledore eventually realized that he was in the wrong. Grindelwald did not, and actually tried to put into action their plan to make the world a better place. According to Hermione, "'For the Greater Good' became Grindelwald's slogan, his justification for all the atrocities he committed later." So, to summarize, two people had good intentions (they wanted to make the world a better place); however, they just ended up committing a bunch of atrocities that created a lot of suffering. They didn't understand the world enough to realize why they were in the wrong, and why their actions would only ever make the world a worse place.

The Spirit of Magic by Virgil

As Dumbledore grew older, he became more mature, and he acquired greater wisdom and understanding. As a result, his views regarding what he had to do for the greater good changed dramatically.

Again, I'm not saying that you shouldn't try to make the world a better place until you are a wise adept, because I don't believe that at all and such an assertion is at complete odds with my values and the values at the heart of magic. On the contrary, I believe you should be constantly trying to make the world a better place. Everyone has a little bit of power, and when you use that power to serve Divine Providence by making the world a better place, you show Divine Providence that you are capable of using the power you do have wisely, which makes it more likely that Divine Providence will grant you more power by allowing you to make progress in your magical training. Tutoring struggling schoolchildren, volunteering at soup kitchens, treating others with kindness, standing up for those who are bullied, listening with empathy to the troubled, and cleaning up litter are just a small handful of ways you can make the world a better place, and it's hard to imagine how doing any of these things could be unwise. However, powerful magic can be used unwisely, and can seriously disturb "the Balance and the Pattern" (I like that phrase) if it is used unwisely. The point I am trying to make in this section is that the more power you have, the more wisdom you need, so strive to become wise just as hard as you strive to become powerful.

Wisdom and Power

When power is used wisely, it makes the world into a better place. When power is used unwisely, it makes the world into a worse place.[59] There are many types of power – military power, political power, financial power, magical power, etc. This principle applies to any type of power.

Solomon's Sphere of Influence

King Solomon was a wise king. He made wise decisions as a king, and therefore, his kingdom was blessed. When he died, his son lacked his wisdom, so his kingdom fell apart.

We're not literal kings, but we're all metaphorical kings with metaphorical kingdoms. In modern magical jargon, your kingdom is called your "sphere of influence." It's basically what it sounds like. It's the region of creation that is within your influence. Your sphere of

Chapter 14: Wisdom

influence encompasses your family, your friends, your coworkers, and your acquaintances because all of these people can be affected by your decisions. Just as Solomon made his kingdom blessed, you can make your sphere of influence blessed.

The more progress you make in your magical training, the bigger your sphere of influence gets. Eventually, your sphere of influence will encompass the whole world. Let's say you are an everyday individual living in America. If I pick some random building in China, that building is probably outside of your sphere of influence. However, if you were a magician, you could use the technique of mental wandering to travel to the building and give it a serene atmosphere by modifying the astral environment of the building. Since you can influence the building in this way, it is within your sphere of influence. Daskalos and his students lived in Cyprus, but they often travelled to the Middle East via mental wandering to make the region more blessed.

If it is your nature to bless, then everything within your sphere of influence becomes more blessed.

Developing Wisdom 1: Wisdom via Inner Silence

Divinity is always speaking to us to give us guidance, but oftentimes, we cannot hear the voice of Divinity because of the chaos within us. By chaos, I mean the chaotic nature of our minds and our passions. They are noise that drowns out the voice of Divinity as that voice emanates from our divine essence deep within us and attempts to rise to the level of our normal waking consciousness. When we develop inner silence, then it is easier for us to hear the voice of Divinity that emanates from deep within us. The practice of emptying one's mind of all thoughts (meditation) is greatly conducive to developing inner silence because our mental chatter is one form of noise that destroys inner silence.

Developing Wisdom 2: Wisdom via an Elemental Equilibrium

For reasons discussed in Chapter 2, the closer you are to the center of the Cross of Equilibrated Forces, the easier it is for you to hear the voice of Divinity. To recap, akasha functions as kind of a window to Divinity, and akasha corresponds to the central point of the cross the same way each element corresponds to one of the four arms. The closer you are to the central point, the easier it is for you to hear the voice of

The Spirit of Magic by Virgil

Divinity as it emanates from that central point. When you have an elemental equilibrium, you stand at this central point, which makes it is easy for you to hear the voice of Divinity, and therefore to know what the will of Divinity is. Since wisdom is defined as the ability to know what the will of Divinity is, standing at the central point makes you wise.

Developing Wisdom 3: Wisdom via Understanding (Ourselves)

Since wisdom and understanding are always found together, we can acquire wisdom by acquiring understanding. When it comes to acquiring understanding, you should start by acquiring understanding of yourself. This is done via introspection. As you progress throughout your magical training, you will also gain greater understanding of other things, such as the four elements, the dynamics of the inner planes, the nature of various entities, etc. This will also increase your wisdom, because you will be able to see how to work with these things and how not to work with them.

Developing Wisdom 4: Wisdom via Compassion

As the saying goes, "Fake it 'till you make it." You can become a patient person by forcing yourself to act like a patient person. You can become an organized person by forcing yourself to act like an organized person. Similarly, you can become a wise person by forcing yourself to act like a wise person. The Kabbalists taught that Tiphereth is the child of Chockmah and Binah, meaning that compassion is born from wisdom and understanding. This implies that wise people are compassionate. If you want to become wise, act like a wise person by being compassionate toward others.

Developing Wisdom 5: Wisdom via Prayer

The master Jesus Christ told us "Ask and ye shall receive." Prayer is a powerful form of magic. In the modern esoteric world, many prayers are long and elegantly worded. I prefer short and simple prayers. Many spiritual cultures around the world advocate repeating a short prayer over and over again. This exercise is a powerful catalyst for one's spiritual evolution. The prayers are often counted on a set of beads. In the West, they are called rosaries. In the East, they are called malas. You can

Chapter 14: Wisdom

design your own rosary to use when praying for wisdom and write a short prayer asking Divine Providence for wisdom. Here's a good one.

Lord God Almighty, Creator and Maker of Heaven and Earth, please give me wisdom and understanding, please help me become more compassionate, and please help me become a magician.

As you can see, this prayer is not super fancy or overly poetic. It's respectfully worded and to the point. Repeat it over and over, using your rosary to count.

Wise People Don't Brag About Their Wisdom

Clearly, in the past, the idea of wisdom was considered central to magic. I sincerely want this to be the case again. However, here I must issue a warning. At the present time, there are many false adepts and frauds in the occult community who portray themselves as great mages, adepts, or teachers for the purpose of making money or satisfying their ego. Many of them run orders or groups and are constantly trying to attract more members. If the general magical community ever relearns the importance of wisdom, then in the future, it is only natural for such individuals to go around proclaiming how wise they are. When encountering these individuals, it is important to remember Solomon's teachings – "Do you see a man wise in his own eyes? There is more hope for a fool than for him." Wisdom comes from understanding. The more you understand, the more you realize how much you don't understand. Einstein put it this way – "As the circle of light increases, so does the circumference of darkness around it." People who don't understand much don't understand that they don't understand much. Therefore, they think they understand everything and go around bragging about how wise they are. People who understand a lot understand that there is a lot more to understand, so they don't go around bragging about how wise they are.

Since compassion is so closely tied with wisdom, someone who goes around bragging about how compassionate he is should also be viewed as nothing more than a fool. Truly wise and compassionate people don't brag about how wise and compassionate they are.

Chapter 15: Caring for Your Garden

Love is the source of wisdom, power, and service.

~William Mistele

I am not afraid of demons, larvae, or phantoms. I am, however, afraid of people, because people can be incomprehensibly cruel. The world, as a result, is often a needlessly cruel place. In Chapter 16, we'll discuss rectifying that, but in this chapter, I want to discuss something else. Helping my loved ones, including my family members, survive, grow, and flourish in this world has always been and continues to be one of my primary motivations for pursuing the wisdom and power magic has to offer. In the following sections, I share some thoughts regarding this subject.

On Being Serious

Bill's well-known five-part series of essays "Problems in the Study of Magic" is without a doubt one of the greatest treasures he has given to the worldwide magical community. This series of essays is exactly what it says it is – a discussion of some of the problems students may face when studying magic. This essay series has many aspects, and some of them are particularly interesting. One of these particularly interesting aspects of this essay series is the way it begins – in other words the first paragraph of the first essay in the series.

Bill begins his series of essays with a paragraph establishing a distinction between magic and something he calls "pretend magic." Clearly, he believes that this is an important distinction to make; after all, his essays are clearly intended for students of magic, and not for students of "pretend magic." The concept of "pretend magic" is one I have given a lot of thought to during the years since I first read that paragraph. When confronted with this concept, a number of questions arise in my mind. What is "pretend magic"? What is the difference between "pretend magic" and genuine magic? What is the goal of "pretend magic"?

Imagine an ideal student of magic. Examine him closely. This is the person you think is the perfect candidate for initiation. He is the person who possesses the combination of qualities that will allow him to advance the most rapidly along the magical path. If you could find one

The Spirit of Magic by Virgil

word to describe this person, what would that word be? For me, that word is "serious."

And this word, I think, forms the starting point for any analysis of the differences between "pretend magic" and genuine magic. Genuine magic is a serious matter, a "life-long discipline that engenders encounters with power and profound mystery." On the other hand, "pretend magic" is not serious. It's roleplaying with fancy tools, ego games, drama, dabbling, occult miscellanea, or any number of other frivolous things. The student of "pretend magic" is not serious. The student of genuine magic is serious. What is he serious about? This is an extraordinarily important question. Other ways of asking "What is the student of magic serious about?" include "Why does the student of magic train?" and "What inspires the student of magic to train?" and "What purpose does the student of magic hope to eventually accomplish with the help of his training?".

Seriousness implies several things. It implies organization, focus, and discipline. A good student of magic is a serious student, but one must be serious about something. So what exactly is the student of magic serious about? Why exactly does he train and practice magic? Some magical orders make prospective students answer this question on their application forms, and more often than not, the responses received are just canned responses – "I want to find the light," or "I want to realize my higher self," or something of that sort. These responses are trite and cliché. Very little thought has been given to them, and they are close to meaningless. What is the "light"? What is a "higher self"?

When you are faced with the question of why you are undergoing magical training, it is not difficult to form an intellectually pleasing answer. "I am undergoing magical training to better my life." "I am undergoing magical training to spiritually evolve." "I am undergoing magical training to find the light." On an intellectual level, these are all valid answers to the question of why you are undergoing magical training. If you were walking down the street and someone randomly came up to you and asked you why you were training in magic, then any of those answers would suffice. Of course, you can just refuse to answer and go on your merry way.

But at some point in your magical training, you will be forced to confront that question in a way that will not allow you to just run away from it. Magical training requires a lot of time and effort. When you ask yourself why you are training, you are essentially asking yourself "How can I justify spending all this time and effort on my magical training when there is plenty of other stuff I could be spending it on?" This is

Chapter 15: Caring for Your Garden

when you really have to think. Sure, practicing magic will increase the rate of your spiritual evolution; however, everyone is always spiritually evolving, even if they aren't practicing magic. Magic may accelerate the process, but what's the rush? And yeah, magical training can result in an improved life, but aren't there plenty of other extremely effective ways to improve your life that don't involve magic and that don't come with the same dangers magic does? These are some of the thoughts that may run through your mind when you reflect on the reasons you began training in magic, and whether you should continue doing so.

You're going to encounter obstacles during your training. You're going to find yourself face to face with various troubles. You're going to "spend a lot of time with your personal fears." You're going to experience setbacks. You're going to go through dark times. You may even face problems that literally no human being has ever faced before, because you are going to explore spiritual territories that are very infrequently travelled. You're going to experience many hardships no "pretend magician" would ever go through, and each of these hardships will make you ask yourself whether you should continue training and why. If you are going to continue training, you're going to need a powerful source of inspiration to motivate you to continue training. The desire to bless is one powerful source of inspiration. This desire has many variants. For example, there is the desire to bless another individual by becoming a guardian angel for that individual, which was discussed in Chapter 13. There is also the desire to bless one's family by becoming a guardian angel for your family, as discussed in the remainder of this chapter. There is also the desire to bless society by becoming a guardian angel for society, as discussed in Chapter 16.

The Desire to Bless One's Family

The desire to improve the lives of your family members can be a powerful source of inspiration that will motivate you to continue your magical training when you feel like giving up. There is a fake quote attributed to Buddha that goes "If you like a flower, you pluck it. If you love a flower, you water it daily." Buddha never actually said that. No one knows who first came up with the quote, but who its real author is doesn't matter. It's a beautiful teaching, and it's one of my favorite quotes. Think of your family members as flowers. For some magicians, magical training is simply the process of learning to fill, carry, and use the watering can. This allows them to care for their flowers.

The Spirit of Magic by Virgil

When you really love your family, you have a genuine desire to bless your family. This genuine desire forces you to stay focused on your training. Some people spend years dabbling in a variety of different forms of occultism. However, if you acquire a strong source of inspiration like the desire to bless your family, then you will eventually ask yourself whether all this dabbling is actually helping you to improve the lives of your family members. If you find yourself answering no to this question, then you will begin to reflect on why the answer is no, and what you need to change so that the answer eventually becomes yes.

In his book *Awaken the Inner Shaman: A Guide to the Power Path of the Heart*, José Luis Stevens writes the following about tribal magicians (shamans).

> *They are the world's oldest spiritual leaders; individuals who, among their many duties, heal the sick, perform ceremonies to harmonize the community with the environment, battle negativity, communicate with the ancestors, work with allies for the good of others, gather knowledge, teach through storytelling, act as seers and prophets, and lead their people.*

Most of us aren't part of tribes, but all of us are part of communities. One community we are a part of is our families. The properly trained magician has the ability to serve his family the same way tribal magicians serve their tribes. The magician is a spiritual leader for his family.[60] This doesn't mean he forces his spiritual beliefs onto his spouse and children. That's what a spiritual tyrant does, not a spiritual leader. Being a spiritual leader means that if his spouse and children need help finding the approach to spirituality that works best for each of them, he can give them that help. This requires having an open mind and great genuine wisdom.[61] They best approach to spirituality for an individual may be a religion, an esoteric path, an art like ballet, a hobby like gardening, or any number of other things.[62]

The magician is also a healer. There are many cruel people out there who can inflict inner wounds upon others through their words. We recognize the presence of these wounds when we feel sorrow, grief, shame, a lack of self-esteem, hopelessness, and other similar forms of inner pain. The magician, through his empathy, compassion, support, and encouragement, can help heal his family members of these inner wounds when they are inflicted upon those he loves. The practice of exercises like the Sea of Love meditation can help the magician develop these

Chapter 15: Caring for Your Garden

qualities. This exercise will teach the magician how to embody a boundless ocean of loving watery energy that absorbs emotional pain and nurtures people back to a state of inner health and inner strength.

The magician also helps his family harmonize his family with the environment. There are many ways of doing this. For example, if we are talking about the environment as in nature, the magician can teach his family members about sustainability practices that will help them lower their carbon footprints. If we are talking about a school environment, the magician can provide his children with the social skills and self-esteem they need to be comfortable in the school environment. Remember that a large part of magical training consists of understanding yourself, as discussed in Chapter 3. Understanding yourself will also help you understand others, and will therefore give you a deep understanding of human psychology in general. The result of this, as one adept put it, is that at the end of your magical training, you possess "the ability to understand personal problems from a universal perspective as one or two Ph.D.s in transpersonal psychology might impart." Possessing this level of understanding of human psychology will greatly improve your interpersonal skills, which will allow you to engage any human environment such as a school environment or work environment harmoniously, and teach others to do the same.

The magician also battles negativity. The negativity that is targeted toward your family members can come in many forms. It can come from political leaders, from other children who are bullies to your own children, from criminals, from destructive cultural trends, from malicious entities, and from his own negative traits (which he at least knows about, since they are listed on his black soul mirror). Battling negativity doesn't mean casting a binding spell at every source of negativity that affects your family, which is the naïve approach that many sorcerers try. In general, that's a bad idea. Binding spells have negative energetic side effects, and much of the darkness in our lives exists so that we may grow stronger by overcoming it in the right way. For example, if a magician's child is being bullied at school, the magician may choose to teach his child how to stand up for himself by using assertive statements and verbal judo (yes this exists).

Ancestor work can be a great way of serving one's family. Of course in the present time, the spirits of one's ancestors have all moved on and reincarnated elsewhere, but the magician can use magical methods to travel back in time or to inner realms beyond time to work with his ancestors and aid them in ways that bring harmony and joy to his family. As this is not my area of specialty, I can't provide practical

The Spirit of Magic by Virgil

advice, but there are plenty of Earthzone spirits who could assist you with this sort of work if it interests you.

The magician also works with various spirits who can aid him in blessing his family. If you read the long list of spirits and their descriptions in the second section of PME, you'll realize that all of them have the ability to provide the magician with vast amounts of knowledge. Knowledge is power, and any form of power can be used to help one's family. Of course, the magician also gathers knowledge from other sources besides spirits. Books on interpersonal skills, personal finance, parenting, relationships, and staying organized can all help him be a blessing to his family. Life experiences and other knowledgeable people are other sources of knowledge the magician can tap into.

The magician is also good at teaching through storytelling. In fact, Jesus Christ, one of the greatest magicians in history, was well-known for teaching through parables. Similar parables, fables such as those of Aesop, as well as anecdotes can be powerful teaching tools. One of my friends used to be a very high ranking executive in a large and powerful company. He told me many anecdotes about the sorts of corruption that were occurring at the higher levels of management in that company. These anecdotes taught me a lot about the nature of greed, and I occasionally pass these anecdotes on to others to teach them the importance of being vigilant and aware when dealing with the corporate world. Once while scrolling through Reddit, I came across an anecdote about something that happened at a party. Some person at the party carelessly threw a bag of chips onto the floor because he was too lazy to throw it away. Someone else slipped on the bag of chips, fell, and was paralyzed for the rest of his life. The lesson this anecdote teaches – don't do irresponsible things akin to throwing a bag of chips on the floor, because the consequences may end up being far greater than you anticipated. If I ever need to teach people the importance of acting responsibly, this anecdote is a teaching aid I could use.

The magician is also a seer and a prophet in the sense that he can foresee the effects that will come from each choice he makes, and will therefore be able to make the choices that aid his family. If he foresees danger, he can move his family to another location. If he foresees trouble, he can take measures to neutralize it before it arrives at his doorstep. This isn't a matter of looking into crystal balls and shewstones. It's a matter of vigilance and wisdom.

Finally, the magician is a leader for his family.[63] A leader is not a manager or a tyrant. Managers control others and tyrants oppress others. Leaders enable and empower others. Leaders provide others with the

Chapter 15: Caring for Your Garden

guidance they need to fulfill their highest potential. Leaders maintain peace and harmony, and build communities of love and joy.

Magical training will sharpen your intuition, balance your personality, provide you with wisdom, give you inner strength, force you to become organized, and put you in contact with astounding spiritual resources in the form of the Earthzone spirits and the ruling genii of the planetary spheres. All of this will give you the ability to bless your family, be a blessing to your family, and make the lives of your family members more blessed.

To conclude this section, I want to discuss three figures from literature. Two of them are magicians who were motivated to train and practice magic by a desire to help their family members and loved ones. One of them was given the opportunity to help another but was unable to do so; she lacked the inner strength, skill, and wisdom of a magician.

The first figure I want to discuss is Esther Smetski, from Orson Scott Card's book *Enchantment*. Esther was a magician, and she had a very clear purpose for studying magic. She wanted to help her family. At first, she was uncomfortable with magic because it went against her religion, but she realized that learning magic would allow her to keep her family safe. She and her family lived in an unstable part of Russian during a very unstable time, and therefore, her family was constantly in danger. Fortunately, with the help of her magical abilities, she was able to protect her family from the KGB, and from whatever other sources of danger surrounded them. Furthermore, because of her intuitive and divinatory abilities, she was able to sense that Ruth was not the right woman for her son Ivan to marry. When Ivan brought Katerina home and explained their situation to Esther, she was able to pass her magical knowledge onto Katerina so Katerina could use it to defeat Baba Yaga. Finally, after the final battle between Baba Yaga and the warriors of Taina, Esther continued to protect her grandchildren from harm using her knowledge of magical amulets and protective spells. Esther never became distracted from her goal of using her magic to bless, protect, and assist her family. At one point in the book, she mentions the existence of "pretend magic" and confides in Katerina that the practitioners of "pretend magic," who also call themselves magicians, embarrass her.

Esther had absolutely no desire for fancy titles and ranks. She never wanted to be a "magistra templi" or an "ipsissima." She did not advertise herself as an adept or hierophant. In fact, she knew that her family would be safer the less conspicuous it was, and therefore the less conspicuous she was. Her own husband and son did not realize she was a magician until Katerina came along and Esther agreed to teach her future daughter-

The Spirit of Magic by Virgil

in-law what she knew so she could defeat a great evil. Imagine a crazed Esther muttering "I've got to get some seeds. I've got to get some seeds, right away. Nothing's planted. I don't have a thing in the ground." The idea is ludicrous. Esther planted her garden ages ago and had already prepared herself to combat the dark forces that threatened to destroy her flowers long before those forces reached her doorstep.

Was Esther serious? The answer is definitely a resounding yes! Esther helps illustrate what I mean by serious. She was an individual who knew, willed, dared, and kept silence. As an exercise, consider the ways in which she did each of these things.

At this point, it is necessary that students of magic keep something very important in mind. At several points in time, you might do spells or rituals to help your family, just like Esther did. That's wonderful. Practical magic is a tool you can use to bless your family, assuming you use it at the right time and in the right way. However, no matter how many spells or rituals you do, the vast majority of the benefit your family will gain from your magical training will come from the maturity and the wisdom you develop within yourself while walking the path, and not from your magical skills and abilities. A mature and wise "muggle" father is infinitely better than an immature and irresponsible father that sometimes does spells and rituals to help his family. If we examine Esther, it is easy to see that she was a very mature and wise woman.

The second figure I want to discuss is Tamara, from Lermontov's poem "Demon." In this poem, there's a demon who lives an empty life completely devoid of hope, love, and light. This demon's life is a life that is saturated with despair, loneliness, sorrow, and grief. There is no one in the universe more in need of a blessing than this demon. To take a life like this demon's life and transform it into a life that is filled with joy and love is a profound magical act. The demon sees a princess named Tamara and hopes that Tamara is able to do that.

The problem is Tamara isn't a magician. Because the demon's constitution contains so much negativity and evil, his kiss is poison. When he kisses Tamara, Tamara isn't strong enough to withstand this poison, so she dies, and the demon's life remains just as hellish as it was before. As Bill writes in his beatitudes, "Blessed are those who meet others in their darkest place and walk by their side back into the light; these are the sons and daughters of God – the children of light – for there is no greater or more sacred celebration of light." Tamara met the demon in his darkest place, but was unable to walk by his side back into the light. Magical training teaches us how to find others in their darkest

Chapter 15: Caring for Your Garden

place, and to walk by their side back into the light without getting lost or overwhelmed by the darkness ourselves.

The third figure I want to discuss is Margarita, from Mikhail Bulgakov's book *The Master and Margarita*. This is perhaps my single favorite book, which is really saying something because I'm an avid reader. Margarita is a magician who dearly loves someone. The person she loves is referred to simply as "the master" and we are never given his real name. The master is a writer, but he is an unsuccessful writer and his lack of success makes him live a life of despair and hopelessness. Margarita wants the master to be happy. She wants his life to be blessed. However, she's having a hard time doing this. Why? Well the society they lived in was hellish.

The master and Margarita lived in Russia during the reign of Stalin, who ruled the country with an iron fist. Nothing that went against his views could ever be published. Imagine if Russian society at the time had promoted free speech and open-mindedness. If this had been the case, then the master, perhaps with a little help from Margarita's magic, could easily have become a famous writer, which would have made him very happy. But Russian society wasn't like that. The master's amazing potential as a writer would never be fully developed or appreciated, and there was nothing Margarita or her demon friends Woland and Azazello could do about it.

If Russian society promoted free speech and open mindedness, then it would have been very easy for Margarita to arrange for the master to become a celebrated author, but that is not the case. Russian society at the time was locked in strict censorship and corrupt idealism. These insights hint at an obvious but important truth. If the society your family lives in is blessed, then it is easier for you to build a blessed life for your family. If the society your family lives in is not blessed (we might call it "hellish" or "cursed"), then it is much more difficult for you to build a blessed life for your family. The magician who wants to build a blessed life for his family should therefore devote some of his efforts to blessing the communities his family is a part of, including society overall.

Chapter 16: Heaven on Earth

Es ist eine wunderschöne und heilige Aufgabe, der leidenden Menschheit mit seinen Kräften behilflich zu sein.

~Franz Bardon (Der Weg zum wahren Adepten)

If you are going to acquire genuine divine powers from practicing magic, then it is a really good idea at the outset to have some sort of divine purpose for which you are going to apply those powers.

~William Mistele

In his book *The Magician: His Training and Work*, W.E. Butler states that the password that unlocks access to the mysteries of magic can be found in a simple phrase – "I desire to know, in order to serve." In the play *The Fall of Atlantis*, God asks a magician what he wants, promising that he will give the magician whatever the magician asks for. The magician's reply is "May my will be in harmony with Your own – that all my actions in service to others may arise from the One Light and serve the purposes of Divine Providence." In his book *New Millennium Magic*, Donald Tyson writes that "the only worthwhile use of magical attainment is in service to the light." This idea that magicians serve something greater than themselves out of compassion is common enough to have made it into pop culture. In the movie *The Sorcerer's Apprentice*, the magician Merlin tells the character Morgana "We are but servants."

When the student becomes an initiate by completing his initiation, he gains access to the ruling genii of the Zone Girdling the Earth, more commonly referred to as the "Earthzone spirits." These spirits are knowledgeable in wide variety of subjects. Morech specializes in inventions. Tardoe specializes in methods to develop artistic talents. Baalto specializes in minerals. Pigios specializes in writing. Parmasa specializes in entertainment. Nachero specializes in animals. Amilee specializes in diseases. Butharusch specializes in cooking. The initiate who can access these spirits can learn from them. The knowledge he receives will allow him to play a significant role in the evolution of

The Spirit of Magic by Virgil

science, technology, art, entertainment, or any other aspect of human culture.

Over the past few years, several esoteric authors have written that magic is synonymous with yoga. This is simply not the case. Approaching magical training as if you were training to be a yogi instead of a magician is a choice that will lead you nowhere, yet many people choose to approach their magical training in this way because they do not know any better. Even in the Bardon community, there are individuals who claim that the Bardon system is a system of yoga, and I have seen these claims sabotage the progress of those Bardonists who choose to believe them. The basic exercises of IIH – meditation, introspection, and self-discipline – will benefit you regardless of whether you think you are training to be a yogi or a magician. However, if you continue to train as a yogi, then at some point you will find yourself unable to penetrate any further into the mysteries of magic, as those mysteries are for magicians.

Magic differs from the other esoteric disciplines in that it is oriented toward service. Some people learn this and immediately reject this path, thinking that it means magicians live a life of suffering because they neglect their own happiness and well-being so they can instead constantly focus on helping others find happiness and well-being. This is not true at all. The magician serves Divine Providence by fulfilling her will. It is the will of Divine Providence that the lives of all creatures, including your own, be blessed. Thus, working to make your own life blessed is a way of serving Divine Providence. The magician also serves society by increasing the amount of joy and wonder in society. You are a member of society, so increasing the amount of joy and wonder in your own life is part of serving society. Thus, being a magician doesn't mean you live a life of suffering. However the magician, being a compassionate individual, will not be satisfied serving Divine Providence and society by just improving his own life. He knows he has the potential to do far more than that, and the purpose of magical training is nothing other than to help him fulfill his highest potential.

Some of the other esoteric disciplines, particularly those that are mystical in nature, are only forms of spirituality. Magic is only in part a form of spirituality because it is also in part a form of science, in part a form of art, and in part a form of engineering. The magician is a spiritually awakened individual who is also an artist, a scientist, and an engineer.

The structural engineer applies his understanding of the universe to solve problems. He understands concepts like the equilibrium of forces and the equilibrium of moments. He understands Mohr's circle and the implications of Poisson's ratio. He understands how the eccentricity of a

Chapter 16: Heaven on Earth

load may affect how a beam buckles. He understands how residual stresses may affect the integrity of a structural member. He understands how a beam's elastic modulus affects how much it deflects. Because he understands these things, he can make wise decisions when he improves the world through his engineering feats.

The geotechnical engineer applies his understanding of the universe to solve problems. He understands how the cohesion and internal friction angle of a soil affect its ability to support a foundation. He understands how groundwater can influence the effective stress of soil. He understands the dangers posed by Karst topography and expansive bedrock. He understands how a line load may influence the consolidation of underlying soil. He understands the way a soil's cohesive properties may affect the side resistance of piles driven into the soil. He understands how lateral earth pressures may affect retaining walls. He understands the way rain can affect slope stability. Because he understands these things, he can make wise decisions when he improves the world through his engineering feats.

The air quality engineer applies his understanding of the universe to solve problems. He understands how aerosols can serve as ice nucleating particles that affect the composition of clouds and reduce radiative forcing. He understands that mass in a closed system can be neither created nor destroyed, and that therefore a mass balance can be used to model the transport of air pollutants. He understands Mie theory, and therefore knows how the size of atmospheric particles can influence visibility. He understands ozone chemistry, how the production of hydroxide radicals is reduced, and the way volatile organic compounds are oxidized. Because he understands these things, he can make wise decisions when he improves the world through his engineering feats.

The magician applies his understanding of the universe to solve problems. He understands that the physical, astral, and mental planes often affect each other and imitate each other in accordance with the principle "as above, so below." He understands that the astral body cannot travel past the Earthzone or the astral matrix connecting it to the physical body will snap, resulting in the phenomenon known as "death." He understands that the mental body can travel past the Earthzone only to the extent that it is balanced and mature. He understands the difference between the etheric body and the astral matrix. He understands the way the electric and magnetic fluids give rise to the four elements. He understands the way the four elements produces illnesses when they are not in harmony with each other in the body. He understands the way karma determines the set of influences on our lives that some call "fate." Most importantly, he understands the Balance and the Pattern. He applies

The Spirit of Magic by Virgil

this knowledge and understanding to improve the world through his magical feats.

To walk the path of a magician is to walk the path of an engineer. Engineers find solutions to problems. They solve problems by making wise decisions, and they base their wise decisions on their understanding of the universe. The difference between magicians and conventional engineers is that conventional engineers only understand the physical level of the universe, but magicians understand the physical, astral, mental, and akashic levels of the universe.

The path of the engineer is not a path for everyone, and therefore, neither is the path of the magician. There is no wrong in choosing to walk the path of the engineer because you realize it is the right path for you. There is also no wrong in choosing not to walk the path of the engineer because you realize it is not the right path for you. The only wrong lies in clinging to a path that is not the write one for you because you do not understand the path well enough to realize that it is not the right one for you. If you are training to become a magician, whether through the use of Bardon's magical training system or some other complete, balanced, and efficient system, then you are training to become an engineer. If you do not understand this, then there will always be mysteries in this path you will not understand, no matter how hard you grapple with them.

Divine Missions

One way that the magician blesses society is by fulfilling divine missions. These are long-term projects that improve the world in some major way. An extensive list of divine missions can be found on Bill's site. In this section, I briefly describe four of those divine missions.

<u>Improving the Global Economy</u>

To fulfil this divine mission, you work with a spirit named Ambriel who is one of the ruling genii of the Sphere of Jupiter. Using the techniques described by Bardon in PME, you bring the vibration of Ambriel to the human realm so that it can inspire people who can make a big impact on the global economy. This inspiration will help them "put the financial system in order, avoid needless suffering, accelerate innovation, and empower economic recovery without destroying the Earth in the process." Ego inflation is a potential danger when doing this kind of intense work with the Sphere of Jupiter and its vibrations, but it is only a danger for those who do not have an elemental equilibrium.

Chapter 16: Heaven on Earth

Increase World Peace by Eliminating Unnecessary War

To fulfil this divine mission, you work with a spirit named Achaiah who is one of the ruling genii of the Sphere of Mercury. Using the technique of mental wandering, you travel to Achaiah's domain and learn to embody his vibration, which creates peace and dissolves conflict. Then you hold in your mind a war or conflict and allow Achaiah's vibration to permeate it. This will cause the war/conflict to dissolve and transform into peace and harmony.

Bring the Mysteries of Silence to Humanity

The power of silence holds many profound mysteries, and the currently existing spiritual traditions of the world have barely scratched the surface of any of them. In this divine mission, you learn about the mysteries of silence from many spirits who are experts in this field, such as the gnome Musar and the Earthzone spirit Alosom, and then transmit what you learn to the rest of humanity through writing, teaching, or other means.

Chapter 17: The Golden Key

"The Golden Key" is an initiatory story written by George MacDonald. This means it illustrates the process of initiation through symbols. Each aspiring initiate will see parallels between Tangle's journey and the journey they are currently undergoing as they work through their own initiation. Since each initiation system is different, the story will generate different insights in the students of different initiation systems.

The process of initiation can be divided into distinct stages. Similarly, this story can be divided into distinct stages. Those stages and their corresponding steps of IIH are as follows.

Grandmother's Cottage – Step 1
Old Man of the Sea – Step 2
Old Man of the Earth – Steps 3 and 4
Old Man of the Fire – Steps 5, 6, 7, and 8
Rainbow – PME

Most who read this story can only wonder what adventures befell Mossy and Tangle after entering the rainbow. The individual who has been blessed enough to discover a valid system of magical initiation has no need to wonder. He knows he will learn the answer once he himself also enters the rainbow.

There was a boy who used to sit in the twilight and listen to his great-aunt's stories.

The very first line of the story states that Mossy liked to listen to his great-aunt's stories. In KTQ, Bardon writes the following,

> *For someone initiated into magic and Quabbalah who understands the symbolic language, fairy tales reveal many mysteries, since he is used to looking at all events with quite different eyes than common people do. A hermetic will not be surprised to realize that he was already fond of fairy tales in his childhood, and that he still likes to reflect on their content in later years, since he understands their high and true sense which can only be read between the lines.*

The Spirit of Magic by Virgil

Since Mossy was "fond of fairy tales in his childhood," we can predict that he will grow up to be a great magician. His spirit desires to penetrate into the mysteries of magic, and since he can intuitively sense the profound magical mysteries hidden within fairy tales, he is fascinated with them, and loves to listen to his great-aunt tell him fairy tales. By the time he and Tangle enter the rainbow together, he will have undergone many strange adventures, but all of it will have started with the secret knowledge contained within his great-aunt's fairy tales.

She told him that if he could reach the place where the end of the rainbow stands he would find there a golden key.
"And what is the key for?" the boy would ask. "What is it the key of? What will it open?"
"That nobody knows," his aunt would reply. "He has to find that out."

The golden key represents compassion, and it opens the door to the rainbow. The rainbow represents the planetary spheres that the initiate enters one by one during the work of PME. Only an initiate fully understands the nature of the planetary spheres. Bill, who became an initiate after working through IIH, has spent many years exploring the planetary spheres and talking to the ruling genii of each sphere. He has written many essays about the planetary spheres and their ruling genii to share what he has learned. However, when it comes to understanding the planetary spheres and their inhabitants, Bill's essays can only take you so far. For full understanding, you need to "find that out" yourself by traveling to the planetary spheres. Mossy's great-aunt is not an initiate, so she doesn't know much about the inner realms an initiate enters after obtaining the golden key. Therefore, she can't answer Mossy's questions, but tells him that he must discover the answers to those questions himself.

"I suppose, being gold," the boy once said, thoughtfully, "that I could get a good deal of money for it if I sold it."
"Better never find it than sell it," returned his aunt.

It might be hard to see how, but compassion is a gift from Divine Providence. Consider the following passage from one of Rawn's articles about karma.

Chapter 17: The Golden Key

Karma is best described by the Golden Rule: "Do unto others as you would have others do unto you." The part that's usually left out is: "For surely, what you do unto others will, in the end, be done unto you." This expresses the fact that we live in a reciprocal universe wherein every causation creates an effect that ultimately returns to its source.

When you are compassionate, you treat others with compassion. Since we live in a reciprocal universe, this means that you get treated with compassion too. If you are mean instead of compassionate, then you will be treated meanly by others and your life won't be pleasant. Having compassion prevents you from generating negative karma and helps you generate positive karma. This is just one of many ways compassion is a gift from Divine Providence. If you were to reject this gift by trying to sell it, you would be showing Divine Providence that you don't appreciate this wonderful gift, and Divine Providence would no longer give you gifts. Divine Providence's gifts are all blessings, so this would result in you living a life void of blessings. This is why Mossy's great-aunt tells him "Better never find it than sell it."

And the boy went to bed and dreamed about the golden key.

Stories have a magic of their own. When we listen to them, they can sink into us and transform our inner lives. This is why magicians often need to be careful about what stories they expose themselves to. Our dreams tell us a lot about our inner lives. I remember one time my friends and I went to see a horrifying and violent movie. I didn't want to see that particular movie, but I went anyway because I did want to spend time with my friends. Later that night, my dreams were filled with horrifying and violent images. The story contained in the movie disturbed my inner life. However, stories can also change our inner lives for the better too. The story Mossy's great-aunt told him sunk into his inner life and awakened a desire to obtain the golden key. This is why he dreams about the golden key.

Now all that his great-aunt told the boy about the golden key would have been nonsense, had it not been that their little house stood on the borders of Fairyland. For it is perfectly well known that out of Fairyland nobody ever can find where the rainbow stands.

The Spirit of Magic by Virgil

The creature takes such good care of its golden key, always flitting from place to place, lest anyone should find it!

Fairyland is the world of magic – the world of grimoires, talismans, spells, wands, sigils, spirits, and initiation. I think we all remember the door we used to enter Fairyland. When I was in third grade, I was exploring my elementary school's library and I came across a book about parapsychology. That book was my door to fairyland. I read that book and soon developed an interest in the paranormal, and then an interest in the supernatural, and eventually an interest in hardcore magic. When you do not believe in something greater than yourself or in anything beyond the physical, in other words if you believe that we are matter and nothing more, then you have little incentive to develop virtues like compassion. Instead, you spend your time and energy pursuing material pleasures because there is nothing else you consider worthy of pursuing. A compassionate nature will always remain elusive to such people. However, people who have an exposure to the teachings of magic (have been to the borders of Fairyland) understand the value of compassion and strive to develop it. A compassionate nature is not elusive to them, but is something they will eventually attain through their striving.

But in Fairyland it is quite different. Things that look real in this country look very thin indeed in Fairyland, while some of the things that here cannot stand still for a moment, will not move there. So it was not in the least absurd of the old lady to tell her nephew such things about the golden key.

Fairyland is the land of magic, and its inhabitants are magicians and the beings they work with. Things that seem valuable to non-magicians often seem valueless to magicians, and things that seem valuable to magicians often seem valueless to non-magicians. Compassion is one example of this. Many non-magicians view compassion as a form of weakness, and therefore believe it to be valueless. Magicians, however, know that compassion is immensely valuable. An expensive car might seem extremely valuable to a non-magician. A magician might appreciate an expensive car and think it would be nice to have one, but he understands that in the grand scheme of things, there are many things that are more valuable.

**"Did you ever know anybody find it?" he asked, one evening.
"Yes. Your father, I believe, found it."**

Chapter 17: The Golden Key

Mossy's father found the golden key, but that doesn't necessarily mean Mossy will find the golden key. We all have to search for the golden key in order to find it.

"And what did he do with it, can you tell me?"
"He never told me."

Compassionate people do compassionate things because they want to help others, and not because they want praise. If you see someone going around bragging about the compassionate things he has done, he isn't a compassionate person. He just wants praise and recognition. Mossy's father didn't go around telling others about the compassionate things he did, so his great-aunt has no idea what compassionate things he did.

"What was it like?"
"He never showed it to me."

Mossy's father took measures to do his compassionate deeds in secret. He understood that this ensured that his compassionate actions were truly done out of compassion, and not to garner praise for himself.

"How does a new key come there always?"
"I don't know. There it is."

Everyone has the capacity to become compassionate, so there is a golden key for every person in the world.

"Perhaps it is the rainbow's egg."
"Perhaps it is. You will be a happy boy if you find the nest."

An animal's egg contains that animal in potential. For example, a raven's egg contains a raven in potential. That doesn't mean a raven's egg is a raven. It just means that it could become a raven someday. The rainbow's egg contains a rainbow, or rather the wisdom and knowledge of the rainbow, in potential. In other words, compassion contains within it the potential to blossom into the wisdom and knowledge of all the planetary spheres. This is because with compassion, one can travel to each planetary sphere and acquire wisdom and knowledge from its ruling genii.

The Spirit of Magic by Virgil

"Perhaps it comes tumbling down the rainbow from the sky."
"Perhaps it does."

In the Zohar, the sky is used as a symbol for Kether. The quality of compassion corresponds to Tiphereth. You might notice that many deities associated with Tiphereth, such as Jesus, were highly compassionate. Tiphereth is the reflection of Kether on a "lower" level that is more comprehendible to the human mind.

One evening, in summer, he went into his own room and stood at the lattice-window, and gazed into the forest which fringed the outskirts of Fairyland. It came close up to his great-aunt's garden, and, indeed, sent some straggling trees into it.

The story notes the separation between the forest and the great-aunt's garden. The great-aunt's garden is reminiscent of the Garden of Eden, which represents a state of innocence, naivety, and being sheltered. Those who stay in the garden will be content, but to become strong and achieve gnosis, you must venture out of the garden and into the forest. In the Tarot, this is represented by the innocent and naïve Fool, who is about to step off the cliff and into the unknown.

The forest lay to the east, and the sun, which was setting behind the cottage, looked straight into the dark wood with his level red eye.

The forest is toward the east of the cottage. This is the direction that Mossy must go. This is the direction of the sun, the country whence the shadows fall. The actual literal sun is setting, indicating that a certain period of Mossy's life is ending so that a new period can begin. As soon as you consciously strive for spiritual knowledge, it is indeed the case that a new period of your life begins.

The trees were all old, and had few branches below, so that the sun could see a great way into the forest and the boy, being keen-sighted, could see almost as far as the sun.

In the introduction of his book *The Esoteric Practice*, Daskalos lists five skills that are essential for those who want to begin the sort of spiritual training that leads to initiation. Those five skills are observation, concentration, visualization, introspection, and meditation. Mossy is described as "keen-sighted." There are several layers of meaning

Chapter 17: The Golden Key

contained in this description, but one layer of meaning alludes to Mossy's good observation skills. Most people cannot observe, or rather, they cannot observe accurately. Their biases, prejudices, and preconceptions distort their vision. During our magical training, we must free ourselves from our biases, prejudices, and preconceptions so that we can observe things clearly. This is very difficult because oftentimes, we are not even aware of the biases, prejudices, and preconceptions that we possess. Hopefully when we introspect while creating our black soul mirrors, we succeed in identifying some of them and listing them. Once we are aware of them, it is easier to free ourselves from them.

The trunks stood like rows of red columns in the shine of the red sun, and he could see down aisle after aisle in the vanishing distance.

Entering the forest is the first stage of Mossy's initiatory journey. The trees in front of him are red, alluding to Mars/Geburah, the sphere associated with the concept of self-discipline. This means that the beginning stages of the aspiring magician's initiatory journey will constantly test and develop his self-discipline.

And as he gazed into the forest he began to feel as if the trees were all waiting for him, and had something they could not go on with till he came to them. But he was hungry and wanted his supper. So he lingered.

Mossy feels called to enter the forest and begin his initiatory journey. However, he doesn't do so because he doesn't have a clear purpose in mind. Many people enter the world of magic without a clear purpose in mind. They read magical books and practice magical exercises but they don't really do anything productive because they don't arrange this reading and practicing around a specific goal they are trying to achieve. The magical world has its dangers, and it doesn't make much sense to expose yourself to those dangers for no reason. So, don't enter this world unless you have a good reason to or a goal you are trying to achieve.

Suddenly, far among the trees, as far as the sun could shine, he saw a glorious thing. It was the end of a rainbow, large and brilliant. He could count all seven colours, and could see shade after shade beyond the violet; while before the red stood a colour more gorgeous and mysterious still. It was a colour he had never seen before. Only

The Spirit of Magic by Virgil

the spring of the rainbow-arch was visible. He could see nothing of it above the trees.

The rainbow is composed of seven colors that represent the seven planetary spheres whose vibrations affect the human realm. These planetary spheres are the Sphere of the Moon, the Sphere of Mercury, the Sphere of Venus, the Sphere of the Sun, the Sphere of Mars, the Sphere of Jupiter, and the Sphere of Saturn.

The last color of the rainbow, violet, corresponds to the Sphere of Saturn. Beyond the Sphere of Saturn are many other planetary spheres, but since these do not directly impact the human realm, human magicians don't discuss them very often. In PME, Bardon writes that the magician who is advanced enough to travel to the Sphere of Saturn "will have found out for certain that there exist, beyond the Saturn sphere, numerous other spheres, which have no direct influence on our Earth or on the zone girdling our Earth." This is why Mossy sees "shade after shade beyond the violet."

Some of those shades aren't even in the visible part of the light spectrum. In PME, Bardon writes the following.

> *As soon as he gets near the sphere he plans to visit, he will perceive, by force of transcendental clairvoyance, the colour of that sphere, thus being able to carry through the appropriate accumulation of light power in the universe, before entering the sphere in question. There exist oscillations the colours of which cannot be compared with any of the colours known to us and which therefore cannot be described. Nevertheless, the transcendental eye sees them and can cause the appropriate light oscillation to be evoked in the mental body, making the contact with that sphere and the beings living there.*

The first color of the rainbow, red, corresponds to the Sphere of the Moon. The Sphere of the Moon is actually silver and the Sphere of Mars is red, but in this symbolic story, the Sphere of the Moon is represented by the red part of the rainbow because red is the first color of the rainbow and the Sphere of the Moon is the first planetary sphere the magician visits.

Before the red part of the rainbow, there is another part that is composed of a color "more gorgeous and mysterious still." This is the Earthzone, which encompasses the human realm of everyday life. Mossy

Chapter 17: The Golden Key

has never seen this color before, and it is not difficult to see why. In his book *The Six Pillars of Self-Esteem*, Nathaniel Branden writes the following.

> *In virtually all of the great spiritual and philosophical traditions of the world, there appears some form of the idea that most human beings are sleepwalking through their own existence.*

This is true. In fact, if you examine Step 1, you'll find that it's largely about waking up. The present-mindedness exercise makes you mentally aware and vigilant of what is going on at the present moment. The soul mirror creation exercise also wakes you up to the existence of aspects of yourself that you previously knew nothing about. Even the exercise of washing in cool water in the morning wakes you up in a sense.

Mossy has been sleepwalking throughout his existence, which is why he has never seen the color of the Earthzone before, despite the fact that the human realm of everyday life that he has been living in is within the Earthzone. However, now that he is starting to wake up, he can see the color of the Earthzone and realizes that the Earthzone is more gorgeous and more mysterious than the other planetary spheres. This would implies that one's daily life can be more gorgeous and mysterious than the fascinating realms that exist on the inner planes.

"The golden key!" he said to himself, and darted out of the house, and into the wood.

Mossy now has a purpose to enter the forest. He has seen the rainbow. Similarly, the student who reads PME and learns about the knowledge he can gain once he becomes an initiate will have a good reason to enter the world of magic by pursuing initiation. These students have "seen the rainbow" in a sense, but they are far from being able to enter the rainbow.

He had not gone far before the sun set. But the rainbow only glowed the brighter. For the rainbow of Fairyland is not dependent upon the sun, as ours is.

The Spirit of Magic by Virgil

The rainbow does not depend on the physical sun to exist. The light which sustains the planetary spheres is not the sort of physical light that emanates from the physical sun, but a different light altogether. This light is called "aur" in Kabbalah and it continually pours through Kether to sustain the universe.

The trees welcomed him. The bushes made way for him. The rainbow grew larger and brighter; and at length he found himself within two trees of it.

Mossy wants the golden key, which represents compassion. The universe is making it easy for him to reach the spot of the golden key. When you genuinely strive to become more compassionate, the universe will help you because compassionate love is the purpose underlying the universe.

It was a grand sight, burning away there in silence, with its gorgeous, its lovely, its delicate colours, each distinct, all combining. He could now see a great deal more of it. It rose high into the blue heavens, but bent so little that he could not tell how high the crown of the arch must reach. It was still only a small portion of a huge bow.

Mossy has no idea what the full scope of the rainbow is. Similarly, the student of magic who has just begun his initiation has no idea what the full scope of the inner planes is. You can get a sense of its immensity by reading Bardon's brief description of the planetary spheres in PME, but you won't really know their true scope until you have mastered the technique of mental wandering and begun exploring them yourself.

He stood gazing at it till he forgot himself with delight--even forgot the key which he had come to seek. And as he stood it grew more wonderful still. For in each of the colours, which was as large as the column of a church, he could faintly see beautiful forms slowly ascending as if by the steps of a winding stair. The forms appeared irregularly--now one, now many, now several, now none--men and women and children--all different, all beautiful.

This is one of my favorite passages. In the microcosm, Tiphereth represents one's inner divine nature. The meaning of "Tiphereth" is "beauty." In Chapter 2, I showed that initiation is in part a process of purifying and balancing your personality. When you have a purified and

Chapter 17: The Golden Key

balanced personality (a purified elemental equilibrium), then the light of your inner divine nature can shine outwards without being blocked or distorted by the impurities and imbalances of your personality. Thus, you are perceived as being beautiful.

The people in the rainbow are all initiates. They have purified and balanced their personalities, and as a result, their personalities don't block and distort the light of their inner divine natures as it shines outward. Thus, Mossy perceives them as being beautiful.

The people in the rainbow are "all different." That's because each person's inner divine nature is a unique divine spark. No two are the same, and therefore, no two initiates are the same. People who have not yet liberated themselves from Nahash are subject to the astral currents that flow through society. This means they always jump on the latest bandwagon and join the latest fashion trend like everyone else does. They lose their uniqueness.[64]

He drew nearer to the rainbow. It vanished. He started back a step in dismay. It was there again, as beautiful as ever. So he contented himself with standing as near it as he might, and watching the forms that ascended the glorious colours towards the unknown height of the arch, which did not end abruptly but faded away in the blue air, so gradually that he could not say where it ceased.

Have you ever heard the phrase "so close yet so far." In one sense, Mossy is close to the rainbow because he can see it right in front of him. Yet in another sense, Mossy is far from the rainbow because every time he tries to get closer to the rainbow, the rainbow vanishes.

Students who have just discovered IIH are so close yet so far from entering the planetary spheres. On one hand, they know what they have to do – work through the first eight steps. Thus, they're in a better position than all those aspiring magicians who don't know what they're doing and are just walking in circles. On the other hand, working through IIH isn't exactly something you can do overnight. This is why they're so close yet so far from the rainbow.

When the thought of the golden key returned, the boy very wisely proceeded to mark out in his mind the space covered by the foundation of the rainbow, in order that he might know where to search, should the rainbow disappear. It was based chiefly upon a bed of moss.

The Spirit of Magic by Virgil

This is interesting. The foundation of the rainbow is where the golden key is, and it is "based chiefly upon a bed of moss." This bed of moss alludes to Mossy's name. The golden key is his golden key. It's not his dad's golden key. It's not your golden key. It's not my golden key. It's his golden key. Compassion is a trait. A talent for painting is also a trait. Those who possess this trait express it by painting. No two talented painters paint the same way. Each talented painter has his own unique style. Those who possess the trait of compassion express it by reducing the amount of suffering in the world and increasing the amount of joy in the world. This is essentially what the art of magic is, and each magician will have his own style when it comes to using this art.

Meantime it had grown quite dark in the wood. The rainbow alone was visible by its own light. But the moment the moon rose the rainbow vanished. Nor could any change of place restore the vision to the boy's eyes. So he threw himself down upon the mossy bed, to wait till the sunlight would give him a chance of finding the key. There he fell fast asleep.

The sun is a symbol of Tiphereth and the moon is a symbol of Yesod. When the Tree of Life is used as a model of the microcosm, Tiphereth represents one's inner divine nature, Yesod represents one's personality, and Malkuth represents one's actions. There is a well-known Kabbalistic teaching that the channel between Tiphereth and Malkuth must be clear so that the light of Tiphereth can pass into Malkuth. This means that our physical actions reflect our inner divine nature. In other words, we act in accordance with our inner divine nature. Since Yesod is between Tiphereth and Malkuth, how easily the light of Tiphereth can reach Malkuth really depends on the state of Yesod. When one's personality is unbalanced, it distorts the light of Tiphereth as it tries to reach Malkuth. When one's personality is impure, it blocks the light of Tiphereth as it tries to reach Malkuth. For the light of Tiphereth to reach Malkuth unaffected, one's personality must be pure and balanced. In other words, one must have a purified elemental equilibrium.

This concept is actually one of the most important concepts in traditional Kabbalah. The metaphor most often used to illustrate this concept is that the prince Tiphereth must be married to the princess Malkuth so that Tiphereth can stick his penis into Malkuth and ejaculate his light into her. When your actions reflect your inner divine nature, you are said to be "righteous." The concept of righteousness was associated with Yesod because the state of Yesod determined how easily the light of

Chapter 17: The Golden Key

Tiphereth could reach Malkuth and be reflected outward into the world via one's actions. A righteous person (*tzadik*) was also said to be a pipe (*tzinor*). This was a reference to his personality/Yesod which was a pipe that allowed the light of Tiphereth to pass into Malkuth easily.

The moon blocks the light of the sun, causing the rainbow to vanish. This means that Mossy's personality is unbalanced and impure, and that this prevents him from accessing the rainbow. To have access to the rainbow is to be an initiate. Initiation, as I've shown in Chapter 2, is in part a process of balancing and purifying your personality.

When he woke in the morning the sun was looking straight into his eyes. He turned away from it, and the same moment saw a brilliant little thing lying on the moss within a foot of his face. It was the golden key. The pipe of it was of plain gold, as bright as gold could be. The handle was curiously wrought and set with sapphires. In a terror of delight he put out his hand and took it, and had it.

The planetary spheres are the sephiroth in the macrocosm. There are many theories about the origin of the word "sephirah." One theory is that it comes from the Hebrew word for sapphire. Thus, the sapphires on the handle of the key hint at what the key opens – a doorway to the planetary spheres.

He lay for a while, turning it over and over, and feeding his eyes upon its beauty.

Compassion is indeed beautiful.

Then he jumped to his feet, remembering that the pretty thing was of no use to him yet. Where was the lock to which the key belonged? It must be somewhere, for how could anybody be so silly as make a key for which there was no lock? Where should he go to look for it? He gazed about him, up into the air, down to the earth, but saw no keyhole in the clouds, in the grass, or in the trees.

It opens a door to the planetary spheres, which are on the inner planes. An initiate is, by definition, someone who can travel through the inner planes. To become an initiate, one must undergo initiation, which is a long process. It will be a long time before Mossy is able to use the key to unlock the door it was designed for, but he will get there eventually. So will you if you persist.

The Spirit of Magic by Virgil

Just as he began to grow disconsolate, however, he saw something glimmering in the wood. It was a mere glimmer that he saw, but he took it for a glimmer of rainbow, and went towards it.-- And now I will go back to the borders of the forest.

There are many times in our training when we may feel disconsolate. When this happens, we should follow the guidance of our intuitions. The glimmer Mossy sees comes from an air-fish, which represents his intuition.

Not far from the house where the boy had lived, there was another house, the owner of which was a merchant, who was much away from home. He had lost his wife some years before, and had only one child, a little girl, whom he left to the charge of two servants, who were very idle and careless. So she was neglected and left untidy, and was sometimes ill-used besides.

Magical training will make you stronger and more mature, but you need to already have attained a certain level of strength and maturity before beginning your training. I know I've said that many times already but it's worth repeating. The people who don't have that level of strength and maturity often find themselves stuck on Step 1 and unable to move on until they acquire the necessary level of strength and maturity. This isn't impossible. It just requires effort and a strategic approach.

The hardships we experience in life make us stronger and more mature in some ways. This doesn't mean that we shouldn't try to improve our lives. Positive and joyful experiences nurture our spirits and make us stronger and more mature in other ways. However, if there are hardships we need to undergo to strengthen certain areas of our personality, we should not avoid them but recognize them as the teachers they are. This girl is destined to become a magician, so Divine Providence has given her the experiences she needs in order to become strong and mature. Many of those experiences were hardships.

Now it is well known that the little creatures commonly known as fairies, though there are many different kinds of fairies in Fairyland, have an exceeding dislike to untidiness. Indeed, they are quite spiteful to slovenly people. Being used to all the lovely ways of the trees and flowers, and to the neatness of the birds and all woodland creatures, it makes them feel miserable, even in their deep

Chapter 17: The Golden Key

woods and on their grassy carpets, to think that within the same moonlight lies a dirty, uncomfortable, slovenly house.

Magical work involves weaving balanced and harmonious patterns in the inner worlds that support and manifest balance and harmony in the outer physical world. Since balance and harmony are important values in magic, chaos, messiness, and disorganization are anathema to magicians and to magic. Just as fairyland is the world of magic, the fairies are the personification of magic. Magic does not like chaos, messiness, and disorganization. The well-known Hermetic axiom "As above, so below" is often rephrased "As within, so without." An outer physical mess is indicative of an inner mess, and an inner mess can produce inner blocks that prevent you from making progress in your magical training. Since the outer and the inner reflect each other, cleaning up your outer mess helps you clean up your inner mess, which dissolves some of the inner blocks that may be holding you back in your training.[65]

Even if we ignore magical theory, there are many common sense reasons to stay organized. It is important for the magician to maintain a state of well-being. Needless to say, it is more pleasant to live in an organized house than in an unorganized house. The magician realizes that he has only a few short decades to make a positive impact on the world, and will therefore waste as little time as possible. When your house is disorganized, you waste a lot of time looking for things because you can't remember where you put anything.

And this makes them angry with the people that live in it, and they would gladly drive them out of the world if they could. They want the whole earth nice and clean. So they pinch the maids black and blue and play them all manner of uncomfortable tricks.

Stepping on Legos and tripping on papers are all examples of the physical harm that can come to us as a result of not keeping our homes organized and tidy. Disorganization and messiness really will pinch you black and blue. When you step onto the magical path, you are stepping onto a path of personal development and self-improvement (and service and several other things).[66] The forces and powers underlying the art of magic will assist you, but oftentimes they do it by teaching you lessons the hard way. This is especially true if you ignore those lessons when they are taught to you the easy way because it is usually harder to ignore lessons when they are taught to you the hard way.

The Spirit of Magic by Virgil

But this house was quite a shame, and the fairies in the forest could not endure it. They tried everything on the maids without effect, and at last resolved upon making a clean riddance, beginning with the child. They ought to have known that it was not her fault, but they have little principle and much mischief in them, and they thought that if they got rid of her the maids would be sure to be turned away.

If you do not learn the lessons you need to learn the hard way, then you will have to learn them the even harder way.[67] The maids were disorganized and probably lost many things. Losing those things was supposed to be a hard lesson regarding why it's important to be organized. They didn't learn their lesson, so now they are going to lose a child they were supposed to watch over. They're going to get in big trouble now. Hopefully they learn their lesson this time, or the universe will have to try to teach them this same lesson an even harder way. Maybe one of the maids will trip on a random book on the ground, fall on her back, and lose her ability to walk?

So one evening, the poor little girl having been put to bed early, before the sun was down, the servants went off to the village, locking the door behind them. The child did not know she was alone, and lay contentedly looking out of her window towards the forest, of which, however, she could not see much, because of the ivy and other creeping plants which had straggled across her window. All at once she saw an ape making faces at her out of the mirror, and the heads carved upon a great old wardrobe grinning fearfully. Then two old spider-legged chairs came forward into the middle of the room, and began to dance a queer, old-fashioned dance. This set her laughing and she forgot the ape and the grinning heads.

Courage is an important quality for the aspiring magician to have. It is one of the four pillars of Solomon's temple. Tangle is courageous, and this is why it is not easy to scare her. She sees a bunch of crazy things, but instead of crying from fright, she laughs.

So the fairies saw they had made a mistake, and sent the chairs back to their places. But they knew that she had been reading the story of Silverhair all day. So the next moment she heard the voices of the three bears upon the stair, big voice, middle voice, and little voice, and she heard their soft, heavy tread, as if they had stockings

Chapter 17: The Golden Key

over their boots, coming nearer and nearer to the door of her room, till she could bear it no longer. She did just as Silverhair did, and as the fairies wanted her to do; she darted to the window, pulled it open, got upon the ivy, and so scrambled to the ground. She then fled to the forest as fast as she could run.

Tangle has been reading the story of Silverhair (a parody of Goldilocks) all day, which implies that Tangle likes to read fairy tales. This is a hint that she is drawn towards magic. In IIH, Bardon says that a person is ready to study magic if he is eager to learn the truth and strives toward the truth. In a later step, he writes "But neither fairy tales nor sagas exist for the true adept, because they are to be understood as a sort of symbolism concealing many deep truths." Many future magicians find themselves drawn to fairy tales because they contain, in symbolic form, the truths their hearts strive towards.

Now, although she did not know it, this was the very best way she could have gone; for nothing is ever so mischievous in its own place as it is out of it; and, besides, these mischievous creatures were only the children of Fairyland, as it were, and there are many other beings there as well; and if a wanderer gets in among them, the good ones will always help him more than the evil ones will be able to hurt him.

In the Abrahamic religions, spirits are divided into two types - angels and demons. The angels help people, guide people, and protect them from the demons. The demons harm people and lead them astray. As magicians, we know that the situation is more complicated than that. There are many spirits, such as fairies and elementals, that are neither angels nor demons. However, it is still the case that there are spirits who are benevolent toward humans and spirits who are hostile toward humans. When you work as a magician, you will often find that the benevolent spirits will help you, and will protect you from the hostile spirits. However, many magicians, in their ignorance, inadvertently do things to make the benevolent spirits leave them. For example, the magician may do things so immature that the benevolent spirits are disgusted by him and leave him. Or, the magician may do things so stupid that the benevolent spirits give up on him and leave him. A pure person possesses both maturity and wisdom, and therefore will always have the assistance and protection of the benevolent spirits.[68] This is one of many reasons Emvatibe told Bill that "for the individual whose spirit

The Spirit of Magic by Virgil

is clear, protection is always near."[69] *The Golden Key* actually explores the theme of having a pure "spirit." When your "spirit" is pure, then the light of your inner divine nature can shine outward without being obstructed by impurities in your "spirit."

The sun was now set, and the darkness coming on, but the child thought of no danger but the bears behind her. If she had looked round, however, she would have seen that she was followed by a very different creature from a bear. It was a curious creature, made like a fish, but covered, instead of scales, with feathers of all colours, sparkling like those of a humming-bird. It had fins, not wings, and swam through the air as a fish does through the water. Its head was like the head of a small owl.

This creature has an interesting composition, and there is no one correct interpretation of what it represents. It serves the role of Tangle's intuition. The fish is a symbol of water. In the physical body, the legs correspond to earth, the gut region corresponds to water, the chest region corresponds to air, and the head region corresponds to fire. Our intuition is often referred to as our "gut feeling." The owl is a symbol of wisdom, and intuition is the source of wisdom. Our intuition provides us with guidance and helps us when we are in trouble. Her intuition is behind her, which implies that she is not following it. Therefore, she is going to run into trouble.

After running a long way, and as the last of the light was disappearing, she passed under a tree with drooping branches. It dropped its branches to the ground all about her, and caught her as in a trap. She struggled to get out, but the branches pressed her closer and closer to the trunk.

In her book *The Untraining of a Sea Priestess*, Stephanie Leon Neal takes the reader through the process of becoming a sea priestess, which is kind of a like a magician who specializes in water magic and in the mysteries of the water element. She uses a lot of sea-themed metaphors throughout the book. The first step in the process of becoming a sea priestess is untangling yourself from seaweed. Seaweed represents the overcomplications that you get caught up in. Getting caught up in these overcomplications causes you to miss seeing the important things. In the first chapter of the book, called "Untangle," she writes the following.

Chapter 17: The Golden Key

Now is the time for you to come out of all the tangled seaweed that leads you to everywhere but you. The main purpose for this lesson is to gently untangle you from all overcomplications. Overcomplication is a time and joy thief, designed to rob you of your free will, your Divine thoughts.

Elaborating on this idea in another section of the book, she writes.

Here is the tough part: all outside gifts must be put down. The tarot, stones, herbs, charts, reference books, everything that has a perceived power must be stripped away, so that you may discover your own power, your own voice, and so that you may dig for your treasures, cultivating a direct line to all that is.

It doesn't take long to see overcomplications in the occult world. New information enters the magical world when magicians acquire it through direct experience. New information enters the occult world when occultists overcomplicate existing information through speculation. The tables of correspondences of tomorrow will be twice as long as the tables of correspondences of today. The pseudo-Kabbalistic philosophy of tomorrow will be twice as dense as the pseudo-Kabbalistic philosophy of today. The occult world is constantly generating new seaweed for aspiring magicians to get tangled up in. Stephanie Leon Neal points out that things like correspondences and philosophies do have their uses, but only at the appropriate time. At the beginning of our training, we should forget those things because there are more important matters to attend to. This is the process of untangling oneself from the seaweed.

She was in great terror and distress, when the air-fish, swimming into the thicket of branches, began tearing them with its beak. They loosened their hold at once, and the creature went on attacking them, till at length they let the child go.

Her intuition has helped her untangle herself from the seaweed. Since intuition is a source of wisdom, and since the owl is an animal representing wisdom, we can also interpret this passage to mean that her wisdom helped her untangle herself from the seaweed. If you are at the beginning stage of your magical training that involves untangling yourself from the seaweed, then it is especially important for you to pray daily for wisdom because you will need wisdom to succeed in this endeavor of untangling.

Then the air-fish came from behind her, and swam on in front, glittering and sparkling all lovely colours; and she followed.

She's following her intuition now, which is good. Her intuition will lead her to Step 1.

It led her gently along till all at once it swam in at a cottage door. The child followed still.

She has arrived at Step 1. That is to say, she has found a suitable initiatory system to work through and has just begun doing so.

There was a bright fire in the middle of the floor, upon which stood a pot without a lid, full of water that boiled and bubbled furiously. The air-fish swam straight to the pot and into the boiling water, where it lay quiet.
A beautiful woman rose from the opposite side of the fire and came to meet the girl. She took her up in her arms, and said,--
"Ah, you are come at last! I have been looking for you a long time."

This woman is beautiful, implying that her personality is fairly balanced and pure. She is the archetype of the student on Step 1. Balancing and purifying one's personality is a large portion of the Step 2 work, but it is also part of the Step 1 work. In Step 1, Bardon teaches the student conscious eating, conscious breathing, and magical washing, which are all powerful self-transformation techniques that can be used to balance and purify one's personality. As a result, the student will already have a fairly balanced personality when he moves on from Step 1 and begins the work of Step 2.

She sat down with her on her lap, and there the girl sat staring at her. She had never seen anything so beautiful. She was tall and strong, with white arms and neck, and a delicate flush on her face.

Grandmother is beautiful, again, because the light of her beautiful inner divine nature is able to shine outwards without being completely blocked or too distorted by impurities and imbalances in her personality.

Chapter 17: The Golden Key

Her skin is white, symbolizing purity. There is a "delicate flush on her face," indicating that she is healthy. Magic is not a path that involves ascetic practices that harm one's health. On the contrary, health is very important in magic. The magician should exercise regularly, eat a balanced diet, get enough sleep, and stay hygienic. The healthier your body is, the stronger it is. The stronger your body is, the more easily it can handle the strain of magical work.

The child could not tell what was the colour of her hair, but could not help thinking it had a tinge of dark green. She had not one ornament upon her, but she looked as if she had just put off quantities of diamonds and emeralds.

In *Transcendental Magic*, Levi writes the following.

Are you priests? Are you kings? The priesthood of Magic is not a vulgar priesthood, and its royalty enters not into competition with the princes of this world. The monarchs of science are the priests of truth, and their sovereignty is hidden from the multitude, like their prayers and sacrifices. The kings of science are men who know the truth and them the truth has made free, according to the specific promise given by the most mighty of all initiators.

Elsewhere in the same book, Levi also writes this.

Magic was called formerly the Sacerdotal Art and the Royal Art, because initiation gave empire over souls to the sage and the capacity for ruling wills.

So we see that the magician is royal, but his royalty is hidden from others because he keeps silence. This is why there was "not one ornament" on Grandmother, but "she looked as if she had just put off quantities of diamonds and emeralds."

Yet here she was in the simplest, poorest little cottage, where she was evidently at home.

The Spirit of Magic by Virgil

Adepts tend not to spend money on unnecessary things because that just makes their homes and lives more cluttered. Therefore, the homes of many adepts are quite simple. The student at Step 1 is not an adept, but should learn the dangers of excess consumerism and the value of living an uncluttered life.

She was dressed in shining green.

This green color represents Malkuth, which is the first sephirah. In magical systems that use the Tree of Life as a map of magical advancement, Malkuth represents the first stages of magical advancement. In IIH, these first stages are found in Step 1. Grandmother is the archetype of the Step 1 student.

The girl looked at the lady, and the lady looked at the girl.
"What is your name?" asked the lady.
"The servants always called me Tangle."
"Ah, that was because your hair was so untidy. But that was their fault, the naughty women! Still it is a pretty name, and I will call you Tangle too. You must not mind my asking you questions, for you may ask me the same questions, every one of them, and any others that you like. How old are you?"
"Ten," answered Tangle.
"You don't look like it," said the lady.

In this story, age represent maturity. Tangle is more mature than most people her age, and therefore looks older than most people her age. This is why Grandmother tells Tangle she doesn't look like she's ten.

"How old are you. please?" returned Tangle.
"Thousands of years old,' answered the lady.

Grandmother is extremely mature, despite only being on Step 1. When you undergo magical training, you become more mature at a rapid pace.

"You don't look like it," said Tangle.
"Don't I? I think I do. Don't you see how beautiful I am!"

Maturity comes from spiritual evolution, and spiritual evolution comes in part from balancing and purifying one's personality, which

Chapter 17: The Golden Key

makes one beautiful. Thus, beautiful people are mature and mature people are beautiful.

And her great blue eyes looked down on the little Tangle, as if all the stars in the sky were melted in them to make their brightness.
"Ah! but," said Tangle, "when people live long they grow old. At least I always thought so."
"I have no time to grow old," said the lady. "I am too busy for that. It is very idle to grow old.--but I cannot have my little girl so untidy. Do you know I can't find a clean spot on your face to kiss!"

Grandmother understands the immense value of time, as do all magicians. Therefore, she does not waste time, but always uses it wisely. This is why she says she's busy. Not wasting time doesn't mean you're a workaholic. Rest and leisure can be wise uses of time. It's not about always working but about always using your time wisely.

Grandmother doesn't like that Tangle is untidy because it is important for students of magic to be organized.

"Perhaps," suggested Tangle, feeling ashamed, but not too much so to say a word for herself,--"perhaps that is because the tree made me cry so."
"My poor darling!" said the lady, looking now as if the moon were melted in her eyes, and kissing her little face, dirty as it was, "the naughty tree must suffer for making a girl cry."
"And what is your name, please?" asked Tangle.
"Grandmother," answered the lady.
"Is it really?"
"Yes, indeed. I never tell stories, even in fun."
"How good of you!"

Grandmother understands the value of honesty. Bardon says that those suited to learn magic are "people eager to search the heights of truth and beginning to ripen for it." The student of magic must value truth, and someone who values truth will not serve the principle of falsity by being dishonest. The student is already required to develop the virtue of honesty at Step 1.[70]

"I couldn't if I tried. It would come true if I said it, and then I should be punished enough."

The Spirit of Magic by Virgil

Power can be used to recreate the universe – in other words to rewrite reality. The magician must use his power maturely or he will cause great suffering for everyone and generate large amounts of negative karma for himself. To protect potential abusers of magic and their potential victims, Divine Providence will not give magical power to those who are immature. This is why immature people often find themselves stuck on Step 1 for years. The power of words is analogous to the power of magic. Like magic, words can also affect the world around you. Divine Providence often assesses how maturely you can use magical power by observing how maturely you can use words. People who speak maturely are given magical power. Those who speak immaturely (e.g. by lying, insulting others, boasting, etc.) are not given magical power, and will run into inner blocks that prevent them from making progress in their training. Grandmother is treating her words like they are magic power, and making sure to use them wisely.

And she smiled like the sun through a summer shower.

The sun is a source of blessings. A summer shower, which is a storm, represents trouble. It is the nature of a magician to bless others, especially when they are going through troubling times. It is during one's magical training that one develops the nature of a magician. Here we see that Grandmother's nature is already to bless others, especially when they are going through troubling times. The student of IIH should also develop this nature as early as possible. The sooner you develop the nature of a magician, the sooner you will become a magician.

"But now," she went on, "I must get you washed and dressed, and then we shall have some supper."
"Oh! I had supper long ago," said Tangle.
"Yes, indeed you had," answered the lady,--"three years ago. You don't know that it is three years since you ran away from the bears. You are thirteen and more now."
Tangle could only stare. She felt quite sure it was true.

Tangle ages rapidly. This means she becomes more mature rapidly. Since beginning Step 1 (arriving at Grandmother's house), she has already acquired the same amount of maturity that it takes most people three years to acquire.

Chapter 17: The Golden Key

"You will not be afraid of anything I do with you--will you?" said the lady.

"I will try very hard not to be; but I can't be certain, you know," replied Tangle.

"I like your saying so, and I shall be quite satisfied," answered the lady.

Tangle is honest with herself. She does not erroneously believe herself to be braver than she is. She can only promise to do her best to be as brave as she can be. Grandmother approves of Tangle's honest assessment of herself. It shows good introspection skills. The better you are at introspection, the easier the soul mirror creation process will be for you.

She took off the girl's night-gown, rose with her in her arms, and going to the wall of the cottage, opened a door. Then Tangle saw a deep tank, the sides of which were filled with green plants, which had flowers of all colours. There was a roof over it like the roof of the cottage. It was filled with beautiful clear water, in which swam a multitude of such fishes as the one that had led her to the cottage. It was the light their colours gave that showed the place in which they were.

The lady spoke some words Tangle could not understand, and threw her into the tank.

The fishes came crowding about her. Two or three of them got under her head and kept it up. The rest of them rubbed themselves all over her, and with their wet feathers washed her quite clean.

This cleaning represents a process of unlearning. Students who begin working through the Bardon system with no prior background in magic or esotericism often have an easier time than those students who do have a prior background in these subjects. This is because students without a prior background are in *shoshin* by default. Those who do have a prior background have to do a lot of unlearning, and this takes time, which causes them to progress more slowly. A prior background can be an advantage at later points, but in the beginning, it can result in the student having preconceptions and making assumptions that prevent him from understanding the system he is practicing. This is why it is best to temporarily "forget everything you think you know" at the beginning of your journey through IIH.[71] This is what I mean by "unlearning."

The Spirit of Magic by Virgil

Then the lady, who had been looking on all the time, spoke again; whereupon some thirty or forty of the fishes rose out of the water underneath Tangle, and so bore her up to the arms the lady held out to take her. She carried her back to the fire, and, having dried her well, opened a chest, and taking out the finest linen garments, smelling of grass and lavender, put them upon her, and over all a green dress, just like her own, shining like hers, and soft like hers, and going into just such lovely folds from the waist, where it was tied with a brown cord, to her bare feet.

Tangle has unlearned everything. That is to say, she has forgotten everything she thought she knew. Therefore, she is now ready to really begin working through the first stages of initiation, represented by the sephirah Malkuth on the Tree of Life. This is why she is adorned with colors associated with Malkuth. These stages correspond to Step 1 of IIH.

"Won't you give me a pair of shoes too, Grandmother?" said Tangle.
"No, my dear; no shoes. Look here. I wear no shoes."

Grandmother wears no shoes, meaning she is grounded. She is down-to-earth. She is connected to the world. In the second essay of his "Problems in the Study of Magic" essay series, Bill writes the following.

> *I explore the inner worlds in order to be more active and effective in the outer world. I get around. I slip into all sorts of incomprehensible spiritual domains to check them out, to take their measure, and to contemplate their value and meaning. But it is this world that I share in common with others that I want to make lasting changes—it is this world, the outer world, where my true work lies.*

This passage from Bill's essay shows the importance of being connected to the world. Some occultists live in fantasy worlds filled with delusions. Some mystics want to leave this world behind. The magician serves Divine Providence by carrying out the will of Divine Providence in this world. To do that, he must remain connected to this world.

Tangle doesn't put on shoes at any point during her initiation, so she is always in touch with the world. Throughout the years you spend

Chapter 17: The Golden Key

working through IIH, you must always remain connected to the world. Fulfill your responsibilities to your family, your employers, and your friends. Have your mundane affairs in order.

So saying she lifted her dress a little, and there were the loveliest white feet, but no shoes.

The feet are the part of the physical body that correspond to Malkuth, but white is the color that corresponds to Kether. The white feet of Grandmother allude to the saying "Kether is in Malkuth and Malkuth is in Kether." The practical implications of this saying refer to the reconciliation of the spiritual and the material, which is necessary for balanced progress along the magical path. At the beginning, this means the student must find a balance between the "magical" parts of his life and the "mundane" parts of his life. Grandmother has clearly done this.

Then Tangle was content to go without shoes too. And the lady sat down with her again, and combed her hair, and brushed it, and then left it to dry while she got the supper.

In Teutonic magic, hair was a symbol of magical power, and for this reason, Teutonic magicians grew their hair and beards very long. Although she has just begun, Tangle's power is starting to grow. This process is represented by the tidying of her hair. Mature people acquire power quickly when they walk the magical path, and Tangle is very mature.

First she got bread out of one hole in the wall; then milk out of another; then several kinds of fruit out a third; and then she went to the pot on the fire, and took out the fish, now nicely cooked, and, as soon as she had pulled off its feathered skin, ready to be eaten.
"But," exclaimed Tangle. And she stared at the fish, and could say no more.
"I know what you mean," returned the lady. "You do not like to eat the messenger that brought you home. But it is the kindest return you can make. The creature was afraid to go until it saw me put the pot on, and heard me promise it should be boiled the moment it returned with you. Then it darted out of the door at once. You saw it go into the pot of itself the moment it entered, did you not?"
"I did," answered Tangle, "and I thought it very strange; but then I saw you, and forgot all about the fish."

The Spirit of Magic by Virgil

"In Fairyland," **resumed the lady, as they sat down to the table, "the ambition of the animals is to be eaten by the people; for that is their highest end in that condition. But they are not therefore destroyed. Out of that pot comes something more than the dead fish, you will see."**

Consciousness is always evolving. There are many forms of consciousness that evolve in ways that are difficult for us to understand, but we must let them evolve, and even help them if we can, acknowledging that the way they evolve is different from the way a human spirit evolves.[72] This means we do not try to force them to evolve the way a human spirit would evolve, but assist them in evolving in the manner that is most natural to them, even if this requires us to do things that are seemingly absurd, like eating them.

Tangle now remarked that the lid was on the pot. But the lady took no further notice of it till they had eaten the fish, which Tangle found nicer than any fish she had ever tasted before. It was as white as snow, and as delicate as cream.

The fish is a symbol of Jesus Christ. In IIH, Bardon writes the following about conscious eating.

> *Whoever in the conscious reception of food takes example in the eucharistic mystery, will find an analogy to it here, and remember the words of our Lord Jesus Christ: 'Take and eat, for this is my flesh; take and drink, for this is my blood'; he will seize their true and primary meaning.*

Conscious eating is a form of the Eucharistic mystery. The Bardonist eats patience in order to become patient, eats compassion to become compassionate, eats intelligence to become intelligent, etc. The principles behind conscious eating are the same as the principles behind the practicing of eating Divinity to become divinized, which is what the Eucharistic mystery as practiced in the church is. The symbol of the fish alludes to the Eucharistic mystery, implying that Tangle is practicing conscious eating.

However, conscious eating can be used to develop any positive trait – patience, compassion, intelligence, courage, assertiveness, open-mindedness, etc. Which specific trait is Tangle trying to develop? As we

Chapter 17: The Golden Key

learn later in the story, the fish that Tangle is eating is a very wise fish. Thus, the fish represents wisdom. Tangle is eating wisdom to become wise.

> **And the moment she had swallowed a mouthful of it, a change she could not describe began to take place in her. She heard a murmuring all about her, which became more and more articulate, and at length, as she went on eating, grew intelligible. By the time she had finished her share, the sounds of all the animals in the forest came crowding through the door to her ears; for the door still stood wide open, though it was pitch-dark outside; and they were no longer sounds only; they were speech, and speech that she could understand. She could tell what the insects in the cottage were saying to each other too. She had even a suspicion that the trees and flowers all about the cottage were holding midnight communications with each other; but what they said she could not hear.**

This is a significant passage. According to legend, after God gave Solomon wisdom, he was able to understand the speech of the birds and beasts. By alluding to this legend about Solomon, the story confirms that Tangle is getting wiser because she is using conscious eating to become wiser.

> **As soon as the fish was eaten, the lady went to the fire and took the lid off the pot. A lovely little creature in human shape, with large white wings, rose out of it, and flew round and round the roof of the cottage; then dropped, fluttering, and nestled in the lap of the lady. She spoke to it some strange words, carried it to the door, and threw it out into the darkness. Tangle heard the flapping of its wings die away in the distance.**
> **"Now have we done the fish any harm?" she said, returning.**
> **"No," answered Tangle, "I do not think we have. I should not mind eating one every day."**
> **"They must wait their time, like you and me too, my little Tangle."**
> **And she smiled a smile which the sadness in it made more lovely.**

Cooking and eating a fish brings it to its next stage of evolution, which is an aëranth. Spiritual evolution can be facilitated via magical training, but it cannot be forced or rushed. Therefore, the fish must "wait

The Spirit of Magic by Virgil

their time" before becoming aëranths. Tangle, too, must wait her time before moving on to Step 2.

"But," she continued, "I think we may have one for supper tomorrow."
So saying she went to the door of the tank, and spoke; and now Tangle understood her perfectly.
"I want one of you." she said,--"the wisest."
Thereupon the fishes got together in the middle of the tank, with their heads forming a circle above the water, and their tails a larger circle beneath it. They were holding a council, in which their relative wisdom should be determined. At length one of them flew up into the lady's hand, looking lively and ready.
"You know where the rainbow stands?" she asked.
"Yes, mother, quite well," answered the fish.
"Bring home a young man you will find there, who does not know where to go."

The wisest fish is always the one sent to perform tasks like bringing Tangle and Mossy to Grandmother. Wisdom is the ability to make the best choices, and a fish is more likely to succeed in his task if he makes the best choices. Therefore, the wisest fish is the one most likely to succeed.

A fish that accomplishes its task also goes into the pot, which puts it in the next phase of its spiritual evolution (an aëranth). The wisest fish is the most highly evolved of the fishes, and therefore the one most ready to enter this next phase of evolution.

The fish was out of the door in a moment. Then the lady told Tangle it was time to go to bed; and, opening another door in the side of the cottage, showed her a little arbour, cool and green, with a bed of purple heath growing in it, upon which she threw a large wrapper made of the feathered skins of the wise fishes, shining gorgeous in the firelight. Tangle was soon lost in the strangest, loveliest dreams. And the beautiful lady was in every one of her dreams.

Grandmother is a student who is successfully working through Step 1. She possesses the qualities that are needed to successfully work through Step 1. Tangle is dreaming about her, indicating that these

Chapter 17: The Golden Key

qualities have taken root in her subconscious mind and will soon bloom within her personality.

In the morning she woke to the rustling of leaves over her head, and the sound of running water. But, to her surprise, she could find no door--nothing but the moss grown wall of the cottage. So she crept through an opening in the arbour, and stood in the forest. Then she bathed in a stream that ran merrily through the trees, and felt happier; for having once been in her grandmother's pond, she must be clean and tidy ever after; and, having put on her green dress, felt like a lady.

Tangle is practicing the Step 1 self-transformation technique of magical washing. When you use this technique to wash a negative trait out of your personality, it is out of your personality for good.[73]

She spent that day in the wood, listening to the birds and beasts and creeping things. She understood all that they said, though she could not repeat a word of it; and every kind had a different language, while there was a common though more limited understanding between all the inhabitants of the forest. She saw nothing of the beautiful lady, but she felt that she was near her all the time; and she took care not to go out of sight of the cottage.

She took care not to go out of sight of the cottage, meaning she took care not to move on to Step 2 because she is not yet ready to do so.

It was round, like a snow-hut or a wigwam; and she could see neither door nor window in it. The fact was, it had no windows; and though it was full of doors, they all opened from the inside, and could not even be seen from the outside.

There are no windows, so outsiders cannot look in. To know what is inside the cottage, you must be inside the cottage, which is Step 1. This means that you don't really know what Step 1 is like until you are in the middle of working through Step 1. Reading the Step 1 section of IIH isn't enough to really understand Step 1. You must actually do the exercises contained in this step.

The doors open from the inside, meaning they cannot be forced open from the outside. If you are not ready to undergo initiation, you will not be able to force your way through the steps of IIH. Some people who

The Spirit of Magic by Virgil

aren't ready for initiation spend hours a day practicing the exercises of IIH and make no progress. Their time would be better spent striving to become more mature by introspecting, praying for wisdom and understanding, and using self-transformation techniques like those in the six-pronged attack.

She was standing at the foot of a tree in the twilight, listening to a quarrel between a mole and a squirrel, in which the mole told the squirrel that the tail was the best of him, and the squirrel called the mole Spade-fists, when, the darkness having deepened around her, she became aware of something shining in her face, and looking round, saw that the door of the cottage was open, and the red light of the fire flowing from it like a river through the darkness. She left Mole and Squirrel to settle matters as they might, and darted off to the cottage. Entering, she found the pot boiling on the fire, and the grand, lovely lady sitting on the other side of it.

Anger results when the fire element in the personality is impure. The traits that arise from the impure fire element have little use. Anger leads to murder and other atrocities. It breaks up friendships and pushes one to abuse and hurt others. Anger is bad for your health. It causes others to lose respect for you. In those few instances when it is wise to act angry for some reason, you can act angry without actually being angry. Anger really has little use.

The angry argument between the squirrel and the mole reflects negative impure fire, which is, again, relatively useless. The red light flowing from the cottage represents positive pure fire, which manifests as courage, enthusiasm, faith, conviction, assertiveness, and confidence. This fire boils the pot, indicating that it is useful.

Tangle observes the negative manifestations and effects of the impure fire element by watching the argument. This teaches her how the impure fire element can manifest negatively in her own personality and in her own actions. She then turns her attention to the positive useful fire that is boiling the pot. Once we learn about the negative effects of impure fire by observing these effects in others and in ourselves, we should turn our attention to acquiring pure fire; that is to say, acquiring the useful positive personality traits associated with pure fire.

"I've been watching you all day," said the lady. "You shall have something to eat by-and-by, but we must wait till our supper comes home."

Chapter 17: The Golden Key

She took Tangle on her knee, and began to sing to her--such songs as made her wish she could listen to them forever. But at length in rushed the shining fish, and snuggled down in the pot. It was followed by a youth who had outgrown his worn garments.

Mossy's clothes fit him when he left his great-aunt's garden. He has already grown quite a bit. Children grow bigger as they get older, so this implies that Mossy has gotten older, which means he has already become more mature.

His face was ruddy with health, and in his hand he carried a little jewel, which sparkled in the firelight.

Again, it's good that Mossy is healthy. It is important to stay healthy during one's initiation. Illness is a sign that the elements in one's body are out of harmony with each other. If we examine Bardon's comments about diet in IIH, we find that his approach to diet is not only one of the few sane approaches, but one of the few truly magical approaches too. There are many teachers who will try to tell you what you should or shouldn't eat. For example, some say you shouldn't eat meat. Others say you should avoid sugar. Much of that sort of diet advice arises from various systems of morality that originate outside of the field of magic but that some people are trying to inject into the field of magic to fulfill certain agendas. Bardon doesn't give that sort of advice. All he says is to design your diet so that it is conducive to health. In other words, eat whatever you need to east in order to stay healthy, and try to avoid eating things that make you unhealthy. That's wise advice right there.

The first words the lady said were,--
"What is that in your hand, Mossy?"
Now Mossy was the name his companions had given him, because he had a favourite stone covered with moss, on which he used to sit whole days reading; and they said the moss had begun to grow upon him too.

Mossy "used to sit whole days reading." This indicates that he loves to learn. A love of learning is an important trait for aspiring magicians to have. Remember, however, that while we can learn important things from books, experience is still the best teacher.[74]

The Spirit of Magic by Virgil

Mossy held out his hand. The moment the lady saw that it was the golden key, she rose from her chair, kissed Mossy on the forehead, made him sit down on her seat, and stood before him like a servant.

In one of his essays, Bill writes the following.

So to answer your question about who was Christ the issue is not belief but becoming like him—and his specific revelation on earth was what he in fact was and did—to demonstrate how a person acts whose heart is a sea of love, and there is no limit to the depth and vastness of the compassion within it.

He who is compassionate is like Christ, and this why Grandmother treats Mossy with such respect.

Mossy could not bear this, and rose at once. But the lady begged him, with tears in her beautiful eyes, to sit, and let her wait on him.
"But you are a great, splendid, beautiful lady," said Mossy.
"Yes, I am. But I work all day long--that is my pleasure; and you will have to leave me so soon!"
"How do you know that, if you please, madam?" asked Mossy.
"Because you have got the golden key."

Possessing compassion is a sure sign of maturity, and mature people advance quickly through IIH. Mossy will soon leave Grandmother's cottage and move on to the next stages of his initiation.

"But I don't know what it is for. I can't find the keyhole. Will you tell me what to do?"
"You must look for the keyhole. That is your work. I cannot help you. I can only tell you that if you look for it you will find it."

Initiation is something that is mostly worked through alone. Some people undergoing initiation have a human mentor to provide them with guidance. Bardonists have IIH in lieu of a mentor. However, a mentor cannot do the work for you. A mentor cannot practice visualization exercises for you, meditate for you, or introspect for you. As Grandmother says, "that is your work."

Chapter 17: The Golden Key

"What kind of box will it open? What is there inside?"
"I do not know. I dream about it, but I know nothing."

The golden key unlocks access to the rainbow, which represents the inner plane realms known as the planetary spheres. A student at Step 1 doesn't really know the wonders that lie within the inner planes. However, when we dream, our awareness closes down to the outer world and opens up to the inner world. Therefore, we sometimes can get a sense of what the inner world is like from our dreams.

"Must I go at once?"
"You may stop here tonight, and have some of my supper. But you must go in the morning. All I can do for you is to give you clothes. Here is a girl called Tangle, whom you must take with you."
"That *will* be nice," said Mossy.

It's not a bad idea to spend a bit of extra time on a step just to make sure you really have mastered all of the exercises in the step. However, you shouldn't linger too long, but should move forward as soon as it is clear that you are ready to.

"No, no !" said Tangle. "I don't want to leave you, please, grandmother."
"You must go with him, Tangle. I am sorry to lose you, but it will be the best thing for you. Even the fishes, you see, have to go into the pot, and then out into the dark. If you fall in with the Old Man of the Sea, mind you ask him whether he has not got some more fishes ready for me. My tank is getting thin."

All things evolve. To stop evolving is true death. Initiation is a process of spiritual evolution. It is the best thing for Tangle to move on to the next stage of her own spiritual evolution. As for the fish, they begin in the Old Man of the Sea's tank, and when they are ready to evolve, they go to Grandmother's tank, and when they are ready to evolve some more, they go into the pot to evolve into an aëranth.

So saying, she took the fish from the pot, and put the lid on as before. They sat down and ate the fish, and then the winged creature rose from the pot, circled the roof, and settled on the lady's lap. She talked to it, carried it to the door, and threw it out into the dark. They heard the flap of its wings die away in the distance.

The Spirit of Magic by Virgil

The lady then showed Mossy into just such another chamber as that of Tangle; and in the morning he found a suit of clothes laid beside him. He looked very handsome in them. But the wearer of Grandmother's clothes never thinks about how he or she looks, but thinks always how handsome other people are.

Mossy is very handsome wearing the clothes Grandmother gave him, but instead of thinking about how handsome he is, he thinks about how handsome other people are. One of the great spiritual lessons we all must learn as that every person you meet "is you in another form." Mossy, although still in the beginning stages of his initiation, is already beginning to learn that spiritual lesson.

Tangle was very unwilling to go.
"Why should I leave you? I don't know the young man," she said to the lady.

Tangle is cautious. This is a good trait to possess and was discussed earlier when analyzing The Hermit; the card whose true name is Prudence.

"I am never allowed to keep my children long. You need not go with him except you please, but you must go some day; and I should like you to go with him, for he has the golden key. No girl need be afraid to go with a youth that has the golden key. You will take care of her, Mossy, will you not?"
"That I will," said Mossy.
And Tangle cast a glance at him, and thought she should like to go with him.

A compassionate person never intentionally hurts others. This is why Grandmother knows that it is safe for Tangle to go with Mossy. Compassionate people care for others, which is why Mossy readily agrees to take care of Tangle.

"And," said the lady, "If you should lose each other as you go through the--the--I never can remember the name of that country,-- do not be afraid, but go on and on."

In magical symbolism, to give something a name is to make it real. Shadows are not real. They are illusory, and therefore, the country of

Chapter 17: The Golden Key

shadows does not have a name. This is why Grandmother can't remember the name of the country. We should not be satisfied with shadows. We should not be satisfied being a shadow of what we could be if we fulfilled our highest potential. We should not be satisfied with a life that is a shadow of the life we could live if we pursued our dreams. If we do that, then we are unreal, and the lives we live are unreal. Only things which are real can be meaningful.

She kissed Tangle on the mouth and Mossy on the forehead, led them to the door, and waved her hand eastward. Mossy and Tangle took each other's hand and walked away into the depth of the forest. In his right hand Mossy held the golden key.

Mossy and Tangle continue to go east, which is the direction of the sun. This symbolizes the fact that they are heading in the direction of the Sphere of the Sun, which is the sphere of adepthood. In this story, it is the "country whence the shadows fall."

In traditional magical symbolism, the right side of the body corresponds to the "active" principle of nature while the left side of the body corresponds to the "passive" principle of nature. Mossy holds the golden key in his right hand, meaning he acts compassionately.

They wandered thus a long way, with endless amusement from the talk of the animals. They soon learned enough of their language to ask them necessary questions. The squirrels were always friendly, and gave them nuts out of their own hoards; but the bees were selfish and rude, justifying themselves on the ground that Tangle and Mossy were not subjects of their queen, and charity must begin at home, though indeed they had not one drone in their poorhouse at the time. Even the blinking moles would fetch them an earth-nut or a truffle now and then, talking as if their mouths, as well as their eyes and ears, were full of cotton wool, or their own velvety fur. By the time they got out of the forest they were very fond of each other, and Tangle was not in the least sorry that her grandmother had sent her away with Mossy.

In his book *The Mist-Filled Path*, Frank MacEowen tells the story of Saint Kevin, who would stand in a river every day and read from a holy book. One day, he accidentally dropped the book in the river. An otter dove down to get the book and bring it to him. When Saint Kevin

The Spirit of Magic by Virgil

opened the book, he found it completely dry. MacEowen writes the following about this story.

> Many modern people, on hearing such a story, would immediately consider it just a quaint fairy tale. Through the lens of primal Celtic tradition, however, we see it in a different light. We see that if we lean toward life willing to give ourselves over to being shaped, as the many druids, Celtic shaman-poets, and saints have done over time, that life also leans back toward us, as in the example of the otter helping Kevin.

Self-transformation on the magical path has a dual nature. Part of it involves taking the initiative and transforming ourselves using the six-pronged attack. However, another part of it involves giving ourselves over to life and letting life shape us. To do this, it is imperative that we do not hide from life in our oratories, but engage life by living fully.

At length the trees grew smaller, and stood farther apart, and the ground began to rise, and it got more and more steep, till the trees were all left behind, and the two were climbing a narrow path with rocks on each side.

Their path has become narrower, meaning they have less choice regarding what direction to go in. The introspection work they are about to do next is vital, and this is why aspiring magicians have to do it. There is no way around it, and their paths force them to go through this work.

Suddenly they came upon a rude doorway, by which they entered a narrow gallery cut in the rock. It grew darker and darker, till it was pitch-dark, and they had to feel their way. At length the light began to return, and at last they came out upon a narrow path on the face of a lofty precipice. This path went winding down the rock to a wide plain, circular in shape, and surrounded on all sides by mountains. Those opposite to them were a great way off, and towered to an awful height, shooting up sharp, blue, ice-enameled pinnacles. An utter silence reigned where they stood. Not even the sound of water reached them. Looking down, they could not tell whether the valley below was a grassy plain or a great still lake. They had never seen any space look like it.

Chapter 17: The Golden Key

They find themselves standing over a giant mirror-like plain filled with shadows. This represents their black soul mirrors. It is circular. The circle is a symbol of the universe, and therefore represents the concepts of completeness and wholeness. Their black soul mirrors are relatively complete because they did a thorough job when making them. They wrote down every single negative trait they could think of, no matter how small it was. Remember that 100 traits on the black soul mirror is the standard goal to aim for. This might seem like a lot, but it is a perfectly reasonable goal. Appendix B contains an actual soul mirror with 166 traits.

The way to it was difficult and dangerous, but down the narrow path they went, and reached the bottom in safety. They found it composed of smooth, light-coloured sandstone, undulating in parts, but mostly level. It was no wonder to them now that they had not been able to tell what it was, for this surface was everywhere crowded with shadows.

Each of these shadows is a negative trait. The light of your inner divine nature shines outward. Your personality transmits some of it perfectly and dulls some of it. The rays of light transmitted perfectly by your personality are the personality traits listed in your white soul mirror. The rays of light dulled by impurities in your personality are the personality traits listed in your black soul mirror. These dull rays are like shadows of the bright rays emanating from your inner divine nature. Your inner divine nature possesses all positive qualities. One ray emanating from it might be assertiveness, but if this ray of assertiveness is dulled when it passes through an impure personality, then the dull ray that ends up externalized is not assertiveness but aggression, a darker form of assertiveness. Similarly, confidence may be dulled into arrogance. Humbleness may be dulled in insecurity. Bravery may be dulled into recklessness.

The mass was chiefly made up of the shadows of leaves innumerable, of all lovely and imaginative forms, waving to and fro, floating and quivering in the breath of a breeze whose motion was unfelt, whose sound was unheard. No forests clothed the mountainsides, no trees were anywhere to be seen, and yet the shadows of the leaves, branches, and stems of all various trees covered the valley as far as their eyes could reach. They soon spied the shadows of flowers mingled with those of the leaves, and now and then the shadow of a

bird with open beak, and throat distended with song. At times would appear the forms of strange, graceful creatures, running up and down the shadow-boles and along the branches, to disappear in the wind-tossed foliage. **As they walked they waded knee-deep in the lovely lake. For the shadows were not merely lying on the surface of the ground, but heaped up above it like substantial forms of darkness, as if they had been cast upon a thousand different planes of the air.**

It is not enough to create one's soul mirrors. One must go through one's soul mirrors, analyzing and studying them carefully. So, after you've created your soul mirrors, make photocopies and then go through each photocopy, annotating it. Underline things. Highlight things. Draw arrows to show connections between different traits. Write comments in the margins. Go through your entire black soul mirror this way regularly, studying and reflecting upon each trait carefully. This is what Mossy and Tangle are doing. The better you understand the dark side of your personality, the easier it will be to transmute this side of your personality when you engage in the Step 2 work of self-transformation. This is why Mossy and Tangle are doing this work before they reach Step 2 (the realm of the Old Man of the Sea).

Tangle and Mossy often lifted their heads and gazed upwards to descry whence the shadows came; but they could see nothing more than a bright mist spread above them, higher than the tops of the mountains, which stood clear against it. No forests, no leaves, no birds were visible.

There are three veils in the Tree of Life. The most well-known of these is the Veil of Paroketh, which some have even called the "Mists of Paroketh." This could be the mist that Tangle and Mossy see; however, it is more likely that this mist is the so-called "Veil of Physicality" that exists between Malkuth and Yesod. They are below this veil, which makes sense since they are in Malkuth, the realm of everyday human life. Later when they enter the rainbow and travel upwards to the Sphere of the Moon, they will be able to travel beyond this veil to acquire knowledge and wisdom in the realms above this veil and bring that knowledge and wisdom to those trapped below the veil because they never learned the technique of mental wandering by undergoing an initiation.

Chapter 17: The Golden Key

After a while, they reached more open spaces, where the shadows were thinner; and came even to portions over which shadows only flitted, leaving them clear for such as might follow. Now a wonderful form, half bird-like half human, would float across on outspread sailing pinions. Anon an exquisite shadow group of gamboling children would be followed by the loveliest female form, and that again by the grand stride of a Titanic shape, each disappearing in the surrounding press of shadowy foliage. Sometimes a profile of unspeakable beauty or grandeur would appear for a moment and vanish. Sometimes they seemed lovers that passed linked arm in arm, sometimes father and son, sometimes brothers in loving contest, sometimes sisters entwined in gracefullest community of complex form. Sometimes wild horses would tear across, free, or bestrode by noble shadows of ruling men. But some of the things which pleased them most they never knew how to describe.

The line between the macrocosm and the microcosm is a bit blurred throughout this whole section. The imagery of this section contains lessons about both the microcosm and the macrocosm. In the microcosm, Tiphereth is one's inner divine nature, Yesod is one's personality, and Malkuth is one's actions. In the macrocosm, Tiphereth is the Sphere of the Sun, Yesod is the Sphere of the Moon, and Malkuth is the Earthzone.

Microcosmically speaking, a shadow hints at the nature of the object casting the shadow. Aggression hints that we could be assertive. Recklessness hints that we could be brave. Arrogance hints that we could be confident. A wide variety of shadows hints that there are a wide variety of positive traits that could eventually develop. Similarly, a shadow of a horse hints at the presence of a horse, and the shadow of a human hints at the presence of a human.

Macrocosmically speaking, within the Earthzone we often find hints of what it is like to be directly connected with Divinity. However, these hints are shadows of the experience of Divine union we encounter when we enter the Sphere of the Sun.

Bill, paraphrasing Bardon, writes that "The magician calls many realms his home, and many races consider him one of their own."

For example, once the magician enters the Kingdom of Earth and works with the gnomes, he penetrates into the mysteries of the earth element. He further refines the earth aspect of his personality and learns to work with the earth element the way a gnome does. Thus, the gnomes consider the magician a gnome because he possesses the traits of a

The Spirit of Magic by Virgil

gnome and can do the things that gnomes can do. Of course, the magician is also a salamander, an undine, and a sylph, but that is beside the point. Part of the poem "How to Meet a Gnome" is written from the perspective of a gnome musing about human magicians. The gnome says "If he thinks like a gnome, perceives like a gnome, feels like a gnome, [and] has the silence of a gnome, then he is one of our own." Thus, the gnomes consider the magician to be a gnome, even though he is also a salamander, a sylph, and an undine.

When you learn to travel outside of the Earthzone and enter the planetary spheres, the exact same phenomenon occurs. For example, when you travel to the Sphere of the Sun, you ask the ruling genii of this sphere to teach you whatever they can to help you spiritually evolve. They are highly spiritually evolved beings themselves, and so they teach you to become highly spiritually evolved in the same way they are highly spiritually evolved. You essentially become like these beings. You're still a salamander, a sylph, an undine, and a gnome, but you're also a solar spirit.[75]

Regarding the process of working with the ruling genii of the Sphere of the Sun, Bill writes the following.

> *Part of the price of interacting with these spirits is to learn to do what they do: to embody in yourself the pure emptiness of akasha, so deep, so vast and pure, that the divine can be reflected through you without distortion and without destroying civilization in the process.*

This is an intense, spiritual, and magical experience. You sometimes experience shadows of this experience during your daily life. For example, some very beautiful and profound works of art may engender within you a shadow of this experience. However, if you want the full experience and not just the shadow, you need to travel to the country whence the shadows fall – the Sphere of the Sun.

About the middle of the plain they sat down to rest in the heart of a heap of shadows. After sitting for a while, each, looking up, saw the other in tears: they were each longing after the country whence the shadows fell.

"We *must* find the country from which the shadows come," said Mossy.

Chapter 17: The Golden Key

Regarding the Sphere of the Sun, Bardon writes the following.

As soon as the sphere magician is master of the Sun sphere, there exists no problem anymore which he would not be able to solve in the right way. His knowledge has no gap and by means of this sphere he is able to become a perfect Adept. For a magician acquainted with Quabbalah, it becomes now clear why the Quabbalistic initiations tell that the connection with the Godhead will be accomplished on Tiphereth, which is the Sun sphere according to the Quabbalistic Tree of Life, in which the magician can obtain the union with God.

This is the country whence the shadows fall. This is the sphere where the initiate becomes a genuine adept. This is where Mossy, Tangle, and every other aspiring magician working through an initiation process aspire to one day be.

"We must, dear Mossy," responded Tangle. "What if your golden key should be the key to *it*?"

It is. Tangle is very intuitive.

"Ah! that would be grand," returned Mossy.--"But we must rest here for a little, and then we shall be able to cross the plain before night."
So he lay down on the ground, and about him on every side, and over his head, was the constant play of the wonderful shadows. He could look through them, and see the one behind the other, till they mixed in a mass of darkness. Tangle, too, lay admiring, and wondering, and longing after the country whence the shadows came. When they were rested they rose and pursued their journey. How long they were in crossing this plain I cannot tell; but before night Mossy's hair was streaked with gray, and Tangle had got wrinkles on her forehead.

Again, age represents maturity, and old age represents great maturity. Mossy and Tangle are extremely mature, and they're not even on Step 2 yet!

The Spirit of Magic by Virgil

As evening grew on, the shadows fell deeper and rose higher. At length they reached a place where they rose above their heads, and made all dark around them. Then they took hold of each other's hand, and walked on in silence and in some dismay. They felt the gathering darkness, and something strangely solemn besides, and the beauty of the shadows ceased to delight them. All at once Tangle found that she had not a hold of Mossy's hand, though when she lost it she could not tell.

"Mossy, Mossy!" she cried aloud in terror.

But no Mossy replied.

A moment after, the shadows sank to her feet, and down under her feet, and the mountains rose before her. She turned towards the gloomy region she had left, and called once more upon Mossy. There the gloom lay tossing and heaving, a dark, stormy, foamless sea of shadows, but no Mossy rose out of it, or came climbing up the hill on which she stood. She threw herself down and wept in despair.

There is no room for evangelism in magic. As a Bardon-trained magician, I want the world to be a blessed place to live in. I work hard to make the world a blessed place to live in, but this is not something I can do alone. Whenever another individual finishes working through IIH, becoming a genuine magician, that is a big win for me because now there is another magician out there also helping me in the work of making the world a blessed place to live in. If another individual finishes working through a magical training system that is not IIH, that is an equally big win for me. It is not about persuading others to choose your magical training system, but about helping them find the magical training system that suits them best, because this is the one they will work through the most easily, meaning they will become a magician more quickly if they use this training system than if they use a training system that does not suit them very well.

Imagine that you are an engineer and that you want to improve the world by designing a bridge that will make traffic less congested. Designing an entire bridge is a difficult task. If you have another engineer working with you, that is a big win for you because now you only have to do half as much work. It doesn't matter if the other engineer got his degree at the same university as you got your degree from. If the other engineer had gone to a university that he didn't like, he would have dropped out and never become an engineer, which means he would not be currently helping you. It's in your best interest, as an engineer, to help aspiring engineers find the university they like best so they are more

Chapter 17: The Golden Key

likely to successfully become engineers who can help you instead of dropping out because they hate their university. Similarly, it's in your best interest as a magician to help aspiring magicians find the magical training system that is best suited for them so they don't give up on their training before they succeed in becoming magicians who can help you make the world a better place.

The beginning stages of all magical training systems are very similar. They all teach you how to meditate. They all teach you how to introspect. They all force you to get your life together. However, after the beginning stages, different magical training systems can look very different. Tangle and Mossy have separated. They both walk different initiatory paths. The initiatory path Tangle walks is very similar to the initiatory path Bardon lays out in IIH, as we'll soon see when we examine the rest of the story. The initiatory path Mossy lays out is different, and the story doesn't tell us much about it.

However, all initiates walk into the same rainbow at the end of their initiation. Mossy and Tangle will meet up again in front of the rainbow and walk into it together, and when you complete your initiation, you will walk into it too.

Suddenly she remembered that the beautiful lady had told them, if they lost each other in a country of which she could not remember the name, they were not to be afraid, but to go straight on.

We must always go on. We must practice daily. We can take breaks if we need to, but we must return to our training as soon as we are able to. Otherwise, we will never reach the rainbow.

"And besides," she said to herself, "Mossy has the golden key, and so no harm will come to him, I do believe."

In Chapter 13, we discussed the idea of genuine spiritual danger and mentioned that the most extreme form of spiritual danger is being cut off from Divine Providence. This only happens when a person does atrocious things, but a compassionate individual would never do atrocious things and therefore would never be cut off from Divine Providence.

She rose from the ground, and went on.

The Spirit of Magic by Virgil

Before long she arrived at a precipice, in the face of which a stair was cut. When she had ascended half-way, the stair ceased, and the path led straight into the mountain. She was afraid to enter, and turning again towards the stair, grew giddy at sight of the depth beneath her, and was forced to throw herself down in the mouth of the cave.

When she opened her eyes, she saw a beautiful little figure with wings standing beside her, waiting.

"I know you," said Tangle. "You are my fish."

"Yes. But I am a fish no longer. I am an aeranth now."

"What is that?" asked Tangle.

"What you see I am," answered the shape. "And I am come to lead you through the mountain."

"Oh! thank you, dear fish--aeranth, I mean," returned Tangle, rising.

When Tangle feels lost in a time of darkness and despair, her intuition guides her and helps her to find her way.

Thereupon the aeranth took to his wings, and flew on through the long, narrow passage, reminding Tangle very much of the way he had swum on before her when he was a fish. And the moment his white wings moved, they began to throw off a continuous shower of sparks of all colours, which lighted up the passage before them.--All at once he vanished, and Tangle heard a low, sweet sound, quite different from the rush and crackle of his wings. Before her was an open arch, and through it came light, mixed with the sound of sea-waves.

She hurried out, and fell, tired and happy, upon the yellow sand of the shore. There she lay, half asleep with weariness and rest, listening to the low plash and retreat of the tiny waves, which seemed ever enticing the land to leave off being land, and become sea. And as she lay, her eyes were fixed upon the foot of a great rainbow standing far away against the sky on the other side of the sea. At length she fell fast asleep.

Even when Tangle is exhausted, her eyes are still fixed on the rainbow, meaning she is still focused on her goal. You must always keep your eyes on the rainbow. That way, you won't see the many things that could distract you and cause you to stray from the path. The various

Chapter 17: The Golden Key

distractions you encounter along the path might be interesting, but they are not nearly as interesting as what lies within the rainbow.

When she awoke, she saw an old man with long white hair down to his shoulders, leaning upon a stick covered with green buds, and so bending over her.
"What do you want here, beautiful woman?" he said.

Tangle is beautiful, meaning her personality has already been purified and balanced significantly because of her work with the conscious eating, conscious breathing, and magical washing exercises of Step 1.

"Am I beautiful? I am so glad!" said Tangle, rising. "My grandmother is beautiful."
"Yes. But what do you want?" he repeated, kindly.
"I think I want you. Are not you the Old Man of the Sea?
"I am."
"Then Grandmother says, have you any more fishes ready for her?"
"We will go and see, my dear," answered the old man, speaking yet more kindly than before. "And I can do something for you, can I not?"

The Old Man of the Sea can be seen as the archetype of the Step 2 student or even as the embodiment of Step 2. He speaks more kindly to Tangle when he learns that she has passed through Grandmother's house. The work of Step 2 is easier for those who have completed Step 1.

"Yes--show me the way up to the country from which the shadows fall," said Tangle.
For there she hoped to find Mossy again.
"Ah! indeed, that would be worth doing," said the old man.
"But I cannot, for I do not know the way myself. But I will send you to the Old Man of the Earth. Perhaps he can tell you. He is much older than I am."

A person at Step 2 can't say much about the Sphere of the Sun or about the methods of entering this planetary sphere. He still has a long way to go before he can begin the PME work of travelling to the planetary spheres.

The Spirit of Magic by Virgil

Leaning on his staff, he conducted her along the shore to a steep rock that looked like a petrified ship turned upside down. The door of it was the rudder of a great vessel, ages ago at the bottom of the sea. Immediately within the door was a stair in the rock, down which the old man went, and Tangle followed. At the bottom the old man had his house, and there he lived.

A ship's rudder is what allows it to be steered. A ship will never reach its destination unless it can be steered toward that destination. An aspiring magician will not reach adepthood unless he steers himself towards adepthood by forcing himself to follow a route that leads to adepthood. Some adepts have laid out such routes for aspiring magicians in the form of magical training systems. Tangle is on one of these routes. She is not going in circles, but steering herself toward the rainbow.

As soon as she entered it, Tangle heard a strange noise, unlike anything she had ever heard before. She soon found that it was the fishes talking. She tried to understand what they said; but their speech was so old-fashioned, and rude, and undefined, that she could not make much of it.

The speech of the fishes is ugly. You can often tell how mature someone is by how maturely he speaks. Mature people speak maturely. Immature people speak immaturely. Since the speech of the fishes is ugly, they are probably ugly. Ugly means they are not highly spiritually evolved. The beautiful initiates Mossy saw within the rainbow, on the other hand, are highly evolved, which is why their inner divine natures (microcosmic Tiphereths) shine outward and are seen in their actions and in their personalities.

"I will go and see about those fishes for my daughter," said the Old Man of the Sea.
And moving a slide in the wall of his house, he first looked out, and then tapped upon a thick piece of crystal that filled the round opening. Tangle came up behind him, and peeping through the window into the heart of the great deep green ocean, saw the most curious creatures, some very ugly, all very odd, and with especially queer mouths, swimming about everywhere, above and below, but all coming towards the window in answer to the tap of the Old Man of the Sea.

Chapter 17: The Golden Key

The fish are indeed ugly. The story makes sure to emphasize that their mouths are ugly too, representing the fact that ugly speech comes out of these mouths.

Only a few could get their mouths against the glass; but those who were floating miles away yet turned their heads towards it. The old man looked through the whole flock carefully for some minutes, and then turning to Tangle, said,--
"I am sorry I have not got one ready yet. I want more time than she does. But I will send some as soon as I can."
He then shut the slide.
Presently a great noise arose in the sea. The old man opened the slide again, and tapped on the glass, whereupon the fishes were all as still as sleep.
"They were only talking about you," he said. "And they do speak such nonsense!--To-morrow," he continued, "I must show you the way to the Old Man of the Earth. He lives a long way from here."

The fish are gossiping about her. Gossip is one example of ugly speech. Lying, boasting, and insulting are other examples of ugly speech. Initiates who have brought forth their inner divine natures and identify with their inner divine natures speak beautifully. Their words educate, heal, and bring joy and wonder to those around them.

"Do let me go at once," said Tangle.
"No. That is not possible. You must come this way first."

The domain of the Old Man of the Earth represents the stages of initiation that encompass Steps 3 and 4. Tangle wants to move on to these steps, but she cannot because she has not yet completed the work of Step 2.

He led her to a hole in the wall, which she had not observed before. It was covered with the green leaves and white blossoms of a creeping plant.
"Only white-blossoming plants can grow under the sea," said the old man. "In there you will find a bath, in which you must lie till I call you."
Tangle went in, and found a smaller room or cave, in the further corner of which was a great basin hollowed out of a rock,

The Spirit of Magic by Virgil

and half-full of the clearest sea-water. Little streams were constantly running into it from cracks in the wall of the cavern. It was polished quite smooth inside, and had a carpet of yellow sand in the bottom of it. Large green leaves and white flowers of various plants crowded up and over it, draping and covering it almost entirely.

In the Epic of Gilgamesh, Gilgamesh learns of a plant living under the sea that will bring immortality to those who eat it. In some versions of the epic, the plant is a white flower. The technique for becoming immortal involves purifying yourself of those things that lead to death. These white flowers, therefore, indicate that she is about to undergo a process of purification.

No sooner was she undressed and lying in the bath, than she began to feel as if the water were sinking into her, and she were receiving all the good of sleep without undergoing its forgetfulness. She felt the good coming all the time. And she grew happier and more hopeful than she had been since she lost Mossy.

This bath represents the astral work of Step 2, which involves purifying one's personality of its negative traits. The longer she remains in the bath, the happier she is. This shows that self-transformation does not have to be a painful practice. In fact, it can be a very joyful process that leads to even more joy. I used to be irascible, disorganized, and socially awkward. When I eliminated these traits from my personality while working through Step 2, my life improved immensely and became more joyful. I was filled with hope that I could succeed in all the endeavors that these negative traits previously forced me to fail in.

But she could not help thinking how very sad it was for a poor old man to live there all alone, and have to take care of a whole seaful of stupid and riotous fishes.

Tangle possesses the quality of empathy, which is an important trait to have.

After about an hour, as she thought, she heard his voice calling her, and rose out of the bath. All the fatigue and aching of her long journey had vanished. She was as whole, and strong, and well as if she had slept for seven days.

Chapter 17: The Golden Key

In the Epic of Gilgamesh, Utnapishtim tells Gilgamesh to stay awake for seven days. Gilgamesh fails, and Utnapishtim explains that because he is unable to stay awake for seven days, he is not ready to become immortal. Here, Tangle feels as refreshed as if she had slept for seven days. This means that if she wanted to, she could stay awake for seven days. She has greatly purified herself.

Returning to the opening that led into the other part of the house, she started back with amazement, for through it she saw the form of a grand man, with a majestic and beautiful face, waiting for her.
"Come," he said; "I see you are ready."

The Old Man of the Sea is about to direct her to the Old Man of the Earth. Having purified her personality, she is now ready to practice the elemental accumulation exercises of Step 3.

She entered with reverence.
"Where is the Old Man of the Sea?" she asked, humbly.
"There is no one here but me," he answered, smiling. "Some people call me the Old Man of the Sea. Others have another name for me, and are terribly frightened when they meet me taking a walk by the shore. Therefore I avoid being seen by them, for they are so afraid, that they never see what I really am. You see me now.--But I must show you the way to the Old Man of the Earth."

Other people cannot see the beauty of the Old Man of the Sea. Tangle can. In other words, she can see things other people can't. This represents the fact that she is becoming clairvoyant. In Step 7, Bardon provides the student with exercises to develop his astral senses (clairvoyance, clairaudience, and clairsentience). However, these exercises aren't meant to develop his astral senses from scratch. Bardon's comments on these exercises are as follows.

The magician's astral senses have been trained and developed in any case in the course of all the preceding exercises; nevertheless there is need of an extraordinary drill in cases of poor abilities for one or the other faculty, because every human being has different talents. Therefore it will be

The Spirit of Magic by Virgil

opportune to quote exercises here that enable the magician to develop the sense of the astral body fast and without difficulty.

In other words, the exercises of the steps preceding Step 7 have caused the student to begin developing clairvoyance. The Step 7 clairvoyance exercise only finishes the process of clairvoyance development. This process begins with the Step 2 plastic imagination work. The imagination can be used actively to change the inner planes, but it can also be used passively to perceive the inner planes. This is basically how your astral senses work.

He led her into the cave where the bath was, and there she saw, in the opposite corner, a second opening in the rock.
"Go down that stair, and it will bring you to him," said the Old Man of the Sea.
With humble thanks Tangle took her leave. She went down the winding stair, till she began to fear there was no end to it. Still down and down it went, rough and broken, with springs of water bursting out of the rocks and running down the steps beside her.

Near the beginning of IIH, there is an image showing Bardon's rendition of the first Tarot card. This card summarizes, in symbolic form, everything the magician is supposed to attain as he works through the ten steps of IIH. In this image, we find mastery of the four elements represented by four streams of light, mastery of the electric and magnetic fluids represented by the sun and the moon, evolution of consciousness represented by the lotus, the experience of the infinite and eternal represented by the letters AUM, and the development and integration of the masculine and feminine principles represented by the tantric act within the glass globe. We also find the philosopher's stone within the lotus flower. This, too, is an attainment of the student once he has worked through this system of initiation. Therefore, we see that the process of initiation is in part a process of spiritual alchemy.

Within alchemy, the key to acquiring the philosopher's stone is found in the acronym V.I.T.R.I.O.L., meaning *"Visita Interiora Terrae Rectificando Invenies Occultum Lapidem"* (Visit the interior of the Earth, and by rectifying, you will find the hidden stone). Tangle's journey downward is a clear reference to this acronym. She will continue to journey downward to the fiery core of the Earth, where she will meet

Chapter 17: The Golden Key

the Old Man of the Fire. At this point, she will be ready to ascend again, and will do so via the rainbow.[76]

It was quite dark about her, and yet she could see. For after being in that bath, people's eyes always give out a light they can see by. There were no creeping things in the way. All was safe and pleasant though so dark and damp and deep.

Since there is no light, Tangle is using clairvoyance to see. The story mentions that the bath is instrumental in the development of her clairvoyance. The bath is the process of purifying one's personality. In IIH, Bardon writes that the quality of one's clairvoyance depends on the purity of one's personality. In Step 2, the student not only trains his plastic imagination, but also purifies his personality. Therefore, the magician who has completed the work of Step 2 has taken some big steps toward the development of clairvoyance and the other astral senses.

Daskalos had great clairvoyance and guided his students through the process of developing their clairvoyance. Visitors often came to him and asked him to help them develop their clairvoyance. He'd always laugh when that happened. Like Bardon, he knew that the quality of one's clairvoyance depends on the purity of one's soul and spirit. If you are blind and suddenly you regain your vision, your vision will be useless if it's so blurry you can't make out anything. You might as well be blind. Daskalos taught his students that when your astral body and mental body are impure, then you constantly think negative thoughts and harbor negative feelings. These negative thoughts and feelings pollute the astramental environment around you and create a dark mist that surrounds you. It is difficult to see beyond this mist, which is why clairvoyance is useless for those who are surrounded by such a dark mist. If you were surrounded by a dark physical mist that you couldn't see beyond, then your physical eyes would be equally useless, and you might as well be blind. When you purify yourself, you no longer harbor negative thoughts and feelings. The dark mist around you dissipates, and you can see beyond it.

At last there was not one step more, and she found herself in a glimmering cave. On a stone in the middle of it sat a figure with its back towards her--the figure of an old man bent double with age. From behind she could see his white beard spread out on the rocky floor in front of him. He did not move as she entered, so she passed round that she might stand before him and speak to him.

The Spirit of Magic by Virgil

He does not move as she enters. He is focused on what he is doing. By the time you reach these steps, your ability to concentrate should be well-developed.

The moment she looked in his face, she saw that he was a youth of marvelous beauty.

He is beautiful because his personality is pure and balanced. That was the astral work of Step 2.

He sat entranced with the delight of what he beheld in a mirror of something like silver, which lay on the floor at his feet, and which from behind she had taken for his white beard.

The mirror represents his personality. The act of looking into the mirror represents introspection.

He sat on, heedless of her presence, pale with the joy of his vision.

The concept of "joy" corresponds to Tiphereth. When the Old Man of the Earth introspects, he sees many positive qualities. These are the qualities of his inner divine nature. The more pure your personality is, the more it reflects the light of your inner divine nature. The more pure the moon is, the more it reflects the light of the sun.

She stood and watched him. At length, all trembling, she spoke. But her voice made no sound. Yet the youth lifted up his head. He showed no surprise, however, at seeing her--only smiled a welcome. "Are you the Old Man of the Earth?" Tangle had said. And the youth answered, and Tangle heard him, though not with her ears:--
"I am. What can I do for you?"
"Tell me the way to the country whence the shadows fall."
"Ah! that I do not know. I only dream about it myself. I see its shadows sometimes in my mirror: the way to it I do not know. But I think the Old Man of the Fire must know. He is much older than I am. He is the oldest man of all."

There are a few shadows in his mirror, indicating that there are still a few minor negative traits in his personality. These minor negative traits are not bad enough to prevent him from safely accumulating the

Chapter 17: The Golden Key

elements, but they will prevent him from safely accumulating the electric and magnetic fluids. Before he gets to Step 8, he will have to root them out.

"Where does he live?"
"I will show you the way to his place. I never saw him myself."

The Old Man of the Earth has never seen the Old Man of the Fire. This is because the Old Man of the Fire is the future form of the Old Man of the Earth. When you are on Step 4 of IIH, you do not know what you will be like when you are on Step 8. The Old Man of the Fire has rooted out the shadows in the mirror.

So saying, the young man rose, and then stood for a while gazing at Tangle.
"I wish I could see that country too," he said. "But I must mind my work."

The Old Man of the Earth is halfway through IIH. Reaching the Sphere of the Sun is halfway through PME. Those who are halfway through IIH should not waste their time wondering what it is like to be halfway through PME. Instead, they should focus on their own work so they can one day reach that level. In the Bardon community, you will find many people who worry about the work of PME when they have barely made any progress through IIH. This shows a lack of focus.

He led her to the side of the cave, and told her to lay her ear against the wall.
"What do you hear?" he asked.
"I hear," answered Tangle, "the sound of a great water running inside the rock."
"That river runs down to the dwelling of the oldest man of all-- the
Old Man of the Fire. I wish I could go to see him. But I must mind my work. That river is the only way to him."
Then the Old Man of the Earth stooped over the floor of the cave, raised a huge stone from it, and left it leaning. It disclosed a great hole that went plumb-down.
"That is the way," he said.
"But there are no stairs."
"You must throw yourself in. There is no other way."

The Spirit of Magic by Virgil

She turned and looked him full in the face--stood so for a whole minute, as she thought: it was a whole year--then threw herself headlong into the hole.

To throw oneself into the work of initiation is a sign of commitment. Commitment is important, because your training becomes more time-consuming during these steps. In Step 1, you were just meditating for ten minutes each day, conscious breathing for ten minutes each day, and studying your soul mirrors a few minutes each day. The exercises of the intermediate steps of IIH are more intense. Your daily practice routine will get longer. Your magical training becomes a bigger commitment, but you must make this commitment if you want to reach adepthood.

Working through Steps 3 and 4 is not something one does overnight. In this story's timeline it takes Tangle a whole year, which undoubtedly represents a much longer period of time in the real world.

When she came to herself, she found herself gliding down fast and deep. Her head was under water, but that did not signify, for, when she thought about it, she could not remember that she had breathed once since her bath in the cave of the Old Man of the Sea. When she lifted up her head a sudden and fierce heat struck her, and she sank it again instantly, and went sweeping on.

Gradually the stream grew shallower. At length she could hardly keep her head under. Then the water could carry her no farther. She rose from the channel, and went step for step down the burning descent. The water ceased altogether. The heat was terrible. She felt scorched to the bone, but it did not touch her strength. It grew hotter and hotter. She said, "I can bear it no longer." Yet she went on.

Some types of suffering make our personality stronger. The severity that helps our personalities become stronger is represented by the sephirah Geburah on the Tree of Life. The fiery river Tangle is passing through represents this severity and will make her personality strong. This severity is not evil, but divine. It serves an important purpose. Again, that purpose is to make Tangle strong.

Not all suffering makes us strong. Sometimes, suffering doesn't make us strong in any way that we are not already strong. Other times, suffering may weaken us if we have already been through too much and are at our breaking point.[77] When the divine purpose of making people

Chapter 17: The Golden Key

strong is removed from Geburah, Geburah becomes an empty shell. This type of shell is called a "qlippah" in Kabbalah. Geburah, severity filled with a purpose, becomes the qlippah Golohab when the purpose at its heart is removed from it. Golohab is purposeless severity – a source of unnecessary suffering.

At the long last, the stair ended at a rude archway in an all but glowing rock. Through this archway Tangle fell exhausted into a cool mossy cave. The floor and walls were covered with moss--green, soft, and damp. A little stream spouted from a rent in the rock and fell into a basin of moss. She plunged her face into it and drank. Then she lifted her head and looked around. Then she rose and looked again. She saw no one in the cave. But the moment she stood upright she had a marvelous sense that she was in the secret of the earth and all its ways. Everything she had seen, or learned from books; all that her grandmother had said or sung to her; all the talk of the beasts, birds, and fishes; all that had happened to her on her journey with Mossy, and since then in the heart of the earth with the Old man and the Older man--all was plain: she understood it all, and saw that everything meant the same thing, though she could not have put it into words again.

The more you advance along the magical path, the more wisdom and understanding you acquire. At this point of the story, we see that Tangle has acquired a very high level of understanding. Since wisdom and understanding always go hand in hand, this means she has also acquired a very high level of wisdom.

The next moment she descried, in a corner of the cave, a little naked child sitting on the moss. He was playing with balls of various colours and sizes, which he disposed in strange figures upon the floor beside him. And now Tangle felt that there was something in her knowledge which was not in her understanding. For she knew there must be an infinite meaning in the change and sequence and individual forms of the figures into which the child arranged the balls, as well as in the varied harmonies of their colours, but what it all meant she could not tell. He went on busily, tirelessly, playing his solitary game, without looking up, or seeming to know that there was a stranger in his deep-withdrawn cell. Diligently as a lace-maker shifts her bobbins, he shifted and arranged his balls. Flashes of meaning would now pass from them to Tangle, and now again all

The Spirit of Magic by Virgil

would be not merely obscure, but utterly dark. She stood looking for a long time, for there was fascination in the sight; and the longer she looked the more an indescribable vague intelligence went on rousing itself in her mind.

In Step 5, the student learns to create spheres made from the elements. He uses the fire element to create a sphere, moves this sphere around, and then dissolves it. He then practices the same exercise but with the other three elements.[78] Once they have become proficient at this exercise, Bardon has students practice the same exercise with more complex shapes like pyramids, cylinders, and cubes. These highly condensed buildups of energy are called "dynamides."

The domain of the Old Man of the Fire represents the stages of initiation that encompass Steps 5 through 8. The Old Man of the Fire himself is an initiate who has completed these steps. He is not just working with the spherical dynamides. He is "playing" with them. This means he is able to work with them effortlessly because he has achieved a high level of proficiency in this exercise.

For seven years she had stood there watching the naked child with his coloured balls, and it seemed to her like seven hours, when all at once the shape the balls took, she knew not why, reminded her of the Valley of Shadows, and she spoke:--

Seven years is a long time, but as I've written before, the steps of IIH are not completed overnight. It seems like seven hours because time flies when you're having fun. To succeed in your magical training, you must enjoy your magical training. I've mentioned before that some people have written that the exercises of IIH are very dry and boring. It's certainly the case that some may find them dry and boring, but not everyone shares this opinion. I find them to be fun and exciting, as I wrote in the chapter about thought-observation.

"Where is the Old Man of the Fire?" she said.
"Here I am," answered the child, rising and leaving his balls on the moss. "What can I do for you?"
There was such an awfulness of absolute repose on the face of the child that Tangle stood dumb before him.

Each sphere has certain virtues associated with it. One of the virtues associated with the Sphere of the Sun is "a stillness that embraces the

Chapter 17: The Golden Key

universe." The Old Man of the Fire, having been to this sphere and having learned from its ruling genii, has internalized this virtue. The look of absolute repose on his face reflects this "stillness that embraces the universe" that he has internalized.

He had no smile, but the love in his large gray eyes was deep as the centre.

The Sphere of the Sun is the sphere of compassion.[79] Having mastered the lessons of this sphere, the love of the Old Man of the Fire is incredibly deep.

And with the repose there lay on his face a shimmer as of moonlight, which seemed as if any moment it might break into such a ravishing smile as would cause the beholder to weep himself to death. But the smile never came, and the moonlight lay there unbroken. For the heart of the child was too deep for any smile to reach from it to his face.
"Are you the oldest man of all?" Tangle at length, although filled with awe, ventured to ask.

We all know people who could be described as "shallow." They are boring, and there is not much to them. The initiate is deep. There is always more to him. His lover can explore him for a lifetime and never know him thoroughly because there is just too much to know. He has been through many fantastical experiences and penetrated into many profound mysteries.

"Yes, I am. I am very, very old. I am able to help you, I know. I can help everybody." And the child drew near and looked up in her face so that she burst into tears.

The initiate is more mature than the students who are in the middle of working through their initiations and have not yet become initiates.
Many students of magic begin their magical training because they want to acquire the power to help others. When they finish their magical training, they do acquire the power to help others.

"Can you tell me the way to the country the shadows fall from?" she sobbed.

269

The Spirit of Magic by Virgil

"Yes. I know the way quite well. I go there myself sometimes. But you could not go my way; you are not old enough. I will show you how you can go."

Tangle must first travel to the Earthzone, and then to the Sphere of the Moon, and then to the Sphere of Mercury, and then to the Sphere of Venus, and then to the Sphere of the Sun. Once she is able to do this proficiently, she can travel to the Sphere of the Sun directly without passing through the lower spheres first.

"Do not send me out into the great heat again," prayed Tangle. "I will not," answered the child.

Severity teaches us important lessons, but once we have learned a lesson, there is no need for us to go through that severity again.

And he reached up, and put his little cool hand on her heart. "Now," he said, "you can go. The fire will not burn you. Come."

This is perhaps the single most important line in the whole story. The desert Tangle is about to enter represents the inner planes. If you enter the desert before you are ready to, you will get burned. The energies within the inner planes can be intense. One must be strong to withstand them, and strength comes from having an elemental equilibrium. By this point, Tangle has a superb elemental equilibrium.

In *A Bardon Companion*, Rawn writes the following at the end of his comments about Step 8.

> *In the introduction to both PME and KTQ, Bardon states that the student must have completed Step Eight of IIH before beginning the work of magical evocation and/or kabbala. Please consider for a moment the degree of training and magical maturity of one who has genuinely made it to this stage. Such a one will possess an absolute magical equilibrium, be capable of the three-part action, be able to journey with their mental body with ease, and have absolute control over the Elements and Fluids. All these attributes are essential for success with evocation and kabbalistic speech. Anyone who dares to begin work with PME and KTQ before*

Chapter 17: The Golden Key

reaching this stage risks great harm to their mental, emotional and physical well-being.

The Old Man of the Fire has absolute control over the elements and fluids, which is why he can effortless create and manipulate dynamides made from the elements and fluids. He is also extremely old, indicating that he has a high degree of magical maturity. Tangle also has those attributes now that she has completed the stage of her initiation represented by the domain of the Old Man of the Fire. If she didn't, she would risk great harm to her "mental, emotional, and physical well-being" when she walked out into the desert. This is what I mean when I say she would be burned.

He led her from the cave, and following him through another archway, she found herself in a vast desert of sand and rock. The sky of it was of rock, lowering over them like solid thunderclouds; and the whole place was so hot that she saw, in bright rivulets, the yellow gold and white silver and red copper trickling molten from the rocks.
But the heat never came near her.
When they had gone some distance, the child turned up a great stone, and took something like an egg from under it. He next drew a long curved line in the sand with his finger, and laid the egg in it. He then spoke something Tangle could not understand. The egg broke, a small snake came out, and, lying in the line in the sand, grew and grew till he filled it. The moment he was thus full-grown, he began to glide away, undulating like a sea-wave.
"Follow that serpent," said the child. "He will lead you the right way."
Tangle followed the serpent. But she could not go far without looking back at the marvellous child. He stood alone in the midst of the glowing desert, beside a fountain of red flame that had burst forth at his feet, his naked whiteness glimmering a pale rosy red in the torrid fire. There he stood, looking after her, till, from the lengthening distance, she could see him no more. The serpent went straight on, turning neither to the right nor left.

This serpent is the serpent Nehushtan, which God tells Moses to erect in the desert. The people of Israel were frustrated and impatient with their long journey from Egypt and began to speak ill of Moses and

The Spirit of Magic by Virgil

God. God sent "fiery serpents" to punish them by biting them. These fiery serpents are the seraphim, the angels of Geburah – the embodiment of severity. They were to teach the people of Israel to be patient and not to speak ill of Moses or God.

Some people repented after they were bitten by the fiery serpents. Since they had learned their lesson after being bitten, any additional suffering from their bites was unnecessary suffering. For these people, God told Moses to build a bronze statue of a serpent. Whoever repented and looked at the serpent would be cured of their wounds. This serpent is Nehushtan.

Nehushtan was made of bronze, which is an alloy of copper and tin. Copper is the metal of Venus/Netzach and tin is the metal of Jupiter/Chesed. Thus, bronze is the metal of the Pillar of Mercy, and it alleviates the suffering caused by the seraphim of the Pillar of Severity.

Since Nehushtan eliminates unnecessary suffering, it is a source of blessings. Tangle walks in the path of this serpent, meaning she too will bless others. Within this serpent we see the Pillars of Mercy and Severity combined. The Pillar of Mercy is found in the alloy bronze. The Pillar of Severity is found in the serpent shape. Combined, they allude to the Pillar of Mildness, and especially to Tiphereth.[80]

The serpent leads Tangle to the rainbow. All of the resources in the rainbow, including the knowledge held by the spirits of the Earthzone and the planetary spheres, serve to help the magician bless society. Tangle has completed Step 8 of IIH and is ready to move on to the work of PME.[81]

Meantime Mossy had got out of the Lake of Shadows, and, following his mournful, lonely way, had reached the sea-shore. It was a dark, stormy evening. The sun had set. The wind was blowing from the sea. The waves had surrounded the rock within which lay the old man's house. A deep water rolled between it and the shore, upon which a majestic figure was walking alone.

Mossy went up to him and said,--

"Will you tell me where to find the Old Man of the Sea?"

"I am the Old Man of the Sea," the figure answered.

"I see a strong kingly man of middle age," returned Mossy.

Then the old man looked at him more intently, and said,--

"Your sight, young man, is better than that of most who take this way. The night is stormy: come to my house and tell me what I can do for you."

Chapter 17: The Golden Key

Mossy's sight is better than that of most people because he can see on three planes (he is clairvoyant) while most people can only see on the physical plane. While Tangle followed an initiatory path that is similar to the path Bardon lays out in IIH, Mossy seems to have followed a different initiatory path. Step 7 is the step of IIH where the student finishes developing his clairvoyance. Mossy, being clairvoyant, seems to have reached the point in his training that is the equivalent of Step 7 of IIH. After Step 7 is Step 8, which is the step where the student learns mental wandering.

Mossy followed him. The waves flew from before the footsteps of the Old Man of the Sea, and Mossy followed upon dry sand. When they had reached the cave, they sat down and gazed at each other.
Now Mossy was an old man by this time. He looked much older than the Old Man of the Sea, and his feet were very weary.

Mossy is extremely mature. He has been walking a long time, but he hasn't been walking in circles like many aspiring magicians. He has been walking toward adepthood.

After looking at him for a moment, the old man took him by the hand and led him into his inner cave. There he helped him to undress, and laid him in the bath.[82] And he saw that one of his hands Mossy did not open.

Compassionate people do not show off their compassion in an effort to look good and gain praise from others. Mossy keeps his golden key concealed.

"What have you in that hand?" he asked.
Mossy opened his hand, and there lay the golden key.
"Ah!" said the old man, "that accounts for your knowing me. And I know the way you have to go."

The quality of one's clairvoyance depends on the purity of one's soul and spirit. Compassion is a sign of a very pure soul and spirit.

"I want to find the country whence the shadows fall," said Mossy.
"I dare say you do. So do I. But meantime, one thing is certain.

The Spirit of Magic by Virgil

What is that key for, do you think?"
"For a key-hole somewhere. But I don't know why I keep it. I never could find the key-hole. And I have lived a good while, I believe," said Mossy, sadly. "I'm not sure that I'm not old. I know my feet ache."

I feel sad every time I read this passage. Daskalos once told his students "you must always be aware that good is never lost." Compassion is never useless, and in the grand scheme of things, there is nothing more useful than compassion.

"Do they?" said the old man, as if he really meant to ask the question; and Mossy, who was still lying in the bath, watched his feet for a moment before he replied,--"No, they do not. Perhaps I am not old either."
"Get up and look at yourself in the water."
He rose and looked at himself in the water, and there was not a gray hair on his head or a wrinkle on his skin.

Step 8 is the step where the student masters the electric and magnetic fluids. These fluids are symbolized by the sun and the moon in alchemical images. These alchemical images hint that mastery over the electric and magnetic fluids is the key to rejuvenation.

"You have tasted of death now," said the old man. "Is it good?"

The process of remaining in the bath also represents Mossy's training in mental wandering. The work of PME is the work of using mental wandering to travel to the planetary spheres to meet their ruling genii.[83] This work is represented in symbolic form in the second card of the Major Arcana – The High Priestess. In Bardon's rendition of The High Priestess, two paintings depicting Nephthys and Isis hang on the wall of the temple. Nephthys was the goddess of death. Isis was the goddess of rebirth. In Egyptian mythology, these two goddesses protected those who were undergoing the process of dying and transitioning into a new life. This is a process of leaving your body and entering a new body. The process of mental wandering is like that, only you return to the same body. This is the reason the concept of an "initiation" is often seen as a process of death and rebirth. Now that Mossy has mastered mental wandering, he knows what it is like to leave his body, so he has a taste of what it is like to die.

Chapter 17: The Golden Key

"It is good," said Mossy. "It is better than life."
"No, said the old man: it is only more life.--Your feet will make no holes in the water now."

He can walk on water, meaning he can walk on the astral ocean without drowning. Many people who attempt to enter the astral ocean get caught up in the currents and "drown." To use a Hermetic metaphor, Mossy now has the winged sandals of Hermes.

"What do you mean?"
"I will show you that presently."
They returned to the outer cave, and sat and talked together for a long time. At length the Old Man of the Sea rose, and said to Mossy,--
"Follow me."
He led him up the stair again, and opened another door. They stood on the level of the raging sea, looking towards the east. Across the waste of waters, against the bosom of a fierce black cloud, stood the foot of a rainbow, glowing in the dark.

He's still going east; even after all these years the journey continues. He has always been walking east, the direction of adepthood. This is why he has always been continually getting closer to adepthood. Had he been walking in circles or walking in the wrong direction, he would never have reached his current location, which is close to the rainbow.

"This indeed is my way," said Mossy, as soon as he saw the rainbow, and stepped out upon the sea. His feet made no holes in the water. He fought the wind, and clomb the waves, and went on towards the rainbow.

He has the strength to fight the wind and climb the waves because of his elemental equilibrium.

The storm died away. A lovely day and a lovelier night followed. A cool wind blew over the wide plain of the quiet ocean. And still Mossy journeyed eastward. But the rainbow had vanished with the storm.

The Spirit of Magic by Virgil

Sometimes we need brief reminders of what awaits us once we have finished our initiation. These brief reminders motivate us to keep going. I interpret Mossy seeing the rainbow for a short period of time as one such brief reminder.

Day after day he held on, and he thought he had no guide. He did not see how a shining fish under the water directed his steps.

The fish is a symbol of Jesus, and therefore of Tiphereth, which is associated with the concept of divine guidance. This is because our primary source of divine guidance is our Holy Guardian Angel, and the concept of the HGA is associated with Tiphereth. Our HGA's give us plenty of guidance throughout our initiation, but we are often unaware of that guidance on a conscious level.

He crossed the sea, and came to a great precipice of rock, up which he could discover but one path. Nor did this lead him farther than half-way up the rock, where it ended on a platform. Here he stood and pondered.--It could not be that the way stopped here, else what was the path for? It was a rough path, not very plain, yet certainly a path.--He examined the face of the rock. It was smooth as glass.

Some people succeed in exteriorizing their mental bodies despite not going through proper initiation. They often use things like drugs to force their mental bodies out of their physical bodies. These people might be able to wander around the lower levels of the inner planes, but they won't be able to enter any of the more sublime realms. Mossy can go further.

But as his eyes kept roving hopelessly over it, something glittered, and he caught sight of a row of small sapphires. They bordered a little hole in the rock.
"The key-hole!" he cried.
He tried the key. It fitted. It turned. A great clang and clash, as of iron bolts on huge brazen caldrons, echoed thunderously within.

Compassion unlocks many doors in magic. Magicians serve Divine Providence by fulfilling the will of Divine Providence on Earth. They simultaneously serve society because it is the will of Divine Providence that society be blessed. The desire to bless society arises from

Chapter 17: The Golden Key

compassion, and the more eager you are to bless society, the more readily you will penetrate into the mysteries of magic. A genuine desire to serve society always arises from compassion.

He drew out the key. The rock in front of him began to fall. He retreated from it as far as the breadth of the platform would allow. A great slab fell at his feet. In front was still the solid rock, with this one slab fallen forward out of it. But the moment he stepped upon it, a second fell, just short of the edge of the first, making the next step of a stair, which thus kept dropping itself before him as he ascended into the heart of the precipice. It led him into a hall fit for such an approach--irregular and rude in formation, but floor, sides, pillars, and vaulted roof, all one mass of shining stones of every colour that light can show. In the centre stood seven columns, ranged from red to violet.

In the Book of Proverbs, it is written,

Wisdom hath builded her house, she hath hewn out her seven pillars. She hath killed her beasts; she hath mingled her wine; she hath also furnished her table. She hath sent forth her maidens: she crieth upon the highest places of the city, "Whoso is simple, let him turn in hither." As for him that wanteth understanding, she saith to him, "Come, eat of my bread, and drink of the wine which I have mingled. Forsake the foolish, and live; and go in the way of understanding.

Mossy has entered the house of wisdom. That is to say, he has become wise. At the very beginning of his path, when he was staying in Grandmother's house, he used conscious eating to begin the process of becoming wise. He never stopped striving to become wiser, and now he is actually within the house of wisdom.

There is a bit of confusion here regarding terminology. The story's description of the hall says it has pillars and seven columns. The seven columns allude to the seven "pillars" in the house of wisdom mentioned in the Bible quote above. But what are the pillars in the hall in addition to the seven columns? The story does not say how many pillars there are, but the perceptive Bardonist will immediately realize that there are four pillars. In IIH, Bardon writes,

The Spirit of Magic by Virgil

Knowledge, daring, volition, silence: these are the four pillars of Solomon's temple, i.e., the microcosm and the macrocosm upon which the sacred science of magic is built. According to the four elements, they are the fundamental qualities which must be inherent in each magician if he aspires to the highest perfection in science.

All good magical training systems teach their students to develop knowledge, daring, volition, and silence; even if they don't explicitly call them that, or specifically identify those traits as being special. In one way or another, they're woven into the system.

And on the pedestal of one of them sat a woman, motionless, with her face bowed upon her knees. Seven years had she sat there waiting. She lifted her head as Mossy drew near. It was Tangle. Her hair had grown to her feet, and was rippled like the windless sea on broad sands.

As mentioned previously in this commentary, hair is a symbol of magical power in some cultures. Tangle's hair is really long, meaning she has a great deal of magical power.

Her face was beautiful, like her grandmother's, and as still and peaceful as that of the Old Man of the Fire. Her form was tall and noble. Yet Mossy knew her at once.

Like the Old Man of the Fire, she is an initiate.

"How beautiful you are, Tangle!" he said, in delight and astonishment.

You too will be beautiful when you have completed your initiation. That is to say, your microcosmic Tiphereth will be visible to everyone because its light will not be blocked by a dark and impure personality.

"Am I?" she returned. "Oh, I have waited for you so long! But you, you are like the Old Man of the Sea. No. You are like the Old Man of the Earth. No, no. You are like the oldest man of all. You are like them all. And yet you are my own old Mossy! How did you come

Chapter 17: The Golden Key

here? What did you do after I lost you? Did you find the key-hole? Have you got the key still?"

She had a hundred questions to ask him, and he a hundred more to ask her. They told each other all their adventures, and were as happy as man and woman could be. For they were younger and better, and stronger and wiser, than they had ever been before.

When you have completed your initiation, you too will be "younger," better, stronger, and wiser than ever before. You will be "younger" because you will have regained the curiosity, open-mindedness, and desire to pursue one's dreams you had as a child. You will be better because you will have used the six-pronged attack to develop many positive traits such as intelligence, charisma, organization, assertiveness, and courage. You will be stronger because you will have an elemental equilibrium, which is where true inner strength arises from. You will be wiser because initiation is just as much a process of acquiring wisdom as it is a process of acquiring magical power.

It began to grow dark. And they wanted more than ever to reach the country whence the shadows fall. So they looked about them for a way out of the cave. The door by which Mossy entered had closed again, and there was half a mile of rock between them and the sea. Neither could Tangle find the opening in the floor by which the serpent had led her thither. They searched till it grew so dark that they could see nothing, and gave it up. After a while, however, the cave began to glimmer again. The light came from the moon, but it did not look like moonlight, for it gleamed through those seven pillars in the middle, and filled the place with all colours.

They have purified and balanced their personalities. The moon transmits the light of the sun without blocking it or distorting it in any way. The light of the moon doesn't look like moonlight because, for all intents and purposes, it is actually sunlight. This is also why it causes the rainbow to appear. Moonlight cannot create a rainbow, but sunlight can.

Each of the seven pillars leads to one of the seven planetary spheres whose vibrations reach the human realm. These are the Sphere of the Moon, the Sphere of Mercury, the Sphere of Venus, the Sphere of the Sun, the Sphere of Mars, the Sphere of Jupiter, and the Sphere of Saturn. The initiate learns to travel to each sphere in that order. However, before he can travel to the Sphere of the Moon and learn from its ruling genii,

The Spirit of Magic by Virgil

he must travel to the ruling genii of the Earthzone and learn from them first.

And now Mossy saw that there was a pillar beside the red one, which he had not observed before. And it was of the same new colour that he had seen in the rainbow when he saw it first in the fairy forest. And on it he saw a sparkle of blue. It was the sapphires round the key-hole.

This is one leads to the Earthzone.

He took his key. It turned in the lock to the sound of Aeolian music.

There is a correspondence between the four planes and the four elements. The physical plane corresponds to earth. The astral plane corresponds to water. The mental plane corresponds to air. The akashic plane corresponds to fire. They are in their mental bodies and on the mental plane (hence why the technique is called "mental wandering"). This is why the music surrounding them is described as "Aeolian."

A door opened upon slow hinges, and disclosed a winding stair within. The key vanished from his fingers.

This physical key has vanished, but the true golden key will always be a part of him, just like it was always a part of Tangle.

Tangle went up. Mossy followed. The door closed behind them. They climbed out of the earth; and, still climbing, rose above it. They were in the rainbow.

Do you remember in the beginning of the story when Mossy couldn't get too close to the rainbow because he was "so close yet so far" from it? He has finally entered the rainbow.

Far abroad, over ocean and land, they could see through its transparent walls the earth beneath their feet. Stairs beside stairs wound up together, and beautiful beings of all ages climbed along with them.

Chapter 17: The Golden Key

There are many systems of initiation. Some of them like Bardon's can be worked through alone and are available to everyone. Other systems are designed to be worked through with a teacher and are only known about in certain magical circles. However, one true initiation system is as good as another. All initiates enter the same rainbow at the end of their initiation and begin their real learning when they access the spiritual resources within the rainbow like the ruling genii of the Earthzone and the planetary spheres.

They knew that they were going up to the country whence the shadows fall.
And by this time I think they must have got there.

To all sincere students of any complete and balanced system of initiation, I assure you that you too will reach the country whence the shadows fall.

Chapter 18: Becoming Hermes Trismegistus

There are only a few people in our physical world, who, with their spirit, are able to penetrate the borders of human existence and to proceed to other zones. People who are able to do this consciously are called initiates from the point of view of Hermetics.

~Franz Bardon

According to legend, there once was a civilization in which scientist, poet, politician, warrior, and magician all shared the same heartful inspiration. The time has come for this to return.

~William Mistele

Three hundred years ago, a man named Abraham desperately sought instruction in genuine magic. He travelled to many lands. In his travels, he studied with many individuals revered as adepts, and although some of them could perform marvelous wonders, he did not find the object of his search within their teachings. He also read many books purporting to be about magic, only to conclude "that the greater number of magical books are false and vain," and that "not one of these books is worth an obolus." By the time Abraham succeeded in becoming an adept, he had come to a very important realization. He had realized that much of what passes for magic in the world has very little to do with magic, falling instead under the category of sorcery. The dawning of this realization in Abraham's mind is well-documented in the first of the three books of the sacred magic of Abramelin the Mage. It is a realization that all students of magic should grasp early on in their training.

In Step 8, Bardon gives instructions for the basic technique that is the foundation of many truly advanced magical working methods. This is the technique of accumulating the electric and magnetic fluids in one's body. Before he gives the instructions for this technique, he writes the following.

The Spirit of Magic by Virgil

In the previous steps I have always pointed out how very important it is to ennoble the soul, to be free of passions and to try to reach the magic equilibrium. If an unrighteous and passionate person who has not yet reached the full magic balance wished to perform these exercises, he would only increase his passions by activating them. He would hardly be able to control his passions, which could become fateful for him. Everybody will see that these warnings are not mere words or a simple moral lecture. A well-balanced personality, however, has nothing to fear. On the contrary, he will have every opportunity to ascend and be fortunate enough to realize his highest ideals.

There are some key takeaways from this passage. Someone with an unbalanced and impure personality is not capable of safely practicing this technique, and if he were to try, then his personality would only become further corrupted. On the other hand, someone who has strengthened his personality by balancing and purifying it through the diligent practice of the exercises of the first seven steps "has nothing to fear" and "will have every opportunity to ascend and be fortunate enough to realize his highest ideals." This idea that the personality must be strengthened is understood by every adept. Human spirits incarnate in order to grow, and this in part entails growing strong. Besides practicing exercises like elemental pore breathing before you are ready to, there are plenty of other ways of using magic to weaken your personality, or at least impede its growth. Using magic to banish away your problems prevents you from becoming stronger by overcoming the challenges you come across in life. Sorcerers do not understand the nature of spiritual evolution, nor do they understand the full range of consequences any inner action can have. Therefore, they use their fragments of magical knowledge to dissolve any storm in life that may make them stronger, and banish away any hardship that may teach them valuable lessons. Magic requires strength – enough strength to withstand the intense energies of the inner planes without being burned. When Tangle followed the snake into the burning desert, she was strong. Had she been weak, she would have been consumed by the fire. The practice of sorcery is a crutch that its practitioners eventually come to depend upon, thus growing exponentially weaker. The practice of magic is empowering, and will eventually turn its practitioners into co-creators of the universe, giving

Chapter 18: Becoming Hermes Trismegistus

them the "capacity to move as a divine being among other divine beings and on occasion to participate directly in the divine workshop engaging in highly creative activity."

Sorcery is not magic. Neither are the occultism, pseudo-Kabbalistic teachings, and New Age nonsense that are often peddled as magic. Much of modern Western magic as we know it has its origins in the French occult revival. One of the more celebrated works on this subject, Christopher McIntosh's book *Eliphas Levi and the French Occult Revival*, gives a very enlightening view of this movement, and does much to explain many of the detrimental trends and attitudes that still plague the esoteric world. McIntosh ends his informative book by writing the following.

> *Though there was a continuation of occult activity which connects with the present day, it is possible to discern the setting up of a new momentum after the First World War. If occultism tends to flourish in a period of impending crises, when the crises actually arrives, the opiates of occultism cease to be effective and men must turn their minds to the preservation of their lives or the defense of their country.*

Let the meaning of that passage sink in because it is a powerful series of statements with many implications. Genuine magic is about disillusionment. It is about learning the truth. It is about getting real. Occultism is an opiate. It is fascinating and interesting. It distracts people from the real world when they cannot handle the truth. Magicians solve problems. Occultists prefer to keep problems out of their minds, and they do this by immersing their minds in the study of tables of correspondences, metaphysical philosophy with no practical value, and pseudo-Kabbalistic teachings. In the meantime, the problems they ignore continue to grow. Occultism flourished right before the French Revolution. It flourished around the world wars. And according to McIntosh, it is beginning to flourish again right now in modern times. If we are standing on a train track and there is a train barreling down towards us, then we can put a blindfold on so we don't see the train and become less scared. It will make us feel better, but it won't stop the train from hitting us. Occultism is that blindfold.

In the past, people have accused me of being overly harsh and judgmental when assessing the state of modern magic, but to understand

The Spirit of Magic by Virgil

my point of view, know that much is at stake. The governments of most major countries are run by corrupt politicians. The atmosphere and the world's oceans are treated like sewers. Poverty and starvation hold many less developed countries in their grasp. Terrorism is rampant in large areas of the world. It is becoming increasingly difficult to find safe ways to dispose of nuclear waste. Furthermore, many of our natural resources are being depleted at an alarming rate.

Within the inner planes, there are vast spiritual resources that can help our race overcome these problems. These resources include extremely knowledgeable spirits, such as the 360 ruling genii of the Earthzone, who are tasked with guiding humanity and willing to teach us. Each of the 360 Earthzone spirits is an expert in a specific subject and they are all ready and waiting to instruct those (genuine!) magicians who communicate with them, either by evoking them to our realm or by mental wandering to their realm.[84] The subjects these spirits specialize in are diverse and vast. Some Earthzone spirits specialize in mundane subjects. Nachero, who rules the twenty-seventh degree of Libra, specializes in milk, while Hipolopos, who rules the fifteenth degree of Scorpio, specializes in games and jokes. Other Earthzone spirits specialize in magical subjects. Hahadu, who rules the twentieth degree of Aries, specializes in water magic. Paguldez, who rules the thirteenth degree of Taurus, specializes in nature magic.

In this book, I have given no magical techniques for making others' lives more blessed. If you want to learn such techniques, go learn them from Kofan. In this book, I have given no magical techniques for healing others. If you want to learn such techniques, go learn them from Radina. In this book, I have given no magical techniques for dissolving conflict. If you want to learn such techniques, go learn them from Erimites. In this book, I have given no techniques of magical protection. If you want to learn such techniques, go learn them from Kibigili. In this book, I have not given you any sigils that can be drawn on talismans. If you want sigils you can use for talismanic purposes, ask Jugula for some. But before you reach out to these spirits to learn, make sure you are strong, and that you are Hermes Trismegistus. Has the Old Man of the Fire placed his hand upon your heart and confirmed that the fire will not burn you?

These days, experiencing pareidolia is considered the same as evoking a spirit successfully. Dabblers try to evoke a spirit, see a vague humanoid shape in the incense smoke the same way some people see Jesus on burnt toast, and then "feel an impression" that further convinces

Chapter 18: Becoming Hermes Trismegistus

them there is an entity in front of them communicating with them. Because of these low standards for what constitutes a successful evocation, many people find it difficult to believe that you can talk to spirits. They may acknowledge that it's possible in theory, but assert that it's unlikely to ever actually happen because, well, we don't live in a fairy tale.

This skepticism toward the possibility of meaningful interactions with spirits has even infected the Bardon community. In the Bardon community, you often see lively debates about which famous yogi, mystic, or magician was Bardon's teacher and provided him with his magical knowledge, including the knowledge he transmitted to future generations of students via his books. In *Memories of Franz Bardon*, Dr. M.K. states that Bardon would go to a secret location every single night and evoke an entity. The entities he evoked are the same knowledgeable entities he describes in PME. It is obvious that these entities provided Bardon with most of his magical knowledge. However, many members of the Bardon community continue to argue over who Bardon's teacher was. These members neither believe nor disbelieve the assertion that Bardon learned from spirits. They literally can't wrap their minds around the idea that Bardon learned from spirits, and therefore can't even think about the idea in order to decide whether or not to believe it. This is what happens when feeling "impressions" generated by spirits that aren't even there is what passes for a successful evocation these days.

There are many knowledgeable spirits dwelling on the inner planes, and there are many properly trained magicians learning from those spirits and using their knowledge to improve the world in real tangible ways. I think if more students could wrap their minds around the fact that it is possible to learn from spirits, then more students would be motivated to stay focused on their training, and the question of where some of the greatest adepts in history acquired most of their magical knowledge would no longer be such a mystery.

There is one particular incident in my past that really highlighted to me the problems with the low standards of modern evocation. A certain individual, whom I will call Paul, sent me a message with several questions about magical healing. There is an Earthzone spirit named Radina who specializes in magical healing. In Bill's book *Twenty-Five Earthzone Spirits*, there is a chapter about Radina in which Bill shares some of the knowledge he received from this spirit. Since the answers to some of Paul's questions could be found in this chapter, I directed Paul to an online version of the book and told him to read the chapter. Paul

The Spirit of Magic by Virgil

read the chapter and then sent me another message with some very baffling comments. Paul said he disagreed with Bill's "theories" about the nature of Radina. Radina is the ruling genius of the twenty-sixth degree of Scorpio in the Earthzone. Paul explained to me that Scorpio is traditionally associated with concepts like violence and destruction. Therefore, according to Paul, a spirit associated with Scorpio could not be a healer. Paul also stated that Bill probably did not know this fact before he tried to write an essay about Radina.

Wow! The information about Radina in Bill's book did not come from speculation. Bill used mental wandering to travel to Radina's domain in the Earthzone. He actually met Radina and conversed with Radina. This fact is something Paul found utterly impossible to wrap his head around, and although I could not understand why then, I do now. It is very common to speculate about a spirit's nature based on its astrological correspondences or the gematria of its name. But of course no one would ever consider the possibility of actually evoking the spirit or mental wandering to the spirit's domain for a chat. That's impossible, after all, only a genuine initiate could do that, and no one has the time to undergo genuine initiation these days, right? I don't agree. Becoming proficient in magic by meaningful standards may require daily practice over many years; however, so does becoming proficient in acting, ballet, or any similar art. If there are people with the self-discipline needed to learn those arts, then there are people with the self-discipline needed to undergo magical initiation.

Hermes Trismegistus is the symbol/archetype of the ideal initiate. "Trismegistus," meaning "thrice-great," refers to the initiate's mastery over the physical, astral, and mental planes. "Hermes" alludes to the Greek god Hermes, whose winged sandals symbolize the ability to fly through the inner planes. Just as Hermes was the messenger between the gods and mankind, the modern initiate must also bring the teachings, instructions, and knowledge of the 360 Earthzone spirits to the rest of society. The caduceus contains two snakes, representing the electric and magnetic fluids. Hermes carries a caduceus, symbolizing his ability to wield the electric and magnetic fluids. In the Bardon system, students learn to wield the electric and magnetic fluids in Step 8. Step 8 is also the step where students learn the technique of mental wandering, thus becoming initiates. Bardon says that students of his system must complete Step 8 of IIH first before beginning the work of PME. Students of other magical training systems should reach an equivalent level of

Chapter 18: Becoming Hermes Trismegistus

magical advancement before beginning extensive work with evocation and travelling on the inner planes.

When I first began training in magic, I imagined myself one day doing rituals to bring about world peace, end world hunger, and heal the environment. Now I know that I can't single handedly fix the world's major problems, especially when many of them are caused by the group karma of the human race. However, with the guidance of the Earthzone spirits, I regularly do magical workings to make the world a better place. Many other magicians do the same, oftentimes with amazing results. For example, with the guidance of the Earthzone spirit Cigila, Bill used magic to prevent a nuclear explosion that would have killed many people.

However, when it comes to the role of magic in making the world a better place, magicians doing magical rituals and workings to improve the world is just a small part of this. With the guidance of Tigrapho, initiated engineers could learn to build safer buildings and bridges that are more structurally sound and resistant to natural disasters. With the guidance of Peekah, initiated cooks could create delicious new recipes. With the guidance of Tolet, initiated dieticians could discover new principles underlying health and pass on this spirit's knowledge to the rest of the world. Initiated comedians could study with Parmasa. Initiated singers could learn from Riqita. Initiated parents could learn from Adae how to keep their families in a state of peace, harmony, and love. No matter what your occupation is, there is some Earthzone spirit who is able to teach you how to excel in that occupation and work in a way that blesses human society and advances human culture. If more people were genuine magicians and capable of accessing the knowledge and guidance of the Earthzone spirits in this way, society would be more blessed. This is what Bardon envisioned. This is what he had in mind when he wrote his books.

There are magical lineages, traditions, and orders that claim exclusive access to certain powerful spirits who will not work with anyone not a part of their special little group. This exclusive access is often waved in front of potential members to entice them into joining. Lineages, traditions, and orders are human creations. The 360 ruling genii of the Earthzone exist beyond human society, so humans are unable to put restrictions on them. Therefore, no lineage, tradition, or order will ever be able to truthfully claim exclusive access to them. The magician does not command these spirits and order them to fulfill his petty desires. The magician also does not give up his freedom to them in exchange for

The Spirit of Magic by Virgil

illusory power via a pact such as the one members of the FOGC Lodge have with its demon patrons Belphegor and Ashmedai. The relationship between the magician and the ruling genii he works with is one of mutual respect and friendship. The respect of these spirits, however, must be earned. It cannot be bestowed upon another through initiation ceremonies or decree. Since they exist beyond human society, they exist outside whatever internal hierarchies humans have created amongst themselves. Lofty titles, lamens, sashes, or signifiers of status and rank in such hierarchies are meaningless to them. People in your company may see you as a CEO or boss, but the Earthzone spirits will assess for themselves how seriously to take you. People in your magical order may address you as a hierophant or an adeptus exemptus, but the Earthzone spirits will assess for themselves what your real level of magical advancement is. Each of these spirits is united with Divine Providence and seeks to fulfill various divine missions. A genuine magician and an Earthzone spirit working alongside each other are two friends who have partnered together to better serve Divine Providence. The sum is greater than the parts, and many more blessings will flow through their collaborative work than either could produce alone.

It is no small task to use the spiritual resources on the inner planes to serve society, and the person who wishes to play such a role cannot afford to get caught up in the sea of distractions that is the modern occult world. The more focused you are on your training, the sooner you will reach the level where you are able to access the spiritual resources on the inner planes. These days, not only do students of magic become distracted easily, many students of magic actively seek out distractions. This approach to magical training leads nowhere. Stay focused. Magical training is long, and can be difficult and tiring at times. At one point in Tangle's journey to the rainbow, she collapsed from exhaustion. However, even as she lay on the ground losing consciousness, she was still looking at the rainbow. That was her goal. That's what she was focused on reaching. So if you're a Bardonist, don't neglect to master thought-observation because you're tempted to practice some chakra exercise you found in a random New Age book instead. Don't fail to master your asana because instead of sitting in your asana each day, you practice Enochian rituals because you are curious to see what will happen. Don't forget to introspect regularly because you are too busy reading books about candle magic. Don't refrain from practicing pore breathing because it's more fun to absent-mindedly draw pentagrams in the air and vibrate divine names. To students of other magical training

Chapter 18: Becoming Hermes Trismegistus

systems, I offer the same advice in more general form. Don't let the irrelevant books and exercises you stumble across distract you from assimilating the knowledge of your system and mastering your system's practices. There are many magical training systems. There are many directions an aspiring magician can approach the rainbow from. However, you must keep your eyes on the rainbow to make sure you are always walking in the right direction.

And besides staying focused, there is one other thing that is essential. We must understand the story of why Solomon became a great magician. We must understand that those who reach only for power will never receive it, but that those who reach for wisdom will receive both wisdom and power. Wisdom and understanding are always found together. To receive wisdom is to receive understanding and to acquire compassion, which is born from those two qualities. This is the golden key that will bring students destined for success to the rainbow, and then to the country whence the shadows fall.

Epilogue

If you've reached this point, I want to congratulate you on finishing this book. Some of you may have spent many years walking in circles by using the shotgun approach, practicing the wrong exercises, or working through incomplete and unbalanced systems. For those in this situation, parts of this book must have been painful to read. Your decision to read those parts anyway shows great open-mindedness and courage. Those two traits are essential for success when walking the path of systematic magical training, so do not despair. You are well-equipped to begin walking in the right direction. You cannot turn back the hands of time, but by making wise decisions in the present, you can make up for anything you've lost through the inefficiencies of the past. I wish you all the best in your efforts to find a complete, balanced, safe, and efficient magical training system that is compatible with the circumstances of your life and resonates well with you.

In bringing this book to a close, I want to share with you a well-known Taoist parable – the parable of the cicada and the wren. The following version of this parable comes from Huston Smith's book *The Religions of Man*.

> *When it was suggested to the wren and cicada that there are birds that fly hundreds of miles without alighting, both quickly agreed that such a thing was impossible. 'You and I know very well,' they said, 'that the furthest one can ever get even by the most tremendous effort is that elm tree over there; and even this one cannot be sure of reaching every time. Often one finds oneself dragged back to Earth long before one gets there. All these stories about flying hundreds of miles at a stretch are sheer nonsense.'*

A few esoteric authors in the past, including Bardon, have described in their writings the faculties and capabilities possessed by genuine initiates. There will always be people who dismiss these descriptions as fantasies, basing their assessment on their own faculties and capabilities. Not having worked through a solid system of initiation, their own faculties and capabilities are quite limited, and therefore, their perception of what is possible is also quite limited. In short, it is difficult for those who are not Hermes Trismegistus to see and comprehend the full capabilities of Hermes Trismegistus.

But regardless of what the cicadas and wrens believe to be possible or impossible, there will also always be those who strive to become falcons and hawks, flying hundreds of miles at a stretch and feeling no worse for the wear. Not everyone is capable of becoming such a bird. As Bardon writes in IIH, this requires the student to possess "an enormous, almost superhuman, amount of endurance and patience, a tenacious willpower, and secrecy regarding his progress." However, even if you do not possess these qualities and therefore do not currently have what it takes to become an initiate, there is absolutely no reason you cannot acquire these qualities through your own efforts. You now know how to introspect in order to learn which of these vital qualities you are lacking. You also know how to use the six-pronged attack to transform yourself into someone who does possess those qualities. Use these tools. In time, you will find that you are not the person you once were. You are more; you can do more; and you can fly farther. If you remain patient and continue to persist, then one day you will wake up able to fly hundreds of miles without alighting.

Virgil

Appendix A: Summary of IIH

Step 1

Mental:
 1. Thought-observation
 2. Present-mindedness
 3. Concentration
 4. Vacancy of mind

Astral:
 1. Creation of the black soul mirror
 2. Creation of the white soul mirror

Physical:
 1. Conscious eating
 2. Conscious breathing
 3. Magic of water
 4. Living a healthy lifestyle

Step 2

Mental:
 1. Plastic imagination with eyes closed
 2. Plastic imagination with eyes open

Astral:
 1. Character transformation with the help of autosuggestion, analysis, and volition

Physical:
 1. Asana
 2. Pore breathing
 3. Conscious pore breathing
 4. Control of the body in everyday life

Step 3

Mental:
1. Plastic imagination with multiple senses
2. Plastic imagination with familiar and unfamiliar landscapes
3. Plastic imagination with animals and people

Astral:
1. Accumulation of the elements via pore breathing

Physical:
1. Transferring consciousness into various body parts and pore breathing through them
2. Accumulation of the vital force

Step 4

Mental:
1. Transplantation of consciousness into objects
2. Transplantation of consciousness into imagined animals
3. Transplantation of consciousness into people

Astral:
1. Condensing elements into body parts by accumulating it in the body first
2. Condensing elements into body parts via transplantation of consciousness
3. Exhaling an element from a body part by spreading it through the body first
4. Exhaling an element from a body part directly into the universe
5. Accumulation of the elements in their associated regions of the body

Physical:
1. Finger rituals

Step 5

Mental:
1. Transplantation of consciousness into the depth point of objects

2. Transplantation of consciousness into the depth point of animals and other humans
3. Transplantation of consciousness into the depth point of items not in view
4. Transplantation of consciousness into your own depth point

Astral:
1. Breathing elements into a room through the solar plexus
2. Breathing elements into a room through the whole body
3. Breathing elements into a room through specific body parts (emphasis on hands)
4. Creating dynamides from the elements and moving them into a room via the solar plexus
5. Accumulating the elements into a room directly through the universe
6. Creating dynamides from the elements directly through the universe

Physical:
1. Levitating the fingers and then the arm
2. Exteriorizing the hand
3. Communicating with spirits via a pendulum, planchette, writing, and finger lifting.

Step 6

Mental:
1. Examining the functions of the spirit (will, intellect, feeling, and consciousness)
2. Concentrating on the mental body moving the astral body moving the physical body
3. Concentrating on the mental body sensing the world through the astral and physical bodies

Astral:
1. Filling the body with akasha
2. Filling the body with akasha with the intent of attaining mastery over the elements

Physical:

1. Creation of thoughtforms (mental plane entities)

Step 7

Mental:
1. Balancing the four functions of the spirit

Astral:
1. Development of clairvoyance
2. Development of clairaudience
3. Development of clairsentience

Physical:
1. Creation of elementaries (astral entities)
2. Animation of pictures and statues

Step 8

Mental:
1. Exteriorizing the mental body
2. Short distance mental wandering
3. Long distance mental wandering

Astral:
1. The Great Now
2. Inductive control of the electric fluid
3. Inductive control of the electric fluid for the purpose of ennobling oneself
4. Inductive control of the magnetic fluid
5. Inductive control of the magnetic fluid for the purpose of ennobling oneself
6. Deductive control of the electric fluid
7. Deductive control of the magnetic fluid
8. Loading the electric and magnetic fluids into their corresponding regions of the body

Physical:
1. Fluid condensers
2. Making magic mirror

Appendix B: An Example Black Soul Mirror

[Author's note: The following is an example black soul mirror that should give you a general idea of what a black soul mirror is. Note that the traits listed are as specific as possible. Note also that in addition to writing down a trait, I often include specific examples in braces. This isn't necessary, but I've found it helpful. Further comments about this soul mirror can be found in my book *The Elemental Equilibrium: Notes on the Foundation of Magical Adepthood*]

(#1) I masturbate too much. [Fire, 3]

(#2) I get turned on very easily. [Fire, 2]

(#3) I daydream too much at work and get little done as a result. [Air, 3]

(#4) I am too shy/socially awkward. [Air, 3] {Feel awkward standing in line at Starbucks because I'm surrounded by people}

(#5) I am bashful. [Air, 2] {Pam, European history}[85]

(#6) I smile/laugh when I feel awkward, which is very often. [Air, 2]

(#7) I lash out impulsively when angry. [Fire, 3] {Shouting "for fuck's sake" at Peter}

(#8) I am messy. [Air, 3] {Desk, apartment in Seattle}

(#9) I waste a lot of time listening to music. [Earth, 2]

(#10) When I think of a trait to add to my soul mirrors, I don't always write it down immediately. As a result, when I go to update my soul mirrors, I often forget what the trait was. [Air, 1]

(#11) I almost never have any cash in my wallet. If I ever really needed to buy something at a place that doesn't accept credit cards, I wouldn't be able to. [Air, 1]

(#12) When someone surprises me, I make a loud gasping sound. It's kind of weird. [Air, 1] {At Giant Eagle when the box fell off the shelf and almost hit me}

(#13) I swear too much. [Air, 2]

(#14) When I see an attractive woman, I spend a second or two staring at her. If people notice, this could be embarrassing for me. [Water, 2]

(#15) I am not good at pacing myself. I often try to tackle big tasks all at once instead of spreading out the work. [Fire, 2]

(#16) I'm semi-addicted to running. This causes me to waste a lot of time doing it. [Air, 2]

(#17) I put off important things, sometimes until it's too late. [Air, 2] {Giving Duquesne Light a call seconds before deadline}

(#18) I often forget that it's the thought that counts and not the physical gift. [Earth, 1] {When Mark gave me a copy of *Demons*, I was disappointed that it was a book I had already read, but instead I should have been grateful for his kindness.}

(#19) When I'm on the computer, I get distracted a lot by random stuff on the internet. [Air, 2]

(#20) I often feel like I need to listen to music before going to sleep. If I didn't do this, I'd get a lot more sleep each night. [Air, 3]

(#21) I sleep in a lot, and therefore find it hard to get up early. When I do wake up early, I stay in bed daydreaming or listening to music because I am too lazy to get up. [Earth, 2]

(#22) I often feel a need to do everything in the ideal place. [Water, 1]

(#23) I am not comfortable/familiar with the workings of computers. [Air, 2] {Struggled to remove that virus and had to ask Lukas to do it. Be more like Lukas.}

(#24) I never do anything with spare change. I just put it in some random place until it eventually gets lost. Now there are coins everywhere in my car and house. [Air, 1]

(#25) I don't brush my teeth in the morning or floss. [Earth, 2]

(#26) I get angry too easily over little things. [Fire, 1] {Mark's April Fool's Day joke}

(#27) When people treat me kindly, it never occurs to me that they are just doing so in order to manipulate me, despite the fact that this has happened several times already. [Water, 1]

(#28) When using timers I am anxious about them going off. [Air, 1] {Microwave timers}

(#29) When packing up in a hotel while preparing to leave, I don't do a thorough job of making sure I've packed everything. [Air, 1] {Left vibrator in Hilton}

(#30) I don't organize my papers very well. [Air, 3] {Constantly have to reprint papers after misplacing them}

(#31) I don't do my laundry as often as I should. [Air, 1]

(#32) My grasp of chemistry is shaky. [Air, 1][86]

(#33) Things send me off into a daydream easily. [Air, 2] {Looking at that *Enter the Dragon* movie poster}

(#34) It is hard for me to come down from a daydream and regain my focus. The daydream has a momentum of its own. [Air, 2]

(#35) I am passive aggressive. [Water, 2] {Trying to manipulate Mark into feeling bad for scratching my laptop}

(#36) I lack confidence in myself when I do my magical exercises. [Water, 2]

(#37) Falling in love can make me do silly things impulsively. [Water, 2] {Writing a bunch of creepy poems and sending them to Jill}

(#38) I don't make an effort to eat healthy when travelling. [Earth, 1] {Getting a side of fries instead of vegetables every time I ate at that one restaurant in Toronto}

(#39) I snack too much. [Air, 1] {Nuts, cookies, Cheez-its}

(#40) I get really nervous before job interviews. [Air, 2] {Duquesne Light, PNC bank}

(#41) I take too many breaks when working. Some are long. Some involve long walks. [Air, 2]

(#42) I leave my soul mirrors out on my desk when I take a break from working on then and go to the restroom. If someone walks into my office, they could see them and read them. [Water, 1]

(#43) I have an irrational fear of spiders. [Water, 1]

(#44) I don't "seize the day". [Earth, 2]

(#45) I don't actively and continually strive for excellence. [Water, 2]

(#46) I scratch/pick at my hair a lot. [Fire, 1]

(#47) I get upset about imagined situations. [Fire, 2] {Imagining Nick telling everyone about me and ill because it seemed like something he would do, and then getting upset about it}

(#48) I don't keep silent about projects I am working on. [Air, 2] {My novel}

(#49) I complain a lot. It doesn't do anything. [Air, 2] {Coworkers, the long drive home}

(#50) I check my email too much. [Air, 1]

(#51) I get angry when I read conversations on the internet and see someone being stupid. [Fire, 1] {Conversation on that grappling forum with the misogynistic remarks}

(#52) When I am determined to do something, it is hard for me to stop in the middle and ask "Hold on a second, is this really a good idea?" [Fire, 2] {Sending email complaining about Dave}

(#53) It is often hard for me to see both sides of an argument. [Fire, 2] {Hard time/refusal to see/acknowledge Mark's argument for not sending the email}

(#54) I have a hard time admitting I'm wrong or I messed up. [Fire, 2] {After that close call while driving on Christmas, Emma said I should have slowed down. I insisted the guy shouldn't have been on the road. She was right.}

(#55) I'm not outgoing and charismatic. [Air, 3] {Interviews}

(#56) I am sometimes in a hurry to get things over with when I could get better results from taking my time. [Fire, 2] {Writing cover letter for Duquesne Light job application}

(#57) I'm on Facebook too much. [Air, 3]

(#58) When I'm stuck at a certain point of a written project, I don't move on to another section and come back to it later. I continue to just stare at the screen.[Earth, 2] {Every essay I've ever written}

(#59) I let my weirdness show itself in situations when it would be in my best interest to pretend to be normal. [Fire, 2] {Weirding out Dave's cousin and that Asian girl}

(#60) I sometimes skim texts it would be better for me to read thoroughly. [Fire, 1] {Instructions for using that cooking contraption at Mark's place}

(#61) I often stay up ridiculously late on Friday and Saturday nights. [Fire, 2]

(#62) I sometimes lose steam or give up near the end of a long project. This jeopardizes all the hard work I've put in previously. [Water, 2]

(#63) I sometimes decide what to do based on what others do when it shouldn't matter. [Water, 1] {Deciding to wear jeans at work just because everyone else was doing it when I find them really uncomfortable}

(#64) I don't do a good job of backing up important files. [Air, 2]

(#65) I sometimes impulsively say hurtful things. [Fire, 3] {How my friendship with Nigel ended}

(#66) I keep trying to change people who are dead set on not changing. [Fire, 1] {Mark and Dom}

(#67) I get caught up in the current of arguments. [Fire, 2]

(#68) I get offended too easily. [Fire, 2] {Being offended when Rose accused me of being afraid of encountering Jill}

(#69) I often give too much information when explaining something. [Air, 1] {Explaining directions to Seth Street to the guy on the bike, explaining why I was late to Mark's Christmas party}

(#70) I sometimes ask unnecessary dumb questions. [Air, 1] {Asking guard at the park if I needed to show my ID}

(#71) I get angry when reading internet articles. [Fire, 1] {The one about Megan Fox's ex-husband ruining her life}

(#72) I have a problem staying disconnected from the online world. [Water, 3] {Get nervous about how people will react to each article on my green living blog after sharing it on Facebook}

(#73) I need to learn to let go of certain old attachments. [Water, 2] {Been thinking about Emily for months now. Time to let her go}

(#74) There are still traces of occultism in my life. [Air, 2] {Some occult websites still bookmarked on computer, visit occult blogs occasionally}[87]

(#75) I am uncomfortable with my body. [Air, 3]

(#76) I think that I can use spells to solve all my problems and shape my life into however I want. [Air, 1] {Thinking my sigils would get me the job and writing a crappy cover letter as a result}[88]

(#77) I want revenge for perceived wrongs. [Fire, 1] {Trying to get back at Joe for wasting my time even though what happened was more my fault than his}

(#78) I use the word "however" too much. [Earth, 1]

(#79) I immaturely try to show people I am upset with them by giving them the silent treatment. [Fire, 2] {Avoiding Peter}

(#80) I'm slightly afraid of the dark. [Air, 2]

(#81) I am very ticklish. [Air, 2]

(#82) I listen to the same songs over and over again instead of trying new songs. [Earth, 2]

(#83) When I miss the very beginning of a video or song, I go back to the beginning, even if it was only a second or two. [Fire, 1]

(#84) Every now and then, there is a day where I get absolutely nothing done whatsoever. [Water, 2]

(#85) I don't pray often enough. [Earth, 1]

(#86) I have a slight interest in martial arts. [Fire, 1] {Occasionally watch martial arts related videos on YouTube.}[89]

(#87) I am easily convinced. [Water, 2]

(#88) I often feel moved to involve myself in other people's fights for some reason. [Fire, 1] {Getting involved in Pedro's fight with Anthony for no good reason}

(#89) I'm often too lazy to read reviews of a product before ordering one online. [Air, 1] {Should have read some reviews of the air pump so I would have known not to buy it}

(#90) I don't go about magical training in a strategic organized fashion. [Fire, 2] {Try to master a bunch of exercises at once. Need to make lists when doing plastic imagination stuff}

(#91) I don't have confidence in my own intellect. [Water, 2] {Intimidated by smart people}

(#92) I waste a lot of time reading comics. [Earth, 2] {Garfield, Wizard of Id}

(#93) I find it hard to be productive after dinner and late at night. [Earth, 3]

(#94) When working with a group on a project, I often take advantage of others and don't pull my weight. [Air, 2] {Writing the pseudocode for the printer}

(#95) I don't retrospect at the end of each day. [Earth, 2]

(#96) When I want to make a point about something I am passionate about, I can be overly aggressive. [Fire, 1] {First draft of the op-ed I wrote}

(#97) I still use the word "retarded." [Air, 2] {Saying the magazine picture looks retarded. Calling Nick retarded}

(#98) I feel a need to entertain others when I am not obligated to. [Water, 2]

(#99) I talk about others behind their backs. This is dangerous. What if they are nearby? [Air, 3] {Calling Nick a snob}

(#100) I can be overly generous. [Water, 2] {Letting Bill keep my knife when I still needed it for a lot of things}

(#101) I can be overly afraid of disappointing others. [Water, 2] {Afraid Beth would be disappointed that I wasn't coming to the came}

(#102) I make up lies in order to excuse myself when I think I am disappointing others. [Air, 3] {Telling Beth I was ill}

(#103) I feel awkward/uncomfortable when I pass by people. The uncomfortable/awkward feeling seems to be bigger around woman. [Air, 3]

(#104) When I breathe in a bad smell, I have to visualize it coming out of my nostrils and dissolving. [Water, 1]

(#105) I am often late to appointments. [Air, 2] {Dentist appointment on 7/7/03}

(#106) I fear emotional pain. [Water, 2] {Avoiding some places or people because being there or seeing them makes me feel emotional, Jill, the top floor of the library}

(#107) I often use unnecessarily dramatic wording when conveying simple points. [Fire, 2]

(#108) I'm bad at cooking. [Air, 2]

(#109) I'm bad at tying ties. [Air, 3]

(#110) I get upset when I think about past incidents. [Fire, 1] {Ashley thinking Christianity is superior to other religions and trying to force me to believe this}

(#111) I daydream before falling asleep. If I didn't, I'd get more sleep. [Air, 3]

(#112) I can be overly suspicious. [Air, 2] {Thinking coworkers made another secret chat just so they didn't have to put up with me}

(#113) I watch a lot of porn. [Fire, 3]

(#114) I pack at the last minute when preparing to travel somewhere. [Air, 1]

(#115) I am not an interesting person. [Earth, 3] {Conversations with me usually die out fast}

(#116) I use "Audentes Fortuna iuvat" to justify my intent to do something stupid. [Water, 3] {Asking Jill out when I knew she was already seeing someone}

(#117) I get involved in conversations of a religious/spiritual nature and even say stupid pointless things. [Fire, 2] {Jumping into that conversation about religion between those two people on the bus}

(#118) I am bad at taking notes. [Water, 2] {The notes I took during the meeting in Seattle were so bad}

(#119) I tell lies to impress others. [Fire, 2] {Telling Steve I've been skydiving before when he asked me}

(#120) I often forget I can adjust the mirror in my car when doing so would be really helpful to me. [Air, 1]

(#121) I am not good at parking. [Water, 3]

(#122) I'm on my phone too much. [Air, 3]

(#123) I submit forms at the last minute. [Air, 2] {Application form to be a sub}

(#124) Anger causes me to do things impulsively. [Fire, 2] {Emailing that French person}

(#125) I get annoyed when people try to portray themselves as lone rangers. [Fire, 1] {Calvin, Austin}

(#126) I sometimes forget to use my turn signal. [Air, 2]

(#127) I am slightly superstitious. [Air, 1]

(#128) I am uncomfortable with my sense of smell. [Air, 3]

(#129) I am sadistic. [Fire, 2] {Reading about Drummer the falcon}

(#130) It takes a while for me to calm down and return to a state of peace after becoming angry. [Fire, 3]

(#131) I don't use the magic of water when washing my hands at work. [Air, 2]

(#132) I have a tendency to ridicule people. [Air, 3] {Ridiculing Sarah when chatting with Mark, ridiculing Target's marketing team when chatting with Sarah}

(#133) I have a tendency to express my annoyance, even if it isn't going to help the situation and might create conflict. [Fire, 2]

(#134) I get offended when people think I am not competent enough to do a job that I am in fact competent enough to do. [Fire, 1] {Fixing the lamp}

(#135) I always want to win arguments, even when they are pointless. [Fire, 3] {Trying to win that argument about hockey with Megan}

(#136) I get nervous and worried easily. [Air, 3] {Those three phone calls in a row from the unknown number}

(#137) I flinch easily. [Air, 2]

(#138) I lose things easily. [Air, 2] {Mechanical pencil, ID card}

(#139) I find it difficult to smile for a camera. My facial expression is either dead serious or cracking up. [Earth, 1]

(#140) I don't take full advantage of the situation when I have the meeting room to myself. [Water, 2]

(#141) I make up stuff to make my life seem worse than it really is when complaining to others. [Air, 2] {Telling dad my neighbor's dog's barking keeps me up all night when it only keeps me up half the night}

(#142) I daydream sometimes while driving. [Air, 3] {Any time I've had a really stressful day at work}

(#143) I get dragged into religious conversations easily. [Water, 1] {Those evangelists coming up to me and talking to me in Boston}

(#144) I am not assertive enough to say no when people ask me to do things I am not obligated to do. [Water, 2] {Evangelists in Boston asking me to meet for coffee so they could finish trying to convert me, not wanting to go on a date with Anna but doing so because I felt bad about saying no}

(#145) I swear impulsively. [Fire 2] {When I dropped my iPod}

(#146) I don't adopt a "Better Safe than sorry" approach. [Water, 2] {Not taking my laptop with me when leaving the building when the fire alarm went off, even though it occurred to me to do so because there might actually be a real fire this time and it might burn the building down}

(#147) I don't do a good job of organizing bookmarks in my computer. [Air, 2]

(#148) I apologize too much. [Air, 2]

(#149) I scratch and pick at my skin a lot. I do this in public, and even flick away pieces of it. [Fire, 2]

(#150) I feel awkward and uncomfortable around music in public. [Air, 2]

(#151) I sometimes forget to put food back into the refrigerator for a while after taking it out. [Air, 1]

(#152) When I read, I get up often and walk around while daydreaming about what I've read. [Air, 1]

(#153) I don't read each new post of the Archdruid Report the week it comes out. [Air, 1]

(#154) I only read Archdruid report posts once. I should read each twice. [Air, 1]

(#155) I don't stretch in the morning. [Air, 2]

(#156) My body isn't flexible. [Earth, 2]

(#157) I crack my knuckles a lot. [Fire, 1]

(#158) I spit sometimes when I talk. [Fire, 2]

(#159) My voice is scratchy. [Earth, 1]

(#160) My voice is soft and often people can't hear me. [Air, 2]

(#161) When I see something that catches my attention, I immediately stop and stare. Sometimes, this might be rude. [Air, 2] {Girl with twisted leg at Giant Eagle}

(#162) I waste too much time watching videos on YouTube. [Air, 3] {Spending entire Saturday watching Equals Three}

(#163) I am not careful enough to avoid being overheard while repeating affirmations out loud when using autosuggestion. [Air, 1] {Using autosuggestion to improve my concentration in the YMCA bathroom when someone else was in there and I didn't notice}

(#164) I don't wash my hair frequently enough. [Air, 2]

(#165) I spend too much time proofreading things I write. [Earth, 2] {Emails, articles}

(#166) I am afraid of being by myself. I'm afraid that there is some murderer hiding in the room. [Air, 1]

Appendix C: A Council of Angels

[Author's note: The following story was written by Bill, who has been generous enough to let me include it in this book. It can also be found in his own book *Stories of Magic and Enchantment*.]

A Council of Angels by **William R. Mistele**

And seven mighty angels, lords of creation, stood before the throne of the Creator. And their spokesman steps forward and says, "Almighty, maker of heaven and earth, you who are beyond all understanding, ineffable and shrouded in mystery; you for whom all the stars and galaxies are but a faint echo of your joy and glory, hear our petition.

"We have a problem that resists solution. It interferes with our commission to bless all beings, to insure their lives are fulfilled, to grant them opportunities to attain to their highest paths in life, and to decide what part they wish to play in the unfolding of the universe."

The Creator says, "Go on."

The angel explains, "The problem is that some convert the blessing we give them to a dark purpose. We give the ability to understand others and to negotiate fair and just agreements, but this gift only makes them arrogant. They use their heightened insight to dominate and to make others' choices for them. They feel the gifts they are given are owed to them and that they should have been given more right from the start.

"If we offer them wealth and abundance, they waste it on selfish pursuits. If we give them the ability to love, they use their empathy to enchant others so they submit to them. If we give them purposes to fulfill that produce things of value that endure through all ages of the world they produce instead weapons of war. There is no end to their greed. They live as if their will is the only thing that is real. They set aside no time to celebrate the divine, the beauty of the universe, or the joy of being alive.

"Consequently, our attempts to bless them and to fulfill their lives result in failure. We humbly ask for a few suggestions."

And the Creator, who sits upon a throne that exists neither in space nor in time but rather is beyond, replies, "Did I not create the blue sky?"

And the angel replies, "Yes, you did."

And the Creator asks, "Why did I do so? I could have left above the earth darkness and clouds of dust and ash, or else impenetrable mists of sulfur and acids."

And the angel replies, "You created the sky by day so that in one single glance men might see that regardless of the raging storms of life, regardless of being surrounded by death on all sides, and regardless of the horrors that pursue them from the moment they are born, the mind itself is open, pure, and clear."

"Is that it?" asks the Creator with a tone of voice implying the angel is missing the main point.

And angel, good at improvisation, replies, "And, in contemplating the sky that embodies freedom and the enlightened mind, there shall come a time when each man shall find the universe reflected inside of him."

And the Creator asks, "Did I not create the sky by night filled with countless stars?"

And the angel replies, "Yes."

And the Creator asks, "Why?"

And the angel replies, "So that in one single glance men might perceive that the mind is infinite."

The Creator says, "And?"

The angel replies, "And if they persist in contemplation,

perceiving without thoughts intervening, they shall sense a great stillness embracing the universe in which the beginnings and ends of all things are united in peace and harmony.

And the Creator asks, "Did I not create the oceans and the seas encircling the earth?"

And the angel says, "Yes, you did."

And the Creator asks, "Why do you suppose I did so? I mean,

I could have placed the earth outside the goldilocks zone so that it was either too hot or too cold to have liquid water on its surface encircling the planet."

And the angel says, "So that in one single glance men might
behold in front of them extending from horizon to horizon a love
that has nurtured life on earth for billions of years. In its very
essence it gives without asking for anything in return. All
embracing and with infinite receptivity, it seeks to fulfill any
being's deepest dreams and the visions hidden within their hearts."

And the Creator asks, "How is that going?"

And the angel replies, "Not good. They glance a lot at the sea but the love that it embodies is not yet one of their discoveries."

And the Creator asks, "Why do you suppose that is?"

And the angel replies, "When they can create love through force of concentration so that it emanates from their own bodies filling the space around them for miles, then truly they will awaken and perceive that the oceans of the earth and the sun that shines down upon it emanate a love that extends to the ends of the universe."

And the Creator asks, "Did I not create mountains, trees, forests, plants, hills, and plains?"

And the angel replies, "Yes."

And the Creator says, "Why would I bother to do that? Does it not strike you that the earth with its material forms that change and fade away are separate from what is celestial and spiritual and so not worthy of serious attention or investigation?"

And the angel replies, "You created matter in its densest form so that men might have material to build a home where love, light, and life are celebrated in the ordinary moments of the day when they gather to eat, share, and sleep."

And the Creator says, "There must be more to it than that."

The angel responds, "Lightning is in the heartbeat, winds in the breath, seas in the bloodstream, minerals and the densest matter are part of the body supporting and sustaining consciousness. By being aware of the physical body, they shall realize that the forces unfolding the universe are within and a part of them."

And the Creator asks, "Why did I create a void so empty the density is less than one hydrogen atom per cubic meter and the temperature is just above absolute zero?"

And the angel responds, "So that any intelligent being in one glance at this darkness that lies between the stars might comprehend what it is to be absolutely and totally receptive—to be consciousness without form or image, without space or time to give it definition."

The Creator says, "And?"

The angel replies, "And, in that moment of complete detachment, to perceive the infinite possibilities that surround us. In so doing, to create something worthy, something glorious and magnificent filled with awe and wonder, as a small token of appreciation for the beauty of the universe in which we exist.

The Creator asks, "Anything else going on here with this void?"

And angel replies, "Yes. When things go wrong each being that possesses intelligence and consciousness might know how to return to the beginning and in so doing to restore life to what it is meant to be."

And God said, "Why have I commissioned you to bless men?"

And the angel replies, "Because it is the essence of your being to bless all things, to see that life is fulfilled in every conceivable way. You offer men the opportunity to choose a destiny so they become like you possessing the ability to make all things new."

And then the Creator says, "Now what would you suppose might be the best thing to do if when you bless men your blessings they refuse?"

And the angels replies, "Take away one by one the things they have until they reach the point where they are grateful simply to be alive and to have little things—like heartbeat, breath, their five senses, their ability to feel, to think, to love, and to share. Then they will be ready to begin again their lives without corrupting the deepest purposes of life."

And the angels asks, "But if they still refuse choosing to persist in their desire to dominate and harm others, what then?"

And the Creator says, "Then give them what I myself am: an infinite void that can create an entire universe in order to share love and that is equally content in being absolutely nothing."

"Let them then make their own choice whether they wish to be like me—nothing at all—or else to discover everything life can be.

"The creative void that I am is within every sense perception, every form of substance and energy, and in every thought and feeling. There is no end to my being or my originality.

"As I have always said and which the planets and constellations proclaim, 'Life is a gift. Use it well. Satisfy your desires and meet your needs. Fulfill your dreams. But for each man there shall come a day of reckoning—through the choices he makes he shall shape his fate, whether to create without limitation or give his attention to his ego which is destined to fade.'"

And the angel asks, "Is this confrontation with the consequences of their actions something we should make happen sooner or later?"

And the Creator says, "Use your own discretion. Sometimes to solve a problem you have to create an original solution. But my suggestion to you is that when it comes to learning from experience, sooner is better than later.

"One other thing. Encourage them to ask the right questions as I have encouraged you.

Appendix D: A Conversation with an Archdemon

[Author's note: The following passage comes from an upcoming book by Bill called *Ten Rules for Spiritual Beginners*. It is spoken by an archdemon who is giving instructions on how to put an end to peoples' spiritual development. I include it to emphasize the importance of open-mindedness and of not accepting anything as dogma, including the ideas of those you consider to be adepts. Always explore, be open to new points of views, and draw your own conclusions.]

"The spiritual laws governing the operation of spiritual communities are indisputable. It does not matter how loving a community is or how productive and helpful it is in serving others. All we require to put an end to any spiritual development of any kind in an individual is to control one of three things – either what people think, that is, their beliefs, what they feel, or their actions.

Have you joined a loving community where everyone cares for each other with genuine affection? It does not matter. Get these people to accept without question any set of doctrines, no matter how profound, and that spiritual community now falls under demonic jurisdiction. Without freedom of thought, the heart is like a beautiful song bird imprisoned in a gilded cage.

Do you have a group of people whose thoughts are free, independent, and completely benevolent, who are generous and philanthropic? It does not matter. There is no elevation of their consciousness occurring. All you need to do is have them feel vulnerable, insecure, unsure of themselves, and easily threatened by others whose beliefs are different from their own. You see, they have no access to inspiration because they are frightened of anything new and unknown."

Appendix E: Useful Articles and Essays

This is a list of articles and essays available on the web that contain valuable information for aspiring magicians. Of course links change, and in time, it could be that some or all of the links below will be broken. However, nothing on the internet ever really goes away. That's why you should be very careful about what you post on social media. You should be equally careful about what you write in your emails. Treat all your emails as if they were public, because they might one day become public. You never know when an email you send will be forwarded to another person without your knowledge. And remember that if you pull someone into an email conversation, that person can see the whole history of that conversation. If a link is broken, do a Google search of the essay or article's title and you should be able to find the new site the essay/article is hosted on.

(#1) A Mirror at an Angle – Or Why Not to Read About Your Holy Guardian Angel, by Frater Acher

https://theomagica.com/blog/a-mirror-at-an-angle-or-why-not-to-read-on-your-holy-guardian-angel

Many students of magic erroneously believe that reading more is always better, but this is not true. Oftentimes, the more you read, the more you sabotage your own progress. This article explains why. Don't think that you should avoid reading altogether, because that's not true. You just need to make wise decisions regarding what to read and how to process the things you do read.

(#2) Amtophul – The Salamander, by William Mistele

http://www.williammistele.com/amtophul.htm

There are various types of power the magician works with. Some types of power arise from the water element, others from the fire element, others from the air element, and others from the earth element. The concept of power in general, however, corresponds to the fire element. This essay will give you an insightful introduction to what power is and how it is used in magic. It will also help you see why many of the most famous occultists in history who remained enslaved to their egos their whole lives failed to attain to any level of magical power that is significant by meaningful standards.

(#3) Chapter 1, Mental Level Exercises, by William Mistele

http://williammistele.com/ch1mental.html

The four mental exercises of Step 1 are not just a part of Bardon's system, but a part of all good magical training systems. If you don't believe me, then name one genuine adept who isn't aware of what is going on in his mind, can't focus, and can't still his mind. You won't be able to, because these are fundamental and essential mental skills that all magicians must possess in order to do their work competently. In this essay, Bill provides his comments about the four mental exercises of Step 1. Since these are exercises that all students of magic practice in some form, this essay will be useful to all students of magic, and not just to Bardonists.

(#4) Franz Bardon's Hermetics – An Interview with William Mistele: Part I

http://www.falconbookspublishing.com/franz-bardons-hermetics-interview-william-mistele/

This is an interview with Bill carried out by my publisher, Falcon Books Publishing. In this interview, Bill discusses a number of subjects, including the challenges aspiring magicians will face, what it means to have an elemental equilibrium, and the purpose of magic. There's a lot of great information packed in here.

(#5) Gomah, by William Mistele

http://williammistele.com/gomah.html

This evocation account by Bill will give you a sense of what an evocation is like when carried out by a properly trained magician. Do you think an untrained dabbler who just downloads a PDF of the *Goetia* and messes around with the conjurations in it could ever have such a powerful, intense, intimate, instructive, and transfiguring experience? Not a chance!

(#6) Problems in the Study of Magic, Part I, by William Mistele

http://williammistele.com/problems1.htm

This is the first essay in Bill's well-known five-part essay series about problems students of magic may face during their training. The introductory paragraphs provide some insightful information about magic in general. Most of the essay addresses the subject of becoming balanced. In the Bardon system, the process of becoming balanced is often thought of in terms of the elements, which is why Bardonists often refer to the state of being balanced as an "elemental equilibrium." What I find interesting about this essay is that Bill chose to think of the process of becoming balanced in terms of the chakras instead. This alternate angle provides new insights into the process and further deepens the student's understanding of what it means to be balanced and what it takes to become balanced. Remember that whether you adopt the elemental point of view, the chakra-themed point of view, or the zodiacal point of view (also common), it is the same process you are looking at.

(#7) Problems in the Study of Magic, Part II, by William Mistele

http://williammistele.com/problems2.htm

This is the second essay in Bill's five part series. When it comes to deciding whether or not the magical path is the right path for you, you need to assess whether the values woven into this path are the same as your own values. What I like about this essay is that it presents many of the values at the heart of magic. Learning about these values will allow you to determine whether they are the same as your own values. It will also allow you to see the ways in which magic differs from the other disciplines that fall in the general category of esotericism.

(# 8) Redemption, the Discipline of Karma, by Rawn Clark

http://abardoncompanion.de/Redemption.html

It's very important for the magician to understand what karma is and how it works. Karma generates many of the limitations the magician will face when he works magic. For example, the magician will be able to heal some illnesses very easily, but will be unable to heal others because they are generated by negative karma that the sick individual must work through first before being healed. This article by Rawn presents an excellent overview of karma, and will help you begin understanding karma.

(#9) Subjective and Objective Perception, by Rawn Clark

http://abardoncompanion.de/Perception.html

Perception is an important subject for magicians to understand. The magician is not some hermit living in a forest cave meditating his whole life while completely indifferent to the state of the world. The magician's compassion causes him to take an active role in improving the world in real, meaningful, and tangible ways. Good intentions alone never make a difference in the world. Only actions make a difference in the world. Our actions are based on the information we have, and the type of information we have depends on the way we perceive. Reading this article will allow you to take the first few steps toward understanding perception and the different types of perception.

(#10) On the Path of the Ritual Lone Practitioner, by Frater Acher

https://theomagica.com/the-lone-practitioners-path/

Many of the comments Frater Acher makes apply to all lone practitioners, and not just to those who walk ritual-oriented magical paths.

(#11) The Five Senses, by William Mistele

http://williamrmistele.com/uploads/fivesensepractice.pdf

Unlike some spiritual disciplines that teach you to deny your senses, ignore your senses, or view your senses as your enemies, magic holds that the senses are powerful gateways through which information and power can flow in and out of your being. This makes them very useful tools for the magician, and the adept magician should be able to wield these tools with great mastery. This essay by Bill will give you insights on how you can explore your senses and discover all the magic they have to offer.

(#12) How to Develop Your Astral Senses – Or Breaking Free from Fantasies, by Frater Acher

https://theomagica.com/blog/how-to-develop-your-astral-senses?rq=presence

This article will reveal some additional magical benefits to exploring the senses in the way Bill describes in the previously mentioned essay.

(#13) On Defining Hermeticism

http://abardoncompanion.de/Hermeticism.html

This article by Rawn provides a concise summary of some key magical principles and teachings.

(#14) A Fourth Key to Magic – Or the Order of Unlearning

https://theomagica.com/blog/2011/6/22/a-fourth-key-to-magic-or-the-order-of-unlearning.html

This article will give you much to think about. Aspiring magicians often take it for granted that they should learn as much as possible. The idea that sometimes they need to be doing the exact opposite rarely crosses their minds.

(#15) Body Awareness Meditation, by William Mistele

http://williammistele.com/body1.htm

In Chapter 7, I explained that practicing thought-awareness has many benefits, and that one of these benefits is that you become friends with your mind, which is a benefit that produces benefits of its own. Similarly, practicing body awareness also has many benefits, including becoming friends with your body, which is a benefit that produces benefits of its own. These benefits will greatly facilitate the aspiring magician's rise to mastery over his art.

(#16) The Spirit of 26 Degrees Virgo in the Earthzone, by William Mistele

http://williammistele.com/hyrmiua.htm

In this essay, Bill shares some of the knowledge he received from the Earthzone spirit Hyrmiua regarding mental health and mental clarity. This knowledge will be very useful to aspiring magicians; after all, mental training is one of the three components of magical training.

(#17) The Lunar Spirit Emvatibe, by William Mistele

http://www.williammistele.com/emvatibe.htm

There are three reasons I recommend this essay. The first reason I recommend this essay is that it will give the reader a better understanding of what the planetary spheres are and how they are each unique. Bill describes both the Earthzone and the Sphere of the Moon, comparing and contrasting them. Although you won't be entering the planetary spheres until you have completed Step 8 of IIH or reached the equivalent level in another magical training system, it's still nice to have a basic understanding of what they are so you have an idea of what sort of experiences you'll be having and what sort of realms you'll be exploring after finishing your initiation. The second reason I recommend this essay is that I think the reader will find it interesting to learn about Emvatibe's approach to magical protection and to compare it to the common approaches of magical protection seen in the modern magical world. The third and main reason I recommend this essay is because it touches upon a method of working with spirits that so far I haven't seen outside of the Bardon system, and I think the greater esoteric community would benefit from at least gaining exposure to this concept, although not everyone is capable of putting it into practice. The two main ways magicians work with spirits are receiving knowledge from them and requesting them to complete tasks. Bill does both, and discusses both in this essay. For example, he writes about how he received knowledge about magical protection from Emvatibe, and he writes about how he requested a gnome friend of his to divert a magical attack away from him. However, Bill mentions a third method of working with spirits that, as I wrote previously, seems to be unique to the Bardon system, and that some might consider the heart of the work of PME. Rather than merely receiving information from a spirit or requesting that the spirit complete a task for you, this method involves developing the powers of a spirit and embodying the spirit's nature. Emvatibe's nature is such that his very presence immediately shuts down hostile attacks. If a conventional magician is being attacked, he might try to apply knowledge he receives from Emvatibe to stop the attack or ask Emvatibe to stop the attack himself. If the magician has learned to embody the nature of Emvatibe, however, then his very presence will also immediately shut down any hostile attacks directed against him. If you attack such a magician, it will be as if you are attacking Emvatibe himself, and after reading this essay, you will see that this is a very bad idea indeed.

Not everyone is capable of safely embodying the nature of a powerful lunar spirit like Emvatibe. When you embody the nature of a lunar spirit like Emvatibe, this new nature is not meant to override your human nature. Rather, it is an addition/add-on to your human nature. You still remain human, but you have the capacity to act with the powers and nature of an Emvatibe-esque lunar spirit to accomplish tasks like divine missions if you need to. To prevent a spirit's nature from overriding your human nature, you need to be firmly established in your human nature. The essence of human nature is, to use a term from the Bardon system, "tetrapolar." During the beginning steps of IIH, the impurities and imbalances clouding your essential tetrapolar nature are removed. Then, during the intermediate and advanced steps, your tetrapolar nature becomes strengthened and refined as you work with the four elements and akasha. Note that the four elements and akasha are the five things that correspond to the points of the pentagram, the symbol of human nature. Once you have become firmly rooted in the tetra-polar nature that defines you as a human while working through IIH, then you can safely and productively start working with the spirits of PME by learning to develop their powers and embody their natures without fear that their natures will override your human tetra-polar nature. In this way, while remaining a human, you also become like an Earthzone genius, a lunar genius, a genius of the Sphere of Mercury, etc. Eventually, you acquire "the freedom and discretionary power of a spirit who watches over and guides human evolution."

References

Anonymous. "The Hermetic Arcanum." *The Hermetic Arcanum*. *Sacred* Texts, n.d. Web. 12 June 2016.

Atteshlis, Stylianos. "Introspection." *Researchers of Truth*, Researchers of Truth, www.researchersoftruth.org/teachings/introspection.

Atteshlis, Stylianos. *The Esoteric Practice: Christian Meditations and Exercises*. Imprinta, 1994.

Atteshlis, Stylianos. *The Esoteric Teachings: a Christian Approach to Truth*. Imprinta, 1992.

Bardon, Franz. *Initiation into Hermetics: A Course of Instruction of Magic Theory and Practice*. Wuppertal, Western Germany: D. Rüggeberg, 1987. Print.

Bardon, Franz. *The Key to the True Quabbalah: The Quabbalist as a Sovereign in the Microcosm and the Macrocosm*. Wuppertal, Western Germany: D. Rüggeberg, 1986. Print.

Bardon, Franz. The Practice of Magical *Evocation: Instructions for Invoking Spirits from the Spheres Surrounding Us*. Wuppertal, W. Germany: D. Rüggeberg, 1991. Print.

Branden, Nathaniel. *The Six Pillars of Self Esteem*. Bantam Books, 1995.

Bulgákov, Mijail Afanasievich, Richard Pevear, and Larissa Volokhonsky. The Master and Margarita. London: Penguin, 1997. Print.

Card, Orson Scott. *Enchantment*. New York: Ballantine Pub. Group, 1999. Print.

Clark, Rawn. "A Bardon Companion." *A Bardon Companion*. A Bardon Companion, 2014. Web. 12 June 2016.

Cornelius, Agrippa Von Nettesheim Heinrich, Robert Turner, and Petrus. Henry Cornelius Agrippa. *His Fourth Book of Occult Philosophy of Geomancie, Magical Elements of Peter De Aban: Astronomical Geomancie; the Nature of Spirits; Arbatel of Magick ; the Species or Several Kindes of Magick*. London: Printed by J.C. for the Rooks,1665. Print.

Crowley, Aleister. *Eight Lectures on Yoga*. Dallas, TX: Sangreal Foundation, 1939. Print.

Crowley, Aleister, Mary Desti, Leila Waddell, and Hymenaeus Beta. *Magick: Liber ABA*. Boston, Md: Weiser, 1997. Print.

Curzan, Anne. "20 Words That Once Meant Something Very Different." *Ideas.ted.com*, Ideas.ted.com, 30 Dec. 2015, ideas.ted.com/20-words-that-once-meant-something-very-different/.

Denning, Melita, and Osborne Phillips. *The Sword and the Serpent: the Two-Fold Qabalistic Universe*. Llewellyn Publications, 2005.

Evola, Julius, and Michael Moynihan. *Introduction to Magic: Rituals and Practical Techniques for the Magus*. Rochester, VT: Inner Traditions, 2001. Print.

Fulcanelli. *The Dwellings of the Philosophers = Les Demeures Philosophales: Et Le Symbolisme Hermétique Dans Ses Rapports Avec L'art Sacré Et L'ésotérisme Du Grand-œuvre*. Boulder, CO: Archive and Communications, 1999. Print.

Grosche, Eugen. "THE SATURNIAN WAY OF REALIZATION." *Ordo Saturni: THELEMA*. Orient Toronto of the Ordo Saturni, n.d. Web. 26 Aug. 2016.

Gundarsson, Kveldulf. *Teutonic Magic: The Magical and Spiritual Practices of the Germanic Peoples*. Llewellyn Publications, 1990.

Hartmann, Franz. *In the Pronaos of the Temple of Wisdom. Containing the History of the True and the False Brothers of the Rose Cross*. Universal Pansophic Soc., 1934.

Helmond, Johannes, and Gerard Hanswille. *Alchemy Unveiled: for the First Time the Secret of the Philosophers Stone Is Openly Explained*. Merkur, 2000.

Ivanits, Linda J. *Russian Folk Belief*. Armonk, NY: M.E. Sharpe, 1989. Print.

Levi, Eliphas, and W. Wynn Westcott. "The Magical Ritual of the Sanctum Regnum." (2009): n. pag. *The Magical Ritual of the Sanctum Regnum*. Hermetics.org, 21 July 2000. Web. 12 June 2016.

Levi, Eliphas. *Transcendental Magic*. Newburyport: Red Wheel Weiser, 1968. Print.

Lindquist, Galina. *Conjuring Hope: Magic and Healing in Contemporary Russia*. New York: Berghahn, 2006. Print.

Macdonald, George. "George MacDonald." *The Golden Key*. Macdonald Society, 1995. Web. 12 June 2016.

MacEowen, Frank. *The Mist-Filled Path: Celtic Wisdom for Exiles, Wanderers, and Seekers*. New World Library, 2002.

Markides, Kyriacos C. *Fire in the Heart: Healers, Sages and Mystics*. Penguin, 1991.

Markides, Kyriacos C. *The Magus of Strovolos*. Penguin Books, 1985.

McIntosh, Christopher. *Eliphas Lévi and the French Occult Revival*. London: Rider, 1972. Print.

Min, Tzu. *Chinese Taoist Sorcery: The Art of Getting Even*. Los Angeles: Vision Films, 2000. Print.

Mistele, William. "Franz Bardon Hermetics, Fairy Tales, and Transpersonal Psychology." *Bardon Home Page*. William Mistele, n.d. Web. 12 June 2016.

Neal, Stephanie L. *The Untraining of a Sea Priestess A Practical Journey to Connect With Cosmic Water Wisdom*. Turning Stone Pr, 2017.

O'Donohue, John. *Anam Cara*. Cliff Street Books, 1997

Puttock International Pty Ltd. "Public Domain Story Files - The Golden Key. by George MacDonald." *Printable Page From Public-Domain-Poetry.com*, www.public-domain-poetry.com/stories/george-macdonald/the-golden-key-1927.

Rochman, Bonnie. "Hitting Your Kids Increases Their Risk of Mental Illness." *Time*, Time, 2 July 2012, healthland.time.com/2012/07/02/physical-punishment-increases-your-kids-risk-of-mental-illness/.

"Overtraining." *Wikipedia*, Wikimedia Foundation, 14 July 2018, en.m.wikipedia.org/wiki/Overtraining.

Rodenburg, Patsy. *The Second Circle: Using Positive Energy for Success in Every Situation*. W.W. Norton & Company, 2017.

http://www.public-domain-poetry.com/stories/george-macdonald/the-golden-key-1927

Rowling, J. K., and Mary GrandPré. *Harry Potter and the Deathly Hallows*. New York, NY: Arthur A. Levine, 2007. Print.

Smith, Huston. *The Religions of Man: a Clear and Objective Description of the Great Religions and Their Appeal to the Spiritual Aspirations of the Different Peoples of the World*. Harper & Row, 1964.

Sadhu, Mouni. *Concentration, a Guide to Mental Mastery*. New York: Harper, 1959. Print.

Sadhu, Mouni. *The Tarot; a Contemporary Course of the Quintessence of Hermetic Occultism*. London: G. Allen & Unwin, 1962. Print.

Sheinkin, David, and Edward Hoffman. *Path of the Kabbalah*. New York, NY: Paragon House, 1986. Print.

Sherwin, Byron L. *Kabbalah: An Introduction to Jewish Mysticism*. Lanham: Rowman & Littlefield, 2006. Print.

Sivananda. *Conquest of Anger*. Yoga-Vedanta Forest Academy, 1962.

Stevens José. *Awaken the Inner Shaman: a Guide to the Power Path of the Heart*. Sounds True., 2014.

"The Book of Lambspring." *The Hermetic Museum, Vol I: The Book of Lambspring*, Sacred Texts, www.sacred-texts.com/alc/hm1/hm113.htm.

Tyson, Donald. *New Millennium Magick: a Complete System of Self-Realizatin*. Llewellyn Publications, 1996.

Zalewski, Pat. *Talismans & Evocations of the Golden Dawn*. Leicestershire, England: Thoth Publications, 2002. Print.

Bonus Content

Dear Reader,

The following chapter is from a book I am currently in the middle of writing. It is a compilation of many of my insights into the exercises of IIH. As I worked through each step of IIH, I was forced to come to my own understanding of the exercises in order to find an approach to them that worked for me. My goal is to share my understanding with Bardonists via the book in hopes that it will prevent them from encountering the same unnecessary frustrations that I encountered.

At the moment, my life is really busy, and progress on the book has been slow. It may be a long time before I finish it and submit it to my publisher to be proofread and published. However, as a way of thanking you for buying the second edition of *The Spirit of Magic*, I want to give you the opportunity to read a chapter from a book I am currently working on early. The following chapter comes from the book's manuscript and contains crucial information that all Bardonists should know. Even if you are not a Bardonist and have decided that another magical training system suits you better, you will still benefit from the information in this chapter because the four mental exercises of Step 1 are found in all systems in some form. They are indispensable because they develop three mental abilities that all magicians should have – the ability to know what is going on in one's mind, the ability to concentrate, and the ability to still one's mind.

Best,
Virgil

Chapter 3: The Importance of Present-Mindedness

Some people remain stuck on Step I because they are not mature enough to move on to Step II. In this chapter, I assume that you do have the maturity needed to move on to Step II, and that the reason you are stuck on Step I has to do with the way you are approaching the exercises of Step I.

Which Exercises Aren't Holding You Back?

Let's determine which Step I exercises aren't the ones holding you back.

The astral exercises are clearly not holding you back. These exercises consist of making the black and white soul mirrors. You should come up with at least 100 items for your black soul mirror and at least 100 items for your white soul mirror. If you have decent introspection skills, you should be able to think of ten items per day. If you build your mirrors at a rate of ten items per day, then you should be able to come up with the items for both mirrors in twenty days. You also need to spend a few days categorizing the items into the four elements and assessing their severity on a scale from 1 to 3. However, this shouldn't take more than a few days. Therefore, you should be able to finishing building both soul mirrors in about a month.

Let's say you are really bad at introspection and you are only able to think of one item per day. Even if you work at a rate of one item per day, you should still come up with all of the items for both mirrors in 200 days. Even if it takes you a few weeks to categorize the traits and assess their severity, you are still going to complete your soul mirrors in under a year because a year is 365 days. Clearly, making the soul mirrors isn't the exercise that causes people to remain stuck on Step I for several years.

The physical exercises aren't holding you back either. There are no standards of mastery for these exercises. Therefore, no one can say "I need to remain on Step I because I have not yet met Bardon's standards of mastery for conscious eating and conscious breathing." You just practice these physical exercises every day until you have mastered the mental and astral exercises. Then, you move on to Step II.

Since the astral and physical exercises aren't the reason people remain stuck on Step I for years, the source of the problem must be the mental exercises.

Why are You Unable to Master the Step 1 Mental Exercises?

If you could complete the four Step I mental exercises, you would be able to move onto Step II. After all, as we have seen in the previous section, the physical exercises don't have standards of mastery so they are freebies, and you can complete the astral soul mirror exercises in less than a year, even if you generate the mirrors at a rate as slow as one item per day.

There are four mental exercises in Step I.

Exercise 1: Be aware of the thoughts passing through your mind. The standard of mastery for this exercise is that you must be able to do this for ten minutes without becoming distracted or absent-minded in any way. I will refer to this first exercise as the "thought-awareness exercise."

Exercise 2: Keep your attention/awareness centered on the present moment. I will refer to this second exercise as the "present-mindedness exercise."

Exercise 3: Let your mind encompass one thought, and one thought only. Do not allow other thoughts into your mind. I will refer to this third exercise as the "concentration exercise."

Exercise 4: Keep your mind empty of all thoughts. I will refer to this fourth exercise as the "VOM exercise."

Ok, so let's go back to the question of why you are unable to master the four mental exercises of Step I. The answer is that you are not practicing the present-mindedness exercise seriously enough.

If you can't master the thought-awareness exercise, it's because you aren't practicing the present-mindedness exercise seriously enough.

If you can't master the concentration exercise, it's because you aren't practicing the present-mindedness exercise seriously enough.

If you can't master the VOM exercise, it's because you aren't practicing the present-mindedness exercise seriously enough.

The present-mindedness exercise overlaps with the thought-awareness exercise. Therefore the present-mindedness exercise complements the thought-awareness exercise. The better you get at the present-mindedness exercise, the better you will get at the thought-awareness exercise.

The present-mindedness exercise overlaps with the concentration exercise. Therefore the present-mindedness exercise complements the concentration exercise. The better you get at the present-mindedness exercise, the better you will get at the concentration exercise.

The present-mindedness exercise overlaps with the VOM exercise. Therefore the present-mindedness exercise complements the VOM exercise. The better you get at the present-mindedness exercise, the better you will get at the VOM exercise.

All Four Exercises Require Being Attentive

All four exercises require you to remain attentive for an extended period of time.

The thought-awareness exercise requires that you be attentive to the contents of your mind for ten minutes.

The concentration exercise requires that you be attentive to the contents of your mind for ten minutes. The only difference between the concentration exercise and the thought-awareness exercise is that your mind has only one thought in it when you practice the concentration exercise and that it is full of thoughts when you practice the thought-awareness exercise.

The VOM exercise requires that you be attentive to your mind for ten minutes. The only difference between the VOM exercise and the thought-awareness exercise is that your mind is empty when you practice the VOM exercise and it is full of thoughts when you practice the thought-awareness exercise.

Note that these three exercises all require that you be attentive to something for ten minutes straight, regardless of whether it is a mind filled with thoughts, a mind with only one single thought in it, or a mind with no thoughts in it.

The present-mindedness exercise involves being attentive to what you are presently doing. The better you get at the present-mindedness exercise, the better you will get at being attentive. The better you get at being attentive, the better you will get at any exercise that involves being attentive, including the thought-awareness exercise, the concentration exercise, and the VOM exercise.

A Quick Note

The present-mindedness exercise involves being attentive to what you are presently doing. Please note that what you are presently doing could be a physical action or a mental action. Examples of physical actions include the following.

Cooking
Doing the laundry
Driving
Practicing a karate kata
Mowing the lawn
Tidying the house

Examples of mental actions include the following

Using mental math to calculate how much you should tip the waiter
Reflecting upon a past incident
Planning the week ahead
Planning your novel
Contemplating whether to break up with your girlfriend
Realizing you should break up with your girlfriend
Contemplating what your next move will be while playing chess
Brainstorming ideas for a book about magical training

Regardless of whether you are doing something physical or mental in nature, you are attentive to what you are doing.

The Present-Mindedness Exercise and the Thought-Awareness Exercise

Have you ever gotten into a car to drive to a location and found yourself at that location with no recollection of how you got there? Obviously, you and your car didn't just teleport to the location. You did drive there. However, you don't remember driving there because while you were driving, you weren't aware that you were driving. Perhaps you were absent-minded. Perhaps you were distracted. Those are just two possible states you might be in when you are not in a state of awareness. We can only be attentive to what we are doing if we do it in a state of awareness. Therefore, practicing the present-mindedness exercise requires that we be aware, and develops our ability to remain aware for extended periods of time.

When you practice the present-mindedness exercise, you are in a state of awareness. When you practice the thought-awareness exercise, you are in a state of awareness. In the end, awareness is awareness. If you become better at one awareness exercise, you become better at all awareness exercises. If you want to master the thought-awareness exercise, then practice the present-mindedness exercise seriously.

The Present-Mindedness Exercise and the VOM Exercise

The present-mindedness exercise and the VOM exercise both involve being attentive. However, they are similar in another way. The present-mindedness exercise and the VOM exercise are both stillness exercises.

Think of your mind as an ocean. Each thought that passes through your mind is a wave (vritti) on the ocean. "Vacancy of mind" (VOM) can also be phrased as "stillness of mind."

Ok, forget about VOM for a second. I want to introduce you to the symbol/concept of the point. This is a symbol/concept that you will become familiar with during your magical training. The more you progress in your magical training, the more your understanding of the point will grow.

Let's start with the basic teachings concerning the point.

(#1) The point is the only thing that exists. You exist, so you are the point. I also exist so I am the point. However, there is only one point, so you and I are the same point. We are one. Everything is one. The entire created universe is represented by the Tree of Life, yet the nine lower sephiroth are contained within Kether, which is a point. The whole universe is a point, and points are dimensionless. The dimensions of space and time are illusions.

(#2) The point is immovable. Movement only makes sense when it is presented as being relative to a reference point. Since the point is the only thing that exists, there is nothing else in existence that can be used as a reference point. Since there is nothing for the point to move relative to, the point cannot be moved. Because the point cannot be moved, it is perfectly STILL (≋ key word here). Later on in your training, you may come across some dark forces, people, and entities who will try to "move" (manipulate/control/influence) you. When you notice this happening, you should be able to become the point so that you cannot be moved. This is one effective method of defense.

(#3) The point is the point at which opposites unite. The point is where spirit and matter become one. The point is where fire, water, earth, and air merge and become one (in other words the central point of the Cross of Equilibrated Forces). The point is where the uncreated and the created merge and become one. The point is also the point where the past and future merge and become one. In other words, it's the present moment. On one side of the present moment is the future. On the other side is the past. The present-moment itself is an infinitely small point in time. All points are one point, which is THE point. Therefore, the present-moment is THE point, and since the point is perfectly still, the present-moment is a position of perfect stillness in the temporal dimension.

When you practice the present-mindedness exercise, you center your awareness on the point. Since the point is perfectly still, this makes you perfectly still as well.

Stillness is stillness. When you get better at one stillness exercise, you get better at all stillness exercises. Therefore, if you want to get better at the VOM exercise, practice the present-mindedness exercise seriously.

What Does Practicing the Present-Mindedness Exercise Seriously Mean?

By now, it should be clear to you why getting better at the present-mindedness exercise will also make you better at the thought-awareness, concentration, and VOM exercises. To get better at the present-mindedness exercise, it is not enough to practice the exercise. You must practice the exercise seriously.

Practicing the present-mindedness exercise seriously means you strive to be present-minded every waking moment. At the beginning, you can start by trying to be present-minded for just five or ten minutes. However, you should increase the amount of time you remain present-minded each day, gradually working up to the point where you are present-minded every waking moment.

If you practice the present-mindedness exercise every waking moment, you will get better at it quickly. This will also cause you to get better at the thought-awareness exercise, the concentration exercise, and the VOM exercise because those three exercise overlap with the present-mindedness exercise.

In the beginning, you will have to try to remain present-minded because present-mindedness is not your default state. However, eventually, you will no longer have to try to remain present-minded because it will be your default state. This means your default state is a state of attentiveness. When you've reached this point, it should be easy for you to remain attentive to a filled mind, a single thought, or an empty mind for ten minutes. Therefore, the thought-awareness exercise, the concentration exercise, and the VOM exercise will be very easy to master.

Obstacles to Present-Mindedness

Making present-mindedness your default state is largely a matter of rooting out the tendencies that draw you out of a state of present-mindedness. There are several of these tendencies. Three of them are as follows.

Tendency to be distracted
Tendency to become absent-minded
Tendency to fall into a daydream unintentionally

You can rid yourself of these tendencies by breathing them out using the magical exhalation, or by washing them away using magical washing.

Four Tips for Becoming Present-Minded

In the following sections, I give four tips that will help you remain present-minded. Remember that if you remain constantly present-minded, present-mindedness will eventually become your default mental state, which is good for the reasons discussed in the previous sections. The first two tips I give are ones I also give in the present-mindedness chapter of my book *The Covert Side of Initiation*. I am giving them again in this book because they are relevant and I want those who don't have *The Covert Side of Initiation* to also know these two tips.

Tip 1: Use the Magical Exhalation to Breathe Out Distracting Thoughts

Use the magical exhalation to breathe out irrelevant thoughts that are distracting you and pulling your attention away from what you are presently doing. This makes things easier because instead of fighting these distracting thoughts (which can be exhausting), you can just breathe them out of you. For example, if you are gardening in your garden at home but thoughts about your job fill your mind and prevent you from remaining attentive to your gardening, then just breathe out those job-related thoughts.

Tip 2: Trace Back Your Train of Thought After Becoming Distracted

Many times, if we are practicing present-mindedness and realize we have started daydreaming or thinking about other things, we immediately turn our attention back to the present moment. Instead of doing this, trace back the sequence of your thoughts to the point of its departure from the present-moment. This increases your mental awareness and your understanding of the distraction process, which helps you avoid becoming distracted again in the future. In a sense, it also "undoes" the process of becoming distracted, which might seem like a weird idea to wrap your head around, but when you try it, you will see what I mean.

Consider the following hypothetical example. Let's say that I am taking a walk and trying to remain present-minded throughout the walk. Suddenly, in the middle of the walk, I realize that I am thinking about the movie Ip Man 3, and therefore, am obviously not present-minded. Instead of turning my attention back to the present-moment, I trace the train of my thoughts back. Before I was thinking about Ip Man 3 in general, I was thinking about a specific scene in the movie where Ip Man (temporarily blinded) uses his hearing to evade Cheung Tin Chi's attacks and defeat him. Before I was thinking about that scene, I was thinking about a scene in Rogue One where Chirrut Îmwe (who is blind) uses his hearing to sense the location of the clone troopers and defeat them in battle. I thought of this scene because I heard the sound of a dog behind me. I didn't see the dog because I was facing in the other direction, but I knew it was behind me because I heard it.

So now I know that realizing a dog was behind me after hearing it reminded me of the scene in Rogue One where Chirrut Îmwe uses his hearing to sense the position of the clone troopers. Because Donnie Yen plays Chirrut Îmwe as well as Ip Man, this reminded me of the scene in Ip Man 3 where Ip Man uses his hearing to evade Cheung Tin Chi's attacks. This is why I was thinking about Ip Man 3 in the middle of my walk. Having followed my train of thoughts back to the moment when they departed from the present, I can resume being attentive to the present.

Tip 3: Use the Mantra "Every Second Counts"

"Every second counts" is a mantra that I used to help myself stay present-minded. Staying present-minded improves your ability to concentrate, increases your mental discipline, and helps you make progress in the mental component of your training. In fact, every second you remain present-minded improves your ability to concentrate, increases your mental discipline, and helps you make progress in the mental component of your training. That's what I mean by "Every second counts." Whenever I felt my mind was losing its state of present-mindedness, I'd repeat to myself "Every second counts" and this would motivate me to retain my state of present-mindedness for a bit longer.

Tip 4: Use Affirmative and Imperative Autosuggestion

Affirmative autosuggestion is repeating the affirmation "I am present-minded" over and over again. Imperative autosuggestion is repeatedly telling yourself "Be present-minded." Use one of these types of autosuggestion throughout the day, especially when you realize you have become distracted or absent-minded.

[1] Many people use the phrase "Bardon system" to refer to the work of IIH; in fact, I probably do that a few times throughout this book. However, technically speaking, the Bardon system refers to the work of all three books and not just to the work of IIH.

[2] I'm not sure why Bardon chose this spelling. It is not the standard spelling used in English texts. However, I have seen a few other German texts that also spell it "Quabbalah," so perhaps that was just the standard spelling amongst German and Czech esotericists. It's also possible that Bardon deliberately chose a strange spelling to highlight the fact that what he was teaching was not the same as traditional Kabbalah or the "Hermetic Qabalah" taught in Golden Dawn style orders. Rawn has his own thoughts on the subject. See the link below.

http://abardoncompanion.de/Quab.html

[3] See the chapter on asana in *Liber E vel Exercitiorum*.

[4] If you spend time in the esoteric world, you will occasionally come across lengthy hatchet jobs written about genuine adepts or the magical training systems they created. Not everyone has the self-discipline (or maturity) needed to work through a good magical training system and become a magician. As Aesop's fable about the fox and the grapes shows, we often attack what we are unable to attain as a way of soothing our egos. This applies just as much to success in working through a magical training system as it does to fruit on a tree. However, if you are in this position, there is one VERY important thing you must know. Self-discipline is a quality that can be increased, improved, and strengthened. All you need to do is regularly exercise self-discipline and in time, you will find that your level of self-discipline is higher than it was before. It goes without saying that the time one spends writing a hatchet job could be better spent exercising one's self-discipline.

In more general terms, there is a key lesson to take away from this. You will encounter many problems during your magical training. Not having the self-discipline (or maturity) needed to undergo magical training is a problem, but it's really no different from any other problem you might encounter in your training, and therefore, you should deal with it the same way you would deal with any other problem you might encounter in your training. Seek to understand the problem. Then come up with a strategy for solving it. Then work to solve the problem by implementing the strategy you came up with. Not having enough time to train and not being able to get the hang of certain exercises are examples of other problems that you might encounter, and you deal with those problems using the same three-part plan given above.

[5] IIH contains extensive work with the elements, so people who are interested in the elements and eager to do element-related work are often attracted to the Bardon system. Actual work with elemental energies does not appear until Step 3, where Bardon has you accumulating them in your body via pore breathing. Bardon warns multiple times that you need to establish an elemental equilibrium in Step 2 before practicing these elemental accumulation exercises "unless you wish to do mischief to yourself." Many Bardonists read this warning and believe it, but are still impatient to work with the elements. Therefore, while they are on Step 1 or 2, they practice other elemental exercises from other systems and sources outside of the Bardon system. It seems like they are heeding Bardon's warning because they are not practicing the Step 3 elemental accumulation exercises; however, Bardon's warning actually applies to all exercises that involve working with elemental energies, and not just to the Step 3 elemental accumulation exercises. Therefore, these impatient students still end up doing mischief to themselves.

[6] The text of IIH reads "Should anyone wish to use these exercises of physic carriage for the purpose of developing the will-power, he may make out various carriages at his own discretion, provided he is able to sit relaxed and comfortable

without any disturbance at all for a full hour. [...] We need a certain position for our magical development, no matter which one, the simplest being that which we described above." In other words, after you have mastered an asana so you can use it to do the later exercises, you can then continue to master other asanas for the purpose of strengthening your willpower if you want to. However, the primary reason we master an asana is not to develop willpower. It's because "we need a certain position for our magical development." In other words, we need a certain position that we can remain in comfortably when we do our magical exercises – concentration, meditation, visualization, etc.

[7] "In all of Bardon's exercises, it sometimes helps to imagine you have already mastered the exercise. This is an exercise in imagination. It gives you a chance to feel what it is like to do something you do not yet know how to do. And there is a sense that if you can imagine it then you can get it. The thought or image of already being able to do something creates energy which generates momentum and success." – William Mistele

[8] If you don't own a copy of Patsy Rodenburg's book *The Second Circle: How to Use Positive Energy for Success in Every Situation*, I highly encourage you to get one. It's a book every student of magic should own. The description of the Second Circle body's spine in the sixth chapter of Rodenburg's book is a good guide to how your spine should be when sitting in the throne posture. A slouched spine is in First Circle. A spine pulled up too far is in Third Circle. You want your spine to be in Second Circle.

[9] I am simplifying in this chapter by assuming that all of the traits are the same "size." However, in real life, some traits are major and some traits are minor or even close to trivial, so having the same amount of traits in each elemental category doesn't necessarily mean you are balanced.

[10] Other common names for the elemental equilibrium include "magical equilibrium," "elemental equipoise," and "astral equipoise." If you see any of these phrases, they are synonymous with "elemental equilibrium." Mouni Sadhu calls it "pentagrammatic freedom" because a person with an elemental equilibrium is represented by an ideal pentagram and is free from the sorts of influences that can easily overcome those who are impure and unbalanced.

[11] Conscience, intuition, wisdom, memory, and inspiration are others.

[12] "You are called to be king of air, water, earth and fire; but to reign over these four living creatures of symbolism, it is necessary to conquer and enchain them." – Eliphas Levi

To conquer and enchain the elements means to ensure that all the elemental traits, positive and negative, are under the control of your will. Thus, when you will yourself not to do something, your elemental traits can never force you to do it anyway.

[13] Some call this the Cross of Equated Forces. "Equilibrated" is a better word. Fire and water are in a state of equilibrium, meaning they balance each other. They are not equated with each other. This would imply they are the same element, which is not the case.

[14] It is sometimes represented by the river Naher, which gives rise to the four elemental rivers that flow into the created universe to nourish, sustain, and continually recreate it. Each arm of the cross corresponds to one of the rivers.

[15] When Archimedes said "Give me a point on which to stand and I will move the Earth," he was revealing a profound magical teaching. The point in this statement refers to the point at the center of the Cross of Equilibrated Forces. If you stand at this point, then you are in a position of balance. This balance gives you the stability needed to move the anima mundi (astral light / lit. "soul of the world").

[16] The classification Claude de St. Martin gave to people completely under the influence of Nahash was "L'Homme du Torrent." This translates to "Man of the Torrent," and refers to the torrents (powerful currents) of the astral plane. These people do not design and create their destinies using reason and will, but are simply carried along by the currents flowing through their lives.

[17] Trismegistus means "thrice-great." According to Daskalos, this refers to Hermes's mastery of the three planes – physical, astral, and mental. Hermes is not actually a specific figure, but the general archetype that represents an initiate. This is why some ancient texts referred to multiple people as Hermes Trismegistus. It simply means all these people were initiates.

[18] If you didn't understand the quote by Levi about continence in the previous section, it might make more sense now.

[19] For the record, I am aware that physical strength is far from being the only thing that determines the outcome of a fight, and that there are martial arts that center on using an opponent's strength against him. In general, however, my statement is true.

[20] Mouni Sadhu also writes that if the elemental equilibriums of two magicians are equally strong, then the one with the stronger nervous system will be the winner in a duel. This statement also has a lot of truth. It illustrates the importance of the physical aspect of training. The exercise of pore breathing the vital force revitalizes and strengthens the nervous system.

[21] If someone who does not possess an elemental equilibrium tries to activate a ritual circle and succeeds (perhaps through some natural affinity for magical power), then the ritual circle becomes an extension of his lack of balance. Any magic he does with it will be unbalanced, and unbalanced magic has a number of negative effects. It will exacerbate the magician's own imbalances. It will attract parasites. It will disrupt the balance of the macrocosm/universe. The list goes on and on. Fortunately, most ritual magic performed by those who are not properly trained is just inert theatrics.

[22] The phrase "pretend magic," which I will discuss in a later chapter, comes from the first essay in Bill's well-known "Problems in the Study of Magic" series of essays.

http://www.williammistele.com/problems1.htm

[23] I highly recommend reading Bill's book *Mermaids, Sylphs, Gnomes, and Salamanders: Dialogues with the Kings and Queens of Nature.* In fact, if you are using a magical training system that has you working with the elements of fire, water, earth, and air, then this book is a must-read. There are hundreds, if not thousands of books in the esoteric world about the elements. The information in most of those books comes from speculation and conjecture about the elements, and is therefore of questionable accuracy. This book is unique because the information about the elements contained in this book comes from Bill's personal experience working with the elements, entering the elemental kingdoms, and conversing with the sovereigns of those kingdoms. For this reason, you can be sure that the information about the elements contained in this book is accurate. There is quite a bit of information packed into this book, so by the time you are through with it, you will have enough knowledge about the elements to easily complete the second phase of the soul mirror creation process.

[24] Dragging a suitcase full of altars, wands, censers, pentacles, and swords with me every time I wanted to fly somewhere just wasn't going to work out.

[25] The other reason IIH was one of the few systems compatible with my life concerned privacy. This isn't an issue if those close to you are open-minded and supportive of you finding your own spiritual path, but that wasn't the case for me. Many

of the people I was in close proximity to were narrow-minded and hostile to anything related to esotericism, and I didn't have a lot of privacy. Rather than stressing over how to hide altars, wands, and robes, and worrying constantly that they would be discovered, I opted to choose a system that didn't require me to work with a large array of ritual tools I needed to hide from prying eyes.

[26] You can't fully understand the Bardon system unless you work through it. However, at the beginning, you do need to understand enough of it to be able to make an educated guess regarding whether or not it is the best system for you. Reading through IIH and PME will give you a basic understanding of what working through the Bardon system entails. After that, I highly suggest you read through the second edition of Rawn Clark's book *A Bardon Companion*. This book will help you deepen your understanding of the Bardon system, which will help you make an even more informed decision about whether or not to ultimately choose this system.

[27] Note that some magical schools/orders/traditions try to attract new students by promising them magical knowledge they claim is only possessed by that school/order/tradition and can be found nowhere else. Remember that whatever amount of magical knowledge these schools/orders/traditions might possess is minuscule compared to the amount of magical knowledge possessed by the ruling genii of the Earthzone and of the planetary spheres.

[28] http://williammistele.com/negative.html

[29] Which makes you wonder what is going on in the heads of those people who cherry-pick the intermediate or advanced exercises from IIH to practice or to recommend to others.

[30] It is imperative for the magician to have a strong astra-mental body. If the magician's astra-mental body is weak, it will easily become strained when working magic. A magician with a strong astra-mental body can move large amounts of magical energy around without fear of injury. A magician with a weak astra-mental body will always find his astra-mental body becoming strained, even when working with small trickles of energy. The effects of this astra-mental strain often "overflow" onto the physical level, leading to disturbances in the physical body as well. These disturbances are usually most visible in the subtle aspects of the physical body like the nervous system and endocrine system, and less visible in the denser aspects like the skeletal system.

In Step 3, Bardon has you accumulating the elements within yourself via pore breathing. When you first move onto Step 3, if you try to accumulate 30 breaths of an element, your astra-mental body will become strained because it is not strong enough to hold that intense of an accumulation. That's why Bardon has you begin by accumulating 7 breaths of an element, and slowly working your way up to 30 breaths by increasing the number of breaths by one each day. When you reach the point where you can accumulate 30 breaths of an element, your astra-mental body has become considerably stronger.

I am unaware of any other single magical exercise that can increase the strength of the astra-mental body as rapidly or effectively as Bardon's elemental accumulation exercises. Without a doubt, others see this too, which explains why so many authors have cherry-picked this exercise from IIH to recommend to those who want stronger-astra-mental bodies so they can work with greater amounts of magical energy without becoming strained. However, we must always remember the phrase "One man's meat is another man's poison." There is a reason the elemental accumulation exercises are found in Step 3 and not in an earlier step. To those who have completed the work of Steps 1 and 2, the exercises of Step 3 will be meat. To those who have not completed the work of Steps 1 and 2, the exercises of Step 3 will be poison.

[31] Remember that magical advancement will not begin until you have first grasped the lesser mysteries. Until you have developed qualities like compassion, patience, humility, and honesty, you stand no chance of penetrating into the greater mysteries. In *The Esoteric Teachings*, Daskalos writes "In our system we stress the full development of the personality; becoming a moral and ethical individual before developing the gifts of clairvoyance and the kind." Now you know why his system (and Bardon's) are set up that way.

Daskalos and Bardon could both heal people of diseases the doctors of their day considered incurable, peer into the inner realms with flawless clairvoyant sight, and use their wills to manipulate the physical plane directly (as evidenced by Daskalos changing the trajectory of Skylab and Bardon dissolving thunderstorms and accidentally shattering a mirror by accumulating too much energy into it). You'd think more people would pay serious attention to the teachings of adepts of their caliber, but because people are impatient, they insist on trying various exercises to force their astral senses open before they have even grasped the lesser mysteries, let alone reached the necessary level of magical advancement.

[32] Any Bardonist who is past Step 8 can tell you that the opposite is true; those Bardonists are not theorizing or speculating. They are speaking from experience.

[33] In the Bardon community, this exercise is often called VOM, meaning "Vacancy of Mind." I use this abbreviation to reference this exercise periodically throughout this book.

[34] Everyone is different, so the comments in this paragraph don't apply to everyone. Many people sit down to practice thought-observation for the first time and are able to observe their thoughts right off the bat. These people are already able to see. There's a good chance you're one of them. However, a lot of people aren't able to do this. They need to learn to see. In other words, they need to get the hang of observing their thoughts. Only then will they be able to observe their thoughts for five minutes and gradually work their way up to observing their thoughts for ten minutes.

[35] In my opinion, you don't have to master the first mental exercise before beginning to practice the second mental exercise (present-mindedness). In fact, I think the practice of present-mindedness will greatly compliment your efforts to master thought-observation. Practicing present-mindedness will teach you to be continually attentive to the present-moment. This will also help you become continually attentive to what is going on in your mind. Mastering the first exercise requires that you be continually attentive to what is going on in your mind for ten minutes.

[36] I am using the word "mastered" pretty loosely here to mean you meet the proficiency requirements needed to move on to the next exercise.

[37] http://williamrmistele.com/uploads/fivesensepractice.pdf

[38] http://williammistele.com/body1.htm

[39] At least this is the case for me. The reason is that objects are three dimensional while symbols are two dimensional. The extra dimension makes it easier to "grip" the visualized image and hold it in your mind's eye. Not sure if this makes sense in writing, but if you experiment around with visualization, you will probably notice the same phenomenon.

[40] E.g. *Concentration: A Guide to Mental Mastery*, by Mouni Sadhu; *A Bardon Companion*, by Rawn Clark; *The Second Circle: How to Use Positive Energy for Success in Every Situation*, by Patsy Rodenburg

[41] I have nothing against approaching chakra work properly. However, most New Age chakra exercises were created by authors who have no real understanding of what the chakras are and how to open them safely.

⁴² https://www.ecosophia.net/blogs-and-essays/the-well-of-galabes/foundations-of-magical-practice-ritual/

⁴³ Ted Wong, one of Bruce Lee's students, once gave the following advice - "Take what you have and think of a way to improve it or simplify it." This is what Bardon did to his system with each iteration. Simple systems tend to be efficient, while unnecessarily complicated systems are inefficient. Bardon simplified his system by cutting out unnecessary exercises like the previously mentioned color exercise. He also simplified it by simplifying the exercises themselves. This is a good idea because simple exercises tend to be more beneficial than complicated exercises. This is why the simple concentration exercises in IIH are more beneficial than the standard "Druidic Kabbalistic past life chakra exercise" or "Pleiadian angel Kundalini balancing exercise" you find in many occult or New Age books. I am reminded of a Hermetic axiom – "Whatever may be accomplished by a simple method should not be attempted by a complicated one." If you can learn concentration from a simple concentration exercise such as the ones found in IIH, why would you try to learn concentration from an unnecessarily complicated concentration exercise?

⁴⁴ The quote from Bardon that I give in the second epigraph of this chapter illustrates this well. I do want to make a few comments about this quote, however, because it is easy to misinterpret it. Bardon is not saying to hate yourself or be abusive toward yourself. Such behavior is not conducive to one's mental or physical health, and it is important for the student to remain mentally and physical healthy. I remember reading a study some time ago in which various artists from different fields were interviewed. Some were actors. Others were violin players. Others were dancers. The study showed that the artists at the top of their field always hired coaches who gave them lots of (constructive) criticism, constantly challenged them, and constantly forced them to test their limits. Since magic is an art, and since Bardon anticipated that many students would work through IIH alone, he urges the student to act as his own coach. This is what he means when he says to "be relentless and hard" with yourself.

⁴⁵ Otherwise it would be your fear of punishment, instead of your will, that would hold you back from punching him. In this case, your will would not be strengthened because it wouldn't be doing the work.

⁴⁶ Read Randy Pausch's book *The Last Lecture*.

⁴⁷ Many conversations on Bardon forums consist of Bardonists giving each other ideas on how to make their training unnecessarily time-consuming.

⁴⁸ Read the section titled "Dead-End Jobs" in Chapter 29 of Rodenburg's *The Second Circle: How to Use Positive Energy for Success in Every Situation*. The fate of the librarians she describes illustrates the dire consequences of succumbing to this fear. Courage is one of the four pillars of Solomon's Temple. It is a necessary quality for magicians to have, so those who succumb to this fear are in an unfavorable position when it comes to making progress along the magical path. Some fears like the fear of danger or the fear of injury are reasonable and keep us safe, but a fear of failure usually just prevents us from being productive. Most major successes are preceded by numerous failures, or rather, valuable learning experiences.

⁴⁹ For a basic introduction to the concept of presence, read Frater Acher's article "How to Develop Your Astral Senses."

https://theomagica.com/blog/how-to-develop-your-astral-senses?rq=presence

Searching the word "presence" in Theomagica's search bar will also bring up all of Frater Acher's articles that mention the concept of presence. John O'donohue also discusses the concept of presence at various points in his books, and Patsy Rodenburg's book *The Second Circle* is entirely about the subject of presence.

⁵⁰ The first eight steps of IIH involve learning how to become a salamander, gnome, sylph, and undine. As a human being, you can work with and master all four elements instead of just one. In fact, to maintain your balance, you do need to work with all four, and not one exclusively.

⁵¹ PME is not a guide to contacting spirits. It is a guide to contacting spirits productively. When we are prepared to contact spirits, then contacting them is a productive activity because we can learn from them. When we are unprepared to contact spirits, then trying to contact them is an unproductive activity, even if we succeed in establishing contact with them. You occasionally see evocation accounts written by people who contacted spirits before being properly initiated. Many of these accounts are unremarkable compared to the evocation accounts of genuine initiates, and after reading some of these accounts, you'd be under the impression that spirits can't teach you anything you don't already know, or do anything more than create some cool flashes and bangs. This is an erroneous assumption, but if we are not prepared to receive the knowledge and guidance of a spirit because we lack the level of maturity and development needed to do so, then the spirit will refrain from giving us the knowledge and guidance we think we desire. The following text is a passage from one of Bill's Facebook posts.

"You may use psychic abilities to contact these spirits. But without adequate training, talking to them will not necessarily get you anything. You risk being 'bitterly disappointed.' Well, it is worse than that. You might assume you actually understand what they are saying to you and, on the basis of your assumption that they're guiding you, end up making horrible mistakes in your real world decisions."

⁵² "Body, Spirit, and Soul. Now, I tell you most truly, cook these three together." The Book of Lambspring makes it clear that these three should be cooked together and not separately one at a time. Yet, there are still systems out there telling students to cook these three one at a time.

⁵³ The four cardinal virtues are prudence, strength, temperance, and justice. Strength, temperance, and justice have cards named after them, so it seems odd that there is no card named after prudence. This led to speculation that there initially was a card named after prudence, but that the card's name was later changed. This card is said to be the card we now know as The Hermit.

⁵⁴ If you possess a copy of *The Universal Master Key*, the third chapter in the fire section, which is about bravery, illustrates what I'm saying very well. Many of the views presented in this chapter are not magical teachings, but ideas inspired by toxic masculinity. Bardon made it clear that students of magic should take care of themselves, look after their own well-being, and do their best to stay healthy. This necessitates that you go to your doctor if you think there is something wrong with your body. A pain in your gut that you ignore and don't tell anyone about could later grow into a lethal tumor. A feeling of nausea that you choose to suffer through and not tell anyone about could be a sign of a heart infection that will kill you if it is not treated. A mild blurriness in your vision could grow into permanent tunnel vision if you do not get it treated right away. A strange lump on your body could be a sign of cancer that is more likely to kill you the longer you wait to get it removed. These sorts of things happen all the time because people ignore the signals from their body that there is something wrong and they need to look into it and seek healing.

Regarding *The Universal Master Key* overall, I think it's an ok book and can be a useful tool for those engaged in the work of self-transformation. However, no book is perfect, and the chapter about bravery is especially problematic.

⁵⁵ You cannot succumb to the temptation to abuse akashic magic if you aren't capable of using akashic magic. This is why many Bardonists encounter obstacles in

their training that prevent them from progressing to the intermediate steps of IIH where they learn akashic magic through depth-point meditation and by pore breathing akasha. When they are mature enough, those obstacles will be removed and they will be able to make progress in their training once more. The obstacles are placed in their training to protect them from themselves.

[56] Self-esteem is an important trait for anyone to have. It doesn't come from baseless praise and compliments. It comes from successfully overcoming challenges and solving problems, because doing these things inspires confidence in one's abilities. This is another reason you should not prevent your ward from overcoming challenges and solving problems. You would be preventing your ward from developing self-esteem. Learn to discriminate between helpful challenges/problems and sources of serious danger.

[57] Which is, of course, all the time

[58] "She knew nothing of the Balance and the Pattern which the true wizard knows and serves, and which keep him from using his spells unless real need demands."
~Ursula Le Guin (A Wizard of Earthsea)

[59] When you are an adept, you will have a great amount of magical power. Oftentimes, you will be working together with extremely wise spirits who will give you guidance when it comes to using that power, which is nice. However, magic requires us to be independent (a fire trait). So while we should take advantage of the wisdom of the spirits who guide us, we should not grow dependent upon them, which means we should also acquire wisdom and understanding ourselves. On the practical level, there will often be times when you have to use power immediately (e.g. emergencies) and won't have time to consult with wise spirits like the ruling genii of the Earthone. In those situations, you must rely on your own wisdom to ensure that you use your power wisely. Acquiring wisdom is also a part of spiritual evolution, which we all go through, so we must constantly acquire wisdom for that purpose too.

[60] Note that I write "a spiritual leader" and not "the spiritual leader."

[61] I purposely write "genuine wisdom" instead of just "wisdom" to emphasize that I am talking about wisdom and not other things, such as knowledge, that are often mistaken for wisdom but are not wisdom.

[62] Humans of New York did an interesting interview with a man who was unable to find any genuine spirituality in the church, but took up ballet and found in this art a way of celebrating and connecting with God. If you ask most Christians what their idea of spirituality is, they will probably say going to church regularly and praying regularly. If you ask most students of magic what their idea of spirituality is, they will probably say practicing magical exercises. Our idea of spirituality is heavily influenced by the way we ourselves approach spirituality, so it may be hard to see that there are an infinite number of forms of spirituality and many of them are quite different from each other. At the end of the day, spirituality is not about going to church, praying regularly, practicing the exercises of IIH, or doing rituals. It's about finding a way to make your life meaningful. If the physical world was all the existed and we were nothing but matter, it would be impossible to find meaning in life. Anything that brings meaning into our lives, regardless if it is a religion, a magical training system, an art, a hobby, volunteering, or a way of life, does so because it connects us to spirit. So when I say a magician is a spiritual leader for his family, what I am really saying is that if his family members need help finding meaning in their lives, he can give them guidance if they want him to.

[63] Note that I write "a leader" and not "the leader."

[64] Sometimes a magician will choose to jump on the latest bandwagon and join the latest fashion trend because life is often easier if you fit in and aren't perceived as a

weirdo, but for the magician, it is a conscious choice based on reason and not a blind impulse.

[65] Who would have thought that spring cleaning could have massive magical benefits?

[66] Magic is highly multifaceted. I discuss many facets of magic in this book, but you will constantly be discovering new facets during your training and during your work as a magician.

[67] "Suffering is always a warning. So much the worse for him who does not understand it! When Nature tightens the rein, it is that we are swerving; when she plies the whip, it is that danger is imminent. Woe, then, to him who does not reflect." – Eliphas Levi

[68] By "pure person," I mean someone with a purified elemental equilibrium, as discussed in Chapter 2.

[69] There are other reasons. Note that spirits exist outside of the magician. In other words, despite the claims of some occultists, they don't exist only in the mind of the magician. The individual who has purified himself will also have access to sources of protection from within, and some of those internal sources of protection are powerful indeed. In the cases of impure individuals, the activity of those internal sources of protection is obstructed by the presence of impurities in the personality.

[70] Note that yoga, which is not a magical discipline but is still an esoteric discipline, also entails a search for truth, and that developing the quality of *satya* is part of the very first rung of the yogic ladder.

[71] Quote comes from Karl Mordo

[72] "Let me say it again so it is clear beyond any doubt: anyone who interferes with my work by default falls under my jurisdiction. You see, the core of my power and the duties I have been authorized to perform arise from a source human evolution cannot comprehend. For this reason I can blend with more subtlety into the mind of a magician than air with lungs or blood with veins. "- The Chief Judge of Saturn
http://williammistele.com/saturn.html

[73] Unless you make some really bad choices and redevelop that negative trait

[74] Read Frater Acher's article "A Mirror at an Angle – Or Why Not to Read About Your Holy Guardian Angel"
https://theomagica.com/blog/a-mirror-at-an-angle-or-why-not-to-read-on-your-holy-guardian-angel

[75] You're also an Earthzone spirit, a lunar spirit, a Merucian spirit, and a Venusian spirit because you have to pass through those spheres first before reaching the Sphere of the Sun. Otherwise, you won't be ready to enter the Sphere of the Sun. Bardon's warning about trying to enter the Sphere of the Sun before you're ready to was quoted in Chapter 12 of this book.

[76] There are many books, such as the Mutus Liber, that contain instructions for creating the philosophers stone. These instructions are not written in English, but in the so-called "symbolic language of alchemy." These books were written for those who had been taught the symbolic language of alchemy, and were not intended for those who did not know the symbolic language of alchemy. Those who did not know the symbolic language of alchemy often tried to decode these books, but to no avail. When it comes to books like the Mutus Liber, there are numerous different interpretations of the symbols in the book because each person who has tried to decipher it has come up with his own interpretation of the symbols. However, the book was not meant to be interpreted. It was meant to be read, and it can only be read by those who know the language it was written in. A person who does not know German will never be able to read a book written in German no matter how long he stares at the words and tries to

decipher their meaning. Until the Rosetta Stone was found, no one was able to read the writing of the ancient Egyptians. Yet people who do not know the symbolic language of alchemy still spend their whole lives trying to read a book written in a language they do not know in order to learn the process of creating the philosopher's stone.

There is no need for this, and there is no need for those who do not know the symbolic language of alchemy to abandon all hope. The instructions for creating the stone can be found in another language – plain English. The rendition of The Magician placed at the beginning of IIH depicts all that the magical training system in the book will allow you to attain, and we see the red stone in the midst of the open lotus, symbolizing the attainment of the philosopher's stone through the expansion and evolution of consciousness – a process Bardon has you accomplishing through the completion of ten steps.

[77] Hence, there are some types of storms that you can sail around or dissolve using magic, as mentioned in Chapter 9.

[78] There is a sentence in Step 5 of IIH that is often joked about within the Bardon community – "Consequently the magician must know exactly how to produce a fireball, a ball of air, one of water, and an earth ball." If you see jokes about Bardonists being able to throw fireballs, they're references to this sentence. During one online discussion where this sentence was brought up again, my friend Crystalf noted that the fire element produces the emotion of anger. Therefore, if someone was attacking you and you threw a "fireball" into him, the "fireball" would probably have the effect of making him angrier, and therefore would make your situation worse. Water is associated with serenity, so throwing a ball of water into him might get him to calm down.

[79] Process begins with Step 1

[80] In the Gospel of John, Jesus compares himself to Nehushtan.

[81] See Figure X in the Book of Lambspring.

[82] See Figure VIII of The Book of Lambspring.

[83] Or of using evocation to call those ruling genii to our realm

[84] I've heard many people who have been practicing evocation for years claim that it's impossible to have the sort of deeply enriching and transformative evocation experiences described by Bardon in PME. I agree with them. It is indeed impossible, but only for those who have not worked through IIH. For the true initiates who did have the patience, will, and perseverance required to work through an initiation system like IIH, the deeply enriching and transformative evocation experiences described by Bardon in PME are not fantasies, but regular occurrences.

[85] References to an incident involving someone I used to know named Pam and an incident involving a history class I took in college.

[86] Some tasks for my job require knowledge of chemistry to complete.

[87] There is nothing inherently wrong with being interested in occultism, but I decided that for me it would be better to leave that subject in my past, forget about it, and develop other interests.

[88] Boy have I changed.

[89] Again, nothing inherently wrong with being interested in martial arts (obviously), but I decided it would be better for me to leave my interest in the subject in my past.

www.ingramcontent.com/pod-product-compliance
Lightning Source LLC
Chambersburg PA
CBHW070945180426
43194CB00040B/962